ROUGH
GUIDES

TRAVEL THE
LIBERATION
ROUTE
EUROPE

**SITES AND EXPERIENCES ALONG THE PATH
OF THE WORLD WAR II ALLIED ADVANCE**

Liberation
ROUTE
EUROPE

Written by
Nick Inman and Joe Staines

Contents

Preface by
William Boyd

Novelist and screenwriter

The D-Day landings of 6 June 1944 still astound. The slightest acquaintance with the scale and risk involved, the monstrous complications of the logistics and the strategy, not to mention the mind-boggling bravery of tens of thousands of young soldiers, is a humbling experience to contemplate and examine. The whole enterprise seems, in military terms, almost hubristic. How could anyone have dreamed up such a plan – the largest seaborne invasion in the whole history of warfare, never to be surpassed? How could such a start to the liberation of western Europe have been contemplated given the enormous, cataclysmic consequences of failure?

Time has passed and hindsight's 20/20 vision does not lessen the admiration – on the contrary: if anything our respect and wonderment have increased. Were the stakes higher then? Undoubtedly. Were we braver people then? Probably. D-Day and its aftermath cast a light on our own times –

and sometimes that candid illumination is not flattering.

Nothing better, then, than to retrace the events of that day and the weeks and months that followed and vicariously relive a small fragment of twentieth-century history.

D-Day on the beaches of Normandy leads on to the slow but steady liberation of western Europe – other invasions, other battles fought, most won, some lost, but the progress towards victory seemed unwavering. And let's not forget that Nazi Germany was caught in an inexorable pincer attack of its own making. Hammer blows from the East as well as the West. Throughout Europe, the many sites and memorials still speak to us with clarion voices. It is remarkable, three-quarters of a century on from 1944, that Europe remains united and at peace, albeit under new pressures. Remembering D-Day, the liberation of Europe and the cause it represented, is a potent spur to that remaining the case, forever.

Preface by
Richard Overy
Professor of History at the University of Exeter

The Liberation of Europe in 1943–45 from the menace of German occupation and oppression was a defining moment of the last century. That liberation required a colossal military effort, almost unimaginable today. Allied armies from the west, east and south slowly drove back the Axis forces until by 1945 they decisively destroyed German military power in Germany itself. The German armed forces surrendered on 7 May.

Liberation Route Europe is a unique organization dedicated to keeping alive the memory of that momentous victory and the terrible cost in lives and treasure that it demanded, not only from those powers engaged in the fighting, but from the people and cities in the path of the advancing armies who were bombed or shelled or starved by the circumstances of the war. Tracing the path made by the Western Allies from the prelude to D-Day in 1944 to the final invasion of Germany in March 1945 is to follow a route of campaigns and battles that hung in the balance on many occasions – the defence of the narrow Normandy beachhead in June, the crisis at Arnhem in September, the Battle of the Bulge in December when Hitler ordered one last surprise assault against the Allied line. The Liberation Route recaptures those key moments and shows just what an exceptional effort was involved in crossing northern Europe against a determined foe.

Liberation was also the language used by the Soviet Union as the Red Army stormed across Eastern Europe. Here at least the genocidal German regime was defeated, but liberation meant something different for the peoples brought suddenly under the rule of Soviet-sponsored dictatorships. Here liberation in the same sense as the West was postponed until the 1990s. The liberation that mattered in shaping the development of the continent after the war was the liberation of northern and western Europe. This laid the foundation for today's European Union and the reconciliation of the peoples of Europe. Liberation Route Europe is not only about reconstructing the key historical moment when freedom returned, but a way of reinforcing the ideal of a united and peaceful Europe in the present.

Richard Overy.

Foreword by the Liberation Route Europe

A continuously growing, international remembrance trail, the Liberation Route Europe (LRE) connects important milestones from modern European history. It forms a link between the main regions impacted by the Liberation of Europe in 1943–1945 and is managed by the Liberation Route Europe Foundation.

Origins of the Liberation Route Europe

The LRE's roots lie in a small regional project that began in the Arnhem–Nijmegen area of the Netherlands, where Operation Market Garden and Operation Veritable took place in 1944–1945. In 2008, three of the area's museums – the National Liberation Museum 1944-1945 in Groesbeek, the Airborne Museum "Hartenstein" in Oosterbeek and the War Museum in Overloon – joined forces with the Regional Tourist Board Arnhem Nijmegen (RBTKAN) to raise awareness of local World War II history by telling its stories and promoting its remembrance sites.

In Arnhem and Nijmegen, plenty of recognized sites remembered the war and the Liberation – museums, cemeteries and so on – but other important locations were almost completely unknown. Commemorative years witnessed veterans returning to the region with their families, eager to show them where they fought; some were airdropped during the war and keen to identify their landing areas. Unfortunately, many of their stories were unmarked, lost in the fields and forests that blanketed the land. "It was difficult to find all the relevant information, the stories, the bigger picture; we had to do something to keep this history alive," explains Jurriaan de Mol, one of the project founders.

In response, a network of listening locations called "audiospots" were devel-

LRE audiospots

The LRE currently has around two hundred audiospots disseminated in six provinces of the Netherlands, as well as in Kreis Kleve in Germany. Audiospots are planned in several other Dutch provinces, and the network is constantly expanding. At each audiospot, poignant stories of wartime experiences are offered in three languages using a mobile application or a local phone number. Throughout this book, audiospots are marked with the headphones symbol 🎧. You can listen to the thought-provoking stories at www.liberationroute.com/audiospots.

oped, where visitors could listen to – and read about – the forgotten and hidden stories of World War II. Accessed using a smartphone or by calling a specific phone number, in time these audiospots became local monuments, maintained by local communities. Tour companies and their guides began incorporating the spots on their routes, connecting story and place to give meaningful insight into the Liberation of Europe.

The LRE trail today

The initial project met with enthusiasm, and quickly spread to provinces all over the Netherlands. Its immediate popularity prompted the founders to investigate the possibility of expanding into other European nations. When they had successfully joined together with partners from five other countries, the idea of creating a transnational remembrance trail was born, linking the regions, sites and stories of the Liberation across Europe. LRE's chairwoman, Victoria van Krieken, has compared the route to a pilgrimage – dedicated to the memory of those who fought and lost their lives during World War II.

The LRE, in its international form, was officially inaugurated in Arromanches on the shores of Normandy on 6 June 2014 to mark the 70th anniversary of D-Day. Today, as presented in this book, the trail connects sites – museums, cemeteries, memorials, fortifications, monuments and audiospots – in nine European countries: Italy, the United Kingdom, France, Belgium, Luxembourg, the Netherlands, Germany, the Czech Republic and Poland. But the route is still far from complete. The LRE Foundation is committed to extending the trail, especially into parts of eastern and southern Europe, in

A legacy project

The LRE is all about "remembrance and reflection," says project founder Jurriaan de Mol. "Without the sacrifice of all those men and women in the Second World War, we would live in a totally different world." The LRE uses a multi-perspective approach, bringing together many different points of view to explore the sensitive history of World War II and the Liberation, presenting our shared European past in all its complexity.

The message of the LRE is to encourage people, and especially the younger generations, to visit local remembrance sites and to experience history firsthand. Victoria van Krieken's hope is that "young people will consider this history as a reminder that this should never happen again and to be aware that freedom is not to be taken for granted." The route inspires reflection, awareness, sensitivity and a meditation on the importance of freedom.

order to add yet more perspectives to the story of the Liberation.

Route companions

Touring the Liberation Route Europe is even easier with the book in your hands. This helpful companion brings together two parties in a one-of-a-kind partnership: the expertise of Rough Guides as a long-standing travel publisher and the LRE Foundation, promoting remembrance tourism and international cooperation.

You can read more personal stories on the LRE website (liberationroute.com), as well as finding descriptions of over four hundred sites, suggested places to visit and offers from relevant tour operators. A mobile

The Europe Remembers campaign raises awareness of the 75th anniversary of the Liberation of Europe

application also allows you to create your own itineraries (available for download from the Apple Store or Google Play).

It is also possible to travel the route with a professional tour guide specializing in the history of World War II. The LRE Guide Network is a collection of tour operators, from Normandy in France to Berlin in Germany, Arnhem in the Netherlands to Bastogne in Belgium. The guides work to bring visitors the most interesting on-site experiences, as

The vfonds

The Dutch National Fund for Peace, Freedom and Veterans Support (vfonds) was created in the 1970s, its mission being to care for war veterans – especially members of the Netherlands Association of Military War Victims. It focuses on the following social areas: promoting the recognition of veterans and other uniformed persons; keeping the memory of war and peace missions alive; remembering and commemorating victims of conflicts; and celebrating freedom. The vfonds supports war and resistance museums and a number of commemorative projects, as well as providing information on military operations and their consequences for civilians and soldiers. Their work is carried out with the wider aim of preserving peace, democracy and the rule of (both national and international) law. For more information, visit www.vfonds.nl.

well as placing each in its historical context. Find out more about LRE Guides at www.liberationroute.com/guides.

The Liberation Route Europe Foundation

The Liberation Route Europe Foundation was established in the Netherlands in January 2011, with a special team dedicated to implementing the initiative. The foundation is a membership organization, gathering relevant parties – museums, local government teams, tourism boards and veteran associations – into a multidisciplinary network of stakeholders with the shared mission of preserving the history and heritage of World War II.

The LRE Foundation has been generously supported by the vfonds (Dutch National Fund for Peace, Freedom and Veterans Support) since 2012. Vfonds works across three main areas: historical content development; remembrance tourism tools; and memory transmission activities, with young people as their main audience.

2019–2020: the 75th anniversary of the end of World War II

The years 2019 and 2020 mark the 75th anniversary of the Liberation and the end of World

War II; the LRE Foundation has launched two major projects for these jubilee years.

The first initiative, the Europe Remembers awareness campaign, collates a wealth of information about the commemoration – all in one place and available in six languages. The website europeremembers.com provides an inventory of events organized over the course of those two years, including memorial services, special exhibitions, conferences, festivals and concerts. It also presents suggested itineraries and places to visit – with more than six hundred recommended remembrance sites across nine European countries – as well as tours from LRE guides and offers from partnered tour operators. Illuminating historical background and context completes the picture.

The second initiative is a signed hiking trail, due to launch in May 2020 to commemorate VE Day in 1945. The route will allow walkers to follow in the footsteps of many of the soldiers who liberated Europe at the end of World War II. Developed in partnership with several reputable hiking organizations, the main trail will connect London and Berlin, with branches leading off to reach a wider network of remembrance sites. Beyond 2020, the aim is to extend the route and make it bike-accessible.

The trail will be distinctively signed: the LRE Foundation has partnered with Studio Libeskind to develop a family of markers of different sizes and shapes, inscribed with explanatory text and graphics. Creator Daniel Libeskind explains that the collection of markers, or "vectors", "gives you the sense of direction, but also the sense of unity. It is pointing up to something positive and optimistic. Something that gives you the sense that you are united in this territory with many other people from different walks of life."

Daniel Libeskind

Daniel Libeskind is a Polish-American architect who founded Studio Libeskind in 1989 with his wife, Nina. His buildings include the Jewish Museum in Berlin, the Imperial War Museum North in Manchester, the Military History Museum in Dresden and the Holocaust Memorials in Ottawa and Amsterdam. He is also the master architect for the reconstruction of the World Trade Center site in New York City.

For Libeskind, whose architecture company has designed the signage for the 2020 LRE hiking trail, the markers or "vectors" represent, "the footsteps of the future, of something that we all badly need across the divisions, across the forgetting, the oblivion of forgetting, which gives rise to all sorts of ghosts of history. To remember is to create a better future."

Introduction

Introduction to the Liberation of Europe

The Liberation of Europe that marked the closing stages of World War II saw the defeat of Nazi Germany in one of the largest and most daring operations ever witnessed.

Why is the Liberation important today?

For anyone reared on the internet in the democratic nations of western Europe, World War II can feel like a long time ago, and peace is easily taken for granted. Only a dwindling number of elderly men and women remember the conflict first-hand; most people alive today interact with a war that happened before their parents – or even their grandparents – were born. Far removed from the present, World War II is no more than a history lesson at school or the subject of dreary daytime documentaries.

World War II was the last great global war and has long functioned as the conflict by which all other wars are judged. It is a conflict often represented as an archetypal struggle between good and evil, and while wicked and heroic acts were committed by men and women on both sides, the Liberation of western Europe was essentially a triumph of morality and justice. The campaign was driven by a desire to restore liberty to the nations of occupied Europe that had been stripped of their rights.

Between 1940 and 1943 Nazi Germany controlled much of western Europe. The Liberation was contrived by individuals who, for all their faults, agreed that the Nazi regime could not be permitted to continue. They viewed Germany's racial policies, suppression of opposition and militarized occupation of its neighbouring states with contempt. Nazism's expansionist aims, in particular, prompted an international crisis of titanic proportions. Unable to ignore Germany's ruthless invasions across Europe – and despite many politicians favouring a policy of appeasement towards Hitler – an international coalition of nation-states banded together to stand up to discrimination and destruction. The Liberation is an enduring lesson in collaboration and cooperation.

Nevertheless, World War II witnessed acute hardship and suffering. Its victims were seldom comforted by an arching morality tale, and men, women and children existed in exceptional circumstances, and were pushed to the extreme. The realities of war threw everything into question and tested everyone. Some people faced difficult choices; for others, the choices were impossible. It is important to approach the stories of those who lived through World War II with compassion and empathy – to try to understand the responsibility of an army commander who had to ask thousands of young men to give their lives so that the next generation could be born free or the dilemma faced by a resistance fighter whose actions might bring reprisals on her entire village.

All of this belongs to history, but this book is as much about the present as about times lost. The purpose of the Liberation Route Europe – and the sites along it that provide living memorials to World War II and the Liberation – is to keep memory alive so that the stories, experiences and lessons of the war do not fade.

What exactly was the Liberation?

World War II began in 1939 and ended six years later in 1945. The Liberation was the last phase of the war, when occupied Europe was freed from Nazi rule. The Liberation consisted of three campaigns, one from the west, one from the south and one from the east, which converged on and defeated Nazi Germany.

The army from the west was principally an alliance between the USA, Great Britain, Canada and France. The army coming from the east was that of Soviet Russia, officially the Red Army. Together, all the armies of the Liberation are known as the Allies. En route to Germany, these two armies freed the countries that Germany had occupied in 1939–40: France, the Low Countries (Belgium, Luxembourg and the Netherlands), Poland and Czechoslovakia.

The Liberation only became a feasible enterprise after three-and-a-half years of war – the conditions for success came together in the spring of 1945. After much preparation, the Liberation began on 10 July 1943, with the invasion of the island of Sicily. It ended on 8 May 1945 with the capitulation of Nazi Germany to the Allies.

Complexities of the Liberation

All history is a simplification. There is too much detail in any given day of the past to relate it all; facts have to be selected and compressed into a coherent narrative – otherwise history would be unreadable.

Throughout the Liberation there were a great number of variables that affected the Allied advance: the weather; the availability of basic supplies; the health and morale of troops; the quality of communications; and luck. Not all of these factors can be addressed when describing every battle, so it is important to be aware of what's omitted.

It is easier for historians to ignore complexity and instead relate grand events involving famous personalities – these are the

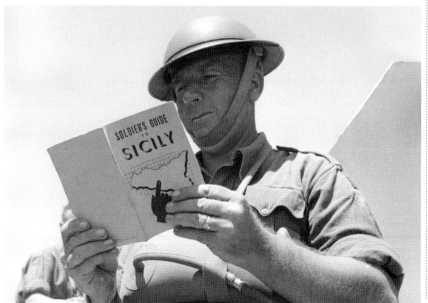

« A British recruit reads the *Soldier's Guide to Sicily*

stories most of us want to read about, after all – but the banal actions of average soldiers and civilians were important, too. The events of the Liberation were at once dictated by large-scale strategic decisions and their implementation "on the ground", altered by the reactions of ordinary men. The difference between the success and failure of an offensive frequently hinged, not on the orders from above, but how the men on the frontline interpreted them in the reality of battle. Did they risk their lives to hold some shell-battered village, for instance, or follow their instincts and retreat? To a platoon of scared young men who didn't want to die, the village was just a coordinate on a map – to a general it could mean the success or failure of a meticulously planned campaign.

War is infinitely complex. Every battle is confusing, and rarely went according to plan, precisely because there were so many variables. With hindsight, it is possible to make sense of the intense and complicated interaction between two opposing forces by comparing the military objectives with the outcomes. It is easy to impose cause and effect on any given phenomenon – that one side prevailed because it was stronger and had better tactics – but that is often to be seduced by a false conclusion. Likewise, it is easy to ignore factors that don't fit the coherent narrative. Sometimes success depended on constantly shifting weather and luck, neither of which is readily quantifiable.

On a practical level, relating history relies on using an accepted system of abbreviations. It is not possible to mention every nationality that fought in any particular episode of the Liberation, and we must make do with terms like "Allies" and "Germans" to describe the armies made up of men and women from a diverse patchwork of backgrounds – of different ethnicities, political persuasions and character. These terms are simultaneously true and imprecise.

Another problem is that we know how things turned out. With hindsight, we know how the war ended, and this can be misleading. Hindsight gives a satisfying shape to a jumble of facts; it joins the dots of cause and effect. It can be hard to understand the decisions made by men and women on the ground who didn't know the end game. In the extreme, hindsight can make an outcome seem inevitable. This is deceptive; the Liberation was not a smooth progression and its conclusion always hung in the balance.

Knowledge on the subject of World War II is also limited – evidence, by definition, is that which is left behind. Any view of the war is dependent on what can be gleaned from original documents, objects, recorded

» East Londoners left homeless by German bombing raids in the first month of the Blitz

«
Burned bodies of the
victims of the
Gardelegen massacre,
perpetrated by the
Nazis in April 1945

interviews and contemporaneous films and photographs. The archive is incomplete and always will be. Additionally, the history of any war is largely written by the victor, who is keen to present a favourable version of events. Myths are easily invented but are hard to dispel. The truth – of course – is that the winner's version is only one interpretation. To see the war from the "other side" demands a leap of comprehension and empathy.

How a person sees the Liberation may well depend on their nationality, ancestry and other allegiances. Its events were felt differently by each country, and by each individual involved – divergent experiences that continue to colour present-day interpretations of World War II.

Writing about the Liberation

Several challenges arise when writing about the Liberation. Its events took place in a number of different places across Europe at the same time, meaning any narrative must move either geographically or chronologically. The liberation of each country (and region) is best considered as a whole, in the order they were freed, but battles were being fought concurrently throughout Europe; it is important to keep both time and place in mind.

Writing about the liberation also involves juggling political and military history. The generals and their troops conducted the war on the ground, but their objectives were set by senior politicians in Washington, London and Moscow. There was not always a clear line of accountability for wartime decisions – which helped many Nazis escape justice after the war (see p.336). The Liberation is a military examination of the troops' various attacks and retreats, as well as the story of the civilians who got caught up in the fighting. The activities of soldiers are generally easy to analyse and reconstruct – armies work in hierarchies and keep meticulous records – whereas civilians frequently slipped beneath the radar;

most of them are mentioned in the history books only as statistics.

When considering the Liberation, there are few stable points of reference. Even the political geography has shifted since the end of World War II. The countries of the time broadly correspond to the nations of today, with some important exceptions. Czechoslovakia has since been divided into two; this book covers only the territory of the Czech Republic. The borders of Poland during the war and the Poland of today are also different. Poland's borders were gerrymandered by the Nazis in 1939; after the war, its borders were altered again to the benefit of the Soviets.

A writer's choice of words matters, too. The very notion of a "liberation" is a value judgement, implying that the Allies were virtuous. We must be wary of depicting one side as wholly right and the other wrong. This is especially important when discussing the actions of the Soviet Union. At the time, the Red Army was often considered an army of liberation in the same way as the USA, but for too many the Soviet "liberation" brought a new kind of subjugation. Wherever possible, it is best to suspend moral prejudgement when reading accounts of the Liberation or visiting its monuments. The accumulation of facts may lead in the same direction, but it is worth leaving a mental space for readjustment. Some actions of the Soviet Union were virtuous; some Nazis defied their stereotype; and some British and American soldiers committed atrocities that must not be whitewashed.

A historical tapestry

For these reasons, it is useful to see the Liberation not as a single coherent event but as a patchwork of accounts – a complex web of overlapping interactions – that is often complicated and contradictory. It is a fascinating period of history with many different stories to tell. It exists in the past, but has a reality today too, kept alive in the memories of those who served in World War II and in the many local and national museums dedicated to the subject.

How this book works

The main section of this book is organized into eight chapters, covering the nine principal countries affected by the Liberation. First, we look at the countries of western Europe: Italy, where the liberation of continental Europe began; the United Kingdom, the launchpad for D-Day; France, liberated through the D-Day landings in Normandy; then Belgium, Luxembourg and the Netherlands – vital territories that had to be controlled by the Allied armies before the invasion of Germany could be launched. Action then shifts east to explain the events that affected Poland (the first country to be invaded by Nazi Germany in collusion with the Soviet Union) and the Czech Republic – countries where Nazi rule was ended by the Soviet Red Army. Last is Germany – straddling western and eastern Europe – where World War II started and where the European war ended in the spring of 1945.

Each chapter recounts the events of the liberation that happened within that country, divided into regions and following a general chronological order as far as possible. The regions contain a range of excellent visitable sites connected with the Liberation; every listing has a helpful description, so you know exactly what to expect. Accompanying country maps – marked with modern borders – pinpoint the location of today's sites, while arrows show the broad sweep of troop movements to help illustrate each country's history.

Dividing the country chapters are eight "in focus" features examining important themes that affected populations across borders: life under occupation; resistance movements; strategic bombing; casualties; atrocities; the Holocaust; the Soviet Union; and displaced persons and refugees.

Before the main countries section, a series of introductory chapters set the Liberation in context. A map provides an overview of the sweep of the Liberation; a timeline chronicles the major events of 1943–45; and an editor's choice suggests the best sites to visit. Directly preceding the country chapters is a discussion of the run-up to the Liberation – the events that shaped Europe between 1934 and 1943 – and an account of the countries that remained neutral in World War II.

Towards the end of the book, the conclusion section explores the legacy of the Liberation, including chapters on reconstruction, justice and retribution, and the world at war – a way of remembering and paying homage to the many non-European countries involved in World War II. We also include a number of personal reflections on the Liberation, offered by people from varied walks of life.

Finally, we have a reference section that supplies some Liberation-themed tailor-made tours around Europe; a selection of films and books for further study; and an explanation of exactly how World War II armies were organized.

Dispersed throughout the book are a number of useful boxes and features offering insights into a range of important themes, from friendly fire to concentration camps, breaking the Enigma code and the Atlantic Wall. All the major personalities are covered too – Eisenhower, Mussolini, Rommel and so forth – as well as some of the people inadvertently caught up in the tragedy of war, such as Anne Frank and Dietrich Bonhoeffer.

« Grave of Polish General Anders at Monte Cassino Polish Military Cemetery

Liberation Route Europe

History is just one aspect of this book. It is also a travel companion, as the fascinating story of the Liberation is brought alive by exploring the landscapes of today. All the sites associated with the Liberation that we have chosen to include in this guide – fortifications, cemeteries, museums, memorials, battlefields, towns, ruined villages – are portals into the past.

It hasn't been easy to decide what to include and what to omit (for want of space), and there are plenty of other interesting places to discover. Some of them don't receive many visitors; some are overgrown with vegetation; some have little or no documentation to explain their significance, but they all have something to say about the people who passed through between 1943 and 1945.

Touring the lands and sites of the Liberation Route Europe, whether through the pages of this book, on the internet, on an independent adventure or as part of an organized trip, is a deeply rewarding experience. History and place intersect to offer a moving, living and connected exploration of World War II and the final Liberation.

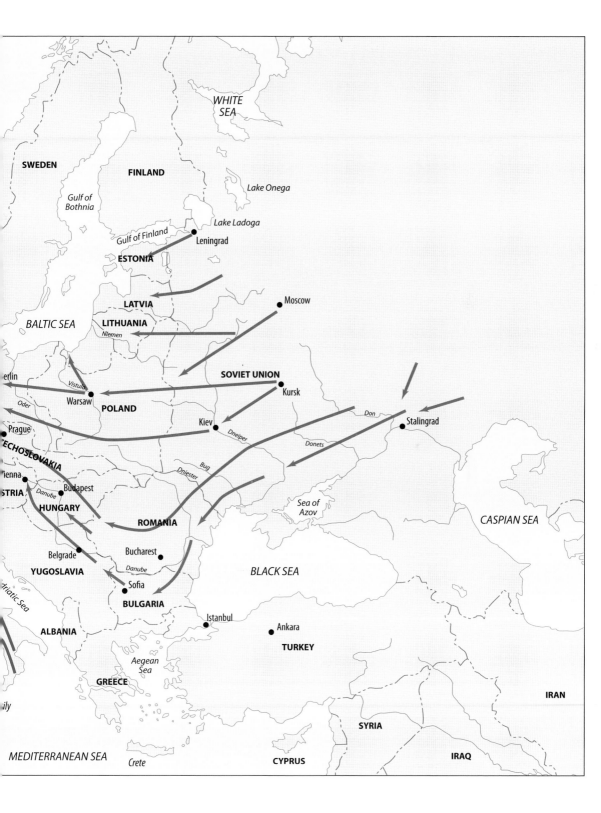

WHITE
SEA

SWEDEN

FINLAND

Gulf of
Bothnia

Lake Onega

Lake Ladoga

Gulf of Finland
Leningrad

ESTONIA

Moscow

LATVIA

BALTIC SEA

LITHUANIA

Niemen

SOVIET UNION

erlin

Vistula

Kursk

Warsaw

POLAND

Oder

Kiev

Don

Stalingrad

Prague

Dneiper

ECHOSLOVAKIA

Donets

ienna

Bug

STRIA

Dniester

Danube

Budapest

HUNGARY

Sea of
Azov

CASPIAN SEA

ROMANIA

Belgrade

Bucharest

YUGOSLAVIA

Danube

BLACK SEA

driatic Sea

Sofia

BULGARIA

Istanbul

ALBANIA

Ankara

TURKEY

Aegean
Sea

GREECE

IRAN

ily

SYRIA

MEDITERRANEAN SEA

Crete

CYPRUS

IRAQ

Timeline of the Liberation of Europe

» 1943

14 January Casablanca Conference begins. Allies agree to demand total unconditional surrender from the Axis powers without negotiation.

2 February A defeated German army surrenders at Stalingrad.

12 May Trident Conference in Washington. Allies agree to an invasion of Sicily followed by an assault across the English Channel in 1944.

13 May German and Italian armies in North Africa surrender unconditionally in Tunisia. Allies turn their attention to continental Europe.

10 July Allied invasion of Sicily by American, British and Canadian forces.

13 July Soviet victory at Battle of Kursk. German army is forced to retreat in what is considered a turning point of the war.

15 July Initial plans for Operation Overlord (the D-Day landings) presented to British Chiefs of Staff Committee.

25 July Fall of Mussolini, who is arrested and replaced by Marshal Badoglio.

17 August German Army evacuated from Sicily to the mainland, leaving the island to the Allies.

3 September Invasion of mainland Italy begins with Operation Baytown. Italy signs secret armistice with the Allies.

8 September Italian armistice made public in a broadcast by Eisenhower.

9 September Allies land at Salerno.

12 September Mussolini rescued by the Germans and transported to northern Italy.

1 October Naples falls to the Allies.

13 October Italy declares war on Germany.

4 November First US troops reach Monte Cassino, an obstacle in the Italian campaign for the next six months.

28 November Tehran Conference begins. Stalin, Roosevelt and Churchill meet to decide how to end the war and divide up influence in the postwar world.

24 December Eisenhower appointed Supreme Allied Commander in Europe and charged with organizing Operation Overlord.

» 1944

4 January Red Army crosses the Polish border.

22 January Anzio beach landing near Rome to relieve troops at Monte Cassino. The breakout proves tougher than expected.

24 March Germans execute Italian prisoners in the Ardeatine caves in Rome as reprisal for a partisan attack.

4 June Rome occupied by the Allies.

6 June D-Day landings launched by the Allies on the north coast of Normandy.

10 June Almost the entire population of Oradour-sur-Glane in France is massacred by an SS unit.

22 June Operation Bagration launched: a huge Soviet offensive against the Germans in Belarus.

9 July Caen in Normandy is liberated.

20 July Bomb plot by members of the German army against Hitler fails.

23 July Lublin, Poland, falls to the Red Army.

25 July Start of Cobra, the Allied operation to break out of Normandy and advance towards Germany.

1 August Warsaw Uprising begins.

4 August Florence falls to the Allies.

15 August Allied troops land on the beaches of Provence in Operation Dragoon, designed to liberate southern and eastern France.

17 August Hitler orders evacuation of German troops in southern France.

19 August Allies reach the Seine. Paris Uprising begins.

21 August End of the Falaise pocket in Normandy, where large numbers of Germans are killed or taken prisoner. Dumbarton Oaks Conference in the USA on the postwar international system formulates the United Nations Organization, including the Security Council.

23 August Romania, previously an Axis power, announces it has signed an armistice with the Allies and declares war on Germany.

25 August Allies take Paris.

2 September British forces cross into Belgium.

3 September The British enter Brussels.

4 September Allies take Antwerp, but not the vital Scheldt estuary.

8 September First V2 rocket bombs launched against Great Britain. Belgian government returns to Brussels.

10 September First Allied soldiers cross into Germany at Roetgen, but progress is halted in the Hürtgenwald.

17 September Operation Market Garden launched in an attempt to capture the bridge at Arnhem.

25 September Market Garden fails in its objective. Troops are evacuated and only a salient of land – but not the bridge – is held.

2 October Warsaw Uprising comes to an end.

7 October Jewish revolt in Auschwitz. Four hundred and fifty prisoners are shot, and four women are later hanged.

14 October Rommel commits suicide.

21 October Aachen becomes the first German city captured by the Allies.

7 November US President Roosevelt elected for fourth term.

8 November Battle of the Scheldt Estuary comes to an end.

12 November The *Tirpitz*, Germany's last battleship, sunk off Norway.

26 November Antwerp opened to Allied shipping.

16 December Ardennes counteroffensive launched, beginning the Battle of the Bulge. Hitler plans to drive through British and US forces and reach Antwerp.

17 December SS unit kills US prisoners of war in cold blood at Malmédy, Belgium.

18 December Fighting in Bastogne, Belgium. The town is held by the Americans and besieged for a week (starting 20 December) by the Germans.

24 December German Ardennes offensive comes to a halt, partly because of German fuel shortages.

≫ 1945

1 January Chenogne massacre in response to Malmédy. German prisoners mown down with machine guns by US troops.

12 January Red Army launches Vistula-Oder Offensive.

15 January Hitler returns to Reich Chancellery in Berlin.

17 January Red Army "liberates" the ruins of Warsaw. Evacuation of Auschwitz; "death marches" begin.

19 January Krakow falls to the Red Army.

25 January End of Battle of the Bulge.

27 January Red Army liberates Auschwitz.

4 February Yalta Conference begins.

9 February Colmar pocket in Alsace, France, is finally cleared.

13 February Fire bombing of Dresden.

3 March Finland declares war on Germany. Churchill visits the Western Front, the first British prime minister to step foot on German soil since Chamberlain in September 1938.

5 March The German Army, short of manpower, calls up all boys born in 1929, some not yet 16.

7 March American forces capture railway bridge across the Rhine at Remagen.

11 March Hitler leaves Berlin for the final time to visit troops on the Oder.

15 March German atomic research ended by Allied bombing of the thorium ore processing plant at Oranienburg (Brandenburg).

17 March Remagen bridge collapses but the Allies are already across the river.

19 March Hitler decrees a scorched earth policy to deny infrastructure and resources to the Allies. He is largely disobeyed.

21 March Gestapo headquarters in Copenhagen bombed. Several bombs are dropped on a school by mistake.

23 March Operation Plunder. Montgomery crosses the Rhine at Rees and Wesel.

25 March American troops take airfields used by German jets. Churchill flies down the Rhine and sets foot on its east bank.

27 March Argentina declares war on Germany and Japan, the 53rd nation to be at war. The last remaining V2 rockets are fired at Great Britain, causing its final civilian casualties of the war.

29 March Red Army reaches Austria.

30 March Danzig (Gdańsk) falls to the Russians.

1 April German Army Group B is surrounded in the Ruhr pocket.

9 April Final Allied offensive in Italy begins.

11 April US soldiers liberate Buchenwald.

12 April Death of Roosevelt, who is succeeded by Truman.

13 April Vienna falls to the Red Army.

15 April Arnhem is finally taken.

16 April Battle of Berlin begins.

18 April Churchill instructs Montgomery to make for Lübeck on the Baltic.

19 April Second British Army reaches the Elbe upstream from Hamburg. Americans take Leipzig.

20 April US takes Nuremberg. German forces isolated in the Netherlands. Berlin is shelled by Russians.

21 April French forces enter Stuttgart. Ruhr pocket surrenders. The commander of the captured German army, Model, shoots himself.

23 April Himmler and Goering each try to take over command from Hitler. Hitler later expels them both from the Nazi party.

24 April Berlin surrounded by Soviet forces.

25 April American and Soviet forces meet at Torgau on the river Elbe. Day of general insurrection in Italy which will become National Liberation Day.

28 April Execution of Mussolini by partisans.

29 April Dachau liberated. Hitler writes his will and testament, blaming "international Jewry" for Germany's misfortunes. Instrument of capitulation signed at Caserta Palace, bringing the war in Italy to an end on 2 May.

30 April Adolf Hitler and Eva Braun commit suicide.

1 May Negotiations for the surrender of Berlin between General Krebs and General Zhukov. Goebbels commits suicide. Bormann escapes but is most likely killed.

2 May Weidling surrenders Berlin to Zhukov. A ceasefire comes into force at 3pm. Wernher von Braun surrenders in Austria and is sent to the United States.

3 May New Germany government under President Dönitz sets up in Flensburg.

4 May Capitulation of German forces in northern Netherlands, northwest Germany and Denmark to Montgomery on Lüneberg Heath. American forces cross Brenner Pass and meet their compatriots coming from northern Italy.

5 May Mauthausen prison camp in Austria is liberated. Prague Uprising begins.

6 May Patton's Third US Army liberates Pilsen, Czech Republic, and parts of western Bohemia.

7 May Jodl signs an instrument of unconditional surrender in Reims, to come into effect on 8 May, henceforth VE Day in Western Europe. The war in Europe effectively comes to an end.

8 May Repetition of the act of capitulation in Berlin for the benefit of the Soviets: their VE day is declared as 9 May.

9 May Soviet army reaches Prague.

11 May Most remaining German resistance comes to an end. Resistance in Prague is over.

23 May Dönitz government dimissed and several of its members arrested.

« Benito Mussolini's corpse (second from left) strung up in Milan

Editor's choice

With so much to see and experience, from world-class museums to sombre memorials, here are twenty Liberation Route sites to prioritize.

Monte Cassino Abbey, Italy
Page 53. Destroyed by a ruthless Allied bombing campaign in 1944, this beautiful abbey has been rebuilt exactly as it was. A small on-site museum explains what happened here.

Sant'Anna di Stazzema, Italy
Page 65. A national peace park marks the spot where the Waffen-SS massacred 560 Tuscan civilians for their links to the Resistance.

Imperial War Museum London, UK
Page 86. The best military museum in the UK capital. Pulling few punches, it chronicles World War II and the Holocaust in vivid detail.

The D-Day Story Portsmouth, UK
Page 92. State-of-the-art D-Day museum on the south coast containing the 90m Overlord Tapestry.

D-Day beaches, France
Page 114. Memories of D-Day abound in Normandy, where more than 150,000 men landed in June 1944 as part of Operation Overlord.

Caen Memorial Museum, France
Page 135. Excellent modern museum charting the rise of fascism in Germany, the resistance and collaboration in France and the major battles of World War II, with a special emphasis on D-Day and its aftermath.

Natzweiler-Struthof Concentration Camp, France
Page 152. A Zyklon B canister is among the sobering items on display at Natzweiler-Struthof Concentration Camp in Alsace.

Bastogne War Museum and Mardasson Memorial, Belgium
Page 175. Belgium's emblematic World War II museum sits opposite the Mardasson Memorial, a monument to the American soldiers who fought and died on Belgian soil.

Luxembourg American Cemetery, Luxembourg
Page 177. General Patton is interred at this US cemetery – along with some 5000 other servicemen – in the country he helped liberate.

Anne Frank House, the Netherlands
Page 206. A poignant and personal evocation of the German persecution of the Jews. Among the moving exhibits is the bookcase behind which the Frank family hid for two years between 1942 and 1944.

Liberation Museum Zeeland, the Netherlands

Page 192. A regional museum with big ambitions and the addition of a new Liberation Park in 2017. There's a special focus on the "forgotten" battle of the Scheldt.

Airborne Museum "Hartenstein", the Netherlands

Page 203. Excellent museum housed in the former headquarters of the British First Airborne Division, where exhibits include a strip of the villa's original wallpaper inscribed with the message "Fuck the Gerrys".

Warsaw Rising Museum, Poland

Page 231. Powerful museum dedicated to the Warsaw Uprising. Outside is a park with a 165m-high wall inscribed with the names of several thousand soldiers who died in the struggle.

Home Army Museum, Poland

Page 242. Poland's only museum dedicated to the government-in-exile and resistance army. Guided tours are highly recommended.

Auschwitz-Birkenau, Poland

Page 245. The notorious concentration and extermination camp offers profound insights into the nature of human evil.

Terezín (Theresienstadt), Czech Republic

Page 266. Heralded as a "model Jewish settlement" by the Nazis, Terezín managed to retain its rich cultural heritage in spite of overcrowding, food shortages and regular deportations to the death camps.

Dachau Concentration Camp Memorial Site, Germany

Page 297. The former Nazi concentration camp on Munich's northern outskirts is entered through an iron gate into which is set the infamous slogan *Arbeit Macht Frei* ("work makes you free").

Dokumentation Obersalzberg, Germany

Page 300. A fascinating exhibition on the rise, fall and crimes of the Nazi movement, its mythology and its association with Obersalzberg.

Historical Technical Museum, Germany

Page 305. Housed in a huge red-brick power station constructed by the Nazis, the Historical Technical Museum charts the development of rocketry at Peenemünde.

German Resistance Memorial Centre, Germany

Page 317. This absorbing exhibition displays a huge collection of photos and documents covering the many and wide-ranging groups who actively opposed the Third Reich – an eclectic mix that included communists, Jews, Quakers and aristocrats.

Before the Liberation: Europe 1934–1943

The Liberation of Europe was liberation from Nazi Germany – arguably the most hateful and destructive regime of the 20th century. The Nazis tyrannized, enslaved and murdered millions of people across Europe and beyond.

By the time the western democracies came to realize the full extent of Adolf Hitler's geo-political ambitions, Germany's reborn military might was already on the move. Central to Nazism was the idea of Germans as part of the Aryan master race, with the right to subjugate those whom they regarded as racially inferior – Jews, Slavs, Roma and Sinti, and black people.

The rise of Hitler

Hitler had come to power through a combination of violence and extreme nationalism. He successfully played on the perception of many Germans that their country had been humiliated at the end of World War I by the punitive Treaty of Versailles. He was determined to overturn the terms of the treaty and reassert Germany as a great world power. Many European politicians saw Hitler as a threat, but they were reluctant to go to war and repeat the cataclysmic events of World War I. There were also those who admired him: it was a common right-wing belief at the time that communism was a Jewish-inspired international conspiracy, which could only be stopped by fascism.

Inspired by Italy's fascist leader, Benito Mussolini, and with the help of Nazi Propa-

ganda Minister Josef Goebbels, Hitler established a leadership cult that many Germans responded to with enthusiasm. By the end of 1934 he was not only Chancellor and head of his party, but also head of state and supreme commander of the armed forces – simply summarised in the title "der Führer" (the leader).

German expansion

Hitler's first significant military action occurred in 1936 when he ordered troops into the Rhineland, a buffer zone between France and Germany that had been demilitarized since the end of World War I. The feeble response of the western democracies encouraged him to go further. In 1938, the Germans annexed Austria – Hitler's birthplace – an event that was broadly welcomed by the populations of both countries. Hitler then turned to the Sudetenland, a territory of Czechoslovakia with a large German-speaking population. This too was annexed, with the connivance of the French and British prime ministers. When the Germans occupied the rest of the country in March 1939, at the invitation – so Hitler claimed – of its president, the reaction of the French and the British was to prove once again indecisive.

The outbreak of war

It was only after the invasion of Poland on 1 September 1939 that Britain and France declared war on Germany. Poland suffered the double blow of being invaded from opposite directions by Germany and the Soviet Union. The two countries had recently signed a non-aggression pact which agreed their future spheres of interest. Their occupying forces then systematically murdered any potential opposition. Neither France nor Britain did much to help the Poles, and the following eight months saw little military action by Poland's allies. An attempt by the British to prevent iron ore reaching Germany by invading Norway ended in failure; instead, Germany occupied Norway, and the British government fell. It was replaced by a coalition led by a new prime minister, Winston Churchill, who had long advocated rearmament and a more aggressive stance towards Hitler.

When the war finally started in earnest for Britain and France, it went wrong rapidly. On 10 May 1940 the Germans began their simultaneous invasion of France, the Netherlands, Belgium and Luxembourg (despite the last three being neutral). It took the Wehrmacht just six weeks to defeat the Allied armies in France. *Blitzkrieg*, the German military tactic based on speed, surprise and co-ordinated attacks, was no less devastating in France than it had been in Poland. The Allied forces that had advanced into Belgium – mostly British and French, with Belgian and Polish support – were forced back and surrounded near the French port of Dunkirk. Many of the stranded troops – 338,000 of them – were picked up and successfully evacuated back to Britain, but the 40,000 fighting a rear-guard action to protect the evacuation were all taken prisoner. Paris fell on 14 June and a week later France was divided into zones: the north and western coastline under German control, most of the south administered by the Vichy government, led by the elderly Marshal Pétain, which collaborated closely with Nazi Germany. To prevent the French fleet, harboured in Algeria, from falling into German hands, Churchill ordered its destruction by the Royal Navy, which was duly carried out with the loss of some 1300 men.

«
German troops advance past a barricade during the invasion of France

Britain at war

Britain, along with its Commonwealth and Empire forces, was now the only substantial military opposition to Nazi Germany. They received significant help from exiled servicemen of the occupied countries. The RAF in particular benefited from an influx of experienced Polish airmen, some of the best pilots of the war. All the occupied countries had resistance networks involved in both intelligence gathering and acts of sabotage. This was vital but highly dangerous work that often resulted in brutal and disproportionate reprisals.

In the summer of 1940, Hitler, who actually admired the British, was still making offers of peace. When these were rejected, the German air force, the Luftwaffe, began a campaign of softening up the British Isles as a prelude to invasion. Beginning on 9 July and lasting until the end of October, the Battle of Britain was a series of aerial battles fought between the RAF and the Luftwaffe over southern England. The RAF's victory was a blow from which the Luftwaffe never completely recovered, and it put an end to Hitler's invasion plans. The war in the air continued, however, with a relentless bombing campaign aimed at Britain's towns and cities. The Blitz, which lasted until May 1941, targeted mostly major ports and industrial centres and was designed to sap morale as well as destroy vital factories and infrastructure.

Lend-Lease and the war in Africa

On 27 September 1940 Germany, Italy and Japan signed the Tripartite Pact, a defensive military alliance which also outlined their shared intention of creating a "new order" in Europe and Asia. At this point the USA was still officially neutral, but providing Britain with huge amounts of vital resources, both military hardware and foodstuffs. This was arranged under the Lend-Lease scheme, whereby US goods were supplied at heavily reduced rates with payment deferred. America was effectively fighting the war by proxy. Meanwhile, the main theatre of war for the British was North Africa, where they were up against both the Germans and the Italians for control of the Suez Canal and access to oil in the Middle East. This was a long and arduous series of campaigns that lasted nearly three years. Two battles at El Alamein were major turning-points: the first, in July 1942, saw the British and Commonwealth Eighth Army halt the Axis advance in Egypt; the second, four months later, resulted in Axis forces being pushed back into Tunisia.

By tying down German troops in Africa, the British had helped take some pressure off the Russians, who since June 1941 had been fighting a desperate defensive war against the Germans. Despite the 1939 non-aggression treaty, Hitler had launched an all-out attack on the Soviet Union (Operation Barbarossa) with an initial force of around three million soldiers. The campaign met with some stunning early victories against unprepared Soviet defences, but was not the quick success Hitler had expected. Barbarossa used up huge amounts of German resources, a situation that became even more critical when Germany declared war on the USA following the Japanese attack on Pearl Harbor in December 1941. Germany was an ally of Japan, but under no obligation to go to war. By doing so, the Wehrmacht was now pitted against the combined military might of the "Big Three" powers – Britain, America and Russia – a formidable opposition.

Shortly after America entered the war, Churchill and US President Franklin D.

Roosevelt met at a conference in Washington DC in January 1942 along with their respective chiefs of staff. It was here that they decided to coordinate Allied military strategy by forming the Combined Chiefs of Staff (CCS), and fight the war under joint command. Roosevelt also agreed to a "Germany First" policy that would prioritize the war in Europe and the defeat of Nazism ahead of the war in the Pacific.

Prelude to the Liberation

The realization by the Allies that German defeat was a real possibility came with the Russian victories at Stalingrad (February 1943) and Kursk (August 1943). Both sides suffered huge numbers of casualties, but whereas Red Army losses could be replaced relatively easily, the Wehrmacht was beginning to run out of manpower and equipment. Stalin had been pressing for a large-scale Anglo-American assault in western Europe, the so-called Second Front, since 1942. The Americans were strongly in favour, but Churchill and General Alan Brooke (his chief military adviser) felt that acting too soon would be potentially disastrous. Victory was fully secured in North Africa in May 1943 following Operation Torch – the Allied invasion of Vichy-controlled Algeria and Morocco, and the first time British and American troops had worked together on a large scale. President Roosevelt had personally ordered the operation in the face of opposition from his chief military adviser, General George Marshall. It had been commanded by Marshall's protégé, a relatively inexperienced general, Dwight D. Eisenhower.

What was to happen next had already been partly decided at the Casablanca Conference of January 1943, attended by Roosevelt, Churchill and their chiefs of staff. After

«
Journalists prepare to interview German Field Marshal Friedrich Paulus, taken prisoner by the Red Army during the Battle of Stalingrad

much discussion, it was decided that nothing less than "unconditional surrender" by the Axis powers could end the war. Pressured by the Americans, the British agreed a provisional date for the invasion of occupied France, but insisted that the Allies first turn their attention to what Churchill thought of as the "soft underbelly of Europe" – an attack on Italy, beginning with Sicily. A conference in Washington in May 1943 finally confirmed that the Normandy campaign (codenamed Operation Overlord) would take place the following May, but Churchill's desire for an Anglo-American Italy campaign received only a vague commitment from Roosevelt. The Sicily campaign was definitely going ahead, however, and preparations for a huge amphibious landing, scheduled for July, were already in place. Once again, overall command would be in the hands of General Eisenhower, with a British general, Harold Alexander, leading the Allied 15th Army Group.

Neutral states

At the beginning of the war, many European governments declared their countries to be neutral.

According to the terms of the 1907 Hague Convention, being neutral meant not participating or assisting countries who were at war, and remaining impartial towards the belligerents and their allies. In turn, warring nations would recognize the non-involvement and impartiality of neutral countries, and respect their territorial integrity.

In reality, no countries were strictly neutral. Some who were, such as the Netherlands (see p.188), Belgium and Luxembourg (see p.177), were invaded anyway; others, for example Romania, altered their positions with changes of government or out of expediency. The USA was technically neutral until December 1941, but provided massive assistance to the British and the Soviets through the Lend-Lease scheme (see p.28). Hungary, Romania, Czechoslovakia, Bulgaria and Yugoslavia – often under pressure from Nazi Germany – were all later signatories to the Tripartite Pact that had bound the three Axis powers (Germany, Italy and Japan) together.

Hitler considered invading more countries than he did, but once Germany had attacked the Soviet Union, and the USA had entered the war, his forces were too heavily stretched. Europe's micro-states, such as Liechtenstein and San Marino, were all affected by the war, but none were of great strategic significance. The role of the Vatican is discussed on p.58.

Switzerland

Bordered by Nazi Germany (including Austria from 1938), Italy and occupied France, Switzerland was quick to mobilize at the start of the war, but managed to stay neutral for its duration. Trade continued with both the Allies and Germany, including accepting gold (much of it plundered) in exchange for currency. Strict border controls were in operation, and although they accepted 60,000 asylum seekers, many, including Jews, were turned away.

Denmark

Declared its neutrality at the start of the war but was occupied by Germany on 9 April 1940 in an operation that took just six hours. As a German "protectorate" it functioned relatively normally up to August 1943, when Danish government resistance to German demands led to direct Nazi rule.

Norway

A neutral country invaded and occupied by Germany in April 1940, shortly after the British had failed to do so. King Haakon VII and the prewar government escaped to London, and a puppet government was established under Vidkun Quisling. It was opposed by a resistance army and many Norwegians fought for the Allies. The occupying German forces capitulated in May 1945.

Sweden

Ostensibly neutral but in fact made concessions to both the Axis and Allies. Sweden supplied Germany with iron ore and allowed German troops to travel through the country. Norwegian resistance troops were trained in Sweden and took part in liberating the north of their country. Sweden was also a haven for refugees, providing transit papers and taking in nearly all of Denmark's eight thousand Jews.

Baltic states

On 18 November 1938, Lithuania, Latvia and Estonia made a joint declaration of neutrality, but in August 1940 all three were occupied by the Soviet Union. They were subsequently invaded by Germany as part of Operation Barbarossa, before being re-invaded and forcibly integrated into the Soviet Union at the end of the war.

Iceland

The country shared a monarch with the Danes, but when Hitler invaded Denmark, Iceland declared its independence. Invaded by the British in May 1940 (with the US taking over thereafter), Iceland became an important air and sea base for the Allies during the Battle of the Atlantic.

Ireland

The Irish Free State, or Eire, was technically still part of the British Empire, but never joined the Allied war effort, although over 30,000 Irishmen volunteered. Hitler and Churchill both considered invasion. Ireland continued to provide meteorological reports to Britain, including the crucial one that enabled D-Day to go ahead.

Spain

The fascist dictatorship of General Franco was highly sympathetic to the Axis powers, but remained nominally neutral throughout the war. Negotiations with Hitler, who wanted to invade Gibraltar, fell through because of Franco's unrealistic demands. Spain provided Germany with tungsten, allowed Axis ships to use its ports, and sent a Division to the Eastern Front. German spies and saboteurs operated openly with impunity. For its fascist leanings, Spain was the only country to be refused Marshall aid after the war.

Portugal

Antonio Salazar was a right-wing dictator who, nevertheless, kept his country out of the war. Portugal supplied Germany with tungsten but also let Britain (its oldest ally) have air bases in the Azores. Portugal's capital Lisbon was the main port for International Red Cross relief supplies and a hotbed of international espionage.

The Balkans

Albania was invaded by Italy in 1939 (before the war started). The Kingdom of Yugoslavia (roughly modern Slovenia, Bosnia and Herzegovina, Kosovo, Croatia, Montenegro, North Macedonia and Serbia) declared neutrality before the war broke out, but signed the Tripartite Pact with the Axis powers in March 1941 following unsuccessful negotiations with the Allies. This resulted in an immediate military coup by those opposed to the pact, which in turn prompted Axis forces to invade.

Greece

The right-wing dictatorship of General Metaxas tried to keep Greece out of the war and repelled an attempted invasion by the Italians in 1940. The Germans invaded in April 1941 and began plundering Greece economically. Communist and other partisan groups offered fierce resistance. The British assisted in defeating the Germans in October 1944, but their subsequent suppression of the communists ignited the three-year Greek Civil War.

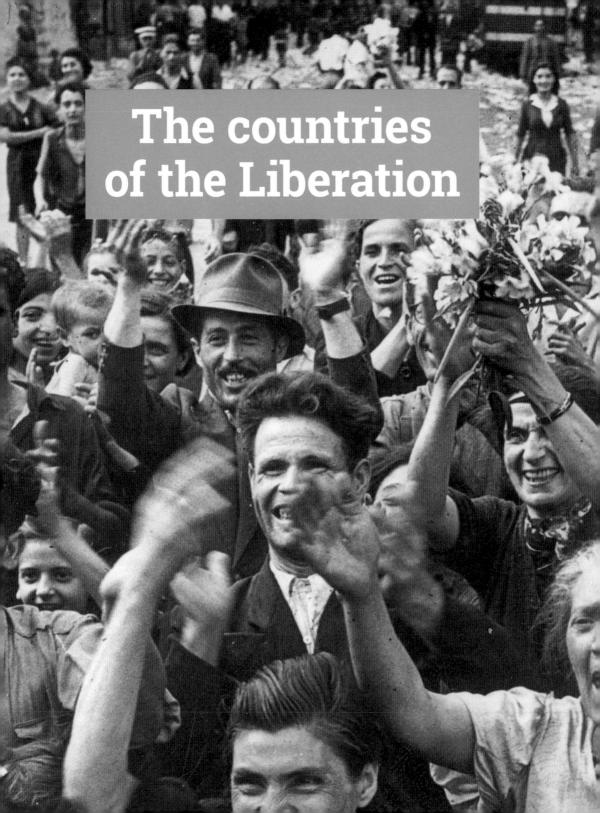

The countries of the Liberation

Italy

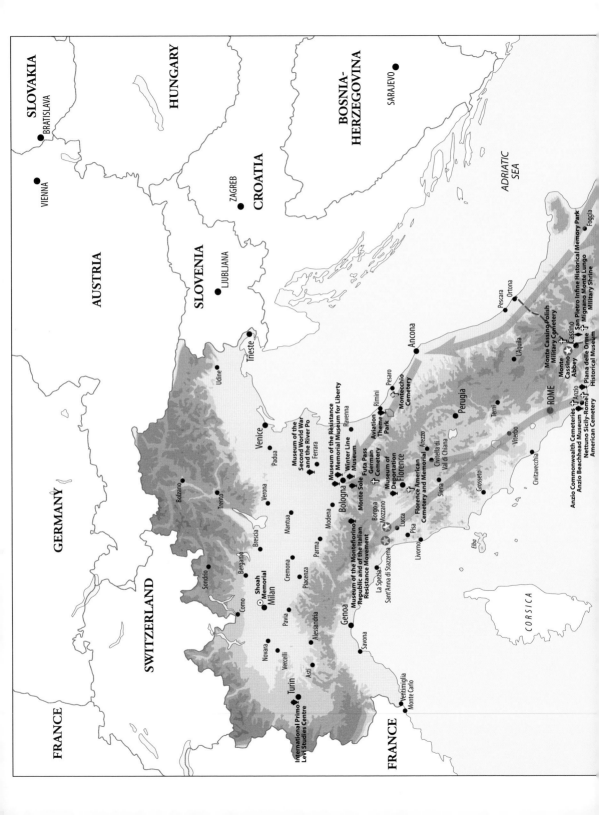

FRANCE

SLOVAKIA
BRATISLAVA

VIENNA

HUNGARY

AUSTRIA

CROATIA
ZAGREB

BOSNIA-
HERZEGOVINA

SARAJEVO

SLOVENIA
LJUBLJANA

ADRIATIC
SEA

GERMANY

Trieste

Udine

Bolzano

Trento

Venice

Padua

Ancona

Verona

SWITZERLAND

Brescia

Mantua

Museum of the
Second World War
and the River Po

Museum of the Resistance
Memorial Museum for Liberty

Winter Line
Museum

Ferrara

Rimini

Ravenna

Pesaro

Aviation
Theme
Park

Montecchio
Cemetery

Perugia

Terni

Sondrio

Como

Bergamo

Cremona

Modena

Futa Pass
German
Cemetery

Monte Sole

Arezzo

Shoah
Memorial
Milan

Pavia

Piacenza

Parma

Bologna

Borgo a
Mozzano

Museum of
Deportation

Florence

Civitella di
Val di Chiana

Novara

Vercelli

Alessandria

La Spezia

Lucca

Florence American
Cemetery and Memorial

Siena

L'Aquila

Grosseto

Viterbo

Monte Cassino
Abbey

Monte Cassino Polish
Military Cemetery

San Pietro Infine Historical Memory Park

Cassino

Mignano Monte Lungo
Military Shrine

Pescara

Ortona

Foggia

Asti

Turin

Museum of the Montefiorino
Republic and of the Italian
Resistance Movement

Sant'Anna di Stazzema

Genoa

Savona

Livorno

Pisa

Elba

Civitavecchia

ROME

Piana delle Orme
Historical Museum

Anzio

Anzio Commonwealth Cemeteries
Anzio Beachhead Museum

Nettuno Sicily-Rome
American Cemetery

Ventimiglia

Monte Carlo

FRANCE

CORSICA

International Primo
Levi Studies Centre

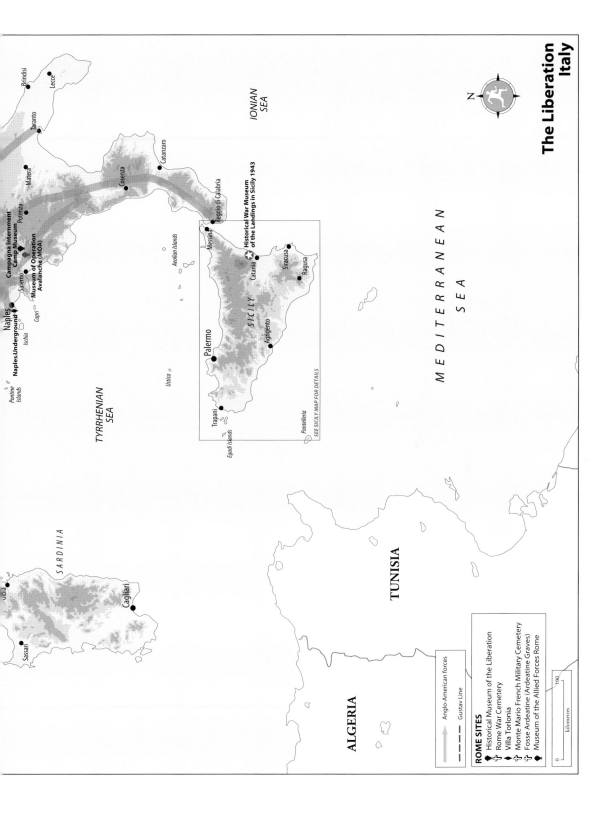

The Liberation
Italy

N

ROME SITES
✠ Historical Museum of the Liberation
✠ Rome War Cemetery
⚓ Villa Torlonia
⚓ Monte Mario French Military Cemetery
⚓ Fosse Ardeatine (Ardeatine Graves)
✠ Museum of the Allied Forces Rome

→ Anglo-American forces
--- Gustav Line

0   100
kilometres

ALGERIA

TUNISIA

SARDINIA

Olbia
Sassari
Cagliari

TYRRHENIAN
SEA

Pontine
Islands

Ustica

Aeolian Islands

Ischia
Capri

Naples
Naples Underground

Campagna Internment
Camp Museum
Museum of Operation
Avalanche (MOA)
Salerno
Potenza
Matera

Cosenza
Catanzaro

Reggio di Calabria

Messina

Catania

Historical War Museum
of the Landings in Sicily 1943

SICILY

Palermo
Trapani
Egadi Islands
Pantelleria
Agrigento
Ragusa
Siracusa

SEE SICILY MAP FOR DETAILS

MEDITERRANEAN
SEA

IONIAN
SEA

Brindisi
Lecce
Taranto

The Liberation Italy

There is some question about whether Winston Churchill ever described Italy as the "soft underbelly" of Axis Europe, but from the autumn of 1942, he certainly saw the country as the most vulnerable part of the occupied continent.

Churchill was confident that fascist Italy would crumble if a direct and strategic attack was mounted by a well-coordinated army, navy and air force. Not all Allied decision-makers were convinced, however. Many doubted the wisdom of invading Sicily, let alone the possibility of continuing the campaign northwards across mainland Italy. High-ranking US military chiefs preferred to conserve resources for a decisive invasion across the English Channel, scheduled for the spring of 1944.

Several convincing arguments were put forward against invading Italy. A mechanized army would be vulnerable to the challenges of central Italy's mountainous terrain, expending great energies for little to no gain. Moreover, a successful invasion depended on knocking Italy out of the war, and the Germans deciding their ally was not worth defending at all costs. Even if these gambles paid off, the Allies could only hope to achieve a small reward for their pains. Rome was a minor prize for the anticipated loss of human life and manpower, even if it did contain the highly symbolic Vatican City, the holy heart of Catholicism. In addition, an impoverished and hungry Italian population could become an unsustainable drain on the Allies' limited supply of imported food and fuel.

Churchill, undeterred, was insistent. He believed it was crucial for the Allies to attack southern Europe in order to take control of the Mediterranean. This would enable military and civilian shipping, maintain the momentum of the war by keeping Allied forces in contact with the enemy and, more urgently, draw German forces away from the Eastern Front to relieve pressure on the Red Army.

Eventually, US President Franklin D. Roosevelt was more willing to listen to the British prime minister than to his own advisors. Allied planners at the Trident Conference in

» Italian fascists

Washington in May 1943 eventually assented to an invasion of the island of Sicily as a compromise. Whether or not the campaign would continue on to the Italian mainland was left undecided. US General Eisenhower, they directed, would decide on the best policy after the Germans had been driven out of Sicily.

Politics and defence in Italy

In 1943, Italy was ruled by Hitler's principal ally in Europe, the fellow fascist dictator Benito Mussolini. Mussolini had joined the war only reluctantly halfway through 1940, believing that his country still needed two more years to fully prepare. Nevertheless, Italy's war aims complemented those of Nazi Germany. Mussolini had pursued a policy of aggressive expansion in southern Europe; without serious opposition, he had occupied the southeast corner of Vichy France, the French island of Corsica, Greece and part of the Balkans. Until his defeat in North Africa in 1943, Mussolini's goal had been to establish hegemony over the Mediterranean and challenge the British Empire in Africa and the Middle East.

The Italian peninsula and islands were defended not only by the country's own (large but ill-equipped) army, but also by a great number of German troops. The German troops were under the nominal command of the Italian generals, but in reality they were controlled by German Field Marshal Albert Kesselring from his base in Frascati on the outskirts of Rome.

Although Mussolini had enjoyed absolute power for eleven years, his success was built on his personal charisma, his ruthless use of force and his conquests abroad. By 1943 the Italian leader's popularity was on the wane, while his political position ultimately depended on retaining the approbation of the king of Ita-

Significant sites are marked on the map on pages 38 and 39

✪ **Historical War Museum of the Landings in Sicily 1943, Catania. See p.48**

✪ **Caserta Palace, Caserta. See p.51**

✪ **Monte Cassino Abbey, Monte Cassino. See p.53**

✪ **Sant'Anna di Stazzema. See p.65**

✪ **Borgo a Mozzano. See p.65**

Significant sites

«

ly, Victor Emmanuel III. Hitler himself was unsure whether he could rely on the strength of Mussolini and his Italian allies. As defeat in North Africa approached, Hitler made contingency plans for the defence of Italy in any eventuality. Three new units were created expressly to serve in Italy, and two experienced existing divisions were dispatched from France, some of them crossing the Strait of Messina to reinforce defences in Sicily.

Preparing Husky

Preparations for the forthcoming invasion of Sicily, codenamed Husky, had to be swift: maintaining an element of surprise was essential. Given Italy was only one possible military target in the Mediterranean, if the Allies could convince the Germans that their attack was planned elsewhere, they would have the upper hand. An ingenious plan, Operation Mincemeat (see p.43), was devised to persuade the Germans that even if there were an invasion in Sicily it would be a diversionary campaign, while the main attack would come in Greece or Sardinia. The success of Husky was to be heavily influenced by two factors: how well Sicily was defended, and how well their task forces and armies would perform in the chaos of battle.

Sicily

The invasion of Sicily in 1943 was, until D-Day eleven months later, the largest amphibious invasion in history.

The ambitious assault on Sicily, codenamed Husky, was the culmination of months of meticulous planning by the leaders of the Allied armies in North Africa. There was much argument about how to go about the task: how many troops would be needed, what their main objectives should be and how air power could best be used in their support.

Eventually it was agreed that a two-pronged offensive would target a number of beaches on Sicily's southwestern and southeastern coasts. The beaches had been covertly surveyed by submarine teams to make sure they were suitable for the large-scale disembarkation of troops and heavy vehicles. The last great unknowns were how strong the enemy's defences would prove and how hard the Italians and Germans would fight to retain control of Sicily.

Build-up to Operation Husky

In preparation for the campaign, a massive amount of men and materials had to be assembled, not just for the invasion itself but to sustain a large army in the most impoverished part of Italy for an indefinite period afterwards. Every detail had to be readied, from medals to be awarded in battle to grave markers for the fallen.

Two task forces were assembled in North Africa under the overall command of General Eisenhower. The Western Task Force was essentially the US Seventh Army – commanded by US General George S. Patton – and the Eastern Task Force was the British Eighth Army, including Canadian divisions, led by British Field Marshal Bernard Montgomery. Each had its respective fleet; altogether around 160,000 men were embarked. Sicily

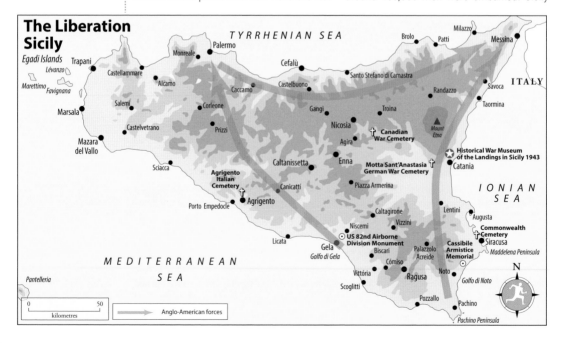

The Liberation Sicily

Egadi Islands
Lévanzo
Marettimo *Favignana*

TYRRHENIAN SEA

Trapani
Monreale
Palermo
Brolo Patti
Milazzo
Messina

Castellammare
Cefalù
Santo Stefano di Camastra

Alcamo
Castelbuono
Randazzo
Savoca
ITALY

Salemi
Caccamo
Gangi
Troina
Taormina

Marsala
Corleone
Nicosia
Mount Etna

Castelvetrano
Prizzi
Agira
† Canadian War Cemetery

Mazara del Vallo
Caltanissetta
Enna
✪ Historical War Museum of the Landings in Sicily 1943

Sciacca
Agrigento Italian Cemetery
Canicattì
Motta Sant'Anastasia † German War Cemetery
Catania

Porto Empedocle
† Agrigento
Piazza Armerina
IONIAN SEA

Caltagirone
Lentini
Augusta

Niscemi
Vizzini
Commonwealth † Cemetery
Siracusa

Licata
⊙ US 82nd Airborne Division Monument
Gela
Golfo di Gela
Biscari
Palazzolo Acreide
Cassibile Armistice Memorial ⊙
Maddelena Peninsula

Cómiso
Noto

Pantelleria

MEDITERRANEAN SEA

Vittória
Scoglitti
Ragusa
Golfo di Noto

N

Pozzallo
Pachino

0 ——— 50 kilometres
→ Anglo-American forces
Pachino Peninsula

» Operation Mincemeat

A successful attack on Sicily depended on keeping German strategists guessing as to where the invasion in the Mediterranean would come. Greece and Sardinia were presumed by German high command to be as likely targets as Italy and Sicily, and Allied planners devised an elaborate deception to disseminate false information. A corpse dressed in the uniform of a Royal Marine major was dropped into the sea and washed up on a beach in Huelva, Spain. Attached to his wrist was a briefcase containing documents that indicated the main attack would be in Greece and Sardinia.

Although officially a neutral state in the war, Spain was ruled by the fascist government of General Franco, which was sympathetic to the Axis cause. The Spanish authorities did what they could to authenticate the documents, then shared the information obtained from the "man who never was" with the Germans. It is believed that the incident inspired the young Ian Fleming, then working for British Naval Intelligence, to create stories for his hero, James Bond. The ruse proved successful: the German Abwehr checked the information fed to them by Operation Mincemeat and accepted it as true.

was defended by the Italian Sixth Army, with an estimated strength of over 200,000, supported by around 32,000 German troops.

Prior to the invasion, the small Italian islands of Pantelleria, Linosa and Lampedusa were captured without any exchange of fire. Bombing raids were carried out on Sicily's two main towns, Palermo and Messina, while airborne troops were dropped inland. The operations carried out by these troops, as well as the naval barrage, were highly significant because they marked the start of the European land war.

The amphibious invasion

The main Allied force was transported overnight on 9–10 July 1943 across 150km of open sea between Tunis and Sicily – a journey which takes around ten hours today. The Western and Eastern task forces were assigned different zones of operation: the Americans to the centre of the island and the British and Canadians to the east coast, pushing past Etna to reach Messina.

The landings in Sicily were largely unopposed. On the first day, a 6.5km-deep beach-head was established and four thousand prisoners were captured; several towns were taken in the opening few hours alone. The Germans staged a counterattack against the Americans at Gela, however, and tenaciously held on to the fortifications they had established in the east. Communication failures, errors and incidents of friendly fire also caused much loss of life. In particular, airborne assaults using parachutes and gliders proved ineffective and costly in fatalities.

The campaign to overcome the island's defenders ran into difficulty at several other points, especially on the east coast. Things were not helped by a tense rivalry between Patton and Montgomery, which hindered co-operation and made it hard to co-ordinate troops. The plain of Catania and the surrounding hills proved a particularly bloody battlefield, and a strong German defensive line was established around the volcano of Etna.

While Montgomery slogged up the east coast, Patton headed north to take Palermo (against light opposition), next turning east to try and reach Messina before the British.

》 Friendly fire

The inadvertent bombing, shelling and shooting of an army's own troops was – and still is – a perennial fact of war. Poor planning, bad weather, faulty information, lax identity checks and general human error were the cause of countless catastrophes during World War II, although the number of injuries and fatalities sustained by friendly fire remains unknown.

There were several instances of friendly fire in the Italian campaign.

During the invasion of Sicily, panicking American ground forces – believing they were being attacked – shot down 23 of their own planes and killed at least 81 paratroopers dropped in as reinforcements. Later, inland from Anzio, American Warhawk planes closed in on the wrong targets. They strafed and bombed their own soldiers, killed and wounding more than one hundred men. The survivors were then pummelled for an additional ten minutes by their own artillery.

Although Patton reached Messina first, his troops were too late to prevent the Germans from evacuating their remaining forces to fight another day.

By the time the campaign was completed on 17 August after 39 days of fighting, more than 5500 Allied soldiers and 9000 Axis combatants had lost their lives. The Allies were mostly greeted as liberators rather than invaders, but as the new occupying force of Sicily, they soon found themselves with problems that would be repeated all over a newly liberated Europe. There was the pressing question of how to deal with civilians who had cooperated with the fascist authorities; another issue was getting Allied troops to treat the local populations with respect.

The invasion of Sicily had important consequences in Rome, as its planners would later claim they'd hoped. While bloody battles were being fought in Sicily, a palace coup d'état in Rome forced Mussolini from power. The new government resolved to secretly negotiate a peace with the Allies, and its prime minister, Pietro Badoglio, opened discussions to this effect. After a pause in fighting, the Allies made their first tentative landfall on mainland Italy on the morning of 3 September 1943. The same afternoon saw the fruition of a long series of negotiations, and an armistice was signed between the two sides at a military camp near Cassibile, on Sicily's east coast.

Sicily sites

Golfo di Gela: western landing beaches

The US Seventh Army landed three divisions on beaches in the Gulf of Gela: at Scoglitti, Gela and Licata. Some of the first troops sent ashore were Italian-Americans, who proved invaluable during the build-up and implementation of Operation Husky. These men supplemented military intelligence with personal recollections and were able to communicate with the locals and help stabilize the newly liberated Italian territories.

Along the coast today – from Porta Aurea at the Valley of the Temples to the streets of Vittoria, through Licata and Gela – you can see a number of surviving military structures including bunkers, strongholds, trenches and pillboxes. Several sombre plaques record mostly individual deaths of combatants, while there are two war monuments in the town of Gela itself.

US 82nd Airborne Division Monument

The 82nd Airborne Division of the US Army faced determined opposition at Ponte Dirillo on the night of 10 July, where they were heavily outnumbered by the German and Italian troops and their tanks. This monument, a large stone tablet located near Gela on the way to Punta Secca, commemorates the 39 paratroopers who died in battle.

Agrigento Italian Cemetery
Agrigento

There are three Italian war cemeteries on Sicily. Besides this one in Agrigento, two others are located at Catania and Acireale on the east coast. Between them, they contain the graves of more than four thousand soldiers who died defending the island.

Palermo

In the prelude to Operation Husky, Sicily's capital was badly bombed, but to little end. Palermo was a more symbolic than useful prize, and the US Seventh Army, who advanced from its landing beaches to take the city, met minimal opposition. Nevertheless, the assault provided useful publicity and a welcome boost to morale. General Patton occupied the grand Palazzo Reale for a few days while he prepared his advance on Messina.

Troina

One of the fiercest battles of the Sicily campaign was fought for control of the small in-

land town of Troina between 31 July and 6 August 1943. Many inhabitants survived in squalor in the crypt of the cathedral; the scenes of horror and destruction that greeted the US liberators would be repeated in countless towns all the way up the Italian peninsula. The end of the battle marked the breaching of the Etna defensive line, but the Germans managed to make an orderly retreat from Troina before the arrival of the US troops.

Golfo di Noto: eastern landing beaches

The British Eighth Army was assigned a series of beaches on the Gulf of Noto, south of Siracusa. Canadian forces came ashore on the west side of the Pachino peninsula; the rest of the Eighth Army landed on stretches between the tips of the Pachino and Maddelena peninsulas. A few memorials stand sentinel in and around Pachino, and at one beach, Fontane Bianche, there's a modern holiday resort.

Cassibile Armistice Memorial
Via Fiume Cacipari, Cassibile

A plaque next to the church in Cassibile records the signing of the Italian armistice in a military camp near town on 3 September 1943, which brought hostilities with the Allies to an end. Preliminary negotiations were undertaken in Lisbon, but the terms were finalized here in Cassibile, with future British Prime Minister Harold Macmillan playing an important role in the process. The document was signed by Walter Bedell Smith, Eisenhower's chief of staff, and Giuseppe Castellano, on behalf of King Victor Emmanuel III and Italian Prime Minister Pietro Badoglio. The armistice and its terms were kept secret

» Crossing the tracks

Italy changed sides in World War II not for moral reasons but pragmatic ones. It hoped to be siding with the winners, who might do less damage to the country than their erstwhile friends, the Germans. The Allies treated the Italians with a mixture of indifference and distain: the years of fascism and collaboration with Hitler were not easily forgiven or forgotten.

Switching sides mid-war was a risk that had harsh consequences for Italy. Most ordinary Italians thought the September armistice meant peace – that the Germans would take it as a signal to withdraw from their country – but that was not the policy issuing from Berlin. In fact, the Germans expected the Italians to surrender. They had long regarded them as duplicitous allies and had made plans accordingly. Overnight, Italian land north of the shifting front line became occupied. German paratroopers entered Rome at the same time as the king and Prime Minister Pietro Badoglio fled the capital.

Having been given no instructions from its government, the Italian military found itself at the mercy of the Wehrmacht. Soldiers who supported Mussolini and fascism were welcomed into the German ranks; all the others were faced with the choice of resisting attempts to disarm them, deserting to join the partisans or accepting their fate. More than 250,000 Italian soldiers were taken prisoner by the Germans and sent to labour camps in central Europe, along with 50,000 Allied prisoners of war. Huge quantities of weapons and vehicles were impounded, although the Italian navy managed to evade capture. The Italian soldiers who chose to fight back – an estimated 20,000 – were massacred by the same combat forces they had been fighting alongside just days before. Italian troops abroad in Greece and the Balkans were treated even more harshly. Around five thousand of them surrendered to their captors and were executed in cold blood. Only on 13 October 1943, too late to be of much use, did the Italian government declare war on Nazi Germany and join the subsequent battles using what manpower and weaponry remained.

Despite the cost, the change of sides meant Italy could recover some of its national self-respect. The partisan movement that flourished in occupied northern Italy would help lay the foundations for the new Italian republic at the end of the war.

for five days as the Italians bought time to prepare for the German backlash. The delay also allowed the Allies to continue planning their invasion of mainland Italy without alerting the Germans to the Italian surrender.

Siracusa Commonwealth Cemetery
Siracusa

British and Canadian forces made their landings in the southeast corner of the island, between Pachino and Siracusa, now the site of a Commonwealth cemetery. The majority of burials belong to men killed during the landings or in the early stages of the campaign – including members of the airborne units that attempted to land west of the town on the night of 9–10 July, when gale-force winds forced sixty of the 140 gliders into the sea and blew others well wide of their objectives. Altogether there are 1059 graves, 134 of them belonging to unidentified personnel.

Biography
Benito Mussolini

Benito Mussolini, known to his followers as Il Duce (the Leader), was the world's first fascist dictator. He came to power in Italy in 1922, while his admirer and imitator Adolf Hitler was still building his power base in Bavaria.

Born into a poor family in Romagna in 1883, Mussolini served in World War I (Italy on that occasion being on the side of the Allies) before becoming a journalist. One of his contemporaries described him as an "orator of the pen", and he naturally understood the power of the media to convey state propaganda.

During the 1930s, Mussolini pursued an aggressive but pragmatic foreign policy, with the aim of making Italy the dominant power in the Mediterranean.

He had some initial success in expanding the Italian empire to include Italian East Africa and Italian North Africa, and gave assistance to Franco's rebel forces in the Spanish Civil War. Mussolini is said to have had great personal magnetism, and a capacity for getting things done. An oft-cited quote claims that Mussolini "made the trains run on time", although he frequently used violence to achieve his political objectives.

In 1937, Mussolini allied himself with Germany and Japan, and it was he who coined the term "Axis powers". But when World War II broke out in 1939, he was reluctant to commit, believing that Italy would not be ready for combat until at least 1942. Nevertheless, on 10 June 1940, Mussolini declared war on Britain and occupied a corner of the soon-to-be-defeated France.

War meant a struggle to retain Italian possessions in North Africa against an Allied army that landed on the coast of Morocco in November 1942 and fought its way eastwards, finally forcing the Italo-German army – cornered in Tunisia – to surrender. Despite being defeated in North Africa, Mussolini's position still looked unassailable on 9 July 1943. "I am like the beasts", he declared, "I smell the weather before it changes. If I submit to my instincts, I never err."

The invasion of Sicily, however, tested the Italian nationalism he had nurtured for twenty years to breaking point. His grip on power, and the loyalty of the king and the political class, were less sure than he believed. Ultimately, Mussolini's personal fate was to be decided by the success or failure of the Sicily campaign.

1943; and a simulator that gives visitors the eerie sensation of living through an air raid.

The museum also functions as a library and research centre, collating books and papers (published and unpublished) about the Sicily campaign, including local resources and eyewitness accounts recorded by Sicilian civilians.

Motta Sant'Anastasia German War Cemetery
Motta Sant'Anastasia

A total of 4561 German military personnel, killed in action in various parts of the island, are buried here. The poignant cemetery is designed like a building, with different rooms representing the different parts of the island where these men fell.

Agira Canadian War Cemetery
Agira

Agira was taken by the 1st Canadian Division on 28 July 1943. The site for this war cemetery was chosen a couple of months later for the burial of all Canadians – a total of 484 – killed in the Sicily campaign. It's permanently open to visitors who want to pay their respects, although the steeply terraced site makes wheelchair access difficult.

Messina

Messina was heavily bombed in the prelude to the invasion of Sicily. The closest island town to the Italian mainland, Messina was a strategic objective for the Allies, who hoped to reach it before the Germans and Italians could evacuate their troops. In the event, the Axis evacuation went ahead virtually unhindered.

Historical War Museum of the Landings in Sicily 1943
Piazzale Rocco Chinnici/Viale Africa, Catania

Despite its mouthful of a name, this museum does a good job of explaining the Sicily campaign, from the beach landings to the battles that allowed the Allies to take the island. Located near the railway station in Catania, it houses a range of evocative displays in a repurposed industrial building.

Exhibits include uniforms, weapons, photographs, video footage and projections of the island's devastated towns, in particular Catania, Palermo and Messina. There are also wax statues of Roosevelt, Churchill, King Victor Emmanuel III, Mussolini and Hitler; a reproduction of the tent at Cassibile in which the armistice was signed on 3 September

Calabria and Campania

Allied hopes were running high after the conquest of Sicily. Italy had been politically destabilized and its government had entered into secret negotiations with the Allies with a view to surrender.

It was assumed that since the Germans had been forced into retreat in Sicily they would not make a determined stand for mainland Italy. Rome was expected to fall within weeks, and the Germans to be driven out of the country with comparative ease. Allied commanders knew they had to press home their advantage and move stealthily northwards. They needed to land sufficient forces on the mainland; keep them on the move; and keep them supplied.

Operation Baytown and the armistice

The invasion of mainland Italy began auspiciously, with a landing (codenamed Baytown) that met almost no opposition. On the morn-ing of 3 September 1943, a contingent of the British Eighth Army crossed the Strait of Messina and landed at Reggio di Calabria. Again, there was little resistance: Italian troops were demoralized by the loss of Sicily and the uncertain political situation after the fall of Mussolini. The German commander Kesselring, meanwhile, had decide not to commit his forces in Calabria in open battle. His strategy would be to slow the Allied advance by blowing bridges and reinforcing established defensive lines further north.

That same afternoon, an armistice was signed between the Allies and the Italian government (see p.44), a capitulation that was kept secret for the next five days while the Italians prepared for the reaction of Germany and the Allies continued strategizing. Since the fall of Mussolini, the Germans had suspected that the Italians were about to renege

« Allied troops in Italy in 1943, having embarked as part of Operation Baytown

on their alliance, even though the new prime minister, Badoglio, assured them that it held firm. On 8 September, the news of the armistice was announced. Hitler had just returned to his headquarters at Rastenburg after his final visit to Russia. He awoke from his afternoon nap to the news that the Italian government had made peace with the Allies.

The armistice had dire consequences for Italy (see p.46). The broadcasted news spread confusion among the Italian armies, who were not given any firm instructions except to cease hostilities with the Allies. Rome was occupied by German troops and the royal family and government fled east, finally taking refuge in Brindisi.

Operation Avalanche at Salerno

In order to maintain their northern progress, the Allies needed to take Naples. Its port would be crucial for importing the vast quantity of supplies necessary to sustain an army on campaign. In the early morning of 9 September 1943, an Allied invasion fleet landed near Salerno, south of Naples, as part of Operation Avalanche. The invasion force, under the command of US General Mark Clark, comprised the US Fifth Army, the 82nd Airborne Division and the British X Corps.

The landings met unexpectedly fierce resistance from the German army. The Allies managed to land and secure a 55km broad beachfront, but on 12 September the German Tenth Army counterattacked the bridgehead; it was barely held. The German counteroffensive led to heavy casualties and, at points, reached the beaches.

For a few critical days there was talk of halting the operation and evacuating the troops. It was hoped that Field Marshal Montgomery would arrive to ease the situation, but advancing slowly from the south, he was too far away to lend assistance until Operation Avalanche had already tipped in favour of the invaders. The German counterattack ultimately failed – mainly because Hitler refused to allow Kesselring to deploy more troops – and on 16 September the tide of battle turned and the German forces withdrew north.

Mussolini is rescued

While the battle of Salerno was being decided, so was the fate of the deposed and imprisoned dictator Benito Mussolini, who was being held in the Hotel Campo Imperatore in the Apennines. He was freed in a daring raid carried out by German paratroopers and commandos on 12 September and flown out of the country. Two days later, German forces were allowed to evacuate the island of Sardinia by the Italian garrison, while a small US force landed to notionally liberate the island.

To maintain some semblance of normality in northern Italy, on 23 September Hitler installed Mussolini as the head of a puppet government, officially the Repubblica Sociale Italiana (Italian Social Republic), but universally known as the Salò Republic, after the town on Lake Garda.

Naples and the Volturno Line

Naples was finally taken on 1 October 1943, giving the Allies a working port. Allied forces continued to press north towards Rome, but their progress was halted by a series of defensive lines established by the Germans. The southernmost of these was the Volturno Line, which ran from Termoli along the Biferno river and through the Apennines to the Volturno river in the west; it was breached on 12 October. The following day, Badoglio's government formally declared war on its old ally, Nazi Germany.

›› Calabria and Campania sites

Salerno

During Operation Avalanche, the Allied army landed on beaches along the Gulf of Salerno from Maiori on the Sorrento peninsula to Agropoli in the south. Most troops embarked on beaches – distinguished and labelled by colour – along the Sele River plain. The British landed north of the river mouth, near Magazzeno, and the Americans near Paestum, to the south.

In town, the Museum of the Salerno Landings (Museo dello Sbarco, Via General Clark 5, salerno1943-1944.com) tells the story of Operation Avalanche through a variety of displays, including unedited video footage, flags, uniforms and weapons. Outside the museum, more substantial military hardware takes the form of two restored Italian anti-aircraft guns and a Sherman tank.

A Commonwealth cemetery lies on the road from Salerno to Eboli.

Museum of Operation Avalanche (MOA)
Via Sant'Antonio 5, Eboli, Ⓦ moamuseum.it

The central feature of the MOA, housed in a fine 15th-century building, is the "Emotional Room", which screens two moving projections. One film shows historical footage narrated by three distinguished personalities: photojournalist Robert Capa, novelist and war correspondent John Steinbeck, and Jack Belden, a war correspondent who landed with the troops at Salerno. The second screen projects images onto a 3D topographical map.

Campagna Internment Camp Museum
Via San Bartolomeo, Campagna, Ⓦ museomemoriapalatucci.it

The Campagna Internment Camp was created in 1940 by the Mussolini government to house foreign Jews fleeing from persecution in Germany, Austria and Poland, and many others who "threatened" the regime. It was never a concentration camp, and only ever held a small population of inmates, reaching just over two hundred at its maximum. When the Allies invaded southern Italy, locals liberated the camp.

Caserta Palace and Cemetery
Viale Giulio Douhet 2/a, Caserta, Ⓦ reggiadicaserta.beniculturali.it

For the greater part of the Italian campaign, the spectacular Royal Palace at Caserta served as headquarters for the Allied armies. The 2nd General Hospital was also located in town from late 1943 until September 1945. Some of the 768 people buried in the cemetery at Caserta died in the hospital, others as prisoners of war before the Allied invasion (there was a POW hospital at Caserta, too).

Naples Underground
Piazza San Gaetano 68, Naples, Ⓦ napolisotteranea.org

The atmospheric complex of tunnels excavated 40m beneath the centre of Naples was begun by the Romans. Many of its passageways were used as air-raid shelters during World War II, and today's Bourbon Gallery contains a good museum where wartime graffiti can still be seen.

Monte Cassino and the Gustav Line

The US Fifth Army left Naples in early October 1943 and moved steadily north. Its commander, General Mark Clark, was confident that Rome would be taken before the end of the month.

Allied planners in Italy, however, had misread the intentions of Kesselring. They believed that the Germans would put up just token resistance in central Italy, before pulling back to defend its north. Instead, the commander of the German forces fought doggedly, understanding that the mountainous topography of the Italian peninsula favoured the defender. During one battle, the American war correspondent John Gunther observed that "both sides are tired, and whereas we are exposed in the plain, the Germans are high up, with good cover." This diagnosis could be reliably applied to almost any Italian confrontation between the Allied and Axis forces over the next year and a half. Kesselring's strategy was to dig in along a series of defensive lines, observing the enemy from altitude and using direct artillery, mortar and machine gun fire to slow the vulnerable attacking troops. In this way, he sought to delay the enemy advance for as long as possible. If his army was forced to retreat, they would simply fall back on the next line of defence. Retreating German troops destroyed bridges and laid mines and booby traps across the roads and paths to hinder the advancing Allies.

Barbara and Winter lines

The defences along the Volturno river were breached on 12 October (see p.50). The next defensive line, the Barbara Line, was crossed with relative ease on 2 November, and a month later the US Fifth Army reached the formidable Winter Line that stretched across Italy from the Tyrrhenian Sea to the Adriatic coast. The Winter Line was a series of three lines, including the Bernhardt Line bulging to the south and the Hitler Line, which arced to the north. The most important part of the Winter Line, however, was the Gustav Line, which stretched for 161km from the River Garigliano in the west to the Sangro in the east. It centred on the ancient Benedictine monastery of Monte Cassino.

Monte Cassino

To approach the Winter Line, fierce battles were fought in December 1943 for possession of San Pietro Infine and Monte Lungo. Crossing the Rapido river proved impossible, and the Allied advance was stalled beneath the formidable abbey of Monte Cassino, standing a lofty 520m above sea level. An initial attempt by the Allies to take possession of the monastery (launched on 17 January and 11 February 1944) was driven back with heavy losses. It was hoped that an amphibious landing at Anzio (see p.56) would unblock the stalemate at Monte Cassino, but this too was unsuccessful. Allied problems were only compounded by the harsh Italian winter.

As early February brought no relief, Allied commanders settled on a radical solution. On 15 February, the abbey was all but obliterated by bombs dropped from US airforce B-17 flying fortresses, killing a large number of civilians sheltering within its walls. The Allies later claimed − and perhaps they really believed − that the Germans were using the abbey as an observation post, but this has been strenuously denied. Another theory is that the Allies were working on faulty intelligence due to the mistranslation of an intercepted radio message. What is certain, however, is that the bombing was counterproductive: the ruins of the abbey provided perfect cover for the German defenders of Monte Cassino when the second frontal assault was launched against them on 16–18 February. A third battle for Monte Cassino was conducted on 15–23 March, again without success for the Allies.

The fourth and final battle for Monte Cassino began on 11 May, codenamed Operation Diadem, reinforced by troops from the British Eighth Army brought in from the Adriatic coast. Finally, the Germans retreated from the Gustav Line on 25 May 1944, and the abbey ruins were overrun by victorious Allied (Polish) troops.

After five months of stalemate, the road to Rome lay open, but the costs were high. It is estimated that the Allies (fielding Australian, Canadian, Free French, Moroccan, Ital-ian, Indian, New Zealand, Polish, South African, British and American troops) suffered around 55,000 casualties; Germany and its ally, the Italian Social Republic, about 20,000.

Monte Cassino and the Gustav Line sites

Monte Cassino Abbey
Via Montecassino, Cassino,
🌐 abbaziamontecassino.org

The abbey of Monte Cassino was founded by Saint Benedict around the year 529, from where its monks spread the word as far away as Britain and Scandinavia. At the start of 1944 the monastery was one of the great medieval buildings of Italy, exquisitely decorated and filled with religious treasures.

Between 17 January and 18 May 1944, Monte Cassino was the scene of unrelenting combat. Lying in a protected historic zone, the abbey itself had been left unoccupied by the Germans, although several Allied commanders believed the abbey was being used

« Monte Cassino Abbey today

as an artillery observation point by the German forces. Despite a lack of clear evidence, the monastery was marked for destruction and on 15 February American bombers reduced the abbey and the entire top of Monte Cassino to a smoking mass of rubble. German officers had already transferred some 1400 precious manuscripts, paintings and other items from the abbey to the Vatican, saving them from the blast.

The destruction of the abbey was one of the greatest military blunders of World War II. Around 230 Italian civilians who had sought refuge in the monastery were tragically killed, while the destruction did nothing to alleviate the Allies' problems. German paratroopers duly occupied the ruins, which provided them with excellent defensive cover.

After the war, the abbey was rebuilt exactly as it was. Today, it's occupied by a monastic community that welcomes both pilgrims and visitors, as well as housing a small museum and video projection explaining the bombing.

Monte Cassino Polish Military Cemetery
Monte Cassino

Only fully completed in 1963, the Polish Military Cemetery at Monte Cassino was officially inaugurated on 1 September 1945, exactly six years after the German invasion of Poland. It takes the shape of an amphitheatre, with an altar and a large cross in the middle of the lawn. At the entrance, a gatepost bears the inscription "For our freedom and yours, we soldiers of Poland gave our soul to god, our life to the soil of Italy and our hearts to Poland."

The cemetery holds the graves of 1052 soldiers of the Polish II Corps who died in the battle of Monte Cassino. After the war, the Corps' Commander General Władysław

» Monte Cassino Polish Military Cemetery

Anders, like many of his soldiers, lived in exile from communist Poland. When he died in London in 1970, he was buried in Monte Cassino according to his will. The Corps was predominantly a Polish unit, but also included Belarusians and Ukrainians. The men had various religious affiliations: most were Catholics, others were Jews and some Eastern Orthodox Christians. The men's religious diversity is reflected on the headstones.

On 18 May 1944, a platoon of the 1st Squadron of the 12th Regiment of the Podolski Lancers were the first troops to enter the ruins of Monte Cassino Abbey. The German defenders were driven from their positions, but at a high cost. The Corps suffered heavy casualties during the Italian campaign: 2301 killed, 8543 wounded and 535 missing.

Winter Line Museum
Palazzo de Utris, Venafro,
Ⓦ winterlinevenafro.it

A small museum in Venafro, created by members of the Winter Line association, brings the Winter Line to life with displays of uniforms, weapons, ammunition and photography. The living conditions of both soldiers and civilians are vividly illustrated.

Mignano Monte Lungo Military Shrine
Mignano Monte Lungo

The Battle of Monte Lungo, also called the Battle of San Pietro Infine, took place between 8–16 December 1943. It was the first engagement of the reconstituted Royal Italian Army following Italy's change of sides in the war.

A new Italian brigade, the First Motorized Group, was attached to the US Fifth Army. Highly spirited but poorly armed, the unit bore the heavy responsibility of redeeming the military honour of the Italian Army. Its troops were ordered to conquer Monte Lungo during the Allied offensive in San Pietro Valley, a mountain occupied by the German 15th Panzer Grenadier Division and blocking the Allies' path. On 8 December 1943, the Italian brigade advanced, together with units of the US II Corps, under cover of the morning mist. As soon as the mist lifted, however, the advancing soldiers were exposed, and the Germans had a clear field of fire. The Italians suffered heavy casualties and the attack was repulsed. A repeat attack on 16 December was better prepared, supported by heavy artillery bombardments, and the peak was conquered by the US and Italian forces.

The current military shrine contains the graves of 974 Italian soldiers killed in battle. Opposite the cemetery, a fine museum exhibits objects related to the role played by the Italian troops in the liberation of their country.

San Pietro Infine Historical Memory Park
San Pietro Infine

In late 1943, the village of San Pietro Infine was completely destroyed by fighting between the advancing US forces – who sought to break the Winter Line – and the defending German troops. The Historical Memory Park, a designated national monument, contains the ruins of the village as they stood at the end of the war. It's an atmospheric place, a ghost town which provided the backdrop for several scenes in Mario Monicelli's 1959 film *The Great War*. A new village was built 3km from the original site.

Anzio

To break the stalemate at Monte Cassino on the Gustav Line (see p.52), Allied commanders decided to open a second front behind the German positions. Operation Shingle was to be an amphibious landing at Anzio, 62km south of Rome.

If the offensive at Anzio went well, the German defenders of the Gustav Line would be outflanked and forced to retreat, the US Fifth Army would be able to break through the Gustav Line, and Rome would quickly fall.

The invasion force of Operation Shingle consisted of 40,000 soldiers and 5000 vehicles under the command of US Major General John P. Lucas. His army landed at three locations: the British Force 9.7km north of Anzio (Peter Beach), the Northwestern US Force at the port of Anzio (Yellow Beach) and the Southwestern US Force attacked near Nettuno, almost 10km east of Anzio (X-Ray Beach). The initial landing on 22 January 1944 met little resistance, but Lucas delayed moving inland immediately to prevent his forces being overextended. Instead, he consolidated his position, but in doing so allowed the German forces to organize their defence. Scattered among the surrounding hills, German artillery units had a clear view of every Allied position.

For many weeks, a rain of shells fell on the Allied bridgehead and the harbour of Anzio. Far from relieving Monte Cassino, the invasion force was pinned down, and became in need of relief itself. A frustrated Churchill commented, "I had hoped we were hurling a wildcat into the shore, but all we got was a stranded whale."

On 22 February Lucas was replaced by General Truscott, and both sides reinforced their armies; Italian troops still loyal to the Axis were deployed by the German army. Despite spirited efforts, the Axis forces were unable to push the Allies back into the sea, but neither did the Allies manage to penetrate inland. The stalemate at Anzio ended on 18 May when the Allies broke through the German line at Monte Cassino.

Anzio sites

Nettuno Sicily-Rome American Cemetery
Nettuno

Inevitably, Anzio – and its surrounding area – is a place of cemeteries. The Sicily-Rome American Cemetery at Nettuno (abmc.gov) is one of only two US cemeteries in Italy. The

» Statue of brothers in arms at Sicily-Rome American Cemetery

«
Piana delle Orme
Historical Museum

majority of the soldiers buried here died in the liberation of Sicily; in the landings at Salerno and the fighting as the Fifth Army made its way northward; and in the landings at Anzio Beach and the expansion of the beachhead. Further graves contain airmen and sailors. The wider complex includes a cenotaph, memorial, map room, pool, peristyle and a chapel with the names of 3095 men declared missing in action. The on-site visitor centre tells the personal stories of combatants as well as showing films, photographs and a number of interesting interactive displays.

Anzio Commonwealth cemeteries

At Anzio itself there are two Commonwealth cemeteries. The larger is the Beach Head Cemetery, north of Anzio town, which contains 2316 graves, 291 of unknown soldiers. It is a place awash with colour: roses, pansies and impatiens grow in front of the tombstones and arbours of wisteria and jasmine flank the pathways.

Anzio Beachhead Museum
Via di Villa Adele, Anzio,
Ⓦ sbarcodianzio.it

Opened in 1994 for the 50th anniversary of the landing, Anzio Beachhead Museum is invaluable for understanding what happened at Anzio. It comprises four sections, divided into American, British, German and Italian sectors. Displays feature authentic uniforms, badges, documents, pictures and other artefacts donated by veterans' organizations.

Piana delle Orme Historical Museum
Via Migliara 43, Latina, Ⓦ pianadelleorme.com

Two pavilions at the Piana delle Orme Historical Museum are entirely devoted to the display of military vehicles from World War II. Dioramas depict how Italy became involved in the war, the course of the North African campaigns, the amphibious landing of the Allied troops near Anzio and the battle for Monte Cassino.

Rome

After the Anzio campaign, US General Mark Clark had two options. His superior, British General Harold Alexander, ordered him to capture as many Germans retreating from the Gustav Line as possible. But Clark had his sights on Rome.

Clark's decision to turn directly towards the capital, rather than to strike a crippling blow to the Germans, is as controversial today as it was then. Did he pass up an opportunity to shorten the Italian campaign in order to win a blaze of glory for himself? Or was he driven by Roosevelt's intimation that Rome must be conquered by American troops? Regardless of his motivations, by moving on Rome, Clark allowed the German Tenth Army to escape and continue its defence of northern Italy.

On 4 June 1944, Rome became the first capital to be liberated from Nazi Germany. It had already been declared an open city and was captured without any loss of life – a welcome relief after the heavy-fought campaign of Cassino. Italian forces fighting alongside the Allied armies were sent to the Adriatic front, meaning they could not participate in the liberation of their capital.

Rome was psychologically and symbolically important to the Allies. Aside from being of tremendous propaganda value, it was hoped that taking the city might draw German troops away from France and the impending D-Day landings – an event that would overshadow the conquest of Rome just two days later.

Rome sites »

Historical Museum of the Liberation
Via Tasso 145, Ⓦ museoliberazione.it

During the Nazi occupation of Rome (11 September 1943–4 June 1944), this museum building functioned as an SS police station under the overall command of Lieutenant Colonel Herbert Kappler. Innumerable

» The Pope and the Vatican

During the 1930s, Pope Pius XI devised a policy intended to condemn the barbarous acts of fascism without exposing the Catholic clergy to danger. This did not always work. In a number of countries, in particular Poland, many priests were brutally murdered by the Nazis.

Throughout the war the Church tried to exercise its spiritual authority without the temporal power to back it up. The Vatican City was treated as a neutral state by both Axis and Allied commanders, and the Nazis deliberately avoided it when they occupied the rest of Rome. But the German occupation, from September 1943, brought the Holocaust closer to home. Italian Jews were deported en masse to concentration camps, even if some were given sanctuary in the monasteries and convents of Rome.

Pope Pius XII, Pius XI's successor, emerged from the Liberation as a figure of national Italian unity – in contrast to the king who was tainted by his collaboration with Mussolini. Since the war, critics have accused the Pope of not doing enough to prevent the evils of the Holocaust, but even they concede that the Vatican's room for manoeuvre was limited. What the Pope failed to publicly denounce was balanced by private acts of admirable religious leadership.

«
Villa Torlonia

unfortunates were brought, many without cause, to be interrogated, detained and tortured. From the station, the only onward destination was Regina Coeli prison; extended captivity in Germany; deportation to another country; or execution at Fort Bravetta. It is estimated that at least 1500 men and more than 350 women passed through during the occupation, some of them partisans, others ordinary citizens. The museum brings together relics, documents and photographs, as well as thoughtful works of art. It has a particularly good collection of underground posters and flyers printed surreptitiously during the occupation.

Rome War Cemetery

Rome War Cemetery lies on Via Nicola Zabaglia, within the Aurelian Walls of the ancient city of Rome. It is reached from the Piazza Venezia, the centre of Rome, by taking the Via dei Fori Imperiali down past the Colosseum and along the Viale Aventino as far as the Porta San Paolo. It lies next to the Protestant Cemetery in which Keats and Shelley are buried.

The war cemetery contains 426 graves, mainly those of the occupying garrison; a few belong to the dead brought in from the surrounding countryside. Some soldiers and airmen who died as prisoners of war in Rome are also buried here.

Villa Torlonia
Via Nomentana 70, Ⓦ museivillatorlonia.it

Mussolini's former residence, Villa Torlonia, is now a complex of three buildings. The main one, the Casino Nobile, has a bomb- and gas-proof shelter built on the orders of Il Duce. A film recounts the history of the villa, including Mussolini's time spent here before his dramatic arrest in July 1943.

»
Nazis carry out the
Fosse Ardeatine
massacre

Monte Mario French Military Cemetery

The Monte Mario French cemetery is located on Via dei Casali di Santo Spirito on the highest hill of the city (but not one of the legendary hills), rising above the right bank of the Tiber. It contains 1709 tombs of men from the French Expeditionary Corps killed between Rome and Sienna. Most of the graves – of which there are 1142 – belong to Muslim soldiers who served in the French army.

Fosse Ardeatine
Via Ardeatina 174,
Ⓦ mausoleofosseardeatine.it

On 23 March 1944, Italian partisans placed a bomb on Via Rasella, on the route taken by a column of Italian policemen who had volunteered to serve with the SS. German Colonel Kappler, chief of police in Rome, requested permission from his superiors to carry out a reprisal for the attack; this was authorized by Adolf Hitler himself, who stipulated that ten civilians must be killed for each dead policeman within 24 hours.

Kappler secretly emptied the jails of men, both condemned and detained, adding Jewish and Italian civilians to reach the required number of 335 – a figure hiked up by a mistake in counting. The men were taken to the tunnels of an old quarry and made to kneel beside the growing pile of corpses. Each was shot in the back of the head to conserve bullets. After the massacre, the Germans blew up the entrance of the Ardeatine quarry to cover their tracks, and most families were told nothing about the fate of their loved ones. It was only after the liberation of Rome that the massacre was discovered; the tragedy is now commemorated by a national mausoleum and museum.

Museum of Allied Forces Rome
Hotel Relais 6, Via Tolmino 6,
Ⓦ 2museumrome.eu/4

This private museum in the Hotel Relais 6 (relais6.com) boasts a good collection of memorabilia connected with the liberation of Rome, including a jeep, motorbike, uniforms and a great many everyday military and civilian items from 1944.

The Adriatic coast

From Salerno, Bernard Montgomery's three British Eighth Army divisions crossed the country to the eastern, Adriatic coast to join up with troops that had landed at the port of Taranto on 9 September 1943.

The first task of Montgomery's men was to capture the airfields of Foggia, which would provide important forward bases for bombing raids into northern Europe. A successful amphibious raid liberated Termoli at the end of the Volturno defensive line on 3 October, allowing Montgomery's forces to continue up the Adriatic coast. His aim was to take Pescara, enabling his troops to traverse the country from east to west via Avezzano to approach Rome. This plan proved over-optimistic.

After crossing the Sangro river with relative ease, Montgomery's advance was halted before Ortona at the Moro river, where Canadian troops were sent into action, with great loss of life trying to cross the final ravine. Ortona itself was only taken after two days of house-to-house fighting – the Germans eventually pulled out and the town was captured on 28 December 1943.

Montgomery's progress was not helped by a surprise German bombing raid on the port of Bari on 2 December, which disabled the port for almost three months. Among the ships sunk was one loaded with mustard gas bombs that the Allies had brought to Italy in case the Germans resorted to chemical warfare. In late December, Montgomery called a halt to the campaign, to be resumed in spring. He flew back to Britain to participate in preparations for D-Day and was replaced by Lieutenant General Oliver Leese.

« Allied soldiers in Italy

»
Canadian infantrymen
preparing an attack
near Ortona, 1943

After the passing of winter, the Eighth Army's advance continued up the Adriatic coast. It was weakened by the transfer of troops and materials to Cassino (see p.52) and to the new offensive in France. However, the port of Ancona was taken after three days of battle (16–18 June 1944) by Polish II Corps. Further north, the British came to the eastern end of the Gothic Line, which was stormed under Operation Olive on 17–21 September, during which Rimini was captured. At the end of the year, in December 1944, Ravenna also fell to the Eighth Army before it paused to overwinter at Faenza.

» The Adriatic coast sites

Ortona

Ortona was almost completely destroyed in the battle that took place here between 21 and 28 December 1943.

Anyone interested in Canada's role in the Italian campaign should visit the Museum of the Battle of Ortona on Corso Garibaldi. Its informative exhibits display memorabilia, photos and war relics, including personal effects of the soldiers. To the south of the town is the Moro River Canadian Cemetery, which contains 1615 graves of men who died during the fighting at Moro river and Ortona – and during the weeks of action that preceded and followed it. In December 1943 alone, the 1st Canadian Division suffered more than five hundred casualties.

Montecchio Cemetery
Montecchio

Montecchio village, near the eastern end of the Gothic Line, was practically razed to the ground during the war and the surrounding countryside was badly damaged. One of the line's anti-tank ditches ran through the valley immediately below Montecchio cemetery. The site, which contains 582 plots, was selected by the Canadian Corps for burials during the fighting to break through the Gothic Line in the autumn of 1944.

Aviation Theme Park
Via S Aquilina 58, Rimini,
Ⓦ museoaviazione.com

This indoor and outdoor museum located southwest of Rimini explores the history of military aviation, with an emphasis on World War II. A number of planes are displayed, along with anti-aircraft weapons and other flying equipment.

Tuscany

> Despite the overshadowing events of D-Day, once Rome was secured the US Fifth Army made its way northwards towards Tuscany.

Two days after the liberation of Rome, Allied commanders delivered their coup de grâce: a massive landing of forces on the beaches of France (see p.114) that would open a western front in Europe. This reduced the Italian campaign to secondary importance in Allied strategy. From D-Day onwards, the Italian battlefields were mostly seen as a way to lure German forces away from France and the Eastern Front, weakening opposition to the main campaign from Normandy to Berlin. Germany was expected to cede the rest of the Italian peninsula without much fight. The US Fifth Army travelled northwards up the west of Italy through Tuscany, while the British Eighth Army was committed in Italy's centre and eastern, Adriatic coast (see p.61).

Lakes Bolsena and Trasimene

The Germans made their first stand after being driven north from Rome at Bolsena. To the east of Lake Bolsena, a tank battle was fought in June 1944 between the 6th South African Armoured Division and the Hermann Goering Panzer Division. The next line of German defences centred on Lake Trasimene, adjacent to Perugia (which was liberated on 20 June). Cortona, north of the lake, was entered on 6 July, the day after Siena (Sienna) had been liberated by Free French forces.

A further German stand at Arezzo in early July 1944 resulted in a dogged struggle before the town was taken on 16 July by the 6th Armoured Division, with the aid of the 2nd New Zealand Division.

The cities of Tuscany

On the coast, the port of Livorno (once known as Leghorn in English) was liberated on 19 July 1944, but not before the departing Germans had blown up its ancient lighthouse. Pisa was liberated on 2 September by the Fifth Army, and Lucca on 5 September. Florence (Firenze), meanwhile, was

« M7 Priest self-propelled gun on the Gothic Line in 1944

attained and liberated on 11 August. Behind the German lines, Italian partisans were increasingly active, incurring great risk to themselves and their communities. Members of the Resistance and the wider civilian population were frequently subject to gruesome reprisals.

The Gothic Line

The Allied advance was checked by the formidable defences of the Gothic Line, renamed as the less grandiose Green Line in June 1944 to allay Hitler's fear that the Allies, if they broke through, would use its name to accent their glories. The Gothic Line was a row of fortifications that ran through the hills north of Florence from the Tyrrhenian Sea to the Adriatic. When it prevented the Allied advance in October 1944, a strategy of "offensive defence" was adopted – the Allies would pause to overwinter until the weather cleared and a spring offensive could be organized. This strategy was disrupted in December, when a last offensive was launched by the German army and troops of Mussolini's Italian Social Republic. The Battle of Garfagnana (officially Operation Winter Storm or Unternehmen Wintergewitter) took place

near Massa and Lucca; Barga was briefly captured by the Germans but as quickly lost again. The episode nevertheless provided a morale boost for Italian soldiers fighting with the Germans, and was promptly utilized for propaganda purposes.

Tuscany sites   «

Civitella di Val di Chiana
🌐 archiviodellamemoriacivitella
valdichiana.it

On 18 June 1944, nine German soldiers entered the recreational club of the village of Civitella, where they were challenged by local partisans. Two Germans were killed in the ensuing confrontation. The villagers pleaded with the German authorities against reprisals, but on 29 June a detachment of paratroopers from the Hermann Goering division – young men, many trained by the Hitler Youth movement – was dispatched to Civitella to exact revenge. The local priest offered his life if others could be spared, but the paratroopers dragged all the men of the village out of their houses and shot them. In total, 149 people were killed, including two

»
History enthusiasts
visit remains of the
Gothic Line

priests; the Germans then set fire to Civitella. Massacres were also carried out in fourteen nearby villages.

Florence American Cemetery and Memorial
Tavarnuzze, Ⓦ Abmc.gov

The Florence American Cemetery, located about 7.5km from Florence near Tavarnuzze, is one of only two American cemeteries in Italy (the other being at Anzio), covering 28 hectares of wooded hills. A bridge leads from the entrance to the main cemetery area, where 4399 headstones are arranged in symmetrically curving rows on the hillside. Most men buried here died in fighting between Rome and the Alps from June 1944 onwards, especially in the Apennines. Above the graves, on the uppermost of the three broad terraces, a memorial is crowned by a large sculptured figure. The memorial's two open *atria* (courtyards) are connected by the Tablets of the Missing, which carry 1409 names. On the southern court is a chapel decorated with fine marble and mosaics; the northern atrium has operations maps (also in marble) showing the movements of the American armed forces in Tuscany and northern Italy. There is also a Commonwealth cemetery near Florence.

Sant'Anna di Stazzema
Sant'Anna di Stazzema,
Ⓦ santannadistazzema.org

On 12 August 1944, troops of the Waffen-SS, assisted by Italian fascists of the Black Brigades, killed 560 people in this Tuscan hill village to punish the civilian population for supporting the Resistance. The massacre is remembered as one of the defining events in the Italian struggle for liberation. In fact, it helped set the political tone of Italy after the war; the new republic would be founded on the struggles of the partisan movement and the German attempts to suppress it. The village now has a national peace park, founded in 2000, while the restored church can also be visited.

Borgo a Mozzano

The Gothic Line ran just south of this village, some 20km north of Lucca, where you'll find multiple examples of excellently preserved military fortifications. Visible bunkers, tank walls and trenches all remain (almost) intact. The town's handsome medieval bridge also survived the war and can be admired still.

Museum of Deportation
Via di Cantagallo 250, Prato,
Ⓦ museodelladeportazione.it

The workers of Prato who were deported to Mauthausen and Ebensee concentration camps in Austria are honoured in this museum, where the exhibits prove that even the most everyday objects can be significant: clothes, posters and photographs speak of life, survival and death in the camps. Prato's labourers – arrested following a general strike in March 1944 – joined Jews, homosexuals, Roma, the disabled and political opponents of the Nazis at the camps. Some were killed on arrival, others were literally worked to death.

Futa Pass German Cemetery
Futa Pass, Ⓦ voksbund.de

The largest German war cemetery in Italy stands near a pass on the Apennines on what was once the Gothic Line. It contains a staggering 30,683 graves.

Bologna and northern Italy

The Allies had hoped to take Bologna before the end of 1944, but the Germans were able to hold the Italian front stable over winter in the Apennines, along the Gothic Line. It was only in the spring of 1945 that the Allies were able to resume their campaign.

To both sides, the outcome of an Allied victory in Italy seemed inevitable – it was just a question of time, and how many soldiers and civilians would die, before peace was declared. By early 1945, General Heinrich von Vietinghoff realized that German defeat was imminent. His troop losses were too great and he was no longer receiving supplies of arms and ammunition from Germany. Vietinghoff began to think of how the war in Italy might be concluded in as favourable way as possible for himself and his armies. In February, on his behalf, SS Obergruppenführer Karl Wolff began secret negotiations with US diplomat Allen Dulles with a view to arranging an armistice. This contravened the terms agreed at Casablanca – that only an unconditional surrender by German forces would be acceptable – and risked offending Stalin, who was not included in the talks or even consulted.

While negotiations were still underway, Operation Grapeshot, the final offensive of the war in Italy, was launched on 6 April 1945. Bologna was heavily bombed in preparation for the Allied ground forces, who approached the city from the south and east. US and Italian troops entered Bologna on 21 April, forcing the German army to retreat northwards, where its route was cut off by the Po river.

» Massed American M10 tanks fire at a German position near Bologna

» The Italian Civil War and the partisan republics

While World War II was drawing slowly towards its conclusion in 1944–5, a war within a war was being waged in Italy. Bands of partisans (*partigani*) fought bravely against Italian fascists (the notorious *Brigate Nere* or Black Brigades) and the German army.

The partisans were organized into autonomous groups, armed with whatever weapons they could find. Among them were communists, socialists, anarchists, liberals, fugitives from the Italian army and sundry foreigners on the run from the authorities. Others simply described themselves as patriots hoping to build a better Italy after the war. All they had in common was their battle-song, *Bella Ciao*, which has since come to represent resistance to all forms of oppression in international popular culture.

The partisans' guerrilla tactics made it hard for the security forces of the German army and the Salò Republic to engage them, so they often chose to punish sabotage by massacring ad hoc groups of civilians instead. This did not prevent the resistance movements of northern Italy from proclaiming a succession of transitory mini-states, called partisan republics. None of the twenty states established was bigger than a valley or a district. They tended to last between a couple of days and a few months before the German occupying forces systematically destroyed them.

The Allies had destroyed the bridge crossings and the German troops were compelled to improvise ways across, leaving their vehicles and heavy weapons behind.

Italy's partisans took the initiative to declare 25 April 1945 a day of general insurrection, and this date is still celebrated as Italy's Day of National Liberation. The cities of northern Italy quickly fell, taken either by Allied forces or liberated "internally" by partisans, some a mixture of the two. Genova (Genoa) was liberated on 25 April; Turin (Torino) and Verona on 26 April; and Milan (Milano) on 28 April. Mussolini and his mistress were captured on 27 April, spelling the end of the Italian Social Republic, and were executed the following day.

By now, the war was being lost on all fronts, and Berlin was close to surrender (see p.320). German high command was determined to conclude a single peace with the Allies, but Vietinghoff defied instructions and flew south to the Royal Palace of Caser-

ta, where he signed an unconditional instrument of capitulation with the Allied victors. The war in Italy ended at 2pm on 2 May 1945, when almost one million German and Italian troops officially surrendered to Field Marshal Harold Alexander.

Bologna and northern Italy sites   »

Museum of the Resistance

Via Sant'Isaia 20, Bologna,
Ⓦ museodellaresistenzadibologna.it

This excellent museum explores the aims and methods of the diverse Italian partisan movements (see above), which played a vital role in attacking the occupying Germans behind their lines. Resistance fighters used underground passageways to move around the city of Bologna; the tunnels can be visited by guided tour.

Memorial Museum for Liberty Bologna
Via G. Dozza 24, Bologna,
Ⓦ museomemoriale.com

A narrative route through five scenes leads visitors through the events of the latter part of the Italian campaign, beginning with the round-up of civilians to build the fortifications of the Gothic Line. The bombings and daily lives of civilians are both explained, and exhibits include tanks, trucks, jeeps and a chilling railway wagon used for deporting Jews.

Monte Sole
Marzabotto, Ⓦ montesole.org

During the summer of 1944, tension among the German occupiers of Italy increased.

>> The fate of Mussolini
Benito Mussolini was immediately arrested by the Italian government after his fall from power in July 1943. He was freed from captivity in a bold raid by German paratroopers shortly after the armistice, and established as the leader of a fascist government in German-occupied northern Italy, known as the Salò Republic. As the Allies advanced northwards, Mussolini's authority waned. On 27 April 1945, he and his mistress Claretta Petacci were captured by Italian partisans while trying to escape to Switzerland; they were executed the next day outside a villa near the shores of Lake Como. Their corpses were taken to Milan where they were defiled by the mob and hung above the forecourt of a petrol station. Adolf Hitler was gravely affected by the way in which Mussolini had been humiliated after his death, and resolved to take his own life and have his body destroyed.

The Allies were advancing slowly from the south and incessant attacks were initiated by partisans hiding in the woods and mountains of the Apennines and the Apuan Alps. Units of the Waffen-SS took revenge on the civilian population in order to discourage the Resistance. The largest single massacre carried out by the Waffen-SS in western Europe took place in Marzabotto on 29 September 1944. The specific number of victims is disputed, but the generally accepted figure is 770 casualties, 150 of them children. The site is now a memorial park with a chapel.

Museum of the Second World War and the River Po
Piazza Municipio, Felonica,
Ⓦ museofelonica.it

Unlike most war museums in Italy, this one tells a story not of battle, but of ignominious retreat. As German and Italian Social Republic troops withdrew northwards from the Apennines and Emilia Romagna, their way was blocked by the broad sweep of the mighty River Po.

The Allies had destroyed the bridges across the river, limiting the German escape routes, while the overwhelming supremacy of Anglo-American aviation forced the retreating troops to move almost exclusively at night, hiding in woods and buildings during the day. Numerous fires and high columns of smoke rose above the southern bank of the River Po between 20 and 24 April 1945. Lucky soldiers were transported to the opposite bank on the few ferries and boats available; others swam or made use of anything that would float: air chambers extracted from the wheels of vehicles, water tanks and barrels, wooden planks and even laundry tubs. Heavy weapons and equipment that could not be carried across had to be abandoned or destroyed. All this and more is explained using a variety of fascinating photographs and objects.

Museum of the Montefiorino Republic and of the Italian Resistance Movement
Via Rocca 1, Montefiorino,
Ⓦ resistenzamontefiorino.it

Italy's resistance movements went further than carrying out acts of sabotage: a scattering of mini-states were set up by partisan groups in liberated corners of northern Italy. There were twenty "partisan republics", which existed for brief periods from two days to a few months before the Wehrmacht arrived to reincorporate them into Mussolini's puppet state, the Italian Social Republic. The Republic of Montefiorino, whose story is told in this medieval castle using documents, photographs and objects, survived for just 45 days from June to August 1944.

International Primo Levi Studies Centre
Via del Carmine 13, Turin, Ⓦ primolevi.it

Jewish writer and chemist Primo Levi's moving personal account of the Holocaust and the Liberation, *If This is a Man*, was published in 1947 (see p.369). Levi formed a partisan group in 1943 but was captured and sent by cattle wagon to Auschwitz. Of the 650 people in his group of deportees, he was one of only thirty who survived the war. This centre is dedicated not only to his memories but also to his thoughtful reflections on war, peace and human behaviour.

≫ Trieste
The Adriatic port-city of Trieste became part of the Salò Republic (see p.50) in September 1943, but was directly controlled by the Germans who installed a concentration camp with a crematorium here, the Risiera di San Sabba (now a museum; risierasansabba.it). During the Liberation, Trieste became a potential flashpoint of east-west confrontation. Marshal Tito's Yugoslav partisans occupied the city from 1 May to 12 June 1945, during which time anti-communist Italians and Slovenian refugees were murdered – some of them simply disappearing. Eventually, Tito reached an agreement with British Field Marshal Harold Alexander, Supreme Commander of Allied forces in the Mediterranean. Trieste and its hinterland were temporarily partitioned into two zones of influence: one under Allied control in the west and the other under Yugoslav jurisdiction in the east. The 1947 Treaty of Paris created the Free Territory of Trieste, but the city was later returned to Italy and the eastern zone incorporated into Yugoslavia (and subsequently divided between Slovenia and Croatia).

Shoah Memorial
Central Railway Station, Milan,
Ⓦ memorialeshoah.it

The word "indifferenza" ("indifference") is spelled out in huge letters along a wall of Milan's memorial to the Holocaust, a stark reminder of fascism's greatest ally. Twenty trains of livestock cars pulled out of Milan station between 1943 and 1945 loaded with Jews and other "undesirables", few of whom were ever to return. Some of the rolling stock used in the transports is on display today.

Life under occupation

For anyone living in a modern democracy in the 21st century, it is hard to imagine what life was like under foreign occupation in the 1940s.

Occupation can seem inconceivable to citizens of countries like Britain, the USA and Australia, who have never shared a land border with an aggressive and dominant neighbouring state. Even for most of continental Europe in the late 1930s, the idea that their autonomous nations could be overrun by the armies of Nazi Germany and administered from Berlin seemed unthinkable. Some countries were convinced that they would be protected by their longstanding declarations of neutrality – a strategy that worked for Switzerland and Sweden but not for Norway, Denmark or the Low Countries. Other nations – notably France – felt safe because of the size and power of their armies, and the presumed strength of their frontier defences.

The map of Europe changed rapidly between 1939 and 1940, in the space of just a year. Territorial expansion was central to the ideologies of both Nazi Germany and Fascist Italy. They extended their borders by means of stealth and manipulation, or – more commonly – by force. As a result, the once autonomous nations of Albania, Belgium, Czechoslovakia, Denmark, Greece, Luxembourg, the Netherlands, Norway and Poland all had to adapt to life under indefinite occupation.

France was occupied by both Germany and Italy, the latter seizing the southeastern corner of Provence. The Channel Islands, dependencies of the British Crown off the coast of Normandy, also fell to, and were administered by, the Nazis. The Baltic states of Estonia, Lithuania and Latvia had a more complicated experience, being occupied initially by the Soviet Union, which also invaded eastern Poland in 1939 (see p.222). In late 1943, Italy went from being an occupying country to an occupied one. Having changed sides in October (see p.46), Italy was unable to prevent its north from coming under German control.

Nazi occupation across Europe

German occupation took many forms, and its severity depended on how the Nazis regarded the

▲
French café life under Nazi occupation

country in question. The Nazis saw the Slavs as an inferior people, and the occupation of Poland was harsher than that of France – a country they admired for its sophisticated culture.

Some territories were regarded in Nazi ideology as rightful parts of Germany to be reincorporated into the Reich, rather than foreign lands to be seized. Austria, Alsace and German-speaking parts of Belgium, Poland and Czechoslovakia were simply being "freed" to rejoin the Fatherland to which they linguistically and culturally belonged. Their experience of "occupation" was therefore less severe – or even almost non-existent – although their young men were conscripted into the Wehrmacht. In "freed" areas of Poland, ethnic Poles were murdered, brutally expelled or ruthlessly Germanized.

In all cases, occupation was dictated on the conqueror's terms. Its essence in the German military mindset was *vae victis* or "woe to the conquered". Nazi rule was not cooperative or consultative; the strong dictated their terms to the weak and defeated, and they were non-negotiable. Occupation was ultimately directed by Hitler's military needs, and resources from Germany's acquired territories were exploited to pay for the war effort and the cost of occupation.

Occupation was particularly disastrous for the Jews – as well

Refugees walking in the street
▼

as several other targeted minorities. Many Jews had escaped from Germany only to find themselves subject to anti-Jewish policies in Nazi-occupied territories such as the Netherlands or Belgium. Under occupation, local authorities and police were expected to round up Jews and dispatch them to the death camps. In Poland, ninety percent of the prewar Jewish population (three million people) was herded into ghettos and camps – and later killed.

Rather than administering conquered territories directly from Berlin, Nazi Germany generally favoured installing puppet regimes. The Vichy government under Marshal Pétain controlled the majority of France, while the Salò Republic was Mussolini's nominal government of northern Italy after the Allied invasion. Regions that were deemed of vital strategic importance – such as the coasts of France and the Low Countries – were placed under the direct jurisdiction of the Wehrmacht.

Defence apart, the main objective of the occupiers was to keep a territory functioning. Agricultural and industrial production were to meet the needs of the German war machine, the railways had to facilitate troop movements, and the subject population must remain compliant in defeat.

Coping with occupation

In certain regions of occupied Europe, life went on much as before, altered by a number of moderate inconveniences and hardships. For others, life was unrecognizably different.

Poland suffered in a way that people in the west were spared. Subject to enforced work programmes and Germanization, the Slavs were regarded as expendable slave labour. Six million Poles – half of them Polish Jews – died as a result of the war, a staggering twenty percent of the population.

A defining experience of all defeated populations was a feeling of powerlessness. The conquered people of Europe were expected to follow Nazi orders. Punishment for disobedience was summary and disproportionate: those who resisted Nazi will were branded criminals and terrorists. The same charge was applied to anyone assisting the resistance or providing safe houses for fugitive Allied airmen. The jails of the Gestapo became overcrowded and executions were carried out as a warning to anyone who dared to defy the occupation authorities.

People faced with life under occupation responded in a number of ways. Some – politicians like de Gaulle and many Polish soldiers and airmen – went into exile to continue the fight from outside the country. Others, typically direct victims of Nazi persecution (Jews, Roma, homosexu-

als and so on), were forced to go into hiding; this was the decision of Anne Frank and her family. Many more chose to resist. An assortment of people helped collect intelligence for the Allies, provide food and shelter for those in hiding and organize strikes and acts of sabotage. Others took to the woods and hills to fight the Germans using whatever weapons they could obtain.

The majority of people, however, stayed and coped as best they could. Accepting the conditions of occupation and continuing life as normally as possible was not easy. There were endless privations and shortages. Travel was difficult – the movement of troops and weaponry took priority and access was forbidden to militarily sensitive parts of each

country. Society, meanwhile, was disrupted as men were sent to work in the Reich – those who had not already been taken as prisoners of war.

Curiously, occupation was to spark both solidarity and distrust among subject populations. There was a common hardship to endure, and resources were often pooled. At the same time, it was almost impossible to know who to trust, and secrets had to be closely guarded.

Living with the occupiers

One of the most troubling dilemmas of occupied life was what attitude to adopt towards the occupying forces. Hostility was futile, but civility seemed inappropriate. Many found there was a fine line between being obedient and obliging.

Some residents were surprised to find that individual occupiers were decent human beings with similar interests to themselves. Not all the Germans were fascists; many were conscripts who secretly abhorred their own government. People with comparable political views found themselves living in close proximity but on opposite sides of the conflict. Were they to ignore each other entirely? Worse still were affairs of the heart. Various young couples fell in love across enemy lines, despite the obvious dangers.

In these situations – and many more – ordinary citizens of

▲
Nazi police confiscate goods from the house of a Polish Jew

the occupied territories found themselves caught between two opposing strictures. If they refused to comply with the Nazis they would be punished for disobedience, but if they complied too readily, society might brand them as collaborators. Life under occupation presented a series of challenges to be delicately managed and requiring endless compromises. Principles and loyalties had to be judged; potential informants had to be avoided or placated; and everyone did what they had to do in order to survive. If an unemployed breadwinner was offered a job by the Germans, he had little choice but to take it. If the resistance asked the same man to steal documents, it might feel difficult to refuse. Could a bartender charm his German customers to keep them spending money? Was a mother able to befriend a German medical orderly to obtain medicine for her sick child? How would a farmer be judged for selling his crops to German troops in order to feed his family?

For children, navigating occupation was even more perplexing. Many had grown up with no memory of what the adults thought of as normality. It was hard for them to understand the nuanced behaviour of grown-ups who had to prepare for two equally possible outcomes: a permanent occupation and its sudden end, when every action would be judged in a new light.

Although most ordinary civilians lived in a grey state of reluctant compliance with the Germans, in every occupied country there were Nazi sympathisers who had no problem with the occupiers. Fascists throughout Europe approved of Nazi ideology and believed it was bringing benefits to their countrymen. They were happy to work with the Germans, to persecute local resistance fighters and to help deport their Jewish neighbours with whom they had long lived in peace. Under occupation, the collaborators thrived, but as soon as their Nazi overlords departed they were utterly exposed.

The Liberation

When a town or city was liberated – often after a devastating period of bombing and shelling – the wartime order was thrown into disarray. Before the courts could be reconvened, an impromptu catharsis of judgement and punishment swept across the newly liberated territories. In France, this was known as the *épuration sauvage*. A frenzy of accusations were directed towards suspected collaborators. Professions of confession or denial were largely ignored, and sentences were passed by angry crowds, many of whom were anxious to relieve their own confused consciences. Punishments were carried out immediately. Women accused of sleeping with Germans had their

▲
Crowds celebrate the liberation of Rome

heads shaved; Gestapo informants were shot or hanged.

For the British and American soldiers of the Liberation, these first reactions to freedom could be bewildering. Feelings of jubilation and relief were usually complicated by a web of other emotions resulting from the intensely charged experience of living under occupation.

United
Kingdom

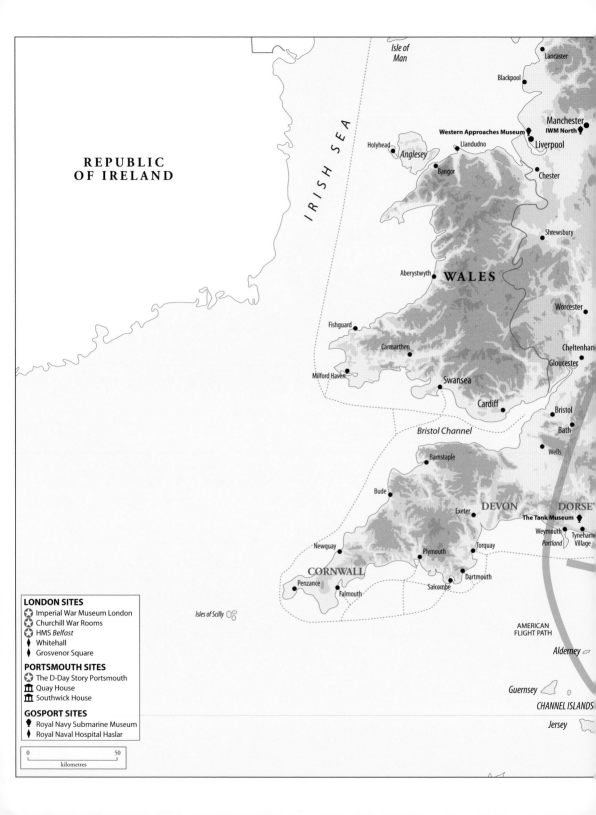

REPUBLIC
OF IRELAND

Isle of Man

IRISH SEA

Lancaster
Blackpool
Manchester
IWM North
Liverpool
Western Approaches Museum
Holyhead
Anglesey
Llandudno
Bangor
Chester
Shrewsbury
Aberystwyth
WALES
Worcester
Fishguard
Cheltenham
Carmarthen
Gloucester
Milford Haven
Swansea
Cardiff
Bristol
Bath
Bristol Channel
Wells
Barnstaple
Bude
DEVON
DORSET
Exeter
The Tank Museum
Weymouth
Tyneham
Portland
Village
Newquay
Torquay
CORNWALL
Plymouth
Dartmouth
Penzance
Salcombe
Falmouth
Isles of Scilly

AMERICAN
FLIGHT PATH

Alderney

Guernsey

CHANNEL ISLANDS

Jersey

LONDON SITES
- Imperial War Museum London
- Churchill War Rooms
- HMS *Belfast*
- Whitehall
- Grosvenor Square

PORTSMOUTH SITES
- The D-Day Story Portsmouth
- Quay House
- Southwick House

GOSPORT SITES
- Royal Navy Submarine Museum
- Royal Naval Hospital Haslar

0   50
kilometres

The Liberation
United Kingdom

Anglo-American forces
Convoy routes

N

NORTH SEA

York
Yorkshire Air Museum
Leeds
:ford
Kingston-upon-Hull

Sheffield

:NGLAND
Lincoln
International Bomber
Command Centre
Skegness

Nottingham

NORFOLK
RAF Air Defence Radar Museum
Great Yarmouth
:lational Memorial
⊙ Arboretum
Leicester
King's Lynn
Norwich
Lowestoft

:mingham
Coventry
Peterborough

Northampton
SUFFOLK

:atford-
:on-Avon
Cambridge
American
Cemetery
Cambridge
Ipswich
Felixstowe

IWM Duxford
Colchester
Harwich

Bletchley Park
ESSEX
Den Haag

Oxford
Combined Military
Services Museum
THE
NETHERLANDS

LONDON
Southend
Middelburg

Chatham
Ramsgate
Ramsgate Tunnels
Antwerp

Canterbury
Dover
Dunkirk

Salisbury
Winchester
KENT
Dover Castle
Romney, Hythe &
Dymchurch Railway
Calais
BELGIUM

:hampton
HAMPSHIRE
SUSSEX
Shoreham
Dungeness
BRUSSELS

THE NEW
FOREST
Gosport
Portsmouth
Newhaven
Boulogne
Lille

:and
:ch'
Isle of
Wight
Hayling Island
Le Touquet

ENGLISH CHANNEL
Arras
Cambrai

BRITISH
FLIGHT PATH
Dieppe
Amiens
St-Quentin

Cherbourg
Le Havre

Normandy Beaches
Honfleur
Rouen
Beauvais
Reims

Bayeux
Senlis

Caen
FRANCE
Châlons-sur-Marne

Coutances
PARIS

The Liberation United Kingdom

By 1943, the British had reasons to be optimistic. In October 1942 they had achieved their first land victory over the Germans at the Second Battle of El Alamein, when the Eighth Army forced German Field Marshal Rommel's elite Afrika Korps out of Egypt.

The victory at El Alamein was followed by the first joint Anglo-American campaign, Operation Torch: a large-scale attack on French Morocco and Algeria. Torch provided invaluable experience in how to organize a large amphibious landing and highlighted some of the problems involved when national armies fought together, such as failures of cooperation and the tendency for top generals to compete with each other. Despite some serious setbacks, the North Africa campaign ended in Allied victory, with the last Axis troops finally surrendering on 13 May 1943.

>>
General Dwight D. Eisenhower addresses paratroopers in England

Planning for D-Day

Though agreement had been reached at the Casablanca Conference in January 1943 and at the Washington (Trident) Conference the following May, the British were still nervous about invading German-occupied France, preferring an Italian campaign to follow the action in Sicily (see p.42). Nevertheless, a team led by Lieutenant General Morgan was already drawing up plans for the French invasion. Presented in July 1943, they identified three Normandy beaches as the best landing sites, rather than Pas-de-Calais (opposite Dover), which would have seemed more obvious. Wherever they chose to land in France, Allied troops would have the challenging task of breaching the massive German coastal defences, known as the Atlantic Wall, which stretched all the way from Norway to Spain.

At the Tehran Conference in December 1943 – the first meeting of Churchill, Roosevelt and Stalin – the Soviet leader agreed to an eastern offensive to coincide with the promised Anglo-American western offensive in order to stretch the German resources to the limit. Shortly afterwards, General Eisenhower was appointed Commander of Supreme Headquarters Allied Expeditionary Force (SHAEF). Setting up his headquarters in London, Eisenhower selected a team of mostly British senior officers to help him refine General Morgan's original plan: Air Chief Marshal Tedder became his deputy; General Montgomery was to command the invading land forces; Admiral Ramsay the naval forces; and Air Chief Marshal Leigh-Mallory the air force. Among the changes to the plan were increasing the invasion area to five beaches between Cherbourg and

Caen, and changing the date from 1 May to early June to allow more landing craft to be assembled and more time for Allied bombers to destroy German supply links – roads and railways – in northern France.

Planning discussions for the invasion (codenamed Operation Overlord) and the amphibious landings (Operation Neptune) were rarely straightforward, and there were major disagreements. Eisenhower threatened to resign unless given full control of all three armed forces, something that RAF Bomber Command, supported by Churchill, tried to resist. Since June 1943 British and American planes had been subjecting German industrial sites and cities to round-the-clock heavy bombing, a strategy that the head of Bomber Command, Sir Arthur Harris, and his US counterpart General Carl Spaatz, believed would ultimately win the war. When Eisenhower, Montgomery and Tedder requested the bombing of French transport systems to prevent rapid deployment of German reinforcements (the Transportation Plan), Harris, Spaatz and Churchill argued against it. In the end, Eisenhower won

Significant sites are marked on the map on pages 78 and 79

✪ **Imperial War Museum London, London. See p.86**

✪ **Churchill War Rooms, London. See p.86**

✪ **HMS *Belfast*, London. See p.89**

✪ **The D-Day Story Portsmouth, Portsmouth. See p.92**

✪ **Imperial War Museum Duxford, Duxford. See p.98**

out and the pre-invasion bombing took place. Although the raids proved effective, they caused substantial civilian casualties.

Build-up on the south coast

On 5 March 1944, General Eisenhower moved his headquarters from Grosvenor Square to Bushy Park in southwest London, partly to avoid the "mini-Blitz" that had hit Central London. He continued to shuttle

» Dieppe Raid

Churchill and his chief military adviser General Alan Brooke were particularly nervous about opening a second front in France because of the failed Dieppe Raid of 19 August 1942, an operation aimed at destroying German defences near the eponymous port in Northern France. It involved around 5000 Canadians – keen to see action – 1000 British, and 50 US Rangers. The ground troops were supported by 237 ships, none larger than a destroyer, and 74 squadrons of aircraft, most of which were fighter planes rather than bombers.

The raid ended in disaster. Reconnais-sance had failed to reveal the German gun emplacements on the cliffs and many of the troops never succeeded in getting off the beaches. The Royal Regiment of Canada suffered particularly heavy losses, several tanks got stuck in the shingle, and those that did cross the sea wall made little impact. Some commandos managed to reach their targets but were ultimately forced back; withdrawal began just five hours after the raid had begun. The only positive was that all subsequent amphibious landings were prepared with much greater attention to detail.

back and forth to liaise with his commanders and Churchill. According to his naval aide Harry C. Butcher, he also visited around twenty divisions, twenty airfields and four US Navy ships in morale-boosting inspections, often accompanied by Churchill.

American troops had been coming to Britain since 1942, and in the run-up to D-Day numbered around 1.5 million. Most arrived at the port in Liverpool. As well as living in vast camps, many soldiers were billeted in people's homes and a degree of culture shock was inevitable. GIs were issued with a pamphlet, *Instructions for American Servicemen in Britain*, with tips such as "Don't Be a Show Off. The British dislike bragging". This huge input of US manpower was essential for the success of Overlord; ongoing campaigns in Italy and the Far East meant the British were running low on troops. All soldiers had to be extremely fit – an infantryman might need to carry as much as half his weight in equipment – and they were subjected to a punishing training regime.

In the months before D-Day, several rehearsal exercises for the amphibious landings were organized. Slapton Sands in South Devon was used for the larger of these because of its resemblance to the Normandy beaches. On 28 April, one such exercise, codenamed Tiger, ended in disaster when eight LSTs (Landing Ship, Tank) filled with troops heading inland were attacked by nine German E-boats (Motor Torpedo boats) with the loss of around 750 US servicemen. The tragedy, which was hushed up for security reasons, did not prevent the even larger Exercise Fabius taking place one week later at several beaches along the south coast, including Slapton Sands. This was a dress rehearsal for Operation Neptune, which ran a whole week and involved 25,000 troops.

Logistical problems

Transporting over 130,000 troops and their equipment – including heavy tanks – across the English Channel, then providing them with sufficient supplies to maintain their effectiveness, was always going to be an enormous challenge. It was a task that many of the best military and scientific brains had been working on for years. Nearly seven thousand ships would be involved, with landing ships and landing craft making up over half of them. Landing craft varied in size according to function – from the enormous LSTs to the smaller British LCAs (Landing Craft, Assault) and the American LCVP (Landing Craft, Vehicle, Personnel). The latter two were mostly made from steel-armoured wood with a shallow enough draft to enable them to land 36 troops in a few feet of water. The advantage of the LCVP – which Eisenhower credited with playing a major role in the success of Overlord – was that it could carry vehicles.

The capture of a French or Belgian port was seen as crucial but unlikely to happen quickly, so British engineers came up with the radical idea of building components for harbours, towing them across to France and assembling them there. This would enable the speedy unloading of vital supplies. Codenamed Operation Mulberry, the harbours were created using floating outer breakwaters (bombardons) and static breakwaters made up of blockships (scuttled ships) held in place by a row of airtight concrete breakwaters (Phoenix caissons) which could be sunk and refloated. Within each harbour, piers were built to transport supplies to the shore. Two were constructed, Mulberry "A" to serve Omaha Beach; Mulberry "B" for Gold Beach.

An equally extraordinary engineering project was the construction of oil pipelines under the English Channel that would supply

Biography
Winston Churchill

He is widely regarded as Britain's greatest wartime leader, but for most of the 1930s, Winston Churchill was on the margins of British political life. The prevailing political orthodoxy was appeasement: making concessions to Hitler in order to preserve peace. Churchill was deeply opposed to this; from early on he recognized both Nazism's barbarity and Hitler's expansionist ambitions. His wasn't a lone voice – many in the Labour Party were anti-fascist – but Churchill's journalism allowed his arguments to be widely heard. When Hitler invaded Poland, having already annexed Austria and occupied Czechoslovakia, Churchill was proved right. His time had come.

Ironically, Churchill became prime minister following Britain's failed invasion of Norway, which he had largely masterminded. He got the job because his only rival, Lord Halifax, didn't seem to want it, whereas Churchill felt it was his destiny. Many more military defeats were to follow, but Churchill's great strength was that he believed wholeheartedly in his cause and had the ability – through charisma and the power of his oratory – to convince most of his colleagues of the same, despite some of them wanting peace with Hitler. The evacuation of Dunkirk, when morale in the country was low and invasion seemed inevitable, prompted his famous "We will fight on the beaches" speech, climaxing with the words "We will never surrender." The speech galvanized parliament and largely united the nation.

Britain's lowest point was Churchill's finest moment. His wit, his affable public face and his trademark "V for Victory" sign came to epitomize the defiant British bulldog spirit. Behind closed doors he was less easy to get along with. He had a prodigious energy for a man in his mid-sixties, in part due to regular afternoon naps, but he could be a bully; he was told off by his wife for being "rough, sarcastic and overbearing" with his staff. He was a better amateur strategist than Hitler, but he still infuriated his generals with his impetuousness and self-belief. The difference was that his generals and colleagues regularly stood up to him.

When the USA entered the war at the end of 1941, Churchill, in his own words, "slept the sleep of the saved and thankful". The Americans had supported Britain financially since the start, but Churchill was convinced that the added manpower and firepower would tilt the balance of the war. He was right, but by the time of the Normandy landings it was the Americans – General Eisenhower and President Roosevelt – who set the agenda for the Liberation of Europe.

» The Channel Islands

The only British citizens to experience occupation were the residents of the Channel Islands, a self-governing Crown dependency 32km west of Normandy. By the time the islands were demilitarized in June 1940 (after the Fall of France), around 25,000 inhabitants had already been evacuated. Most of the remaining 65,000 lived on the two largest islands, Jersey and Guernsey. A Luftwaffe raid at the end of June killed 44 and wounded 70, but once the Nazis realized the islands were undefended, invasion went ahead without further casualties.

The German administration worked in tandem with the existing civil authorities, who were forced to adopt and enforce any new Nazi laws, such as the confiscation of radios in 1942. Law-abiding residents were treated fairly respectfully, but the idea that this was a benign occupation (as some accounts have suggested) is misleading. Any resistance met with severe punishment; over one thousand islanders were imprisoned, two hundred of whom were deported to camps or prisons in Europe.

Although most Jews had left, the thirty or so that remained were subject to punitive laws, passed with little or no fuss from the authorities. Jews had to register themselves, wear the yellow star and relinquish their businesses. Jews were also deported to the Channel Islands, to work as slave labour, along with forced labour from across Europe. Much of the work took place on the isle of Alderney, which had been transformed into four camps, two of which were concentration camps run with excessive brutality by the SS. Work was mostly on fortifying the islands as part of the Atlantic Wall (see p.115) and many defensive structures are still visible. It is estimated that around one thousand people died on Alderney.

Bypassed by Operation Overlord in 1944, liberation finally occurred on 9 May 1945 when HMS *Bulldog* arrived at St Peter Port, Guernsey and the Germans surrendered. Many islanders were on the verge of starvation as a result of the Allied blockade. As with all occupied countries, questions over the extent to which people collaborated remain to this day.

the fuel needed by the Allied armies in France when they moved inland. Because tankers on their own were vulnerable – to bad weather as well as attack – Operation PLUTO (Pipelines Under the Ocean) was developed. The pipes were laid on the Channel floor by unreeling them from a giant drum called a Conundrum, which functioned like a cotton bobbin and was towed by a tug. These were fed by a network of pipelines from all over England culminating in two coastal locations: Shanklin in the Isle of Wight, from where it was pumped along the seabed to Port-en-Bessin, and Dungeness in Kent and then over to Ambleteuse near Boulogne. The operation was shrouded in complete secrecy, with pumping stations disguised as ordinary buildings to reduce the threat of enemy attack.

Intelligence and subterfuge

The Germans were expecting an attack to occur in northern France sooner or later, but it was vitally important to keep them guessing as to the exact time and place. To create as much confusion as possible, the Allies devised elaborate schemes of misinformation. Operation Fortitude South invented an entirely fictitious 1st US Army Group (FUSAG), supposedly stationed in Kent and Essex, to suggest that the invasion would occur at Pas-de-Calais. Inflatable tanks made of rubber, fake landing craft and other military paraphernalia were manufactured at Shepperton studios, and the whole charade was "commanded" by US General George Patton – a soldier so renowned that the Germans were unlikely to think him wasted on a ploy.

To reinforce the illusion, a network of fictitious agents, believed by the Germans to be working for them – but who had in fact been invented by double-agents including Juan Pujol – was supplying German intelligence with convincing information about FUSAG. At the same time, the RAF was dropping more bombs and sending more reconnaissance flights over Pas-de-Calais than over Normandy. The combined effect, so the Allies hoped, was that the Germans would think that the Normandy landings were a prelude to the main invasion rather than the real thing.

One substantial Allied advantage was the fact that Ultra, the code-breaking project based at Bletchley Park, could decrypt the intercepted communications of the Axis powers and provide vital intelligence about the build-up of German troops and their defences in Normandy (see p.115). The French Resistance was also active in the run-up to D-Day, supplying information and carrying out acts of sabotage against crucial infrastructure.

The final days before D-Day

On 15 May 1944, the final Overlord briefing was held at St Paul's School in London, General Montgomery's headquarters. Eisenhower and all the Allied commanders attended, along with King George VI and Churchill. Montgomery gave the main briefing, exuding quiet confidence and expressing the belief that Caen would be captured within 24 hours. All the big decisions about Overlord had now been made, apart from D-Day (the precise date of the invasion) and H-Hour (the precise hour).

As June arrived, Eisenhower moved his Advance Headquarters to Southwick House near Portsmouth, a major naval centre and key embarkation point. He still had plenty of problems to contend with, not least the 69-year-old Churchill's insistence that he be allowed to accompany the invasion – it took the King to persuade him otherwise. A bigger problem was the weather. The ideal situation for a mass landing was a low tide, a clear sky, little wind and a calm sea. The invasion date had been set for 5 June, but as the day approached senior meteorological officer James Stagg predicted a storm for that day. Eisenhower postponed, the storm duly arrived, but then new weather reports suggested a temporary lull and the invasion was back on track. On 6 June 1944 the vast Allied armada – the largest amphibious expedition in history – set out.

» The nationwide war effort

Every part of the United Kingdom made a contribution to the war effort: shipyards in Belfast and Govan; the coal mines of South Wales; munitions and military vehicle factories in Manchester. The port of Liverpool was especially important as the headquarters of the Western Approaches Command (see p.101), charged with protecting merchant shipping during the Battle of the Atlantic – the struggle for control of the ocean which lasted the war's duration. Troops were stationed the length and breadth of the country, but in the build-up to Operation Overlord there was an inevitable gravitation towards the south of England because of its closeness to France. In the months before D-Day, the south coast began to resemble one vast military camp.

London

The Blitz killed thousands and drove millions of Londoners to leave the city, but ministers and the various departments of state stayed put, despite being located within the relatively small area of Westminster and Whitehall.

A near miss at No.10 Downing Street meant that Churchill was forced to move to a ground-floor flat in the New Public Office building (NPO), known as the "No. 10 Annexe". In the basement of NPO were the Cabinet War Rooms (now the Churchill War Rooms), an underground complex that formed the nerve centre of Britain's wartime strategy and policy-making.

The initial military planning for Operation Overlord took place at Norfolk House in St James's Square, but when Eisenhower became Supreme Allied Commander he established his personal headquarters in Grosvenor Square and transferred many of the Norfolk House personnel. Norfolk House

» Churchill's bedroom at the Churchill War Rooms

continued as a planning centre for Overlord's naval commander Admiral Ramsay and the RAF commander Air Chief Marshal Leigh-Mallory. In the run-up to D-Day, SHAEF headquarters was moved to a US Air Base in Bushy Park in the southwest of London.

London was also the temporary home to several governments-in-exile: the Poles at 39 Buckingham Palace Road; the Free French at 4 Carlton Gardens; the Norwegians at Kingston House North, Princes Gate; the Dutch at Stratton House in Piccadilly; and the Belgians at 105 Eaton Square.

London sites   «

Imperial War Museum London
Lambeth Rd, Ⓦ iwm.org.uk/visits/iwm-london

Established during World War I, the Imperial War Museum (IWM) contains a vast collection of objects and documents that show how war has impacted those living in Britain and the Commonwealth. It covers the period from 1914 to the present day, with one of its five floors entirely dedicated to World War II with a separate section on the Holocaust. There is plenty of military hardware on display, but the emphasis is as much on the experiences of civilians and what they had to endure. The IWM also administers the Churchill War Rooms and HMS *Belfast*, and two other museums.

Churchill War Rooms
Clive Steps, King Charles St, Ⓦ iwm.org.uk/visits/churchill-war-rooms

Built as a bunker in expectation of aerial bombardment, the Cabinet War Rooms were completed shortly before war was declared. As

» Women at war

During World War II, most of the prominent figures in politics and the armed forces were men, and it is easy to get the impression that women were relegated to secondary roles in the war effort. Gender inequality in the 1930s and 40s was widespread, but the war demanded a fully mobilized workforce. Countless women made an invaluable contribution to the Allied campaign both at home and abroad.

In Britain, more than 640,000 women were active in the armed forces, most of them working in the Women's Royal Naval Services (WRNS), the Women's Auxiliary Air Force (WAAF) and the Auxiliary Territorial Service (ATS). Many more drove ambulances, ferried aircraft between airfields (nicknamed "ATA-girls") and served as nurses. In the USA, 350,000 women were employed in the organizations of their American counterparts. The Soviet Union – founded on communist ideals which saw men and women as equal – fielded around 800,000 women in the Red Army. More than half of them served as regular troops, but others starred as snipers, fighter pilots and tank commanders.

Women played an integral part in the resistance overseas, too (see p.102). In Britain, just under one third of the Special Operations Executive (SOE) was made up of women. Female special agents and ordinary members of the resistance risked their lives to help the Allied cause in the occupied territories. Gender stereotypes meant women were frequently treated with less suspicion than men, and became excellent couriers, spies, radio operators and saboteurs.

On the Allied homefront, millions of women were employed in war work, taking jobs that were previously reserved for men. More than two million women in Britain, and more than six million women in the USA, joined the domestic war effort. Their jobs were primarily in industry, but women also worked in agriculture, engineering and the auxiliary services. Naturally, many of the jobs in Britain were based in London. In the USA, "Rosie the Riveter" and "Wanda the Welder" became popular characters in propaganda. The increase of women in the workforce did lead to greater opportunity (at least temporarily), but women were consistently paid less than their male counterparts.

In Germany, Nazi ideology preached inequality and women were regarded as mothers and homemakers. Despite this, thousands of German women were employed in industry, primarily in the Nazi munition factories. Women also played an important part in defending Germany's skies, and Hanna Reitsch and Countess von Stauffenberg were two of the Luftwaffe's most prized test pilots.

the main command headquarters of the war, space was at a premium and extra rooms were constantly added: Churchill was given a combined bedroom and office, with his hotline to the US President disguised as a toilet. The War Cabinet met there 115 times, usually when air raids seemed imminent. The most significant space was the Map Room, a military information hub functioning around the clock, which produced daily intelligence summaries for the King, Churchill and the chiefs of staff. A museum since 1984, the rooms provide a unique insight into the pressurized lives of those who worked there. A separate section dedicated to the life and career of Churchill was added in 2003.

Biography
» **General Dwight D. Eisenhower**

Having finally agreed to launch a second front in Normandy, scheduled for May 1944, the Allies were very slow to appoint the hugely important role of supreme commander. The obvious senior generals – the American George C. Marshall or the British Alan Brooke – were considered, but passed over in favour of Marshall's protégé, Dwight D. Eisenhower.

This was the culmination of a meteoric rise for a soldier who had gone from being a mere colonel in March 1941 to commanding the American and Allied forces in North Africa in November 1942 and in Sicily during the summer of 1943. He almost certainly got the job because President Roosevelt realized that as well as being a brilliant administrator, Eisenhower possessed the kind of political acumen that was needed to keep the main Allied powers of Britain, the US and the Soviet Union working together, as well as US public opinion on board.

"Ike", as he was popularly known, also possessed great personal charm, with a smile that one of his subordinates fa-mously said was "worth an army corps in any campaign". His calm demeanour and unifying presence enabled him to mould an excellent Anglo-American planning team in the build-up to D-Day and it won the affection, if not always the respect, of his more egotistical generals.

His own lack of direct battlefield experience meant that some seasoned generals were often withering in their criticism of him. The most regular clashes occurred with leading British general, Bernard Law Montgomery, whose talents as a military commander were matched by his tactlessness and conceit. Montgomery thought that Eisenhower's insistence on a broad front strategy for the Allied drive across Europe was nonsense, feeling – after Normandy – that the quickest way to a German defeat was a single massed attack in the north with preferably himself (or, failing that, the American General Bradley) in command. Eisenhower rejected this, largely for political reasons. The Allies were a coalition of forces and he didn't want one side (or general) taking the credit for victory.

While Eisenhower's management was largely by consensus (which many found frustrating), he was more than capable of making tough strategic decisions when he had to. A good example was his absolute insistence, prior to D-Day, that the bombing campaign of the Allied air forces be diverted from targets in Germany to destroying the infrastructure of northern France. He was also capable of mistakes, but on the whole most of his decisions seemed to have been the right ones, and resulted, finally, in the overwhelming defeat of the Wehrmacht in western Europe.

HMS Belfast
The Queens Walk, ⓦ iwm.org.uk/visits/
hms-belfast

The light cruiser HMS *Belfast* was built for the Royal Navy at Belfast in 1938. *Belfast*'s role on D-Day was as the flagship of Bombardment Force E, opening fire on the German gun battery of La Marefontaine in support of troops landing at Gold and Juno beaches. She remained in action in Normandy for over a month. Decommissioned in the 1960s, HMS *Belfast* is now a museum moored on the Thames and one of only a handful of surviving Royal Navy ships that served in World War II. Visitors can access all nine decks and visit a variety of rooms including the bridge, the operations room, the galley and the huge boiler rooms.

« HMS *Belfast*

Whitehall

Beginning at Trafalgar Square, Whitehall is the street that becomes Parliament Street, which leads to the Houses of Parliament. With its adjacent side roads, Whitehall has long been the location of government offices and departments; some of these were relocated in the war, but most remained. Heading down from Trafalgar Square takes you past several key buildings, including the Admiralty, the War Office (now a hotel), the Ministry of Defence (MOD) and the Foreign and Commonwealth Office. Downing Street, with the prime minister's residence at No.10, is halfway along Whitehall, a short distance from the Cabinet War Rooms in one direction and Parliament in the other.

Whitehall also contains a large number of World War II statues and memorials. In Parliament Square, Winston Churchill defiantly faces Parliament, while both Montgomery and Alan Brooke stand outside the MOD. There are memorials to the Women of World War II in Whitehall (see p.87), and the Royal Tank Regiment in Whitehall Court. Those to the RAF and the Royal Navy Air Service and Fleet Air Arm are both behind the MOD on the Embankment.

Grosvenor Square

Grosvenor Square in Mayfair is about a half-hour walk from Whitehall. During World War II so many official US buildings were located here that the square was nicknamed "Eisenhower Platz". General Eisenhower's headquarters were at No.20, the US Navy was next door at No.18, the Embassy at No.1, the US Lend-Lease Mission at No.3, and the Office of Strategic Studies (OSS) – a US intelligence agency – at No.70. A statue of President Roosevelt was erected on the northeast corner of the square in 1948; it was joined by one of a uniformed Eisenhower in 1989.

Kent

Kent and its neighbouring county, Sussex, make up the southeastern corner of Great Britain, the closest part of the mainland to France. Both counties were important embarkation points for Operation Overlord.

Their proximity to continental Europe also meant that Kent and Sussex were bombed throughout the war – from sea, air and German batteries in France. Coastal towns in particular were under constant attack: Dover and Folkestone in Kent were so badly bombed that the stretch of coastline near them became known as "Hellfire Corner".

A few kilometres down the coast from Folkestone is Romney Marsh, an area near the Kent-Sussex border bounded by the Royal Military Canal on one side and the sea on the other. The Romney, Hythe & Dymchurch Railway runs the length of the marsh's coastline. The area has a long association with military defence and was a key point in Hitler's planned invasion of

» Dover Castle

Britain. Several surviving World War II pillboxes are visible along the canal, and four Advanced Landing Grounds (ALGs) – small temporary airstrips built to support D-Day – were sited in the area. Dungeness, the headland of Romney Marsh, was an assembly point for one of the Mulberry harbours built for the Normandy landings (see p.124), and was also the point from where one of the PLUTO undersea pipelines started (see p.84). A little further up the coast at Littlestone-on-Sea there's an abandoned Phoenix caisson that's visible at low tide.

Kent sites   «

Dover Castle
Castle Hill Rd, Dover, english-heritage.org.uk/visit/places/dover-castle

As the closest point to mainland Europe, Dover and its famous white cliffs became a potent symbol of British resilience in World War II. Dover Castle sits high above the harbour, a major defence against invaders for centuries. During the war its array of tunnels had many uses: Casement Tunnel was Admiral Ramsay's naval headquarters, from where he planned the evacuation from Dunkirk; Annex was a military hospital; and Dumpy was built in 1943 as a regional government centre in case of nuclear attack. Other tunnels were used as air-raid shelters. The castle was also one of the sites of the fictitious 1st US Army Group, created to fool the Germans into thinking the invasion would land at Pas-de-Calais (see p.84). Even after D-Day, Hitler was convinced that the real invasion would be launched from Dover. As a result, the town became the target for some of the heaviest German shelling since the beginning of the war. Remains of Dover's wartime defences

can be seen along the cliffs between Dover and Folkestone.

Ramsgate Tunnels
Marina Esplanade, Ramsgate,
🅦 ramsgatetunnels.org

Ramsgate was another vulnerable Kent town. Before the war started, its farsighted mayor nagged central government to allow him to build Deep Shelter Tunnels as protection against air raids. Four kilometres were eventually built (in addition to the existing railway tunnel). Many people evacuated the town when the heavy bombing started, the remainder sought refuge in the tunnels, which had entry points around the town. Entire families lived there almost permanently, and a whole underground community grew up with shops, street signs, a hospital and even a concert hall. Some of these tunnels can now be visited.

Romney, Hythe & Dymchurch Railway
🅦 rhdr.org.uk

The brainchild of two racing-car enthusiasts, this miniature railway (one-third normal size) has been running along the coast between Hythe and Dungeness since 1928. In World War II the line was requisitioned by the War Office and used to transport material for the building of PLUTO, the undersea oil pipeline (see p.84). Twenty-one kilometres long, the railway has five other stations between Hythe and Dungeness (some of which are request stops) where other wartime sites can be visited.

Dungeness
🅦 theromneymarsh.net/Dungeness

A bleak, windswept expanse of shingle right at the tip of Romney Marsh, Dungeness was one of two sites chosen from where oil pipes were laid under the English Channel to France. PLUTO was a complex engineering project conducted in total secrecy shortly after Operation Overlord was launched. Pluto Cottage, a pumping house built to resemble a small house, still exists at Dungeness and five more disguised installations can be seen at Greatstone-on-Sea, six kilometres up the coast. Fifteen kilometres inland from Dungeness at Brenzett is a small museum, the Romney Marsh Wartime Collection, which details the area's wartime connections.

Hampshire

The county of Hampshire, which lies in the middle of England's south coast, has long historical ties to the navy.

Portsmouth, the home of the Royal Navy, sits almost directly opposite the Cotentin peninsula, and was a major D-Day embarkation point. In June 1940, General Eisenhower moved his headquarters to Southwick House just north of the city. To the west of Portsmouth, the town of Gosport, and to the east Hayling Island, were both important sites in the building of the Mulberry harbour components that were towed across to Normandy. Portsmouth was heavily bombed throughout the war, as was the nearby port of Southampton. In 1940, the Spitfire factory in the Southampton suburb of Woolston, where the plane had been developed, was targeted and completely destroyed by the Luftwaffe.

The New Forest, a unique mixture of heathland, woodland and river valleys, was an ideal area for training in the build-up to D-Day, and many exercises took place there. Three kilometres across a strait of the Channel known as the Solent is the Isle of Wight, one of the sites chosen for Operation PLUTO. The pipeline joined the island at Thorness Bay before connecting to Shanklin and Sandown on the island's southeast coast. From here, fuel was carried under the Channel to Port-en-Bessin, close to Omaha beach.

Hampshire sites 《

The D-Day Story Portsmouth
Clarence Esplanade, Portsmouth,
🌐 theddaystory.com

Located on the seafront close to Southsea Castle, the D-Day Story Portsmouth is a museum entirely dedicated to Operation Overlord, both the events leading up to the invasion and the day itself. It's a large and varied

» D-Day Story Portsmouth exhibit

collection, with many personal artefacts – letters, paintings, photographs and maps – as well as military hardware. There is plenty of child-friendly interactive and audio material that helps bring the events to life, and the museum's excellent website is crammed with a wealth of detailed historical information. The Overlord Tapestry, 34 embroidered panels depicting the unfolding events of D-Day, provides a vivid and colourful climax to the displays.

Quay House
Broad Street, Portsmouth

A half-hour walk northeast from the D-Day Story museum takes you to Quay House on Broad Street. This handsome Art Deco building was used as offices in the 1930s, but in the preparations for D-Day it became the Embarkation Area Headquarters for the Portsmouth sector. Military personnel at Quay House played a vital role in ensuring the campaign ran efficiently, organizing the launches of the Allied troops from four areas across Portsmouth. Recently converted into flats, it can only be viewed from outside.

Southwick House
Southwick, Portsmouth

Eight kilometres north of Portsmouth near the village of Southwick is Southwick House, the final command post of the Supreme Headquarters Allied Expeditionary Force (SHAEF). Admiral Ramsay and General Montgomery moved here from London at the end of April 1944, General Eisenhower on 1 June. A large plywood map of the English south coast and the French coastline from Calais to Brest still adorns the Map Room, where meetings were held and plans final-

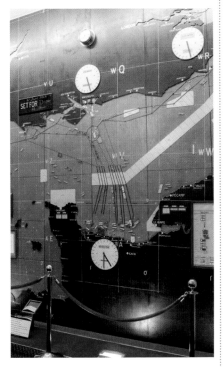

« Southwick House

ized. It was at Southwick House that James Stagg presented the weather report which delayed D-Day by one day (see p.85). Eisenhower's personal headquarters – an office tent and a trailer for sleeping in – was hidden from sight in nearby woods. Visiting the house can only be done by prior appointment; contact the Defence School of Policing and Guarding at DSPG-HQ-Information@mod.uk.

Royal Navy Submarine Museum
Haslar Jetty Road, Gosport, Ⓦ nmrn.org.uk/submarine-museum

The highlight of the Royal Navy Submarine Museum is undoubtedly HMS *Alliance*, an Amphion-class attack submarine of the type used in World War II, although this one wasn't

launched until July 1945. A tour of the submarine takes you through several areas, including the control room, accommodation space and the galley. The museum itself is also worth visiting, especially for its two midget submarines, one of them a British X-Craft similar to those used for surveillance of the Normandy beaches in January 1944, and in guiding landing craft onto Juno and Sword beaches during D-Day.

Royal Naval Hospital Haslar
Haslar, Gosport, Ⓦ haslarheritagegroup.co.uk

The Royal Naval Hospital at Haslar on the Gosport peninsula was founded in 1753 to treat British servicemen. During D-Day and its aftermath it was a key treatment centre for soldiers injured in action. Around 1347 casualties ar-

rived here within three months of the first Normandy landings. Run by the US Military during 1944 and 1945, staff treated both Allied soldiers and German prisoners of war before transferring them to other hospitals around Britain. In 2013 the Ministry of Defence sold the 25-hectare site to a private developer, but there are occasional tours organized by the Haslar Heritage Group. The nearby Haslar Royal Naval Cemetery (entrance in Clayhall Road) is where many of the wounded from D-Day who did not recover are buried.

Hayling Island

Hayling Island, along the shoreline of Langstone Harbour, was one of the places where Mulberry harbours were constructed (see p.82). A wrecked Phoenix caisson, almost broken in half, can be seen just north of the entrance to the harbour. The island is also where Combined Operations Assault Pilotage Parties (COPP) was based. This top-secret unit carried out clandestine reconnaissance missions investigating the beaches and in-shore waters of both Sicily and Normandy. Canoeists and frogmen set out from boats or submarines to gather vital information that would help in the planning of the amphibious landings. A World War II Heritage Trail, beginning near Hayling Island ferry landing, highlights the island's most important World War II sites, including the recently erected COPP memorial.

The New Forest
Ⓦ newforestnpa.gov.uk

The New Forest was a hive of activity throughout the war and in the run-up to the Liberation. Ashley Walk, a remote northern part of the forest, was the site of a major bombing range where most Allied bombs, including the famous Dambusters bouncing bomb, were tested. The forest was also home to several clandestine bases, some of which, like the Hydrographic Survey, were lo-

cated at requisitioned houses along the Beaulieu River. Members of the Special Operations Executive (SOE) received their final training at the Beaulieu Estate before deployment as secret agents in Europe, while the nearby estate village of Buckler's Hard was where motor torpedo boats were built, as well as dummy landing craft used to deceive the Germans about Allied landing plans. Lepe Beach, close to the mouth of the Beaulieu River, was a construction site for Mulberry harbours and the point from which the PLUTO pipeline left the mainland to connect with the Isle of Wight. Many remains of the workings lie scattered along the shoreline. Balmer Lawn Hotel at Brockenhurst was used as an Army Staff College before becoming the divisional headquarters of the 3rd Canadian Infantry Division and an occasional meeting place for key Allied commanders. There were twelve airfields in the New Forest, including four Advanced Landing Grounds, temporary sites built specifically to support troops in Normandy. A memorial to the airfields can be found at the former site of one of them, Holmsley South.

《
Rainbow over
the New Forest

Dorset

Dorset is the coastal county west of Hampshire. Many American troops were stationed here prior to D-Day, with training and exercises taking place across the whole county. This often involved using live ammunition and sometimes required the evacuation of local residents.

Poole, Weymouth and the Isle of Portland were all key D-Day embarkation points, and hundreds of thousands of US military personnel left from these three ports alone. A memorial on Weymouth Esplanade and another in Portland's Victoria Gardens commemorate their departure for Normandy. Two well-preserved Phoenix caissons, towed back from France after the war, stand in Portland Harbour. In 2018, six life-sized sculptures, representing four servicemen and two Portland dockyard workers, were placed on top of them. RAF Tarrant Rushton (now private farmland) was the departure point on 5 June 1944 for six Horsa gliders, each towed by a Halifax bomber, carrying men from the British 6th Airborne Division on a mission to capture the Pegasus bridge at Caen (see p.128).

Dorset sites «

The Tank Museum
Bovington, Ⓦ tankmuseum.org

One of the largest collections of armoured vehicles in the world, the Tank Museum outlines the development of the tank from its beginnings to the present day. There are six

» American M26 Tank at Bovington's Tank Museum

large halls, one of which is entirely devoted to World War II and contains tanks from several of the combatant nations, including the feared German Tigers, and some examples of "Hobart's Funnies" (see box). Several of the tanks are still in working order. Visitors can go behind the scenes to see vehicles being restored, and there are regular talks, events and exhibitions.

Studland Beach
Studland Bay, Ⓦ nationaltrust.org.uk/
studland-bay

Studland Beach was the site of a major D-Day rehearsal, Exercise Smash, that took place on 18 April 1944. King George VI, Winston Churchill and General Eisenhower witnessed the action from the safety of a nearby concrete bunker, Fort Henry. Live ammunition was used and the exercise was an opportunity to try out the new floating tank (see box). Tragically, several of the tanks sank, resulting in the drowning of six men. The area is now part of a National Trust walk on which various World War II defences can be seen, including Fort Henry where a memorial plaque commemorates those who died.

Tyneham Village
Ⓦ gov.uk/government/publications/
lulworth-access-times

In December 1943 the last inhabitants of picturesque Tyneham left their homes, relinquishing their village to the army as a part of a wider area used for military exercises. The villagers were promised that they could return when the war was over, but it never happened. Tyneham was compulsorily purchased and, despite years of lobbying by villagers and others, the Ministry of Defence

❯❯ Hobart's Funnies
Percy "Hobo" Hobart was an irascible Major General and an expert in armoured vehicles who managed to irritate so many people at the War Office that in 1940 he was retired early. He might have spent the rest of the war as a corporal in the Chipping Camden Home Guard had not Churchill intervened, bringing him back and putting him in charge of the 11th Armoured Division. Mutterings and resentment were still directed against him, but in 1943 he was given command of the 79th Armoured Division, with clear instructions to devise specialized armoured vehicles to combat the Atlantic Wall defences during the Normandy landings.

Hobart and his team came up with a number of frequently outlandish but effective ways in which tanks could be modified. These were collectively known as "Hobart's Funnies", and included an amphibious Sherman tank complete with propellers and an inflatable canvas float screen; the Churchill "Bobbin" tank that could lay reinforced matting on ground too soft to support armoured vehicles; the "Crab", which was a Sherman with a flail at the front for clearing mines; the flame-throwing "Crocodile"; and the AVRE which instead of a gun had a mortar capable of destroying concrete obstacles. When used correctly, these proved invaluable during Operation Overlord and later campaigns.

refused to relinquish it. All the buildings are now in ruins except for the church, a poignant memorial to a lost way of life. Public access is permitted on most weekends and a few other times; dates and details can be found on the website.

East Anglia

East Anglia, the bulge sticking out of the east side of England, is made up of the counties of Suffolk, Norfolk and parts of Cambridgeshire and Essex. Its proximity to the European mainland – the Netherlands is about 225 kilometres across the North Sea – and the flatness of the landscape made the area ideal for airfields in World War II.

Over one hundred airfields were built in East Anglia for both the RAF and the USAAF. Airmen from the US began arriving in 1942 and by 1943 there were about 100,000 of them stationed in Britain. Many were based in East Anglia, including all of the Eighth Air Force and some of the Ninth. Nearly all of the airfields are commemorated in some way, and memorials to individual airmen or aircrews can often be found near where their planes

crashed, but the largest resting place for US air personnel is the magnificent American Cemetery near Cambridge.

A handful of airfields are still functioning, but most have been returned to farmland or have been built on. Some stray buildings and bits of runway can also be found, and a few of these have been turned into small museums, such as the Norfolk and Suffolk Aviation Museum near former RAF Bungay, and the Parham Airfield Museum on the site of RAF Thorpe Abbotts. On a much larger scale is the Imperial War Museum at Duxford, the former site of RAF Duxford.

East Anglia sites

IWM Duxford
Duxford, Cambridgeshire, Ⓦ iwm.org.uk/visits/iwm-duxford

From April 1943, RAF Duxford was home to the US 78th Fighter Group, which escorted bombers on raids across Europe and later supported ground troops in Normandy. The airfield closed as an RAF base in 1961 and is now part of the Imperial War Museum as well as home to the American Air Museum; it is still an active airfield and there are regular air shows. There is a wide range of objects on display, but the emphasis is on aviation, with an outstanding collection of planes, many exhibited in the airfield's original hangars. Of the permanent displays, The Battle of Britain and the 1940s Operation Room relate specifically to World War II, while the Normandy landings feature in the Land Warfare Exhibition, with Montgomery's wartime caravan among the exhibits. The American Air Museum displays eighteen planes, including a B-17 Flying Fortress, the famed bomber that took part in many missions across Germany.

»
IWM Duxford

Cambridge American Cemetery
Coton, Cambridgeshire, Ⓦ abmc.gov/
cemeteries-memorials

A few kilometres northwest of Cambridge
is the only permanent World War II American cemetery in Britain, containing the
graves of over 3800 servicemen and wom-
en, among them many who served in the
airfields of East Anglia. Burials began here
in 1943, but it only became an officially
dedicated site in 1956. The 12-hectare
grounds, donated by Cambridge University,
are beautifully landscaped and the surrounding woodland adds to the tranquil atmosphere. A dignified memorial hall of
pristine Portland Stone contains a chapel
at one end and a large marble map at the
other showing the main US areas of action
in Europe and the Atlantic. A separate visitor centre provides further historical context through a permanent exhibition containing personal stories, photographs and
interactive displays.

RAF Air Defence Radar Museum
Birds Lane, Horning, Norfolk,
Ⓦ radarmuseum.co.uk

Radar was an important piece of military
technology in World War II, which enabled
those on the ground and in the air to detect
the approach of enemy aircraft. This small
museum occupies the 1942 radar operations
block that was once part of RAF Neatishead.
It tells the story of radar's defensive use from
the 1930s to the Cold War, with many fascinating exhibits, including much of the original equipment. It is well worth attending the
talks by enthusiastic volunteers, many of
whom worked here when the site was operational and highly secret.

«
Gravestones at
Cambridge American
Cemetery

Combined Military Services Museum
Station Rd, Heybridge, Maldon, Essex,
Ⓦ cmsm.co.uk

Tucked away in a former warehouse, this museum displays an eclectic and extremely impressive collection of militaria from medieval times to the present day. There's a good
selection of material relating to World War II,
with an emphasis on spying and secret operations, including the equipment used by wartime secret agents such as booby traps and
sabotage gear. There's also a display about
Operation Frankton, the raid in 1942 by ten
commandos (the "Cockleshell Heroes") who
planted mines on German ships docked at
Bordeaux. The material includes one of the
original Cockle Mk II canoes used in the raid.

Other locations

Memorials and museums about World War II can be found throughout the British Isles, from Penzance in Cornwall to the Shetland Isles.

The following sites relate to events and operations directly connected with preparing for the Liberation of Europe, most of which took place in the southern half of the UK.

» Other locations sites

International Bomber Command Centre

Canwick Hill, Lincoln, Ⓦ internationalbcc.co.uk

The role of Bomber Command and its commander-in-chief Air Chief Marshal Arthur Harris remain among the most controversial issues of World War II (see p.157), and recognition of the bomber crews' bravery and their contribution to the Allied victory was slow in coming. The RAF Bomber Command Memorial in London's Green Park was only erected in 2012. The International Bomber Command Centre (IBCC) was conceived around that time and opened in Lincolnshire in 2018 – in the county where around a third of all Bomber Command stations were based during the war. The IBCC is both a memorial ground and an education centre. A huge spire – the length of a Lancaster bomber's wingspan – towers over the site, flanked by curved steel walls bearing the names of the 57,871 men and women who died in the command's service. In the nearby Chadwick Centre, personal stories of bombers and air-raid victims are told through film, audios and interactive displays.

Yorkshire Air Museum

Halifax Way, Elvington, York, Ⓦ yorkshireairmuseum.org

The museum occupies the site of former RAF Elvington, which from 1942 to 1944 housed 77 Squadron RAF Bomber Command, and thereafter was home to two French squadrons – the only exclusively French airbase in the country. It is now a sizeable aviation museum with an outstanding collection of planes, ranging from the earliest days of flight to recent times. Among

» Cracking the code

Invented by Arthur Scherbius, the Enigma was an encryption machine that converted plain text into apparent gibberish via three rotors, each wired to scramble the letters every time a key was pressed. The recipient then unscrambled the message by using the same setting on his or her Enigma machine.

Adopted by the German armed forces and intelligence services in the 1920s, Enigma was considered to be an unbreakable system. In fact, Polish mathematicians – including the brilliant Marian Rejewski – had broken the ciphers as early as 1932, using electro-mechanical machines known as "bombes" to search for solutions. The Poles shared their discoveries with the British, enabling them to develop their own version of the bombe. In 1941, Alan Turing succeeded in breaking the German naval Enigma.

The Lorenz, a twelve-rotor machine, was even more sophisticated, becoming the machine of choice for top-secret Nazi communications. Without access to an actual machine, Bill Tutte, another Bletchley mathematician, discovered how it worked from signal traffic.

several World War II aircraft are the Halifax bomber, a Douglas Dakota and the troop-carrying glider, the Waco Hadrian, that could be towed behind it. The museum also acts as the Allied Air Forces Memorial.

National Memorial Arboretum
Croxall Road, Alrewas, Staffordshire,
Ⓦ thenma.org.uk

The National Memorial Arboretum is a place of remembrance containing 350 memorials and over 30,000 trees. In 2014 the Normandy Campaign Memorial was erected to mark the 70th anniversary of the D-Day landings, with a design based on the view of the undulating Normandy coastline as seen by the approaching Allied troops in June 1944. Covering some 60 hectares, the arboretum is not a cemetery but a living monument to those who have served Britain, the Empire and Commonwealth, not just in the armed forces but also in such civil organizations as the merchant navy, the police and the ambulance service.

IWM North
Trafford Wharf Rd, Manchester,
Ⓦ iwm.org.uk/visits/iwm-north

The IWM North is located in Trafford Park, a former industrial site where Lancaster bombers were manufactured during the war, making it a prime target for the Luftwaffe during the Manchester Blitz. The arresting building is by Daniel Libeskind (see p.9), an architect who specializes in memorials and war museums. The design divides the building into three sections representing war on land, sea and air, and is deliberately disconcerting: some floors tilt, there is no grand entrance to the museum, and the emphasis is on the impact of war more than on military hardware.

It's a different approach from IWM London, with more space for contemplation.

Western Approaches Museum
1–3 Rumford Street, Liverpool,
Ⓦ liverpoolwarmuseum.co.uk

A bomb-proof bunker was built into the basement of the 1930s Liverpool Exchange Building, and from 1941 this became the headquarters of the Western Approaches Command. It has now been restored and turned into a fascinating museum. The maze of rooms includes the Map Room, the nerve centre of the Battle of the Atlantic (see p.85), where Women's Royal Naval Service (WRNS) and Women's Auxiliary Air Force (WAAF) personnel worked 24 hours a day monitoring convoy routes, and the Cypher Room where decrypted messages were exchanged with Bletchley Park (see below). Other exhibits include the original Gaumont projector on which Churchill – a regular visitor – watched top-secret footage, and a recreated 1940s street.

Bletchley Park
Bletchley, Milton Keynes,
Buckinghamshire, Ⓦ bletchleypark.org.uk

Bletchley Park is another wartime operation commemorated only recently, in this case because of the highly secretive work that was done there at the Government Code and Cypher School (GC&CS). The place where thousands of code-breakers repeatedly cracked encrypted German messages is now a fascinating museum. The original Victorian mansion has temporary and permanent displays, and some of the huts and blocks have been restored. Alan Turing's office is in Hut 8, while the exhibition in Block B contains a large collection of Enigma machines (see p.100).

REMEMBER

the service and sacrifice of all British, Commonwealth, and Allied forces
who gave so much to liberate Europe.

The Royal British Legion is the UK's champion of Remembrance. We are represented
by the red poppy, a symbol of Remembrance and hope for a peaceful future.

Visit our peaceful woodlands and inspirational monuments at the National
Memorial Arboretum in Staffordshire, the UK's year-round home of Remembrance.

Find our free resources and information at www.britishlegion.org.uk,
or follow us on Twitter, Instagram, and Facebook: @PoppyLegion.

We will remember them.

Registered charity number: 219279

Resistance movements

Resistance organizations across Europe made an enormous contribution to the Allied war effort and the ultimate Liberation.

In the popular imagination, the resistance movements of Europe tend to be seen in one of two ways. They are either mythologized as heroic but hopeless struggles of amateurs, or are marginalized, credited with performing only minor ancillary actions that did not have a decisive impact on the final victory.

The resistance in any given country amounted to a war within a war. Its members carried out activities, usually on a local scale, that are often overlooked when set against the great, decisive battles of the liberating armies. No pan-European resistance movements emerged during the war, partly because totalitarianism proved highly successful at preventing its enemies from uniting. Instead, each country developed its own home-grown opposition to the occupier. These varied according to a number of regional factors, but most shared some common features.

Describing the resistance

It is hard to garner an accurate picture of resistance movements because of their intrinsically secretive nature. Directly after the Liberation, few reporters or photographers took an interest in resistance activities – most kept their focus on the front line, broadcasting to a readership less moved by the skirmishes of provincial backwaters than the glamour of battle. Activists themselves deliberately kept few written records for reasons of personal safety. After the war, the members of the resistance who survived were able to set down their own versions of events – sometimes with no one left to challenge them.

The resistance was multifarious and variegated in almost all senses. Most groups took the form of unofficial, ad-hoc, grassroots movements that defied the conventions of military organization. Resistance fighters were volunteers, motivated by a range of political or pragmatic reasons. They received little training, working in a small band in which comradeship might matter more than discipline. There was often nothing in the way of hierarchy, with no generals or government department to rule on its opera-

▲
Two French spies deny charges of acting as informers for the Nazi Gestapo

tions. Notable exceptions exist, of course. The Polish Home Army, for instance, was a large and co-ordinated force run strictly along military lines.

The resistance was frequently a murky, messy affair in which difficult compromises had to be made. Paramilitary activities shaded into organized crime – which supplied the resistance with black-market weapons and forged documents.

For these reasons, it was a challenge for British and American commanders at the time, and has been for historians ever since, to make sense of the resistance in any uniform fashion. Many of the facts related to the resistance are vague or questionable. Even the simplest information – such as how many members an organiza-tion had – could be disputed, frus-trated by what actually constituted being a member of the resistance. Above all, and in the majority of cases, national resistance move-ments were small and non-hierar-chical. The opposite of static mili-tary armies, the resistance was mobile and agile. As the war pro-gressed and new developments unfolded, many of these grass-roots movements changed their aims, targets and strategy.

Organization of the resistance

Resistance typically began with small, isolated and personal acts of defiance and dissent intended

Yugoslav resistance in Italy
▼

to frustrate the Germans. Pas-sive resistance – strikes and rail go-slows – continued through-out the war. Other individuals decided that, although their gov-ernments had collaborated or fled into exile and their regular armies had surrendered, the war must be carried on by other means. These brave men and women were driven by a variety of motives, sometimes solely united by their conviction that something had to be done.

Several resistance groups op-erated within each country, found-ed on different philosophies. At the heart of many resistance groups were radical political activists, no-tably communists – who had to initially defy the party line from Moscow that sought to honour the Nazi-Soviet non-aggression pact. People of numerous religious de-nominations, predominantly Prot-estants and Catholics, also aided the resistance, fostering a moral duty not to give in to evil.

Women were well represent-ed in resistance movements ev-erywhere, especially when men had been taken as prisoners of war or were forced to migrate for work. When the Nazis introduced measures to send young men to German factories as forced la-bourers midway through the war, membership of the resistance soared: many people went into hiding to avoid being sent abroad.

Although resistance move-ments are often categorized in relation to country – the French Resistance, for instance – in practice, they were often multi-national. Jews, political refugees and deserters from the Allied armies were welcomed to boost numbers. In France, many Re-publicans from Spain, defeated in their civil war, joined the Resis-tance, believing Franco could be toppled after the Nazis were overcome. These fighters brought with them valuable com-bat experience.

Resistance activities

The resistance undertook a variety of functions simultaneously. Espionage and gathering intelligence were incredibly important. Members of the resistance collected what information they could, transmitting their findings back to London to help inform military operations.

Nazi occupation depended on functioning infrastructure, which was therefore targeted by the resistance through acts of sabotage. Repairs to bridges and railway lines interfered with the Nazi deployment of both troops and supplies, whilst also tying up valuable manpower.

There are numerous examples of resistance movements engaging the enemy troops, too. Once the Liberation was underway, it was easy for the resistance to emerge from the woodwork, but it was always risky for a unit to draw attention to itself. As well as staging major urban uprisings and carrying out a number of high-profile assassinations, the resistance was also responsible for the deaths of many German officers. These courageous acts were often met with brutal reprisals. For the Allied military, the resistance also operated escape routes – especially for airmen who had been shot down in the occupied territories. One of the most famous of these routes ran from Belgium to Spain across the Pyrenees.

A final, vital and unspectacular role performed by the resistance was maintaining morale. Undercover organizations across Europe operated clandestine printing presses and distributed anti-German propaganda so that a forbidden "free" politics continued even in the face of Nazi repression. While there was an active resistance, there was still hope to the end of occupation. Intellectual resistance may not have saved any lives, but it preserved the values of a country until they could be revived in peacetime. The resistance also reminded the weak-willed that after the war there would be recriminations against those who had collaborated.

Life in the resistance

To become a member of a resistance organization was seldom an easy choice. It meant living a new and dangerous life. Activists had to decide whether to remain in society incognito, or to take refuge in the forests or hills. In France, the latter approach was taken by the so-called *Maquis*; in the flat and densely populated Netherlands, however, it was nearly impossible to survive in the wild.

Successful members of the resistance were excellent listeners and observers, good judges of

▲
Four Italian resistance fighters wait in ambush in the Apennines in May 1944

character and fluid liars – extemporizing according to need. None of these qualities was of any use without a large dose of luck. However many precautions were taken, the risks remained high. The resistance was, on many occasions, betrayed by informers from within their midst. Double agents, driven by greed for Nazi money and power, or by fear for their families, sent many experienced fighters to the torture chambers and prisons of the Gestapo.

The recompense for too many members of the resistance was incarceration and execution. The German authorities saw them as common criminals and terrorists fighting an irritating but futile war. If the Nazis couldn't identify the instigator of an action against them, the punishment was collective and brutal: a number of hostages were rounded up and executed en masse as an example to the rest of the population. One of the largest reprisals was undertaken in the Ardeatine caves in Rome in March 1944 (see p.60).

The effect of Nazi reprisal, however, was never enough to deny the resistance the support they relied on from ordinary people. In this respect, the resistance was undeniably successful: the occupying troops never felt safe. Any normal civilian could be an operative in disguise, concealing a lethal weapon.

In Germany, the Nazis managed to quash almost all resistance by rounding up their opponents and deporting them to the concentration camps. They cowed the rest of the population with diatribes conflating the ideology of the regime with patriotism. In Poland, Czechoslovakia and Belgium, that was impossible. A police state is never a stable, safe and comfortable country – even for the police.

Assessing the impact

World War II historians still argue over the impact of the resistance in one country or another. The resistance undeniably supported the armies of the Liberation – for example cutting phone lines and blowing bridges before D-Day – but was their contribution vital or just helpful?

The impact of the resistance must be understood on a local scale. Its effect was regional, but significant. Occupied Europe was too large for the great armies to be everywhere at once, and often – as in much of France – it was the resistance that carried out the final liberation. In some places, its members waited for the German garrison to decamp before moving in, to ensure a smooth transition from occupation to a new normality. The resistance was also part of the peace process – which sometimes involved summary executions of local fascists and (alleged) collaborators – but also included a restoration of civic power. Most of all, a country's his-

▲
Members of the *Maquis*, the French Resistance

tory of resistance is its own, not an adjunct to the history of a dominant power overseas.

Brave acts of resistance – the Warsaw and Prague uprisings, the partisan republics of northern Italy or the assassination of Reinhard Heydrich in Prague – provided moments of pride and achievement in what is mostly a dark period of human history.

France

The Liberation
France

PARIS SITES

- Army Museum and Historial Charles de Gaulle
- General Leclerc and Liberation of Paris Museum and Jean Moulin Museum
- ⊙ Shoah Memorial
- ⊙ Drancy Shoah Memorial
- Museum of the Order of the Liberation
- Hotel Meurice
- National Resistance Museum
- Arc de Triomphe and Champs Elysées

Roscoff

Brest   Morlaix

St-Brieu

39-45 Remembrance Museum

Quimper
Concarneau

Vanne

Carnac

ATLANTIC OCEAN

Bay of Biscay

N

A Coruña   Gijón   Santander   Bilbao

⟶ Anglo-American forces

--- Maginot line

0   100
kilometres

SPAIN

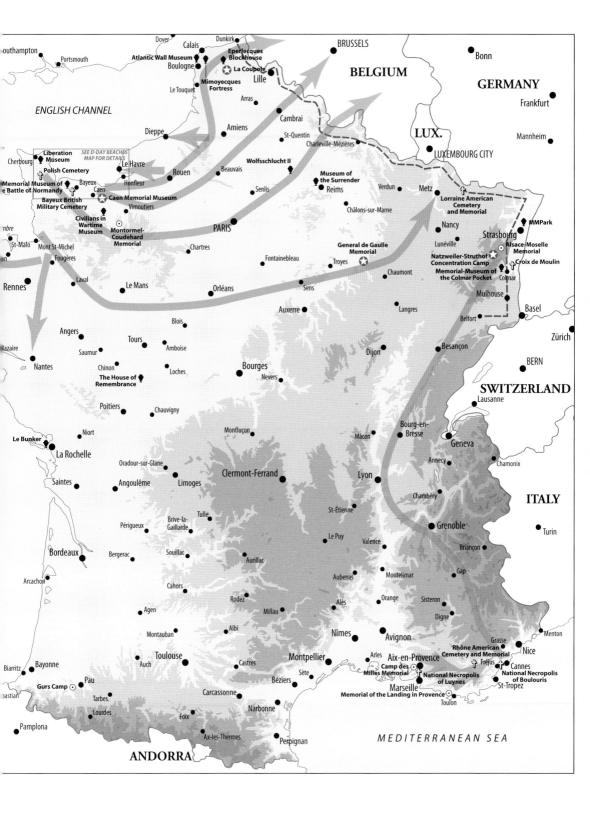

The Liberation France

The defeat of France by Nazi Germany in the spring of 1940 was as inexplicable as it was humiliating. Until then, France had been one of the great world powers, apparently safe behind the defences of the Maginot Line.

In a matter of weeks France was overrun, and the combined forces of the French and British armies that were meant to repel Hitler were forced to retreat to Dunkirk for evacuation. Historians still argue whether Germany's swift victory was due to luck or military superiority, but the result was the same. In May, the French government faced an impossible decision: fight on and risk an even more crushing defeat or sue for peace. The government was split by this choice.

A group of pragmatists and realists – as they thought of themselves – decided to come to terms with Hitler. Both parties to the armistice of 22 June 1940 assumed it would be a temporary arrangement until Britain made its own peace with the Nazis or succumbed to invasion. A sizeable minority in France was always against the armistice, centring on the figure of General Charles de Gaulle. De Gaulle managed to escape to London to rally the French opposition. A government-in-exile was formed, and military personnel who had escaped capture eventually formed the Free French forces that would participate in the liberation of their country.

German occupation

The invasion of Britain never materialized, and the Germans stayed on in France. The French had to get used to a new way of living. Half their country (the north and west) was occupied by enemy troops; the centre, east and south were controlled by the Vichy regime of

» German occupation of Paris, June 1940

Marshal Pétain. Meanwhile, the bulk of the French soldiers, taken prisoner in 1940, were left languishing in German prison camps or put to work in German industry or agriculture.

Occupation meant difficult compromises for almost every French citizen, but it also unleashed the worst of right-wing politics. The authoritarian Vichy regime collaborated closely with the German authorities, aiding the deportation of 76,000 French Jews, of whom only 2500 survived. In November 1942, the Wehrmacht extended the occupation to cover the whole of France. Work began to fortify the west coast against an attempted Allied invasion. A disastrous raid on Dieppe by British and Canadian forces proved how difficult it would be to land an army on the European continent.

German domination also provoked the growth of the French Resistance – a movement of people from divergent political persuasions that became increasingly active as the likelihood of an Allied invasion increased. German reprisals against the partisans were disproportionate and brutal. The invasion of Italy in the summer and autumn of 1943 (see p.49) brought fresh hope to France, especially as it entailed the liberation of Corsica on 4 October 1943, the first French territory to be regained from the occupiers. Unbeknownst to either the Germans or the French – although the Resistance was partially informed – the Allies had set a date of spring 1944 for an invasion of France. This involved meticulous planning and an immense build-up of soldiers and ships. The experience of 1940 was in everyone's mind: there could only be one chance to liberate occupied France, and its success was never a given. It would depend on many factors, predictable and unforeseeable, far beyond the skill of the military commanders.

Significant sites

Significant sites are marked on the map on pages 110 and 111

✪ **D-Day beaches, Normandy. See p.114**

✪ **Caen Memorial Museum, Caen. See p.135**

✪ **La Coupole, Wizernes. See p.142**

✪ **Natzweiler-Struthof Concentration Camp, Natzwiller. See p.152**

✪ **General de Gaulle Memorial, Colombey-les-Deux-Églises. See p.152**

«
Caen Memorial Museum

D-Day beaches

At first light on the morning of 6 June 1944, one of the largest fleets ever assembled appeared in the Baie de la Seine and approached the north coast of Normandy.

Four years after the crushing defeat of France, Belgium and the Netherlands, the Anglo-American Allies finally launched Operation Overlord – the Battle of Normandy. The campaign was kickstarted by Operation Neptune, a massed landing of troops and equipment on the occupied European continent. The invasion would force Nazi Germany to open another front, stretching their resources. In the east, German troops were already locked in battle with the Soviet Union; now they would have to confront an enemy approaching from the west.

Normandy was chosen because of its proximity to the British coast. Allied aircraft would be able to support troops, especially during the landings that would form the ini-

tial phase of the assault. Almost as importantly, Britain would be able to supply the Allied armies as they travelled east. German defences along this stretch of coast were also less formidable than on the beaches of Pas de Calais where the Channel was at its narrowest, and where the Germans expected the attack to come.

A fleet of more than 6900 vessels had been assembled to land more than 156,000 men on five Normandy beaches, which were given codenames (from west to east): Utah and Omaha (US), Gold (British), Juno (Canadian) and Sword (British). About 24,000 airborne troops were also deployed to take control of various strategic points and to prevent German attacks on the flanks of the assault forces on shore. D-Day was mostly an Anglo-American effort: British, American and Canadian troops made up most of the numbers, but no fewer than seventeen Allied countries participated on the ground, in the sea and in the air.

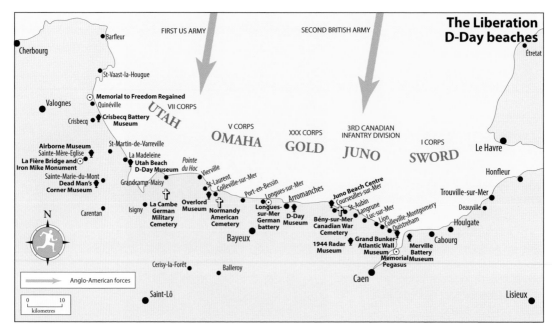

» The Atlantic Wall

Following the abandonment of plans to invade Britain in 1940, the assault on the Soviet Union in June 1941 and the USA's entrance into the war in December 1941, German strategy in the West changed from the offensive to the defensive. Hitler agreed to the construction of a fortified line along the western coastline of the occupied territories, capable of repulsing any Allied attempt to land on the continent. German propagandists would later claim that the Atlantic Wall "stretched from northern Norway to the Spanish border", but it really protected the most vulnerable coastlines of the Netherlands, Belgium and France. For Field Marshal von Rundstedt, commanding the western German ground forces, that still meant building defences along almost 5000km of coast.

Construction work of the Atlantic Wall began in March 1942 around the major European ports and in the French region of Nord-Pas-de-Calais, with the building of submarine bases, batteries, garrison bunkers and radar stations. The work was carried out under the auspices of the Todt Organization, but was of varying quality – the submarine bases being the best fortified – and by the end of 1943 the objective of 15,000 concrete structures was far from complete, with only eight thousand structures erected.

In January 1944, German Field Marshal Rommel, now in charge of defences in the west, was tasked with inspecting the Atlantic Wall along the French coast. He quickly discovered the system's shortcomings, and in the space of just a few months Rommel constructed more than 4000 structures and 500,000 assorted obstacles on the beaches and in the interior zones.

Before D-Day in June, 2000 structures, 200,000 obstacles and two million mines were installed along the beaches and inland Normandy. Twenty-three German batteries were operational. Among these, the batteries of Saint-Marcouf, La Pointe du Hoc, Longues-sur-Mer and Merville presented real problems for the Allies.

There has been talk of declaring the remains of the Atlantic Wall a French national monument, but so far nothing has come of this. Some fortifications have been preserved and are open to the public, notably at the Grand Bunker Atlantic Wall Museum on Sword Beach (see p.129).

Despite unstable weather conditions and fierce resistance from German units, Overlord maintained its element of surprise until the last minute, and the operation was largely successful. On the evening of 6 June 1944, while not all objectives had been achieved, the Allies had gained a foothold on all five beaches: the invaders were established before the German troops could mount a counterattack.

Today, the shore of Calvados department is still called the D-Day coast, and the beaches have retained their codenames. For the most part, the shore consists of innocuous beaches backed by gentle dunes; it is hard to imagine that this small strip of Europe was won at the cost of 10,000 Allied casualties. There are a great number of memorials, monuments, museums and other sites connected to the events of 1944 that can be visited today.

US airborne landings «

An essential preliminary to the D-Day landings was an airborne assault on the defences of

Biography
» Erwin Rommel

Field Marshal Erwin Rommel was a distinguished German commander, charged with improving the fortifications of the "Atlantic Wall" (see p.115) in 1944. In early June, Rommel drove to Germany to celebrate his wife's birth-day; on 6 June, while he was away, the long-awaited Allied invasion was launched. Rommel's absence from the theatre of war until late in the afternoon on D-Day was an unexpected stroke of good luck for the Allies.

By D-Day, Rommel had come to believe that the war was unwinnable and would lead to the destruction of Germany. He became sympathetic towards the 20 July plot (of the same year) to assassinate Hitler, though his exact role in the events remains uncertain. Three days before the plotters struck, Rommel's car was touring the front line when it was strafed by a Spitfire. Rommel sustained a head injury in the attack.

Whatever Rommel's involvement, the 20 July plot failed spectacularly. Convalescing at home in Germany, Rommel was arrested and given the choice of facing trial or committing suicide by cyanide and saving his family honour. He chose the latter, and duly killed himself on 14 October 1944.

Normandy during the night of 5–6 June 1944. The 82nd and 101st US airborne divisions were tasked with establishing a bridgehead on the western flank of the Allied assault area, behind Utah beach. Under the cover of darkness, 13,348 paratroopers jumped from 821 Douglas C-47 planes, while 4400 more soldiers were transported in gliders. Their mission was to support the American infantry troops when they landed at Utah Beach and to help take Cherbourg as fast as possible.

The 82nd Division, led by General Matthew B. Ridgway, was tasked with taking Sainte-Mère-Église, a village on the main road linking Caen to Cherbourg – the thoroughfare was deemed a likely route for a German counterattack. The paratroopers also blew up a number of bridges to prevent German reinforcements coming in from the south. Other strategically located bridges were protected for future Allied military operations.

The 101st Airborne Division, under General Maxwell D. Taylor, was to secure a safe exit for troops from the landing beaches. Units of this division also conducted raids against inland targets, including the German gun battery in Saint-Martin-de-Varreville and a number of bridges leading to Carentan.

As the transport aircraft closed in on the French coast, scouts marked out six drop zones with beacons and lights. This approach was successful in just one of these sectors: most paratroopers landed outside the designated areas, and chaos ensued as the different units tried to link up. Regardless, the two US airborne divisions accomplished most of their missions; most importantly, Sainte-Mère-Église was liberated in the early hours of 6 June. In the afternoon, the Germans staged a counterattack, but the lightly armed airborne troops held out until the next day when they were reinforced by tanks from nearby Utah Beach.

» US airborne landings sites

Airborne Museum
14 rue Eisenhower, Sainte-Mère-Église,
Ⓦ airborne-museum.org

This museum is essentially dedicated to the memory of American paratroopers from the 82nd and 101st airborne divisions who were dropped over the base of the Cotentin peninsula during the night of 5–6 June 1944. Its vast collection of uniforms, weaponry and other military memorabilia includes an example of the famous troop transportation plane, the Douglas C-47 (also known as "Skytrain"), as well as a Waco glider – the only such specimen surviving in France. A legendary American training and reconnaissance plane known as the Piper Cub has pride of place in the hall of the museum's extension.

D-Day Experience (Dead Man's Corner Museum)
2 village de l'Amont, Saint-Côme-du-Mont,
Ⓦ dday-experience.com

The D-Day Experience is located on a strategic crossroads (Dead Man's Corner) that was fiercely contested on 6 and 7 June 1944. The "Dead Man" in question is Walter T. Anderson, a tank commander whose lifeless body was exposed for all to see while fighting continued around him.

The 101st Airborne Division landed behind German lines just after midnight on 6 June, making them the first Allied soldiers to step foot on French soil. These men would fight for 33 consecutive days of the coming

« Displays at the Airborne Museum in Sainte-Mère-Église

battle. One of the division's first missions was taking Carentan, an essential gain so that tanks would be able to move inland from Utah Beach. St-Côme-du-Mont, the last village before Carentan on the N-131 main road, was defended by an entrenched outfit of Luftwaffe paratroopers who had been ordered to hold their position at all cost. When the first American tank reached the St-Côme-du-Mont intersection and turned towards Carentan, it was hit in the turret by a German rocket. The tank was incapacitated, while its commander hung dead from its hatch; he remained like that for several days as the battle raged.

Today's museum contains a large collection of German and American paratrooper memorabilia.

La Fière Bridge and Iron Mike Monument

One of the essential missions of the 82nd Airborne Division was to take the bridges spanning the Merderet river and those of Chef-du-Pont,

»
Utah Beach today

all located west of Sainte-Mère-Église. Between 6 and 9 June 1944, the area around Merderet – swampy land purposely flooded by the Germans – was the setting of several brutal battles.

On 6 June, at daybreak, a company belonging to the US 505th Parachute Infantry Regiment (PIR), along with soldiers from the 507th and 508th regiments, stormed the manor of La Fière and the bridge over the Merderet river. By the end of the afternoon, German forces, though backed up by tanks, had failed to recapture the bridge. Over the following two days German forces counterattacked repeatedly, but in spite of a lack of ammunition, the American soldiers stood their ground. On 9 June, General James Gavin led a bloody assault through the flooded areas to take control of the road and secure it. Supported by tanks from Utah Beach, American paratroopers managed, finally, to take the village of Cauquigny; the victory put an end to the battle of the Merderet river.

A statue was erected in 1961 to pay tribute to the American paratroopers and infantry men who lost their lives here, baptized "Iron Mike". A similar statue can be seen in Fort Bragg in North Carolina, where the 82nd Airborne Division was – and still is – based.

Utah Beach

Utah Beach was the codename for D-Day's westernmost landing beach, on the east coast of the Cotentin peninsula, which stretches from Sainte-Marie-du-Mont to Quinéville. Here, the US 4th Infantry Division came ashore with the task of establishing a bridgehead at the base of the peninsula, an important assignment in the Allied effort to seize the deep-water port of Cherbourg as quickly as possible. Airborne troops, dropped overnight, cleared the enemy positions that threatened the exits from the beach.

The German strongpoint on the beach at La Madeleine, composed of various shelters and bunkers, a grenade launcher and four cannons designed to withstand tanks, was damaged by the air and naval bombardments of D-Day to such an extent that it offered little resistance to the American assault forces. Although many units landed nearly 2km southeast of their designated areas, creating much confusion, the operation was declared a success by nightfall, with relatively few American casualties.

Utah Beach became especially important after D-Day as a place to land equipment and other supplies. From June to November 1944 an endless stream of men and materials arrived in France via Utah Beach. In total, forty percent of all American troops brought to northwest Europe (836,000 men) came ashore here, along with 223,000 vehicles of all sizes and 725,000 tons of supplies.

» Utah Beach sites

Utah Beach D-Day Museum
Plage de la Madeleine, Sainte-Marie-du-Mont, Ⓦ utah-beach.com

The Utah Beach D-Day Museum stands on the site of the former German strongpoint that was eliminated by the US assault force on 6 June 1944. Today, it displays a wide range of German and American military items related to the landings. The 4th US Infantry Division and its 8th Infantry Regiment – the first men to touch down on the beach – are specially emphasized, but attention is also paid to the US Corps of Engineers that cleared the beach of dangerous obstacles and traps set by the German forces. Space is also reserved for the 101st US

« Utah Beach D-Day Museum

Airborne Division, which liberated the area of Sainte-Marie-du-Mont where the museum stands. A real highlight, and the central exhibit of the museum, is a rare Martin B26 G "Marauder", an American twin-engined medium bomber of which no more than six survive today.

Crisbecq Battery Museum
Route des Manoirs, Saint-Marcouf-de-l'Isle, Ⓦ batterie-marcouf.com

During the occupation of France, the German Navy set up a huge battery of 210mm guns in Crisbecq, a small village located in the Saint-Marcouf district. The battery represented a real danger for the ships transporting American troops to the Utah Beach landing areas, and it was bombarded by Allied aircraft in the early days of spring 1944, as well as during the night of 5 June. Suffering little damage, the battery opened fire on the Allied naval forces on the morning of D-Day. In the

»
Omaha Beach

ensuing artillery exchange the fleet succeeded in knocking out three of the German guns, but the gunners aimed their remaining cannon towards Utah Beach itself. Many American soldiers from the 22nd Infantry Regiment (4th Division) died in a vain attempt to take the German position. The four hundred German soldiers commanded by German Naval Lieutenant Walter Ohmsen stubbornly resisted the American ground troops and paratroopers over the coming days, before finally withdrawing on the night of 11 June.

The battery museum comprises a number of fortified buildings, typical of the structures of the Atlantic Wall, as well as anti-aircraft guns, machine guns and a kitchen for the use of German personnel. Although the large guns have been removed, visitors can probe a wealth of military paraphernalia, including weapons and uniforms. The battery also gives a good insight into the living conditions of German soldiers before the Allied landings.

Memorial to Freedom Regained
18 av de la plage, Quinéville

Everyday civilian life under German occupation is the main focus of this museum, which has a reconstructed street complete with shops, an Atlantic Wall bunker, a cinema and scenes populated by 75 life-sized wax figures.

Omaha Beach

D-Day is chiefly remembered for its success, but one beach stands out for its near catastrophic failure. American troops landing on this 6km strip of shore had to contend with German defences that were still virtually intact, and suffered by far the highest losses of D-Day: 4700 killed, wounded or missing. It didn't take long for the survivors to dub this beach "Bloody Omaha".

The two US infantry divisions that landed here from 6.30am onwards (the 1st Division on the eastern half of the beach and the

29th division on the western half) both came ashore under heavy fire; the first two assault waves were decimated within a few minutes. Engineer battalions responsible for clearing the beaches of obstacles also suffered heavy losses. Amidst the chaos, small groups were still able to infiltrate between the German fortifications and gain a foothold inland. On the evening of D-Day, however, the situation was still precarious.

Several factors help explain the heavy losses at Omaha. Preparatory bombardments had failed to clear the German defences, which in turn protected higher numbers of German troops than the Allies had anticipated. On D-Day itself, Allied landing craft unloaded their human cargoes too far out; soldiers had to wade unprotected for several hundred metres through water that came up to their waists, while the amphibious tanks that would have offered the infantry at least some protection in the early stages of the assault struggled to get ashore, some sinking completely in the rough seas. With little support and a taxing battle to reach the beach, the Allied invaders made easy targets for the German guns. Inhabiting fifteen strongpoints called *Widerstandsnester*, the Germans were perfectly placed to fire mercilessly on Omaha. Standing on the hillsides above the beach today, it is easy to understand why the Allied forces faced such devastating odds.

» Omaha Beach sites

Pointe du Hoc
Ⓦ abmc.gov

By late 1942, the Germans had installed an artillery battery at Pointe du Hoc, a prominent cliff overlooking the English Channel. Composed of six 155mm guns positioned in open concrete gun pits (later under casemates), this battery was able to cover the beaches that had been selected for the landing of American troops: Utah Beach to the west and Omaha Beach to the east. Aware of the threat, the Allies bombed the battery many times before the landing. To ensure its complete destruction, they entrusted the task of scaling the cliff, seizing the fortifications and disabling the guns to the 2nd US Ranger battalion, commanded by Lieutenant Colonel James Earl Rudder.

On the morning of D-Day, after a perilous ascent with rope ladders and grappling hooks, the US commandos clashed with German gunners; only when they had overcome the defenders did the rangers realize that the gun bunkers were empty and the guns missing. A short search revealed the guns hidden in a sunken road nearby.

« Pointe du Hoc

Since 1979, the conservation of this site, threatened by coastal erosion, has been assigned to the American Battle Monuments Commission. Considerable work has been undertaken to allow the public to visit. Amid the lunar landscape created by bombs and large-calibre shells, one can distinguish several concrete buildings: shelters for staff, anti-aircraft artillery positions, bunkers and cannon and ammunition pits. Above the fortifications, at the cliff edge, an impressive memorial offers a splendid view of the coast.

La Cambe German Military Cemetery
La Cambe

Of the six German military cemeteries in Normandy, La Cambe, with 21,200 graves, is the largest and best known. The other German cemeteries are found at Champigny/Saint-André-de-l'Eure, Mont-de-Huines, Marigny, Orglandes and Saint-Désir-de-Lisieux. In total, the remains of 80,000 German soldiers are buried in Normandy; some died before the Battle of Normandy, others in captivity after it. La Cambe dates from the summer of 1944, when the US Army established two temporary cemeteries on the battlefield near the village of La Cambe, one reserved for US soldiers, the other for German troops. After the war, the American Battle Monuments Commission decided to move the remains of the US soldiers to the cemetery of Saint-Laurent-sur-Mer.

In the 1950s, the administration of German cemeteries was entrusted to the Volksbund Deutsche Kriegsgräberfürsorge, a private humanitarian organization charged by the Federal Republic of Germany with taking care of the German war dead abroad, under the motto "Versöhnung über den Gräbern" or "reconciliation over the graves". Like other German military cemeteries from World War I and II, La Cambe reflects the status of the defeated. The crosses and headstones are hewn of dark stone, in accordance with a convention that the Treaty of Versailles had already established in 1919 for World War I cemeteries. The bucolic character of the present cemetery urges visitors to remember to live in peace.

Overlord Museum
Lotissement Omaha Center, Colleville-sur-Mer, Ⓦ overlordmuseum.com

Tanks, guns, posters, signs, uniforms, documents, personal items and even a V1 flying

» La Cambe German Military Cemetery

bomb are all part of this extraordinary collection. It was gathered together by the late Michel Leloup, who was 15 at the time of D-Day and became fascinated by the history of the liberation of Normandy.

Normandy American Cemetery
Colleville-sur-Mer

Long lines of white marble Latin crosses and stars of David mark the graves of 9380 US soldiers who died in Normandy, particularly in the savage conflict on nearby Omaha Beach. There are no individual epitaphs, just gold lettering for a few exceptional warriors. A half circle of columns, elaborate statuary and a great reflecting pond combine to make a lasting impression, while a semi-circular wall on the east side of the memorial records the names of 1557 soldiers missing in action, whose bodies were not found, let alone identified. Large maps and commentaries in the loggias explain the Allied operations in Normandy and northwestern Europe; an orientation table shows the strategic movements of troops during the first days of the invasion; and a vantage point offers a sweeping panorama of Omaha Beach. A second American Cemetery in Normandy is situated just outside the town of Saint James.

» Gold Beach
The central beach of the D-Day invasion, between La Rivière and Le Hamel, was nominated Gold Beach and assigned to the British XXX Corps. Because of differences in the tide, troops landed here nearly an hour after the Americans on the beaches to the west. Soldiers disembarking on Gold had a relatively easy time – certainly compared to Omaha – losing 413 (killed or wounded) of the 25,000 men that made it ashore, aided by tanks equipped with flails which were able to clear a path through the minefields. By evening, the XXX Corps had taken Arromanches and penetrated the suburbs of Bayeux. They were able to join up with the Canadians coming from Juno Beach, but not with the Americans from Omaha – that would take three more days. Gold was particularly important to the Allied invasion planners because it was here that they were to install a floating Mulberry Harbour (see p.124), an innovation which would prove vital for supplying the armies moving inland.

Gold Beach sites «

Longues-sur-Mer German battery
39 rue de la Mer, Longues-sur-Mer

The German artillery battery at Longues-sur-Mer was perfectly located to oppose the landings of 6 June 1944. Installed slightly back from the edge of a sixty-metre-high cliff, it sat directly opposite the Allied fleet, and right between Omaha and Gold beaches. The battery consisted of four 150mm guns in concrete bunkers, plus one 120mm gun. Still under construction in May 1944, the battery was operational but the firing command post on the edge of the cliff did not yet have all the equipment necessary for calculating effective fire against naval targets.

On D-Day, the Longues-sur-Mer battery engaged in a protracted duel with the Allied fleet, forcing a number of its vessels to retreat. However, the five guns of the battery were gradually silenced, some destroyed by direct hits. Finally, British troops landing at Gold Beach took the battery on 7 June, capturing the survivors of the battery's 180-strong garrison. Today, the German battery constitutes one of the best-preserved World War II military sites in the country, and is the only one where you can still see some of the original cannons, capable of firing shells weighing 45kg over a staggering 22km. The view from the firing command post, dug into the cliff, offers a vast panorama over the Bay of the Seine.

D-Day Museum
Place du 6 Juin, Arromanches-les-Bains,
Ⓦ musee-arromanches.fr

The first Normandy museum built to commemorate the events of 6 June 1944 (and onwards), the D-Day Museum was funded by the sale of the wrecks that once littered the coastline, and was inaugurated on 5 June 1954. It is located in front of the for-

》 The artificial harbour of Arromanches

While planning the invasion of Normandy (Operation Overlord), Allied command considered it absolutely necessary to have deep-water ports – such as Cherbourg – in order to dispatch reinforcements to the continent. The Canadian assault against Dieppe on 19 August 1942 had shown how thoroughly German command had fortified the ports of the Atlantic coast; they could not be captured without significant loss of life and the harbour facilities would be reduced to ruins in the process.

The ingenious solution of the Allied staff was to manufacture the components for two artificial ports in Britain, to be towed across the Channel and assembled on site. One of them was planned off the American landing zone of Omaha Beach (Vierville-sur-Mer), codenamed Mulberry "A", the second (Mulberry "B") at Arromanches off Gold Beach, a British landing zone.

The 50th British Infantry Division that landed on Gold Beach on 6 June captured Arromanches that same evening. The next day, construction of Mulberry B began. First, a line of floating outer breakwaters (cruciform metal boxes called bombardons) were deployed; next, a pier was constructed by scuttling redundant freighters on the site. The struc-

ture was completed by an alignment of huge concrete caissons, each weighing 1600–6000 tons. The caissons, built in Britain, were towed across the Channel and lain on the seabed. Finally, the surface elements of the harbour were put into position: floating docks and roadways were designed to rise and fall by several metres with the tide.

On 14 June, the first floating road was operational. However, a storm swept through the Channel from 19 to 22 June, damaging the ports. Mulberry A turned out to be completely unusable, though some of its surviving elements were used in repairing Mulberry B, which was less heavily damaged.

In total, the Mulberry harbour at Arromanches functioned for ten months, bringing ashore more than four million tons of supplies. The project was a remarkable technological feat, but with hindsight the endeavour was judged unnecessary and exceedingly costly. The Allies managed to land more men, vehicles and goods by way of a number of small Normandy ports, and even directly onto the beaches. The remains of the floating harbour of Arromanches are still visible today as silent witnesses to this bold gamble and stunning technical achievement.

mer artificial port – or Mulberry harbour – that facilitated the landings of two and a half million men and half a million vehicles. A model inside the museum explains how the port facilities were constructed and used, while a film retraces the stages of design, construction and assembly. Vivid photographs evoke the storm of 19–22 June that nearly destroyed the artificial port. Behind the museum and on the beach, visitors can see the metal remains of the harbour's floating road.

» Juno Beach

The stretch of beach from Graye-sur-Mer to Saint-Aubin-sur-Mer (including the towns of Courseulles and Bernières) was assigned to the 3rd Canadian Infantry Division, led by Major General Rod Keller. Success here was not guaranteed; several issues played out on D-Day morning and the Canadian troops were pitted against determined German opposition. Initial naval bombardment had not been effective, and stormy seas caused delays in landing craft reaching the shore, allowing the Germans, holed up in their bunkers, to organize serious resistance. Many landing craft were hit by gunfire or damaged by underwater obstacles. The Canadian assault units nevertheless succeeded – with tank support – destroying the German positions one by one.

Fighting was particularly heavy at Bernières, and even more so at Courseulles, a small but heavily defended port at the mouth of the Seulles. It was in Saint-Aubin, however, that combat was fiercest. It took a good part of D-Day to neutralize a 50mm gun overlooking the beach, protected by field-fortifications (felled trees) blocking the narrow streets of the village. Saint-Aubin was finally secured during the night of 6 June.

Dogged German resistance led to congestion at the few beach exits. Hampered by the build-up of vehicles, Canadian troops still managed to advance deep inland; they made remarkable progress on D-Day at the cost of 961 casualties (including 319 killed). The following day, their advance was cut short northwest of Caen by the arrival of German armoured reinforcements.

Several VIPs landed on the west beach of Courseulles in the days after D-Day: Winston Churchill on 12 June; General de Gaulle on 14 June, en route to Bayeux; and King George VI, who visited the British troops on 16 June.

Juno Beach sites

Juno Beach Centre
Voie des Français Libres, Courseulles-sur-Mer, Ⓦ junobeach.org

More than a museum dedicated to the landings on D-Day, the Juno Beach Centre remembers the sacrifice of a nation: it recalls Canada's contribution to World War II and the Liberation. The modern museum stands opposite the beach in Courseulles-sur-Mer, on the site of a German strongpoint that protected the harbour entrance and which the 3rd Canadian Division successfully neutralized on 6 June 1944.

Canada entered the war alongside the United Kingdom in September 1939 and made a considerable effort to mobilize its economic and human resources. More than one million Canadians fought for the Allied cause and more than 45,000 lost their lives. At the end of World War II, Canada was transformed, but its national unity remained intact.

The Juno Beach Centre provides a comprehensive overview of Canada's role in the

»
Juno Beach Centre

war through six thematic showrooms. An emotive film, entitled "Dans leurs pas" ("They walk with you"), allows visitors to follow the story of an individual Canadian infantryman.

Bény-sur-Mer Canadian War Cemetery
Reviers

The Canadian War Cemetery called Bény-sur-Mer (but actually located in the town area of Reviers) overlooks Juno Beach. It contains the remains of more than two thousand Canadian soldiers who fell during the first weeks of the Battle of Normandy, notably during the bloody confrontation with the 12th SS Panzer Division Hitlerjugend before the liberation of Caen on 9 July.

A second Canadian cemetery in Normandy is located in Bretteville-sur-Laize, south of Caen. It is the final resting place of 2800 Canadian soldiers killed during the very laborious advancement of the 2nd Canadian Corps towards Falaise between July and August 1944.

1944 Radar Museum
Route de Basly, Douvres-la-Délivrande,
Ⓦ musee-radar.fr

The Radar Museum in Douvres was built on the grounds of a former bunker and – as its name suggests – tells the story of radar during World War II. A new and innovative technology, radar was used by both the Allies and the Axis, particularly by their air forces and navies. Exhibitions also detail life in Douvres during the Nazi occupation, the Liberation and local de-mining operations.

British airborne landings   «
In the early hours of D-Day, the British 6th Airborne Division, under Major General Richard Gale, was dropped behind the German coastal defences of Sword Beach. Its mission, known as Operation Tonga, was to protect the left flank of the landings by gaining control of the area between the Orne and Dives rivers. But that night, with thick clouds impairing the visibility of its pilots, a strong easterly wind scattered the paratroopers over an erroneously large area, causing widespread confusion.

The parachutists were to capture two strategic bridges crossing the Orne River and the Caen Canal; these were taken after just minutes of intensive fighting by five glider crews that had landed close by. The division destroyed several more bridges over the Dives river in a bid to prevent or delay a German counterattack, before attempting to neutralize the German artillery battery of Merville, which would threaten British troops landing on Sword Beach at dawn. The battery was disabled only after fierce combat – which witnessed a casualty rate of fifty percent.

Despite the chaos that surrounded the British airborne landings, all the objectives of Operation Tonga had been achieved when day broke on 6 June, but at a high price.

» British airborne landings sites

Merville Battery Museum
Place du 9ème Batallion, Ⓦ battery-merville.com

Just after midnight on 6 June 1944, a battalion of the 6th British Airborne Division was deployed to destroy the four large guns of the German battery at Merville before they could be used against the landing forces on Sword Beach. Allied intelligence suspected the German battery could greatly hinder the advance of the landing troops as they made their way inland. British Lieutenant Colonel Terence Otway and his 9th Parachute Battalion were tasked with carrying out the daring mission to storm the battery, surrounded by barbed wire, land mines and machine gun nests.

Of the 750 paratroopers who were dispersed in the air, only 150 managed to assemble on the ground. Despite lacking much of their equipment, they went ahead with the assault, and after a half-hour the battery was theirs. Nearly half of the British paratroopers were killed or wounded; of the 130 German soldiers defending the battery, just one quarter survived. Only when the site was taken did it become clear that the intelligence services had overestimated the calibre of the cannon.

A Franco-British partnership founded the Merville Battery Museum in 1983. One of the four emplacements has been fitted with a 100mm field howitzer, identical to the one deployed in 1944. Inside the museum area, visitors can also admire a Dakota plane used in the airborne assaults on 6 June.

Memorial Pegasus
Av du Major Howard, Ranville, Ⓦ memorial-pegasus.org

For the 6th British Airborne Division, the most important mission on 6 June 1944 was to capture the twin bridges that

« Memorial Pegasus tableau

crossed over two parallel stretches of water – the Canal de Caen and the Orne river – intact. This would enable the troops on Sword Beach to proceed rapidly east of the Orne. D-Day preparations were shrouded in secrecy and the element of surprise was key; this mission marked the first Allied action in the British sector.

A company of the 2nd Oxfordshire and Buckinghamshire Light Infantry, commanded by Major Howard and reinforced by sappers, was deployed at 12.20am near the two bridges. One of the six gliders landed a dozen kilometres from the objective, but the other five accurately deployed their assault detachments. At the bridge over the Canal de Caen, the better guarded of the two crossings, Allied troops surprised the small garrison and emerged victorious after a brief but vicious engagement. The bridge over the Orne river, guarded by two German sentries, was taken without a shot being fired. Reinforced by further parachutists during the

night, Howard's men were joined in the early hours of the afternoon by the commandos of the 1st Special Service Brigade, who had landed at dawn on Sword Beach.

Replaced in 1994 to accommodate river traffic, the original bridge (nicknamed Pegasus Bridge) is the focus of the Memorial Pegasus museum. Inside the vaguely glider-shaped building, informative boards explain the attack in detail, accompanied by the expected array of helmets, goggles and medals, as well as photographs and models used to plan the assault. A life-size replica of an Airspeed Horsa glider is also exhibited.

Sword Beach

Sword was the codename for the eastern-most of the five landing beaches, from Langrune to Ouistreham. The objective at Sword was ambitious: troops coming ashore were to protect the left flank of the Allied bridgehead in Normandy – in liaison with the 6th Airborne Division which had landed over-

» Canadian Memorial at Juno Beach

night between the Orne and Dives rivers – and to seize the strategically important city of Caen, 15km inland.

The assault on Sword was led by the 3rd British Infantry Division, reinforced by the commandos of the 1st and 4th Special Service Brigades and supported by specially adapted tanks. The commandos neutralized the German strongpoints by attacking them from two sides. After clearing Ouistreham of hostile units, the 1st Special Service Brigade was able to join up with the paratroopers at Bénouville and take up position on the east bank of the Orne. In contrast, the commandos due to connect with the Canadians from Juno Beach failed to make their rendezvous; they were attacked by the 21st German Panzer Division, which lost fifty tanks in the resultant battle.

Congestion on Sword Beach, and determined resistance by several German strongpoints further inland, prevented the British from capturing Caen on 6 June as they had hoped. More than a month of fighting would ensue before the liberation of Caen, which finally fell to the Allies on 9 July 1944.

» **Sword Beach sites**

Grand Bunker Atlantic Wall Museum
Av du 6 Juin, Ouistreham,
Ⓦ museegrandbunker.com

Housed in a lofty bunker, the Atlantic Wall Museum was headquarters to several German batteries, controlling the entrance to the Orne river and the canal connecting Caen to the sea. It fell to Allied forces on 9 June 1944. The 17-metre-high concrete tower has since been fully restored to its D-Day appearance.

» **Kieffer's commandos**
Only rarely does a military unit assume the name of its commander, but the Commando Kieffer owes its name to Philippe Kieffer, a New York City banker of French nationality. In 1939, at the age of 40, he volunteered as an officer in the Free French Naval Forces, serving at Dunkirk. After the Fall of France in 1940, Kieffer became bored with his administrative duties in London, and was inspired by the British commandos to set up a similar elite French force. Kieffer commanded the only French unit to take part in D-Day, landing on Sword Beach. He was wounded and evacuated to England on 8 June, but returned to take part in the Battle of Normandy, and was one of the first French soldiers to enter liberated Paris. In a tragic twist of fate, at almost the exact same time, Kieffer's eighteen-year-old son, fighting with the resistance, was killed in action near the French capital.

The six floors of the Grand Bunker have been recreated to show what the living quarters would have been like, with newspapers, cutlery and cigarette packets adding a human touch to the explanations of the generators, gas filters and radio room. Other rooms to explore include the dormitory, medical store, sick bay, armoury and arsenal; there's also an observation post equipped with a powerful range-finder. The top floor offers a fabulous 360-degree panorama across Sword Beach and the Bay of the Seine.

Atmospheric photographs, historic documents and weathered items explain the construction of the Atlantic Wall; its artillery and the beach defences are also covered, as are the tactics used by specially trained shock troops who had to find a way through the Wall.

The Battle of Normandy

By nightfall on 6 June 1944, the Allied forces had established a foothold on all five landing beaches. Some troops had even advanced a little way inland, but they had not yet completed the objectives set by their commanders.

At the end of D-Day, the Allied situation was still critical. Forces continued to work on establishing a continuous 80km beachhead along the coast, which was vital for moving further into Normandy. The Allies had underestimated the task, however, and for days the Allied territory in France was unstable and uneven along its coast.

The Allied and Axis forces found themselves locked into a deadly race of strategy and logistics. The battle for possession of Normandy, France and ultimately the European continent was still far from decided. For the Allies, the task was simple: to land sufficient men and weaponry quickly enough to fend off the inevitable German counterattack.

The challenge for the Germans was more complex. In the early days of the invasion, they had more personnel and firepower than the Allies, but this didn't always translate onto the battlefield. Failing to comprehend the gravity of the situation, the German forces were still concentrated in Pas de Calais, where they expected the "real" Allied invasion to come – where the English Channel was at its narrowest. Two further Panzer divisions were in reserve near Paris and could not be moved without express orders from Hitler's headquarters. The delay in releasing these crucial reinforcements gave the Allies valuable time to even the odds.

The Allied advance was propelled by the construction of a huge artificial harbour at Arromanches (see p.124), a provisional arrangement which allowed them to disembark troops and equipment. Capturing the deep-water port of Cherbourg was still important, as was taking the city of Caen, which was of prime strategic value – but which would prove difficult and bloody to liberate.

The Battle of the Hedgerows

Fighting in early July 1944 in the Normandy *bocage* – a fragmented countryside of small fields and orchards divided by leafy hedges and sunken lanes – saw heavy Allied losses. The terrain favoured the German army, being ideal for defensive guerrilla tactics and the operation of snipers. German troops, firmly dug-in, were difficult to see and could pick off Allied soldiers at point-blank range. The high hedges, boggy earth and enclosed fields all caused problems for a modern land army, and rendered the Allied tanks almost useless. The improvisation of front-mounted blades to cut through the hedges eventually paid off, but the Battle of Normandy was an often exhausting process of foot soldiers engaged in close-quarters combat, advancing field by field, orchard by orchard.

Bayeux and Cherbourg

Famous for its extraordinary tapestry showing the conquest of England, the town of Bayeux, 10km from the coast, was the first French city to be liberated on 7 June 1944. Taken so quickly that it escaped serious damage, it briefly became capital of Free France.

The real prize, however, was the deep-water port of Cherbourg, located in the American sector at the end of the Cotentin peninsula. For the Allies, this was a vital gateway to Europe, indispensable for supplying their campaign as it progressed towards Germany. Commandeering the port would enable Allied ships to unload directly in mainland Europe.

After US troops landed on Utah Beach, the Germans blocked the road to Cherbourg. Montebourg was conquered after a bitter offensive, but was almost completely destroyed in the process. On 18 June 1944, American forces reached Barneville, on the west coast of the Cotentin, leaving 40,000 Germans trapped on the peninsula to the north. Some of them surrendered, but the majority retreated around Cherbourg. The Americans rushed towards the city, where they met heavy resistance.

Mass bombings by Allied aircraft and warships weakened the German defences at Cherbourg, and on 26 June the Americans managed to seize Fort du Roule, an imposing citadel clinging to a hillside overlooking the harbour. On the same day, German General von Schlieben, commander of Cherbourg, surrendered to US General Collins. The city was almost intact, but the port facilities had been completely destroyed by the Germans; extensive emergency repairs were started, and the first American ships graced the harbour in late July.

Caen

Caen, capital of Calvados department and the largest city in the proximity of the D-Day beaches, was completely devastated during the fighting of 1944. As an essential road hub, strategically straddling the Orne river and Caen Canal, the city was the main objective for the British 3rd Infantry Division that landed on Sword Beach.

Firmly positioned to the north and west of the city, two Panzer Divisions prevented the Allies from capturing the city in the first two days. General Bernard Montgomery attempted to take Caen by pincer movement, attacking the city from the northeast and southwest. On 13 June the offensive was stalled in Villers-Bocage by German Tiger tanks. A further attack was planned using the British 8th Corps. Operation Epsom brought together 60,000 men who tried to outflank the defenders of Caen by crossing the Odon river, but within a few days the offensive was stopped at the foot of what was dubbed Hill 112.

A few weeks later, Montgomery decided to capture Caen in a frontal attack code-

«
American troops
landing in Normandy

»
British soldiers in
Normandy, 1944

named Charnwood. On 7 July, the city was bombarded by 450 bombers of the Royal Air Force; a total of 2600 tons of bombs were dropped, resulting in the tragic deaths of 300 civilians. On the morning of 8 July, 115,000 men and 500 tanks of the British 1st Corps attacked. British and Canadian troops reached the bridges of the Orne on 9 July. The left bank of the river was liberated, together with the Ilot Sanitaire, an emergency hospital and refuge, which sheltered some 20,000 civilians.

Montgomery launched Operation Goodwood to capture the right bank of the river, and at dawn on 18 July, 6000 tons of bombs were dropped over eastern Caen. Operation

Atlantic, a simultaneous mission entrusted to the Canadians, helped liberate the town entirely on 19 July 1944. Allied planners, who had believed the city could be taken in one day, had been bitterly ambitious. It was a Pyrrhic victory, with a devastating toll: 30,000 British and Canadian soldiers dead; eighty percent of the city destroyed; and three thousand of its inhabitants killed.

The Allied breakout of late July

Control of Cherbourg and Caen meant that the Allies could now contemplate extending their operations to the rest of Normandy. Having established superiority over both land and air, the Allied plan was to outflank the German army to the south before swinging east to advance across northern France. Saint-Lô was captured by the US Army on 19 July after a bitter struggle. The campaign – suspended for the next week because of bad weather – resumed with Operation Cobra on 25 July, which successfully broke through the German lines. Coutances and Granville were liberated and on 31 July, the reactivated US Third Army under General Patton took the vital centre of Avranches, giving the Allies access to Brittany and the rest of western France. An unsuccessful German counterattack failed to cut the Third Army off from its supply lines as they'd hoped, and the Wehrmacht was forced to retreat east, regrouping to plan another defensive against the Allied advance.

Falaise Pocket

In mid-August 1944, Hitler ordered his Seventh Army to mount a stand. It did so in the historic town of Falaise in central Normandy, with disastrous consequences. Falaise was almost entirely destroyed, while the engagement became known as the Falaise

Pocket because the German armies were almost completely encircled by the Allies. Hesitation by the Allied command delayed the final closure of the "pocket" until 19 August, when elements of the 1st Polish Armoured Division met the 90th US Infantry Division coming from the north at Chambois. Surrounded and shelled by Allied artillery, the Germans tried to make their way out of the trap by force, launching desperate attacks on the slopes of Mont-Ormel where they encountered Polish detachments. Both sides suffered heavy losses, but the few hundred Polish soldiers on Mont-Ormel held their positions.

The Battle of Normandy ended with the surrender of part of the German Seventh Army at Tournai-sur-Dive. German losses at Falaise were huge: about 10,000 killed and 40,000–50,000 captured. Despite winning the battle, the Allied victory was mitigated by the great number of German soldiers who escaped the trap – with their vehicles and weapons intact – to continue their retreat eastwards. Even so, the way was now clear to cross the Seine and enter Paris.

» The Battle of Normandy sites

Civilians in Wartime Museum
Place Guillaume le Conquérant, Falaise, Ⓦ memorial-falaise.com

Civilians rather than soldiers are the subjects of this Normandy museum, which looks at the lives of ordinary French people during World War II. On the ground floor, an immersive film of French, British and German archive footage – projected over the ruins of a real bombed house – transports you to the world of an air raid. The museum's other floors deal with the occupation and Liberation.

Montormel-Coudehard Memorial
Les Hayettes, Montormel, Ⓦ memorial-montormel.org

This memorial-museum stands on the high ground of the battlefield of Falaise, giving a fine view over the Vallée de la Dive. It tells the story of the Falaise-Chambois Pocket or "Corridor of Death", beginning with the course of the Battle of Normandy and then covering the climactic events themselves. A meditation room allows for quiet reflection on the universal themes of war, life and death.

Liberation Museum
Fort du Roule, Cherbourg, Ⓦ ville-cherbourg.fr

Cherbourg, as the collection here explains, was exploited by the Germans as an Atlantic port, which made it a prime objective for the Allies following D-Day. Situated 117m above sea level, its Liberation Museum affords a stunning view of the harbour.

Bayeux British Military Cemetery
Bayeux

The largest British World War II cemetery in France holds the remains of 4000 British and 181 Canadian soldiers, as well as a number of Australians, New Zealanders, South Africans, Poles, Russians, French, Czechs, Italians and Germans. Many combatants buried here died in field hospitals to the southwest of town. British tradition prescribes that soldiers are buried with their comrades-in-arms close to where they died, which explains the wide dispersal of British military graves. In the department of Calvados alone, there are nineteen military cemeteries and nearly one hundred monuments. A memorial on the other side of the road bears the names of 1801 Commonwealth soldiers who died during the Battle of Normandy, and those whose remains could not be found or identified. A poignant inscription on the monument recalls William the Conqueror, the duke of Normandy who became king of England in 1066: "Nos a Gulielmo victi victoris patriam liberavimus" ("We, once conquered by William, have now set free the conqueror's native land").

Memorial Museum of the Battle of Normandy
Boulevard Fabian Ware, Bayeux,
Ⓦ bayeuxmuseum.com

Right next to the British military cemetery, this museum relates the bloody ten-week Normandy campaign from the D-Day landings to the withdrawal of the Wehrmacht beyond the River Seine. Covering military strategy as well as what everyday life was like for soldiers and civilians, informative exhibits include mannequins, pictures and weaponry. In addition to the examples of armour outside the museum, a vast hall houses military vehicles and pieces of ordnance, as well as a diorama evoking the decisive struggle in the Falaise Pocket. An archive film recounts the battle in both French and English. The permanent exhibition also deals with aspects of military campaigns that are often ignored: feeding the troops, care for the wounded, logistics, communication and so on. The significant role played by the Allied air forces is remembered, too.

Bayeux was the first French city to be liberated – meriting a visit from Charles de Gaulle himself on 14 June 1944, a highly symbolic event recalled in the museum. His enthusiastic reception led the Allies – and especially US President Roosevelt – to recognize de Gaulle as the only legitimate leader of a free France. A pedestrian path connects to Bayeux's other museums and to its magnificent cathedral, the first home of the Bayeux Tapestry.

»
Flags fluttering outside the Memorial Museum of the Battle of Normandy

Caen Memorial Museum
Esplanade Général Eisenhower,
Ⓦ memorial-caen.com

Just north of Caen, the excellent, high-tech
Caen Memorial Museum stands on a plateau
named after General Eisenhower on a clifftop
beneath which the Germans had their headquarters in June and July 1944. The German
command post – 70m long and 5m wide –
has since been restored.

Originally a "museum for peace", the
brief has been expanded to cover history
since the Great War. It sets out to explain
what happened in Normandy in 1944; to illustrate the scale of World War II, which ultimately led to the death of fifty million people
(half of whom were civilians); and to place
the war in context, from the end of World War
I to its lingering consequences today. One of
a kind in France, the museum asks pertinent
questions about the nature of warfare,
peace, remembrance and human rights.

A large space is dedicated to the varied
individual experiences of men and women
confronted with war: rationing, occupation,
contribution to the war effort, life under aerial attack and direct combat. As the city of
Caen knows intimately, violence against ordinary civilians is a grim reality of war, from
urban bombing campaigns to reprisal massacres and horrific genocides.

Polish Cemetery
Urville-Langannerie

The only Polish cemetery in the region contains 696 graves, mostly those of soldiers
who died during the capture of Caen and in
the battle to close the Falaise Pocket.

Vimoutiers

One of only six surviving Tiger Type E tanks
in the world sits on the roadside outside
Vimoutiers (on the road to Gacé). It was
abandoned or broke down on 19 August
1944 – after which time it was rescued by a
military enthusiast and given to Vimoutiers
town council.

Paris

The iconic French capital was not a strategic target for the Allies, and US General Eisenhower considered it a distraction in his plans. He was thinking of bypassing it altogether as his Allied armies set out in pursuit of the Germans as they retreated eastwards across France.

Eisenhower was sensible to approach Paris with caution. If the city was defended with determination it might be destroyed for all-but symbolic gain, and the already over-stretched Allies would have to feed a huge population of displaced people.

On 19 August 1944, the fate of Paris was decided by an uprising of Parisians and resistance fighters bent on liberating their city for themselves. The German garrison fought back to suppress the rebellion and the precarious situation could easily have de-generated into an uncontrolled guerrilla war of liberation and political feuding – one that risked spreading across the whole of France. Eisenhower couldn't afford anarchy behind his lines or disruption to his carefully orches-trated military campaign.

The French also had a say in the matter. It was imperative they were seen to be taking an active part in liberating their capital. With a sense of historic prescience, de Gaulle dis-embarked at Cherbourg on 20 August, just as the last German troops in Normandy were surrendering to the Allies. Four days later, at dusk on 24 August, an outreach detachment of General Philippe Leclerc's Free French 2nd Armoured Division drove into southern Paris virtually unopposed. The next morning his entire division entered the city.

What followed in the next few hours was to curiously echo the events of the summer of 1940, when the French and Germans de-cided against reducing the City of Lights to rubble. In August 1944, however, Hitler un-equivocally ordered the German military commander of Paris, Lieutenant General Di-etrich von Choltitz, to crush the insurrection and raze the city, as happened in Warsaw (see p.229). If the Allies took Paris, it should be transformed into a prize not worth the ef-fort of taking.

Choltitz chose to disobey his orders, re-fusing to destroy one of the great cities of Eu-ropean civilization. Instead, he yielded Paris intact, and on 25 August, US divisions crossed the Seine and joined Leclerc's troops in clear-ing the last German pockets of resistance. The opposition was sporadic and ineffectual – mainly provided by Germans and collabora-tors who didn't want to fall into Allied hands.

The city's eastern suburbs were bombed, but otherwise Paris survived the war. Choltitz signed an instrument of capitu-lation and ordered his troops to surrender; the following day, de Gaulle led a victory pa-rade down the Champs-Elysées from the Arc de Triomphe. Paris hadn't been scarred by the Liberation, but there was still little light, heat and running water. Gradually normal life resumed, and the city became an adminis-trative centre for the Allies, as well as a plea-sure dome for soldiers on leave.

Paris sites   «

Army Museum and Historial Charles de Gaulle

Hôtel des Invalides, 129 rue de Grenelle, musee-armee.fr

France's Army Museum in the Hôtel des Inva-lides tells the story of the war and Liberation using memorabilia and stirring contempo-rary newsreels. In the basement, the "Histori-al de Gaulle" section plays a high-tech audio-visual tribute to the resistance leader and, later, president. A series of rooms are also devoted to the generals of the Free French forces: Philippe Leclerc de Hauteclocque, Alphonse Juin and Jean de Lattre de Tassigny.

General Leclerc and Liberation of Paris Museum and Jean Moulin Museum
Place Denfert-Rochereau,
Ⓦ museesleclercmoulin.paris.fr

Two essential figures of French history are celebrated at this museum, which recently relocated to new premises. On 25 August 1944 General Leclerc, commander of the 2nd French Armoured Division, drove into Paris, set up his command post in Montparnasse Station and organized the surrender of the city's German garrison. Jean Moulin was the head of the National Council of Resistance. Arrested, tortured and killed in 1943, Moulin died without the knowledge that Paris would later be liberated.

Shoah Memorial
17 rue Geoffroy l'Asnier,
Ⓦ memorialdelashoah.org

Since 1956 this memorial has occupied a sombre crypt containing a large black marble Star of David, with a candle at its centre. In 2005 President Chirac opened a new museum here and unveiled a Wall of Names: four giant slabs of marble engraved with the names of the 76,000 French Jews sent to death camps from 1942 to 1944.

The museum gives an absorbing and moving account of the history of Jews in France, especially Paris, during the German occupation. There are last letters from deportees to their families, videotaped testimony from survivors, numerous ID cards and photos. The museum ends with the Children's Memorial, a collection of photos, almost unbearable to look at, of 2500 French children, each with the date of their birth and the date of deportation.

《
Shoah Memorial

Biography
» **Charles de Gaulle**

Charles de Gaulle served in World War I under Marshal Pétain, where he was wounded, taken prisoner at Verdun and decorated for his bravery. In the interwar years de Gaulle became an advocate for mobile, mechanized warfare and urged his government to rearm with tanks and planes. When the Germans invaded France in 1940 he was charged with an armoured division, but his talent for strategy was recognized and he was promoted to under-secretary of war.

De Gaulle stubbornly refused to accept the armistice that would lead to the creation of the Vichy government, led by his old commander, Pétain, and insisted that France should fight on, whatever the consequences. Keeping his intentions a close-guarded secret, de Gaulle chose exile over surrender, and flew to London –

without any money or resources – to form a government-in-exile. While he was branded a traitor and officially sentenced to death in his absence, on 18 June 1940 he made a stirring radio broadcast, urging the French people not to lose hope. Courageous and single-minded, de Gaulle identified himself with the destiny of France, and obstinately defended his country's interests in the face of Allied politicians and commanders who thought of France as defeated, weak and impotent. De Gaulle had a particularly conflicted relationship with the British; he needed their help to liberate his country but resented having to rely on it.

From London, de Gaulle instigated the formation of the Free French Forces (a rebuilt version of the French army) and the French Resistance (later renamed the French Forces of the Interior). On 20 August 1944 he landed at Cherbourg in time to reach Paris just after its liberation. Here he spoke to the French again, stressing the role of the Free French and all but ignoring the contribution of France's allies. De Gaulle became the acting president of a unified government when the Vichy administration fled to Germany. He insisted on France taking an active part in both the conquest of Germany and the arrangement of the ensuing peace.

Following his instrumental role in World War II, de Gaulle was to become the dominating figure in French postwar politics, eventually becoming French president in 1959. He remained a military man, and although de Gaulle associated himself with the liberation of France, he took a somewhat authoritarian attitude towards democracy.

Drancy Shoah Memorial
110–112 av Jean-Jaurès, Drancy,
ⓦ drancy.memorialdelashoah.org

The Shoah Memorial in Drancy, a suburb of Paris, stands opposite the Cité de la Muette about 10km from the city centre. During World War II, the Cité de la Muette served as an internment camp for the Jews of France before their deportation towards extermination camps. Almost 63,000 people passed through Drancy on their way, principally, to Auschwitz–Birkenau. The memorial here traces the history and function of the camp, as well as the harsh daily lives of the interned.

Museum of the Order of the Liberation
Hôtel des Invalides complex,
Boulevard de La Tour-Maubourg 51,
ⓦ ordredelaliberation.fr

In 1940, Charles de Gaulle created an award for people who participated in the liberation of France. Second only to the better-known Légion d'Honneur, the Order of Liberation was bestowed on fewer than 1500 people for their heroic deeds during World War II. The Hôtel des Invalides complex displays the collections of the Companions of the Order of the Liberation: two thousand objects and documents relate to the Liberation, the deportation of French citizens by the Nazis and the activities of the French Resistance.

Hotel Meurice
228 rue de Rivoli, ⓦ dorchestercollection.com

This no-holds-barred luxury hotel opposite the Tuileries was one of the key locations in the liberation of Paris. In August 1944 it

functioned as the headquarters of Dietrich von Choltitz, the German military governor the city. Hitler is said to have phoned him here to make sure his order to destroy the city was being carried out. "Is Paris burning?" he demanded of Choltitz, who had decided that the preservation of the city was more important than the Führer's command. When the Americans replaced the Germans, this and three hundred other hotels were used to accommodate their officers and offices.

National Resistance Museum
88 av Max Dormoy, Champigny-sur-Marne,
ⓦ cheminsdememoire.gouv.fr

Almost every department of France has its own Resistance archive and centre of interpretation. This museum, in the southeast suburbs of Paris, attempts to present a coherent picture at national level from the inception of the resistance movement to the Liberation. Interesting displays include assorted photographs, documents, paintings and other wartime objects.

Arc de Triomphe and Champs-Elysées

On 14 June 1940, German troops marched from the Arc de Triomphe down the-Elysées – then as now among the most famous streets in the world – to emphasize their unqualified victory after the Fall of France. On 26 August 1944 it was the turn of de Gaulle and the Free French Army, unperturbed by a lone, unidentified sniper firing on the crowd. De Gaulle delivered a rousing speech, praising his countrymen and women for freeing themselves of their Nazi oppressors, but barely acknowledging the contributions of his allies.

Provence

Winston Churchill and the British were bitterly opposed to an American plan to land an army on the French Riviera; they considered Operation Dragoon unnecessary and unlikely to yield worthwhile results.

The British believed an attack on Provence would sap vital resources from Italy (see p.40). Men and equipment would both need diverting, putting an end to Churchill's aspirations to invade Germany from the south. Moreover, if Dragoon succeeded, US troops would dominate the western European theatre of war. Invading Germany via Italy or the Balkans, Churchill argued, would disrupt German oil supplies and help to limit Soviet influence in Eastern Europe. As World War II drew to a conclusion, Churchill saw that military decisions like this would impact British, American and Soviet spheres of influence in postwar Europe.

» Memorial of the Landing in Provence

The US commanders already held the balance of power, however, and Dragoon went ahead. Eisenhower was insistent that the Allies needed another port. Cherbourg had been captured but its harbour facilities needed rebuilding; Antwerp was so far unavailable; Marseilles, therefore, was the obvious place for Liberty ships to unload supplies for the American armies in eastern France and Germany.

The landings in Provence had initially been planned to coincide with Operation Overlord in Normandy (see p.114), in order to stretch the Germans across two French fronts. The demands of launching two major invasions simultaneously were unmeetable, however, and Dragoon was rescheduled for 15 August 1944. The selected beaches – located between Hyères and Cannes – afforded many advantages to the Allies. Their ground troops were supported in the air and by members of the French Resistance, who, emboldened by the Normandy landings, carried out daring sabotage missions directed against General Johannes Blaskowitz and the German Army Group G, charged with the defence of Provence.

The thrust of the invasion was assigned to three divisions of the US VI Corps under Major General Lucian Truscott (part of the US Seventh Army, under Patch) supported by French Army B, led by General Jean de Lattre de Tassigny (usually referred to as de Lattre).

The landings met none of the problems encountered at Salerno or Normandy – only on the right flank was there any serious opposition – and 66,000 men were landed at the cost of less than one hundred fatalities. The French took the task of liberating Toulon and Marseille, which fell to the Allies on 26 and 28 August respectively.

With the whole of southern France now liberated, the Franco–US forces pushed northwards. They proceeded quickly up the Rhone valley in pursuit of the retreating Germans, stopped briefly and bloodily at Montélimar. This was the only pause in an advance that covered 650km of France in under six weeks. On the way, Lyon was liberated on 3 September and Besançon on the 7th. Three days later, patrols from the US Seventh Army coming from Provence met patrols from the US Third Army advancing from Normandy. The progress of Operation Dragoon was only checked by the Vosges mountains of Alsace, where all Allied advancement towards Germany ground to a halt in the autumn of 1944.

» Provence sites

Memorial of the Landing in Provence
Route du Faron, Toulon

The official memorial to the landing in Provence was inaugurated in 1964 by General de Gaulle during his presidency. It pays tribute to the soldiers of the French and American armies who participated in the landings and subsequent Allied attacks. The story of the events of August 1944 as they unfolded is told through a range of audiovisual presentations, archives, models and other exhibits. The role played by troops recruited in France's African colonies is particularly emphasized.

Camp des Milles Memorial
40 Chemin de la Badesse, Aix-en-Provence, Ⓦ campdesmilles.org

Located southwest of Aix, this imposing building in the grounds of Camp des Milles

serves as both a museum and a memorial. It was built in 1939, initially to intern Germans and Austrians living in France. The Germans later used it as a transit camp for Jews. The memorial adopts an educational approach with a view to reinforcing the vigilance and responsibility of citizens to combat racism, anti-Semitism and all forms of fanaticism.

National Necropolis of Boulouris
Saint-Raphaël, Ⓦ cheminsdememoire. gouv.fr/en/saint-raphael-boulouris

This national cemetery contains the graves of 464 combatants – of various nationalities and denominations – belonging to the First French Army who were killed during the landings in Provence.

Rhône American Cemetery and Memorial
553 Boulevard John Kennedy, Draguignan, Ⓦ abmc.gov

This site near Draguignan was chosen to bury the men who were killed on the route of the US Seventh Army's drive up the Rhône Valley. The cemetery contains the graves of 858 American soldiers who fell during the course of Operation Dragoon.

National Necropolis of Luynes

The Luynes necropolis, which lies a few kilometres south of Aix-en-Provence near Les Milles, was completed in 1969. Buried here are 11,424 soldiers who fell during both world wars, including 3077 who died in the wake of the landing on the French Riviera in 1944.

Northeastern France

British General Bernard Montgomery's 21st Army group was responsible for liberating most of northeastern France in the autumn of 1944.

ish ears for its connotations of defeat and military resurrection – held out until the end of the war.

After the Battle of Normandy, US General Eisenhower directed Montgomery's 21st Army Group – consisting of the British Second Army and First Canadian Army – to move north into Belgium, with the objective of taking Antwerp and the River Scheldt (see p.169). On the way, the two armies had to clear northeastern France, including the Channel coast. Dieppe, site of a military debacle for the Allies in 1942 (see p.81), was captured on 1 September 1944 after the German garrison had withdrawn.

A far more important port, Le Havre at the mouth of the Seine, proved a far greater challenge. It was liberated on 12 September after a massive RAF bombing campaign, described as "a storm of iron and fire." The Allies refused to evacuate the town, killing an estimated two thousand people. Le Havre was near-destroyed.

Further north, Montgomery's troops dealt with resistance in the Pas de Calais region, the strip of coast nearest to England. In 1940, Hitler had dreamt of launching an invasion across the English Channel to finish off his last enemy, but "Operation Sea Lion" never took place. Instead, Pas de Calais was heavily fortified, both to deter an inbound invasion and as a base from which to bombard London with Hitler's new long-range weapons, the V1 and V2.

In the early autumn of 1944, British and Canadian troops liberated the Channel ports of Boulogne (22 September) and Calais (1 October). On 15 January 1945, the first civilian train for five years ran from London to Paris via the ferry to Calais. Dunkirk – its name still resonating in Brit-

Northeastern France sites «

Atlantic Wall Museum (Batterie Todt 39/45)
Audinghen, Cap Gris Nez (between Calais and Boulogne), ⓦ batterietodt.com

One of the Third Reich's seven biggest constructions, this fortified gun battery still looks across the Channel at the enemy coast. Originally it had four 380mm guns concealed in casemates, each capable of firing projectiles to a distance of 42km – easily reaching the coast of England. A crew of eighteen men and four officers was needed to operate each gun.

The battery was bombed by the RAF and then stormed by Nova Scotia Highlanders on 29 September 1944. No.2 gun fired a last wild shot at Dover before the assembly was surrendered at 10.30am. Today, the battery is a war museum on three levels. Unique in Europe, a 280mm railway gun is stationed outside, a monstrous 35m in length.

La Coupole
Rue André Clabaux, Wizernes, ⓦ lacoupole-france.com

In 1943, Adolf Hitler decided to destroy London using new weapons. To this end, he ordered five "special constructions" in the Pas de Calais, but all of them were bombed before they could be put into use. The largest of the lot is La Coupole of Helfaut, which has a concrete dome 72m in diameter and 5m thick over what was to be the largest V2 rocket launch pad ever constructed.

Of all the World War II museums in northern France, La Coupole is one of the best, with a labyrinth of 7km of galleries to explore. As you walk around the site of the intended V2 launch pad, individual, multilingual headphones tell you the story of the occupation of northern France, about the use of prisoners as slave labour, and the technology and ethics of the first liquid-fuelled rocket – advanced by Hitler and later developed for the space race by the Soviets, French and Americans. Among the exhibits are an authentic V1 and V2 (restored by a local company). Four excellent films cover all aspects of La Coupole.

Eperlecques Blockhouse
Rue de Sartes, Eperlecques,
Ⓦ leblockhaus.com

Another of the "special constructions" that was built in the Pas de Calais, Eperlecques was planned as a launch site for V2 flying bombs, but never came into operation. Today, visitors are guided around the exhibits – including an authentic V1 launch pad – by a number of talking "sound points".

Mimoyecques Fortress
Between Landrethun-le-Nord and
Leubringhen, Ⓦ mimoyecques.fr

From spring 1943 until the late summer of 1944, the Germans used forced labour to build this secret base for deploying their "supergun", usually referred to as the V3 or the "canon de Londres". Had it been completed, the guns at Mimoyecques would have been collectively capable of firing 1500 shells a day across the English Channel. On 6 July the fortress was hit by lethal Tallboy bombs dropped by the RAF. It was stormed and tak-

«
Tunnel at
Mimoyecques Fortress

en by the Canadians on 5 September, before it was operational.

Wolfsschlucht II
Margival, Ⓦ ravinduloup2.wixsite.com/asw2/w2

After the abortive Dieppe raid (see p.81), Hitler ordered the construction of a western command post from which to co-ordinate the defence of France in the event of an invasion. Much of this complex of 475 bunkers is still intact, but can only be visited on a guided tour lead by enthusiasts of the Association de Sauvegarde du W2. Shortly after D-Day Hitler visited Wolfsschlucht II, the first time he had come to France since 1940. When a malfunctioning V1 flying bomb landed not far from Margival, he cut his visit short and hurried back to Germany.

Western, southwestern and central France

The breakthrough at Avranches in late July 1944 (see p.132) meant the Allies could move freely in France.

The planners of Overlord considered retaking the peninsula of Brittany vital in order to access its deep-water Atlantic ports, and two corps of General Patton's Third Army were assigned to the task. The US 8th Corps moved west across the north of the peninsula towards Brest, while the 20th Corps went south. Both faced enormous supply and communication problems. St-Malo surrendered on 17 August, while the tiny garrison on the island of Cézembre held out until 2 September – only surrendering after being bombed with American napalm. Brest was liberated after a determined struggle on 19 September.

Brittany's ports had been largely destroyed by the Germans, and proved of little use, especially as the Allied advance moved further east. Continuing towards Germany, the ports at Antwerp and Marseilles took on increasing importance. In light of the huge loss of life at Brest, and the ineffectuality of its ports, the Allies decided not to attack the other "Atlantic pockets" (see p.152). Lorient and St-Nazaire were surrounded by the Allies and remained under siege until the end of the war.

The Third Army moved east out of Brittany, liberating Nantes on 12 August without a fight. At Beaugency in the Loire Valley, courageous Resistance activities led German General Botho Henning Elster to surrender two German divisions – numbering more than 18,500 men – to US General Robert Macon.

>> St-Nazaire and the Atlantic pockets

Even before the Allied invasion force had landed in Normandy, Hitler had devised a plan for his troops to take refuge in a series of unassailable fortresses on the Atlantic coast. After the breakout at Avranches at the end of July 1944, these ports took on a new importance. To the Germans, the policy of maintaining the "Atlantic pockets" had both a practical and propagandistic purpose. In theory at least, German submarines had bases from which to operate, but more importantly, unconquered territory in the west provided a morale boost to the citizens of the Fatherland who feared that the war was being lost. They were of equal symbolic value to the French, but proved impossible to conquer by force. The pockets were eventually besieged and bombed by the Allies. St-Nazaire, which held out the longest, only capitulated on 11 May 1945, three days after the surrender of Germany.

Central and southwestern France

The aftershock of the Battle of Normandy and the invasion of Provence was felt throughout France in August 1944. The 220,000 German troops still nominally occupying central and southwest France were now isolated, and the Resistance emerged into the open after months of furtive war. Outlying German units stationed in the countryside retreated to the cities where they grouped together, and preparations were made for an ordered departure. Archives were burned, arms dumps blown up and anything of use to the enemy or incriminating (such as Gestapo headquarters) was destroyed. Columns were formed and the wounded readied for travel.

Liberation in much of France is credited simply to "départ des Allemagnes" – the departure of the Germans. From mid- to late August, the remnants of a once-dominant foreign force set out in haste to join the general retreat in the northeast of France, keen to avoid getting left behind enemy lines. The Resistance did what it could to impede the German evacuation, and feelings of triumph and victory reverberated. The Germans moved out and the Resistance moved in – sometimes on the same day. In this manner, Toulouse was liberated on 19 August, Clermont Ferrand on 27 August and Bordeaux on 28 August. Occasionally there were brief, localized battles, with casualties on both sides, but the result was always a foregone conclusion.

Every major city had its day of liberation, and while most weren't marked by spectacular battles of attrition that beset Normandy and Alsace, they were no less triumphant. Many ordinary citizens had resisted the brutal occupying force with small, uncelebrated acts, while the Resistance network was an ineradicable nuisance to the Germans – for these people, to witness the troops withdraw with little or no fight was no small honour. Battle-hardened Resistance fighters marched through the streets singing the Marseillaise; they formally took control of public buildings and arrested Pétainiste prefects and mayors.

While the military campaigns of the invading Allies and Free French inevitably created the conditions for victory, it was the men and women of the Resistance who took

the cities and ensured continuation of civic authority. In the brief interlude between occupation and the return of routine, between rule according to Vichy decrees and the orders for calm from the provisional government of Charles de Gaulle, prisoners were freed from Nazi jails and a wave of cathartic *épuration sauvage* (rough justice) swept the country. Collaborators were shamed and in some places summarily executed. A few days later the complicated process of reconstructing a civic and political society would begin. Thousands of French prisoners of war who had surrendered in 1940, as well as men sent to Germany as forced labourers, returned to their villages, but most Jews and political prisoners of the Nazis, local individuals who took a conscientious stand aware of the consequences, did not survive.

In the towns and cities of central, western and southwestern France, there are no photographs of fresh-faced young men from Kansas in Sherman tanks being showered with flowers and cakes by the grateful local populace: provincial France quietly liberated itself. Today, there are no strategic bridges and bunkers to commemorate the events, and few "battlefield tourists" visit the local Resistance museums or the *cabanes des maquis* (resistance hideouts) in the woods.

Western, southwestern and central France sites

Le Bunker
8 rue des dames, La Rochelle,
Ⓦ bunkerlarochelle9.wixsite.com/
lebunkerdelarochelle

An authentic German blockhouse stands in the centre of the Atlantic port of La Rochelle. It was built in secret in 1941 as an air-raid

» Oradour-sur-Glane

Some 25km northwest of Limoges, the village of Oradour-sur-Glane stands just as the soldiers of the SS left it on 10 June 1944, after killing 642 of its inhabitants. The ruins have been deliberately preserved as a shrine to the tragic events of that day.

The prelude to Oradour-sur-Glane began two days after D-Day. The 2nd Waffen SS Panzer Division, known as "Das Reich", was ordered to leave its base in Montauban and make its way swiftly to Normandy to reinforce the beleaguered defenders there. Its progress was hampered by the French Resistance, which harassed the division and sabotaged its route. More seriously, resistance fighters attempted to liberate the town of Tulle prematurely, and a detachment of Das Reich troops was sent to reinforce the Tulle garrison and reassert control. By way of reprisal, the SS hanged 99 men from lampposts, some of whom belonged to the Resistance; others were ordinary citizens. Emboldened rather then discouraged, the Resistance kidnapped two SS officers, one of whom was executed.

At about 2pm on 10 June, a contingent of 150 men from the Das Reich division, led by Adolf Diekmann, arrived outside Oradour. They claimed they were checking identities, then that they were searching for secret arms caches belonging to the Resistance. The SS took the men of the village into barns, where they opened fire with machine guns, deliberately aiming low to wound rather than kill, before setting the barn alight – only six men escaped, one of whom was shot dead shortly after. Meanwhile, the women and children were shepherded into the church, where a gas bomb was set off – when this failed, the soldiers let loose with machine guns and grenades, setting the church on fire and killing almost everyone inside. Afterwards the soldiers set fire to the rest of the village. Only a handful of people escaped to tell the story.

Why the SS acted as they did has never been properly explained. It would have been made clear if – like in Tulle – this was an act of reprisal. It is possible that there was a personal motivation on the part of Diekmann for such extreme violence, perhaps to avenge the death of the SS officer killed by the Resistance; alternatively, the town may have been confused with another town called Oradour, not far away.

Diekmann was killed in action in Normandy, three weeks after the Oradour massacre. After the war, a trial failed to establish a motive – or to satisfy the victims' families.

shelter for submarine commanders operating out of the port, and was found intact on the day of the city's liberation, 8 May 1945.

Cézembre

ⓦ saint-malo-tourisme.co.uk

What is now a peaceful island reached by boat from Saint-Malo, Cézembre enjoys the distinction of being the most heavily shelled area of Europe during the Liberation. Covering just 18 hectares, it is estimated to have received 20,000 bombs and projectiles during the summer of 1944, some of them filled with phosphorus and napalm. The German-Italian garrison eventually surrendered to the US 83rd Infantry Division on 2 September 1944.

The House of Remembrance
1 rue de la paix, Maillé,
Ⓦ maisondusouvenir.fr

While Paris was celebrating its liberation on 25 August 1944 (see p.136), the village of Maillé in the Touraine was living through a trauma that still haunts it today. An unidentified detachment of German soldiers – almost certainly of the Waffen-SS – surrounded Maillé and massacred every living being they found there, including the village animals. A total of 124 men, women and children were killed, while a few inhabitants were able to hide or feign death among the corpses. Maillé was then shelled using a rail-mounted gun. The motive for this atrocity has never been established.

The House of Remembrance bears witness to that day. It explores Maillé before and during World War II through testimony, reconstruction and memory. Its archives – documents, images, audio and video recordings – are backed up by good temporary exhibits and events.

39-45 Remembrance Museum
Le Prédic, Plougonvelin,
Ⓦ museememoires39-45.fr

West of Brest near Point St Mathieu (a cape reaching out into the Atlantic), the 39-45 Remembrance Museum occupies the former command post of a naval battery. In August 1944 the guns were pointing out to sea, but their circular turrets were swiveled round to fire on the Americans approaching Brest from the north and east. Displays across five floors explain the Atlantic Wall (of which the battery formed a part) and the Battle of Brest.

Gurs Camp
Gurs, Pyrénées-Atlantiques, Ⓦ campgurs. com

This concentration camp west of Pau was built in 1939 to house Republican refugees from Spain. Before France was invaded in May 1940, the French government also detained Germans here, including a large group of German Jews. Gurs was later used by the Vichy regime to hold its political opponents, as well as Jews awaiting deportation to the death camps. After the liberation it was reopened to house French collaborators and – ironically – Spaniards who had been fighting for the French Resistance lest they cross the border to challenge Franco's regime, with which the new provisional French government was trying to establish friendly relations.

« Gurs Camp

Alsace and Lorraine

As summer 1944 turned into autumn, two Allied armies crossed France on converging trajectories to meet in Alsace.

US General Patton's Third Army (part of the 12th Army Group) moved eastwards from Normandy and Paris, making unexpectedly rapid progress until it reached the Moselle. With supply lines stretched, Patton effectively ran out of fuel and had to call a halt while he established his headquarters at Nancy (liberated on 15 September). The other force came from the south, having landed in Provence as part of Operation Dragoon (see p.140). This was the 6th Army Group, consisting of the Seventh US Army under General Patch and

the First French Army under General de Lattre de Tassigny. It too made quick progress, until being checked by the uplands of the Vosges and the onset of winter.

The two armies met on 10 September 1944 in the northeastern region of Alsace, the only part of France to escape occupation because of its contested identity. Even today, the three departments of Moselle, Bas-Rhin and Haut-Rhin have a culture which is more Germanic than Gallic.

For a long time this territory, sometimes called Alsace-Lorraine, was claimed by Germany. In 1871 it was annexed to the Reich after the Franco-Prussian War, and remained German until the peace at the end of World

» American troops advance in Niederbronn-les-Bains

War I returned it to France. There followed an intense period of francization to counteract the previous four and a half decades of Germanization. In the 1930s, the fortifications of the Maginot Line were built, which emphasized the inclusion of Alsace and Lorraine within France.

In 1940, when Germany invaded France, the Third Reich took what it considered to be its own lands back. Alsace and Moselle were not annexed or occupied; they simply became part of Greater Germany. Their citizens became eligible for military service. Some were willingly to fight for Nazism; most conscripts, however, resented fighting for the other side and became known as the *malgré nous* – meaning "against our will".

In 1944, Alsace was of both military and symbolic importance. Its capture would be a necessary precursor to crossing the Rhine into Germany, but for the French, it meant more than that: they wanted to regain what was theirs, taken in 1940. The battle for Alsace was a bloody struggle, as the Germans considered it an integral part of the Fatherland. To lose it would mean the beginning of the end.

Patton's Third Army had the easier task in the Alsace-Lorraine campaign. Some towns and cities in central northern France were relinquished without a fight by the Germans. Both Reims and Verdun – a mausoleum to some of the most difficult battles of World War I – were taken in August. Elsewhere, the Germans resisted or counterattacked. Tanks clashed at Arracourt between 18 and 29 September in one of the great armoured battles of the war. The city of Nancy was only taken after a bitter clash; once recaptured it became Patton's headquarters. Patton continued his progress towards

» Colmar Pocket

As the American and French armies homed in on Alsace in November 1944, the German 19th Army was surrounded on three sides, with its back against the Rhine. Instead of crossing the river, it stood its ground in a redoubt that came to be known as the "Colmar Pocket": a crude semicircle of land defined by the Rhine in the east and an arc stretching from the south of Strasbourg to the north of Mulhouse in the west. The two sides had much invested in the struggle. According to the Reich, this was officially German soil, while for the Free French Army the pocket represented the theft of a piece of France. Victory at Colmar would be highly symbolic for either army.

The 160km front line proved difficult to break, especially after the 19th Army was reinforced by fresh German troops in December. The Allies were also handicapped by a shortage of supplies, making offensive actions difficult to sustain. Nevertheless, the pocket was gradually reduced in size, and in February 1945 the Germans were forced to evacuate. The Allied victory at Colmar meant that Eisenhower's armies now had control of the west bank of the Rhine from the Swiss border to well north of Strasbourg.

the Rhine by taking Metz on 22 November (although the forts around it held out until 13 December).

Leclerc, meanwhile, with his 2nd Armoured Division of the Free French Army, was directed to enter Strasbourg, which he did on 23 November, although the adjacent bridge across the Rhine remained in German hands. The gains in Alsace – including Strasbourg – were subsequently threatened by the

German Nordwind counteroffensive, launched on 31 December 1944. For a time, a tactical retreat looked likely, but the French were adamant that they would not give up their recaptured territory. By 25 January 1945, the incursion had been repulsed and the Germans driven back across the Rhine. A cornered German army in the so-called Colmar Pocket was slowly and painfully cleared by 9 February, leaving the French and American armies free to bring war to Germany when the order came. For General Eisenhower, the invasion of Germany could only begin when he was sure that the Allies were in control of the battlefields to the north of Alsace in Luxembourg, Belgium and the Netherlands.

» Alsace and Lorraine sites

Museum of the Surrender
12 rue Franklin Roosevelt, Reims, ⓦ
musees-reims.fr/fr/musees/musee-de-la-reddition

Although soon left behind American lines, Reims – situated in nearby Champagne-Ardennes – played an integral role in the conclusion of the war. In the early hours of 7 May 1945, German General Alfred Jodl agreed to the unconditional surrender of the German army here, thus ending World War II in Europe. West of the Porte behind the train and bus station, the Museum of Surrender is based around an old schoolroom that served as Eisenhower's headquarters from February 1945, where the capitulation was signed.

The Soviets were concerned that they had been excluded from the process, however. The Americans had signed their own armistice with the Germans, which was expressly prohibited by US-Soviet agreements. As a consequence, the capitulation had to be formally signed again the next day in Berlin (see p.320). The room in which the armistice was signed has been left exactly as it was (minus the ashtrays and carpet), with the Allies' battle maps on the walls.

Maginot Line

The series of defences built in the 1930s to protect France against invasion – and that failed to do so in 1940 – are a poignant reminder of why the Liberation was necessary. Many Maginot installations in Lorraine and Alsace can be visited. The best of them include three forts – Schoenenbourg (rue commandant Martial Reynier, Hunspach, lignemaginot.com); Four-à-Chaux in Lembach (lignemaginot.fr); and Hackenberg (61 grande rue, Veckring, maginot-hackenberg.com). The Memorial Museum of the Maginot Line of the Rhine in Marckolsheim (route du Rhin, grandried.fr) is also worth a trip.

Memorial-Museum of the Colmar Pocket
25 rue du Conseil, Turckheim, Ⓦ musee.turckheim-alsace.com

An 18th-century arched vault which served as an air-raid shelter during the war has since been turned into a museum explaining the hell of the Colmar Pocket, where fighting continued for several months over the midwinter of 1944–45.

« Imposing Maginot Line defences

Natzweiler-Struthof Concentration Camp

Route départementale 130, Natzwiller,
Ⓦ struthof.fr

A precursor of the horrors to come, Natzweiler-Struthof was the first concentration camp to be discovered by the Allies. It was built in 1940 on the orders of Heinrich Himmler to house forced labourers who worked at a nearby granite quarry. The site, at 800m altitude, was once an outdoor recreation area for the citizens of Alsace.

Natzweiler-Struthof wasn't officially a death camp, but executions were still regularly carried out. In August 1943, 86 Jews were gassed in an outbuilding of a nearby hotel, as a result of a pseudoscientific experiment that would contribute to the Final Solution. In October 1943 a crematorium was built in the camp. The use of one of the camp's concrete structures has never been explained; called the *kartoffelkeller* – potato cellar – by the Germans, it was certainly not designed to store potatoes.

The camp was evacuated between 2 and 5 September 1944, its inmates being transported east to other camps. Soldiers of the US Sixth Army entered Natzweiler-Struthof on 23 November 1944.

Now run as a museum, the camp's primary purpose is to keep the memory of what happened here alive and to educate future generations. Various objects brought from other camps are on display, including a Zyklon B canister from Majdanek.

» Natzweiler-Struthof Concentration Camp

Lorraine American Cemetery and Memorial

Avenue de Fayetteville, Saint-Avold,
Ⓦ abmc.gov

The graves here are of 10,482 American soldiers who were killed in Lorraine and Alsace, mostly while driving the German forces from the fortress city of Metz toward the Siegfried Line and the Rhine river. The memorial, which stands on a plateau to the west of the burial area, includes battlefield maps cast in ceramic.

General de Gaulle Memorial

Colombey-les-Deux-Églises,
Ⓦ en.memorial-charlesdegaulle.fr

In 1934, Charles de Gaulle, ambitious but unheard of, bought property in the town of Colombey-les-Deux-Églises in the department of Haute-Marne, a short hop over into Champagne-Ardennes. When the former French

» The fate of Pétain

When most of France was liberated in August 1944, the divisive government of Marshal Pétain in Vichy lost power to de Gaulle's fledging Free French state almost overnight. For the retreating Germans, the Vichy still had an important, if mostly symbolic value. To see it collapse would be to admit that France had been decisively lost.

On 20 August, Pétain was moved – against his will – to Belfort in the east of France, which remained under German control. The town of Vichy was evacuated on 25 August and peacefully occupied by the Resistance the following day, definitively ending the Nazi wartime puppet government.

With the Americans and Free French approaching Belfort from the south, Pétain was moved again on 8 September to Sigmaringen in southwest Germany. He was a spent figure and as the war approached its conclusion he asked to return to France to face the consequences of his actions. On 23 April 1945 he was taken to Switzerland and handed over by the Swiss authorities to representatives of de Gaulle's government. Pétain was tried after the war for treason and found guilty, but his death sentence was commuted to detention for life on the Ile d'Yeu, off the Vendée coast.

general and president died in 1970, he was buried here in the local churchyard. A modern building was later placed amid this rural landscape to commemorate the man's achievements and legacy. It stands beneath a giant Cross of Lorraine, the double-barred cross that was adopted as a symbol by the Free French in answer to the Nazi swastika. Through multimedia displays and various exhibits, the memorial tells the story of de Gaulle's role in the Resistance and the Liberation, with space dedicated to explaining his military theories.

Alsace-Moselle Memorial
Chauffour, Schirmeck, Ⓦ memorial-alsace-moselle.com

This memorial-museum retraces the history of the region of Alsace and Moselle from 1870 to the present day, with a particular focus on World War II. It is partly dedicated to French-German reconciliation and to European reconstruction after the war.

MMPark
4 rue Gutenberg, La Wantzenau, Ⓦ mmpark.fr

Situated just outside Strasbourg, the MMPark museum displays a huge collection of items related to the armies of World War II. There are literally hundreds of mannequins, armoured vehicles, trucks, motorcycles and personal belongings, as well as an aeroplane and a German speedboat. For more active explorers, there's even a D-Day obstacle course.

Croix du Moulin
Rue d'Ostheim, Jebsheim

During the battle to eliminate the Colmar Pocket, Jebsheim witnessed fighting between 20 and 29 January 1945. It has been called the "Alsatian Verdun", although this is something of an exaggeration. Its modern memorial takes the form of the outline of a cross in the middle of a three-part design, representing the three armies of France, the USA and Germany.

75th ANNIVERSARY
D-DAY AND BATTLE OF NORMANDY

NORMANDY
FOR PEACE

1944 D-DAY
NORMANDY
LAND OF LIBERTY

www.normandy-dday.com

SEE YOU IN NORMANDY FROM MAY TO AUGUST 2019!

Strategic bombing

Bombing developed throughout World War II into a formidable weapon that wreaked devastation upon entire towns, cities and civilian populations.

At the start of World War II, strategic bombing (as opposed to dropping bombs on the battlefield) was still a relatively crude instrument. The Luftwaffe had demonstrated its potential at Guernica in 1937 during the Spanish Civil War.

Even a small strike on a defence-less civilian population could have a massive psychological effect and propaganda reach far beyond the actual physical destruction.

The Luftwaffe applied itself ruthlessly during the Polish campaign of 1939, not differentiating between civilian and military targets. The London Blitz of 1940, following the Fall of France, was intended to be the Luftwaffe's coup de grâce: continuous bombing was expected to demoralize the population and force Britain to sue for peace. It failed to achieve either.

Britain's early bombing campaigns

Before the Liberation was under-way, long-range strategic bombing was the only means for Britain to directly hit its tormentor, Nazi Germany. Daylight raids were advantageous because the German targets were clearly visible, but they exposed Britain's slow-flying bombers to the superior Luftwaffe and anti-aircraft fire from the ground. Nighttime bombing was therefore adopted to reduce the loss of aircraft and crew.

Bombing in darkness, however, was inevitably inaccurate. Only by using the centres of towns and cities as targets could the planes have any chance of dropping their bombs on designated factories and military installations. Both sides quickly came to regard civilians as inhabitants of the legitimate front line, rather than innocents to be avoided at all cost. Even France was repeatedly bombed by the Allies, causing more than 60,000 deaths over the course of World War II.

The arrival of saturation bombing

By the time the Liberation began in 1943, the USA had joined the war on the Allied side. Both the USA and Britain were flying numerous missions to targets all over occupied Europe, mainly from bases in England, but later from airfields nearer the front line as well.

Germany took the brunt of Allied bombing. Despite the fail-

▲ **A man takes statements from bombed-out residents in London's East End during the Blitz**

An RAF pilot in training in the open cockpit
of a biplane
▼

ure of the Blitz, the idea that long-range strategic bombing could win a war – or at least be instrumental in its victory – found ever greater purchase in the top levels of the British RAF and the USAAF. The primary aim of bombing German cities was not to hit military targets or destroy vital industries, although these were desirable side effects. Allied command believed that the German people had allowed the Nazis to take power and, if they suffered enough, would finally bring about regime change.

A "scientific" hypothesis was even created, which suggested that if a certain number of explosives fell on residential areas in Germany, the population would reach a critical state of rebellion. The people would turn on their overlords and demand a negotiated end to the war.

A tipping point never came. Instead, as in the London Blitz, the bombing campaigns merely stiffened the resolve of Germany's inhabitants not to give in to brute force. When they could, German civilians turned their anger on captured Allied serviceman who fell into their hands.

Allied bombing and firestorms

Britain specialized in nighttime raids because its slow-flying bombers were too easily attacked during daylight operations. Heavily armed American bombers, meanwhile, perfected the art of daytime bombing. Combining forces, during the final phase of the war – when the Allies had control of German airspace – the same target could be hit by successive waves of bombers in the space of just a few hours. Horror on the ground increased. Just as a city was recovering from one raid, while fire engines and ambulances were still active, it would fall victim to another.

All this was closely observed by Allied planners, who noticed that incendiary bombs caused much more damage to a city than high-explosive bombs. Dropping a critical number of incendiary bombs together created so many fires that it was impossible to extinguish them. The individual fires blew together to wreak immense destruction – the so-called firestorm that was used to deadly effect in Hamburg (see p.305), Dresden (see p.294) and Kassel.

Casualties

It is well known that being a bomber-crew member meant a short life expectancy. The most dangerous job in all World War II was that of a tail gunner of a heavy bomber, but all men in heavy, slow-flying planes were exposed to the danger of flak from the ground and airborne attack by agile fighter planes. Of the 125,000 aircrew that made up Bomber Command (all volunteers), 51,861 were killed in action, a mortality rate of 44 percent. The average age of death was just 23. Bombers – expensive and time-consuming to build – were lost at an extraordinarily high rate. Of the 7300 Avro Lancaster bombers built, 3200 were lost in action.

Things were far worse on the ground, where civilians died in their thousands. Bombing was an exceptionally unequal and impersonal form of warfare: it was never possible to know which nation had dropped a bomb, let alone the people involved. Loss of life was so prodigious that individual deaths became rolled up in impersonal statistics. Many victims who had nothing to do with the war vanished in the blasts. Bombs fell indiscriminately on civilians, prisoners of war, schoolchildren and concentration camp inmates.

Bombing was feared more than shelling because it didn't come from a particular direction or at a regular rate. It was wholly unpredictable, and the only defence was finding somewhere underground to shelter.

Improving technology

As the war progressed, planes grew bigger and flew further. Heavy bombers had various gun turrets to protect them against fighter planes, but these were of limited use. In case of attack, a crew's best hope was to take evasive action.

Bombs grew larger too. The general-purpose World War II bomb weighed 113kg or 227kg, but in the summer of 1944 the 5443kg "Tallboy" earthquake bomb was introduced for use against forti-

▲
Munition workers at an RAF factory fit components to bombs

fied structures. It March 1945 it was surpassed by the 9979kg "Grand Slam", of which only 41 were dropped by the RAF, on railway viaducts and U-boat pens.

All World War II bombs were sophisticated feats of engineering, with complex structures. Every bomb had to be safe to handle, with thick metal walls protecting the high-explosive or incendiary material until the moment of detonation. Aerodynamic design and tail fins ensured bombs fell straight for maximum accuracy, and most were fitted with contact or impact fuses – causing them to explode when they hit the ground. Far more effective were proximity fuses that detonated above ground level, resulting in greater destruction. Germany also experimented with radio-guided bombs, used to grave effect against Allied shipping during the Italian campaign.

For all the technological advances, however, bombing was not always efficient. A significant number of bombs missed their targets by several kilometres, and an estimated twenty percent of all bombs dropped were duds that failed to detonate. Several have been discovered since the war and subsequently defused or destroyed in controlled explosions.

Bombing: a winning tactic?

The effectiveness of bombing during the Liberation is still debat-ed. Control of airspace was certainly a significant factor in the land war but there is no evidence that strategic bombing had any direct impact on the length of a ground campaign, or that it shortened the war.

Equally, bombing could prove counterproductive. A town, like Caen, was no use to the victor if it was reduced to ruins, while the mountains of debris at Monte Cassino impeded the movement of Allied vehicles and provided perfect cover for the defenders to hide behind.

Only at the very end of the war did strategists of the RAF and US-AAF reluctantly admit that bombing German cities was not producing the results they had expected. A decision was finally made to target synthetic fuel plants and rail marshalling yards instead, in a bid to disrupt supplies reaching the armies in the field.

Ethical issues

In the USA and Britain, there was almost no criticism of the prolonged bombing campaigns that targeted German civilians. Only after the war did people challenge the morality of a policy that sought to annihilate entire towns and cities. Difficult questions asked what the difference was between the premeditated massacre of a village by the SS and the methodically planned deaths of a city full of people by Allied command.

▲
Storage sheds and docks on the lower Seine suffer direct hits

After World War I there had been an attempt to classify all bombing as a war crime, making it illegal under international law. By the end of World War II, bombing a civilian population became an unquestioned military tactic that paved the way for the reluctant public acceptance of Hiroshima and Nagasaki.

Belgium and Luxembourg

The Liberation
Belgium and Luxembourg

N

NORTH SEA

Knokke
Blankenberge
De Haan
Damme
Ostend
Atlantikwall Museum
Bruges
Nieuwpoort
Veurne
Diksmuide
Ghent
Sint Niklaas
Antwerp
**National Memorial
Fort Breendonk**
Kazerne Dossin
Mechelen
Aalst
Dunkirk
Calais
Poperinge
Ieper
Kortrijk
Oudenaarde
BRUSSELS
**Royal Museum of the
Armed Forces and
of Military History**
Mesen
Ronse
Waterloo
Lille
Tournai
Soignies
Mons
Binche
Charleroi
Arras
Couvin
Chimay
Cambrai
Amiens
FRANCE
Laon

0   20
kilometres

Anglo-American forces

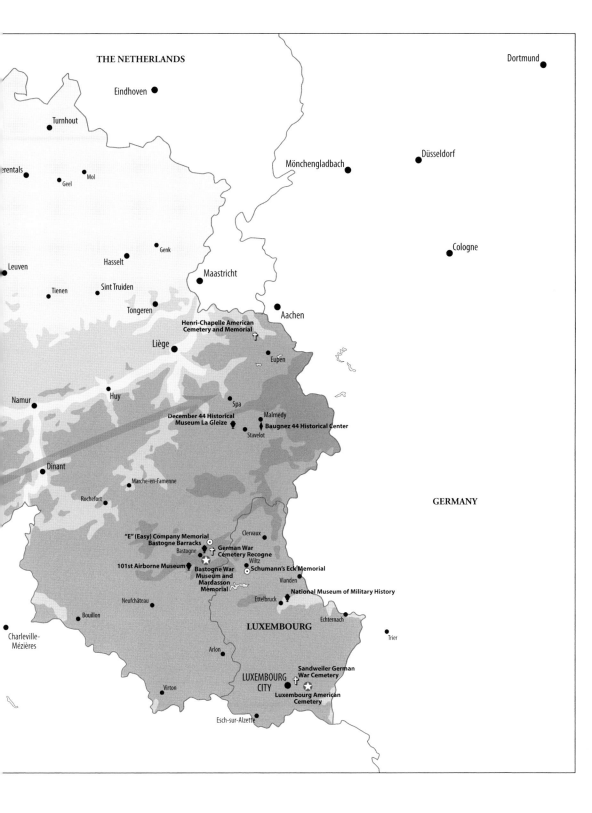

THE NETHERLANDS

Dortmund

Eindhoven

Turnhout

Düsseldorf

erentals

Geel   Mol

Mönchengladbach

Cologne

Genk

Hasselt

Leuven

Sint Truiden

Maastricht

Tienen

Tongeren

Aachen

Henri-Chapelle American
Cemetery and Memorial

Liège

Eupen

Huy

Namur

Spa

Malmedy

December 44 Historical
Museum La Gleize

Baugnez 44 Historical Center

Stavelot

Dinant

Marche-en-Famenne

GERMANY

Rochefort

Clervaux

"E" (Easy) Company Memorial
Bastogne Barracks

German War
Cemetery Recogne

Bastogne

Wiltz

101st Airborne Museum

Schumann's Eck Memorial

Bastogne War
Museum and
Mardasson
Memorial

Vianden

National Museum of Military History

Neufchâteau

Ettelbruck

Echternach

Bouillon

LUXEMBOURG

Charleville-
Mézières

Trier

Arlon

Sandweiler German
War Cemetery

LUXEMBOURG
CITY

Luxembourg American
Cemetery

Virton

Esch-sur-Alzette

The Liberation
Belgium and Luxembourg

After their success in France, the Anglo-American armies swept eastwards across Belgium and Luxembourg in a concerted push towards Germany.

The First US Army crossed the Belgian border on the morning of 2 September 1944, passing through the hamlet of Cendron before liberating the city of Mons the following morning. The British reached Brussels on 3 September and Antwerp the next day; the Americans liberated Liège on 7 and Luxembourg on 10 September. By the middle of the month, both countries were largely free of German troops.

German occupation of Belgium

Belgium had been occupied for four years, ever since May 1940 when the German army invaded and encircled the Allied armies via a daring advance through the Ardennes. The official Belgian response to invasion was divided: Prime Minister Hubert Pierlot and his ministers wanted the king and government to move to France; King Léopold III wished to remain in Belgium. To the disgust of the Allies, the king surrendered to the Germans, prompting his ministers to head for France anyway. When France fell, an attempt at reconciliation by Pierlot was rejected by the king, who now viewed his prime minister as a traitor. Léopold hoped to negotiate with Hitler to achieve some form of autonomy for the country, but failed to do so and his status and influence declined as the occupation continued. Shortly before the liberation in June 1944, he was deported to Germany. Meanwhile, Pierlot and his ministers had formed a government-in-exile in London, but their distant relationship with their homeland

» Belgian women ride on the hood of a jeep after their country's liberation, September 1944

made them less effective allies than the Poles or the Czechs. However, many Belgian soldiers and airmen fought as part of the British forces.

Belgium was governed by a Wehrmacht military administration, presided over by SS-Gruppenführer Eggert Reeder. Most of the day-to-day running of the country was managed by existing Belgian authorities, with key positions in central and local government going to members of the right-wing Flemish nationalist group, the Vlaams Nationaal Verbond (VNV). Wallonia, the Francophone half of the country, also had its own fascist party, the Rexists. Both had paramilitary wings – the Flemish Legion and the Walloon Legion – which sent units to fight alongside the Germans against the Soviets.

Resistance to the Nazi occupiers was sporadic and disorganized, particularly in the early years. Activities increased with greater Nazi oppression and the realization, after the Normandy landings, that the Germans were likely to be defeated. The biggest resistance group was the Armée Secrète (AS), which had ties to the Pierlot government but remained loyal to Léopold III. They were responsible for acts of sabotage and, in connection with the Special Operations Executive (SOE) in London, were part of the organized escape lines for Allied airmen who had bailed out over Belgium. One great motivator for resistance was the German economic exploitation of the country, not just in terms of goods and raw materials, but in the Reich's insatiable demand for labour. By 1943 more than 500,000 Belgians had been forced to work in Germany or France, and many people went into hiding to avoid deportation.

Belgium's Jews numbered between 65,000 and 70,000 in 1940, mostly concen-

Significant sites are marked on the map on pages 162 and 163

✪ **Royal Museum of the Armed Forces and of Military History, Brussels. See p.168**

✪ **National Memorial Fort Breendonk, Willebroek. See p.170**

✪ **Bastogne War Museum and Mardasson Memorial, Bastogne. See p.175**

✪ **Luxembourg American Cemetery, Hamm. See p.177**

trated in Antwerp and Brussels. Many were stateless refugees who had arrived after World War I. Nazi racial laws were applied almost immediately, but with less efficiency or enthusiasm than in other occupied countries. Many Belgians objected to how Jews were treated, including the country's leading Catholic, Cardinal van Roey, but Belgium's administrators were willing collaborators, and there were plenty of anti-Semites happy to join in the Nazi persecution. In April 1941, the VNV and others set fire to two Antwerp synagogues, which the fire brigade was prevented from putting out. Many Jews simply failed to register and others went into hiding, but in July 1942 deportations began in earnest when the Dossin Barracks near Mechelen was converted into a transit camp for Jews. Nearly 26,000 left here on trains to Auschwitz-Birkenau and other camps; fewer than two thousand deportees survived the Holocaust.

Even as they were driven out of Belgium in September 1944, German troops continued committing barbaric acts, often random and disproportionate retaliation for small gestures of resistance. It was a fore-

»

An American soldier
plays during a
memorial service at
Luxembourg American
Cemetery

taste of what was to come during the massive counteroffensive, known as the Battle of the Bulge, that was launched by the Nazis later in the year.

German occupation of Luxembourg

Luxembourg has an area of 2586 sq km, slightly smaller than the US state of Rhode Island and slightly larger than the English county of Dorset. The eastern side of the country borders Germany, with its boundary along the Our and Moselle rivers.

In 1940 Luxembourg had a population of 296,000 but no standing army, making it easy pickings for the Wehrmacht. The invasion took place on 10 May 1940, prompting the reigning monarch, Grand Duchess Charlotte, to leave the country with her ministers. The departure of the government left the state functions of Luxembourg in disarray. For her first two years Charlotte was in Canada and after 1943 in London, from where she broadcast regular morale-boosting messages to her countrymen.

By August the country was under direct German administration, with the Gauleiter of Mosseland, Gustav Simon, put in charge. His role was to assimilate the country into the Reich, a project strongly resisted by a generally hostile population. In October 1941, Simon organized a referendum which posed questions about national identity. Encouraged by the resistance, over ninety percent of citizens declared themselves Luxembourgish, prompting the Nazi regime to become markedly more harsh. All languages apart from German were now banned and citizens were forcibly conscripted into the German armed forces. The following summer a general strike against compulsory national service was only halted after its ringleaders were executed and hundreds of protesters sent to concentration camps. Of those Luxembourgers conscripted, possibly as many as 25,000 died – most shot as deserters.

Northern Luxembourg was devastated during the Battle of the Bulge, as Manteuffel's 5th Panzer Army bombarded US positions in its December push into Belgium, and then again when the Americans forced the Germans back in January and February 1945. Around 3500 homes were damaged or destroyed, some 45,000 people became refugees, and about one-third of the country's farmland was unable to be cultivated.

Brussels and beyond

On 2 September 1944, the British Guards Armoured Division (commanded by Lieutenant Colonel Allan Adair) was stationed in northern France when, late in the evening, XXX Corps commander Lieutenant General Brian Horrocks gave the order to march on Brussels.

Allan Adair and his men set off early on 3 September and by evening had entered Brussels by the Avenue de Tervuren, having covered more than 120km in one day. They were greeted by crowds of jubilant Belgians lining the Boulevard de Waterloo.

That same morning, most of the German troops had taken to their heels. In Brussels – as in other cities – their withdrawal was accompanied by much destruction. Before leaving, German soldiers set fire to the Palace of Justice in order to burn the documents still stored there. Despite efforts to extinguish the fire, the copper dome of the building collapsed, although not before thousands of bottles of wine had been removed from the cellars and distributed among the wildly celebrating crowds. Sporadic fighting was still occurring in some parts of the city, including violent clashes between resistance fighters and German soldiers in the Parc du Cinquantenaire.

The next day saw the arrival of the 1st Infantry Brigade of the Free Belgian Forces, better known as the Piron Brigade after its commander Colonel Jean-Baptiste Piron, who had transformed it into a first-rate combat unit after being put in charge in 1942. As part of the British 6th Airborne Division, the brigade was active in Normandy from 8 August 1944, liberating towns and villages eastward along the coast. Brussels' citizens were pleasantly surprised to discover compatriots among the liberating forces, though some mistook them for French Canadians.

On 8 September, Hubert Pierlot, prime minister of the Belgian government-in-exile in London, returned to Brussels to lead a government of national unity. He was met with almost total indifference by the population. One of the first actions of the new government was to appoint Prince Karel, Count of Flanders, as regent in the absence of his brother, King Léopold III. But faced with the problems of food shortages, controversy over his acrimonious relations

›› Hitler's funeral in the Marolles

The inhabitants of the Marolles district in central Brussels celebrated their city's liberation with a mock funeral for the Führer. On Sunday 10 September they carried a Hitler lookalike in a coffin through the streets on the back of a horse-drawn cart. Printed cards announcing the "sad news" referred to Hitler as the "Grand Chevalier de L'Espace Vital" ("Grand Knight of Living Space"), a reference to his demands for European living space for German settlers. The mourners listed included "Monsieur General Goering, his confidant", while the funeral music was to be conducted by the "well-loved Benito Mussolini". A rag-bag of uniformed followers accompanied the cortege, while the crowd threw an assortment of offerings – flowers, tomatoes, eggs – and occasionally spat at the prone figure. The departure point on the Rue de la Prévoyance from where the procession set off is now marked with a commemorative plaque.

» Radios at the Atlantikwall Museum

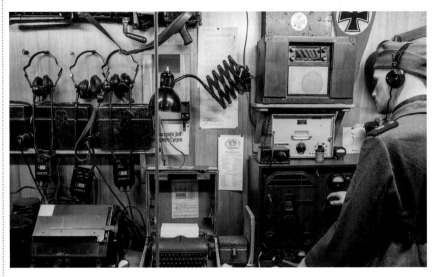

with the exiled king, and his failure to pursue collaborators sufficiently vigorously, Pierlot and his government grew increasingly unpopular. Forced to rely on the British military commander, Major General Erskine, to maintain order in the face of communist-led riots and resistance fighters' refusal to give up their arms, Pierlot's government eventually fell in February 1945.

» Brussels and beyond sites

Royal Museum of the Armed Forces and of Military History
Jubelpark 3, Brussels, Ⓦ klm-mra.be

Located in Brussels' Parc du Cinquantenaire, or Jubelpark, this museum traces the history of the Belgian army from the late 18th century to the present day by means of a vast hoard of weapons, armaments and uniforms. The magnificent Bordiau Gallery (named after the architect of the park and its buildings) is dedicated to the major conflicts of the 20th century. New displays for the World War

II material are currently being constructed, and will cover four main topics: the German occupation of Belgium (1940–44), the Liberation (1944–45), the ideology and race policy of the Nazis (1933–45) and the war in the Pacific (1937–45).

Atlantikwall Museum
Nieuwpoortsesteenweg 636, Ostend,
Ⓦ raversyde.be/en/atlantikwall-0

The Atlantic Wall was a line of German fortifications and gun batteries built to protect the northern European coastline from Allied invasion (see p.115). Much of it still exists, including a well-preserved section along the Belgian coastline, 8km from Ostend. Here among the dunes can be found sixty bunkers (some from World War I), connected by lines of trenches and tunnels. The area was part of an estate owned by the Regent, Prince Karel, who was active in the preservation of the defences. The site is not suitable for those with disabilities or wheelchair users.

Antwerp and around

The taking of such a large and well-equipped port as Antwerp was a hugely significant capture for the Allies, as those ports already liberated in northern Europe were either too small or too badly damaged to solve the Allies' supply needs.

The British 11th Armoured Division, part of the Second Army, rolled into Antwerp at midday on Monday 4 September. By the evening, German forces in the centre of town were routed, the docks saved from destruction by the Belgian resistance, and six thousand POWs locked up in the cages of Antwerp Zoo. Fighting continued, however, and attempts by the division to create a bridgehead across the Albert Canal, a recently completed waterway linking the rivers Scheldt and Meuse (or Maas), were fiercely resisted and resulted in failure.

Having supply lines this far east would now make it that much easier for the Allies to strike into Germany. But for this to happen

effectively, the vast estuary at the mouth of the River Scheldt (part of the Netherlands) would need to be under Allied control. Unfortunately, Montgomery delayed clearing the estuary, instead giving priority to Operation Market Garden (see box). This gave the Germans time to reinforce the estuary island of Walcheren and the Beveland Isthmus on the Scheldt's north shore, thus preventing Allied shipping from reaching Antwerp. Many historians regard Montgomery's oversight as one of the Allies' gravest strategic errors of the entire war.

When Montgomery finally realized just how important clearing the Scheldt was (having had the point emphasized by Eisenhower), he decided to assign the formidable task to the First Canadian Army under the temporary command of Lieutenant General

» Operation Market Garden – Montgomery's daring plan

Having liberated Belgium, Allied commanders were now at odds about the best way to progress. Patton favoured an advance into Germany from the south; Montgomery wanted a concentrated attack through the Netherlands in the north. As their boss, Eisenhower was adamant that a broad front should be preserved (rather than concentrating the bulk of his troops at a single point), but he was intrigued by Montgomery's plan and in the end gave it the green light.

Montgomery's idea was for a two-part operation (codenamed Market Garden) that would entail three airborne divisions landing in the Netherlands and capturing bridges and territory at Eindhoven, Nijmegen and Arnhem, thus creating a cor-

ridor for the British XXX Corps to advance along. The furthest bridge at Arnhem was over the Lower Rhine which, once secured, would open a gateway into the Ruhr – Germany's industrial heartland – that would bypass the massive German Westwall defences.

The starting point for the ground troops in Belgium was at Bridge Number 9 across the Bocholt-Herentals Canal at Neerpelt, which was captured by a unit of the Irish Guards in a surprise attack on 10 September 1944. Thereafter it was named Joe's Bridge in honour of the unit's commander, J.O.E. Vandeleur. The XXX Corps, commanded by Lieutenant General Horrocks, set off from Joe's Bridge on the afternoon of 17 September (see p.197).

Guy Simonds. The ensuing Battle of the Scheldt (see p.190) was won on 8 November, but it was another three weeks before the estuary was finally made safe after a major mine-sweeping operation. The first Allied shipping arrived in Antwerp on 28 November 1944 and by mid-December 23,000 tons of goods per day were being unloaded.

The bombing of Antwerp

While the Germans were able to thwart the use of Antwerp as a working port for almost two months after its liberation, they also instigated a ruthless bombing campaign. Even before the port was up and running, V2 rockets and V1 flying bombs were pointed at the city. A V2 hit the busy central square of Teniersplaats on 27 November 1944 killing 159 people; another landed on the Rex Cinema in the Avenue de Keyser on 15 December. A total of 567 people were killed, over half of them Allied servicemen, and many more were injured. Although the Allied anti-aircraft teams grew adept at hitting the V1s, the silent V2 – which had a maximum speed of 5760km per hour – could not be defended against and caused massive amounts of damage. As much as two-thirds of Antwerp's houses were destroyed in raids that lasted from October 1944 until March 1945.

» Antwerp and around sites

National Memorial Fort Breendonk
Brandstraat 57, Willebroek, ⓦ breendonk.be

Built in the early 20th century as one of a line of forts for the defence of Antwerp, Fort Breendonk is located 20km south of Antwerp. From September 1940 until Belgium's liberation it functioned as a Nazi concentration camp, and about 3500 prisoners were interned here, staying an average of three months before being deported to camps in Germany, Austria or Poland. Jews made up half the number in the first year of the occupation, before Dossin Barracks (see below) was established as a Jewish transit camp in 1942. An austere and forbidding place, surrounded by a huge moat, the fort is one of the best-preserved Nazi camps and is now a memorial and education centre dedicated to all those who suffered here. An audio guide is available for non-French or Flemish speakers, which focuses on the harrowing personal testimonies of individual prisoners. The site is not suitable for young children.

Kazerne Dossin
Goswin de Stassartstraat 153, Mechelen, ⓦ kazernedossin.eu

Ten kilometres southeast from Fort Breendonk is Kazerne Dossin (Dossin Barracks), a former Austrian military base used as a Jewish transit camp. From here, 25,484 Jews and 352 Roma and Sinti were deported to Auschwitz-Birkenau and other camps. Less than five percent of them survived.

Previously housed in part of the barracks, in 2011 a new building was opened nearby as a "Memorial, Museum and Documentation Center on Holocaust and Human Rights". As the name suggests, the focus is not just on the Nazi victimization of Belgium's minorities – the centre places those experiences within the wider and continuing story of persecution and human rights abuses across the world. It's a less raw experience than Fort Breendonk, as the new building relies on interpretation and symbolism to connect you to the horrors of past and present, but the displays are thoughtfully and clearly presented.

The Ardennes

The Ardennes is a rugged, forested wilderness that stretches across southern Belgium and into northern Luxembourg, but also includes parts of Germany and France. It played a crucial role during World War II on two separate occasions.

In 1940 the German army launched a surprise attack through the Ardennes which led to their occupation of western Europe. In the winter of 1944–45, the Germans tried to repeat their earlier success with a similar attack. By this point of the war, however, the balance of power had shifted in favour of the Allies, and the German offensive – known as the Ardennes Offensive (and by the Allies as the Battle of the Bulge) – proved not just unsuccessful but a disastrous setback from which the Wehrmacht never recovered.

The Ardennes Offensive

Codenamed "Wacht am Rhein" (Watch on the Rhine), the Ardennes Offensive was almost entirely the brainchild of Hitler himself. A highly ambitious operation, its aim was to sweep through the Ardennes, seize the bridges over the Meuse River and recapture the key supply port of Antwerp. This would halt the Allied advance into Germany and allow the Nazis to encircle and destroy four Allied armies. Hitler hoped it might even succeed in driving the Allies back to the English Channel and force them to negotiate a peace treaty in the Axis' favour.

Hitler's senior generals were highly dubious about the scale of the plan. General Guderian, for one, felt that stalling the Soviet advance on the Eastern Front was of far greater importance and that a big push in the Ardennes would squander vital men and resources. Model and von Rundstedt, meanwhile, believed that aiming for Antwerp was simply too ambitious.

The Allied lines stretched from Antwerp in the north to southern France, but the Ardennes was undermanned, largely because both Bradley and Montgomery had told Eisenhower that a German attack was highly unlikely, especially in such difficult terrain. When the offensive was launched on 16 December 1944, it therefore had the advantage of surprise. The mist and fog that had descended also benefited the German troops, rendering the vastly superior Allied air power initially ineffective.

The main German force comprised three armies: General Dietrich's Sixth Panzer Army in the north; General von Manteuffel's Fifth Panzer Army in the centre; and a back-up force of General Brandenberger's Seventh Army in the south, tasked with protecting the flank. They would find themselves up against mostly American troops: the US First Army and US Ninth Army (both part of Bradley's 12th Army Group). To maximize American confusion, the Germans formed a brigade of English-speaking soldiers dressed in US uniforms that was sent ahead to infiltrate the US lines – a move which contravened the rules of war and succeeded in generating rumour and paranoia among the Allied troops.

Leading the German attack was the Sixth Panzer Army, commanded by SS-Oberstgruppenführer Sepp Dietrich. It was spearheaded by the 1st SS Panzer Regiment, a combat group (Kampfgruppe) led by Obersturmbannführer (lieutenant colonel) Joachim Peiper, a young SS officer known for his ruthlessness. His task was to reach the River Meuse and secure the bridges at Huy. Under his command were nearly six thousand troops and seventy tanks, including the powerful and heavily armoured Tiger II. Roads that were little more than tracks meant that progress was slower than Peiper expected, and US troops – though unprepared for the assault and struggling to find adequate defensive positions – managed to slow his progress. Many US troops were killed or captured in the fighting, including 86 massacred near Malmédy after surrendering (see p.173).

The Battle of Elsenborn Ridge

Hitler had envisaged a swift Blitzkrieg-style offensive (as in the previous Ardennes assault), but this time the weather, the terrain and shortage of fuel were working against him. More importantly, once the Americans realized what was happening, they put up formidable resistance. On the northern shoulder of the German advance, the Sixth Panzer Army was effectively halted by the 99th and 2nd Infantry Divisions of V Corps (part of the US First Army). The bitter and often confused fighting lasted around ten days. Initially centred on the twin villages of Krinkelt and Rocherath, the Americans withdrew to nearby Elsenborn Ridge on 19 December. From here, a war of attrition ensued with heavy casualties on both sides, but the Americans were well enough dug in to repel almost everything that the Sixth Panzer Army could throw at them.

The Battle of St Vith

The Germans had greater success in the centre, where US troops were outnumbered and gradually overwhelmed by the Fifth Panzer Army. Manteuffel's immediate aim was to capture the towns of St Vith and Bastogne, both important road and rail junctions which would facilitate German progress towards Antwerp. Blocking his route was the recently arrived US 106th Division which was defending a wide front in the rugged and hilly Schnee Eifel on the Belgium-German border. The American soldiers were inexperienced and poorly trained, however, hindered by strategic errors in the command chain as well as bad weather, which thwarted Allied air support. Due to a miscommunication, Major General Jones, the divisions' commander, held fast rather than pulling his troops back, with the result that two regiments were encircled and about seven thousand men were forced to surrender on 19 December.

Two days later, American troops withdrew from St Vith and the town fell to the Germans. For Hitler, this seemed like an enormous success, but he had repeatedly ignored Manteuffel's advice to return to the Siegfried Line in order to continue the attack. American resistance had put the Ardennes Offensive well behind schedule, allowing the Allies to regroup and plan a counterattack.

Eisenhower was already sending reinforcements along the Ardennes front, with a total of around 240,000 men deployed during the last ten days of December. Because the German advance had split the troops of Bradley's 12th Army Group to the north and south of the "bulge", Eisenhower temporarily assigned the American First and Ninth Army from the 12th to Montgomery's 21st Army Group in the north (much to Bradley's annoyance). Montgomery immediately sent four British divisions towards the Meuse to protect the river crossings at Givet, Dinant and Namur.

The Siege of Bastogne

On 19 December 1944, Brigadier General McAuliffe and the 101st Airborne Division arrived in Bastogne, a few hours ahead of three divisions of the Fifth Panzer Army – 18,000

» Malmédy massacre

On 17 December 1944, 140 US soldiers left Malmédy heading south when they ran in to the Peiper Kampfgruppe at the crossroads of Baugnez. After an exchange of fire, the Americans surrendered and around 113 of them, with arms raised, were herded into a snow-covered field. Peiper was apparently not present when, at 2.15pm, the Germans opened fire on the prisoners and then wandered the field shooting them individually at close range. Amazingly, around sixty survived, having played dead until they could make their escape.

The reasons for the shooting remain unclear. Was it a premeditated or a spontaneous act? Had the prisoners attempted to escape, ostensibly justifying the shooting? Was Peiper reluctant to have his progress slowed by having to deal with POWs? One possible clue is that the massacre was not an isolated incident but part of a series of war crimes committed by the same unit through-out the Ardennes Offensive. Other incidents were reported at Bande, Noville, Stavelot, Bourcy, Houffalize, Cheneux, La Gleize, Stoumont, in the region between Stavelot and Trois-Ponts, and in Lutrebois and Petit Their.

In 1946, those accused of the massacre were brought before the Military Tribunal at Dachau. The "Malmédy massacre trial" covered all the war crimes charged to Kampfgruppe Peiper during the Battle of the Bulge, with over seventy people put on trial. Forty-three of the accused were sentenced to death but for various legal reasons nobody was executed; instead, 22 were given life sentences. Peiper, in prison the longest, was released in 1956. After a career in the motor industry, he ended up living in France where one day he was recognized by a former communist resistance fighter and publicly denounced. On the night before Bastille Day 1976, Peiper's house was firebombed. His burnt remains were discovered the next day.

Americans pitted against 45,000 Germans. By 21 December German troops had encircled the town; McAuliffe, his troops and around three thousand civilians were completely enclosed and ammunition and medical equipment were running low. The following day General von Lüttwitz, commander of the XLVII Panzer Corps, issued an ultimatum to the besieged Americans: "There is only one possibility to save the encircled U.S.A. troops from total annihilation: that is the honourable surrender of the encircled town." McAuliffe's official typed reply read as follows: "To the German Commander. NUTS! The American Commander". More days of fierce fighting followed, but McAuliffe and his men held fast, despite suffering heavy casualties. A large consignment of supplies was air dropped to them on 23 December and the weather had improved sufficiently for squadrons of P.47 Thunderbolts to attack the enemy's armoured troops.

Meanwhile, three divisions of Patton's Third Army were heading up from the south, having managed the remarkable feat of turning 90 degrees from their eastward course and pushing north along a 40km front. Unfortunately, Patton's radio security was poor, allowing the Germans to track the divisions' movements and slow them down. On Christmas Eve 1944, German bombers began the first of two raids on Bastogne, but by Boxing Day the first of Patton's troops, the 37th Tank Battalion, finally entered the town.

To the west, the Germans had reached as close to the River Meuse as they would get, capturing the village of Celles, just 9km away from Dinant, on Christmas Eve. Forced back by a combination of the US 2nd Armored Division and VII Corps, the 2nd Panzer Division was dangerously low on fuel, prompting von Manteuffel to order his troops to abandon their vehicles and retreat on foot. Further to the north, Peiper's Panzer Regiment was in the same predicament and had to turn back towards the German lines with 135 armoured vehicles left behind. Of Peiper's original elite force of 5800 men, only about eight hundred remained.

Operation Bodenplatte

The Germans attempted to regain the front foot by launching Operation Bodenplatte on 1 January 1945 – an attack by the Luftwaffe on sixteen Allied air bases in Belgium, France and the Netherlands that was intended to wrest control of the skies from the RAF and USAAF. Though plenty of Allied planes were destroyed, they were replaced in little more than a week, whereas the German losses, both planes and personnel, badly damaged the Luftwaffe – this would turn out to be its last major operation.

It was now the Allies' turn to take the offensive and finally eradicate the salient (or "bulge") in their lines. Troops from Patton's Third Army advanced northwards from the south, while the US First Army headed southwards from the north, the two forces converging on 16 January at Houffalize, or rather what was left of it. Allied bombers had completely destroyed the town, which had been a strategic crossroads on the highway from Bastogne to Liège. St Vith was recaptured on 23 January after which the battle ground to a halt.

Counting the cost

Out of a US fighting force of 600,000, around 19,000 men had lost their lives and approximately the same number were taken prisoner. German casualties are disputed, but may have been as high as 120,000 men killed or wounded and about seven hundred tanks destroyed – very significant losses which did lasting damage to the Wehrmacht.

» 101st Airborne Museum

» The Ardennes sites

Bastogne Barracks
Rue de la-roche 40, Bastogne, Ⓦ klm-mra.be/D7t

Opened as a museum in 2010, the barracks (just outside Bastogne) were the headquarters of the US 101st Airborne Division during the Ardennes Offensive, and the place from where General McAuliffe sent his famous "NUTS" riposte to General von Lüttwitz. A two-hour tour takes in the operational rooms, in which uniformed mannequins and original wartime equipment create something of the atmosphere of this key command centre. There is also a great collection of military vehicles, including Tiger and Sherman tanks, many of them in full working order. In the centre of Bastogne, the main square is named after McAuliffe and contains a memorial bust of the general.

Mardasson Memorial
Route de Bizory 1, Bastogne

The Mardasson Memorial was inaugurated in 1950 and commemorates the US servicemen who risked or lost their lives on Belgian soil in World War II. A temple-like structure, designed by Belgian architect Georges Dedoyard, it takes the form of a huge five-point star supported by tall columns, with the story of the battle engraved in gold on the walls of the open gallery. A walkway on the roof of the memorial provides visitors with a panoramic view of the defensive positions held during the siege of the town. The crypt contains a Catholic, Protestant and Jewish altar, each one decorated with a mosaic by the French artist Fernand Léger.

Bastogne War Museum
Colline du Mardasson 5, Bastogne,
Ⓦ bastognewarmuseum.be

Opposite the Mardasson Memorial is the new Bastogne War Museum, which covers the whole Belgium experience of World War II, rather than just the Battle of the Bulge. The concept of the displays is very high-tech, with a series of "experiences", including one scene set in the Ardennes forest and another set in a café – with the sounds of war all around. The audioguide, provided as part of the entrance fee, continues the multi-sensory, narrative approach by providing the perspectives of a fictional group of people, including a Belgian child and a German soldier. There are plenty of objects on display, but this museum is more about immersive excitement than quiet contemplation.

101st Airborne Museum
Av de la gare 11, Bastogne,
Ⓦ 101airbornemuseumbastogne.com

The 101st Airborne Museum is located in the former officers' mess of the Belgian army in Bastogne, in a historic building that was later used as a hospital by the Red Cross. The museum's focus is the Battle of the Bulge, and the exhibition centres on a number of lifelike tableaux. There's also a recreated bomb shelter, complete with sound and visual effects to help visitors imagine what it was like to be caught up in a raid.

"E" (Easy) Company Memorial, Jack's Wood
Le Bois Jacques, Foy

Le Bois Jacques (Jack's Wood), close to the village of Foy, is where the men of

"E" (known as Easy) Company of the 101st Airborne Division dug themselves in on 19 December as part of the defence of Bastogne. Despite being outnumbered, enduring constant bombardment, and with night-time temperatures as low as −28°C, they managed to hold the enemy at bay. Foy changed hands several times, but was captured by the Americans on 13 January 1945. The "foxholes" and cavities that the soldiers dug in the wood as protection from hostile fire are still visible, and a monument to their courage was unveiled here in 2004.

German War Cemetery Recogne
Recogne 27, Bastogne

In the hamlet of Recogne, close to Foy, is a German war cemetery containing the graves of more than 6800 German soldiers between the ages of 17 and 52. About half were killed during the Ardennes Offensive; the rest were brought here from other battle sites in Belgium and Luxembourg. A simple red-bricked chapel marks the entrance to the cemetery. Over 2500 American troops were also buried at Recogne but were subsequently transferred to the Henri-Chapelle American Cemetery and Memorial at Plombières.

Baugnez 44 Historical Center
Route de Luxembourg 10, Malmédy

With several unique pieces relating to the Malmédy massacre (see p.173), this modern museum evokes the Battle of the Bulge through historic photographs and film footage, military material and vehicles, and fifteen tableaux depicting the life of an ordinary soldier.

December 44 Historical Museum La Gleize
Rue de l'église, La Gleize, Ⓦ december44. com

Sixty kilometres north of Bastogne is the village of La Gleize, where the SS combat group led by Joachim Peiper was halted and forced to abandon its vehicles before retreating through the US lines. One of the group's tanks, a King Tiger, now stands outside a small museum founded in 1989 by local resident, Philippe Gillain, who had been scouring the neighbourhood for wartime remains since he was a teenager. Dedicated to the Ardennes Offensive, the museum has a wealth of military hardware and uniforms on show, many displayed with mannequins set against dioramas.

Henri-Chapelle American Cemetery and Memorial
Rue du Mémorial Américain 159, Plombières, Ⓦ abmc.gov/cemeteries-memorials

At the edge of the Belgian Ardennes, about 30km east of Liège and close to the German border, this 25-hectare US war cemetery contains nearly eight thousand American servicemen who died at the Battle of the Bulge and in Germany. The graves are laid out in gently curving lines on either side of a central pathway.

The memorial itself is a rectangle of pale stone bearing a vast relief sculpture of an eagle with wings outstretched on its front and the insignia of all the divisions that served in Belgium on its back. At the eastern end of the cemetery is a colonnade that, with the chapel and map room, overlooks the burial area. The piers of the colonnade bear the names of 463 soldiers missing in action.

Luxembourg

On 9 September 1944, forces from the US 5th Armored Division crossed the border from France and entered the Grand Duchy of Luxembourg near Pétange.

The next day, on 10 September, the division reached Luxembourg City and the rest of the country was liberated shortly afterwards. It had endured just over four years of occupation, during which time more than five thousand Luxembourgers were killed, around two thousand of whom were Jewish.

» Luxembourg sites

Schumann's Eck Memorial
Rue Grande-Duchesse Charlotte/
Bastnicherstrooss, Wiltz, Ⓦ nlm.lu

During the Battle of the Bulge, Schumann's Eck was a strategically important crossroads. Many American and German soldiers lost their lives here; a monument was erected in their honour on the 50th anniversary of the liberation of Luxembourg. Today's memorial includes several plaques explaining the actions of US units during the battle.

National Museum of Military History
Bamertal 10, Diekirch, Ⓦ mnhm.net

One of the better World War II museums in the region, providing a good historical survey of the Battle of the Bulge (see p.171) with an emphasis on the troops that liberated Diekirch. There's plenty of miltary equipment, but the main draw are the photographs showing both sets of troops. A display entitled "Veiner Miliz" details the activities of the resistance movement

based in Vianden, and there's a room devoted to Tambow, a Soviet camp where many Luxembourgers who had worked as Nazi forced labour at the Eastern Front were incarcerated.

Luxembourg American Cemetery
50 Val du Scheid, Hamm, Ⓦ abmc.gov/
cemeteries-memorials

Located at Hamm, about 6km east of Luxembourg City and the same distance south from the airport, the US cemetery contains the graves of some five thousand American servicemen, including General Patton, who died on 21 December 1945 following a car accident 12 days earlier. Most of those buried here lost their lives in the Battle of the Bulge or in the advance to the River Rhine. It follows the usual pattern of America's European cemeteries, with the pristine white gravestones laid out in curved lines on manicured lawns surrounded by woodland.

Sandweiler German War Cemetery
Rue d'Itzig, Sandweiler

The German burial ground at Sandweiler is a 20-minute walk from the US cemetery. It too is set in woodland, but it's smaller and less grandiose, with the crosses that mark the graves made from a sombre grey granite. Nearly 11,000 German servicemen are buried here, about half of them interred by the Americans. It's a melancholy and moving place, with most gravestones carrying the names of two, or sometimes three, combatants.

Casualties

The Liberation of Europe in 1943–45 was the bloodiest phase of the bloodiest conflict on earth.

It is impossible to give exact figures for how many people were injured and killed during World War II. Some countries kept accurate records of those killed in battle, but failed to record the men and women who died in related circumstances. People disappeared in large numbers, including peasants and civilians whose identities were not documented in the first place; those who never officially existed could not be named in death.

There have been many attempts to arrive at reliable estimates to express the scale of the casualties. It is likely that fifty million people were killed directly by World War II worldwide. This number can be increased to 70–85 million if "war-related deaths" (a vague term) are added, which would mean that three percent of the global prewar population died in the war. The Soviet Union alone lost between 24 and 26 million soldiers and civilians to the war; Germany lost 6–7 million. An incalculably higher number of men, women and children were left scarred by World War II – physically, mentally and emotionally.

An estimated twelve million people were murdered, not only in concentration camps but in atrocities elsewhere, including almost six million Jews (around fifty percent of Europe's prewar population). Up to one million people died as a result of bombing.

These figures are astronomical. Statistics like these, while shocking, can frequently feel removed and clinical – a treatment of suffering as a general condition rather than something that affected individuals in highly personal ways. To truly understand the scale of the catastrophe that was World War II, it is necessary to relate these horrifying figures to particular human stories.

Frontline soldiers

Death in wartime is of a chaotic and unpredictable nature, and the soldiers and civilians of World War II could only do so much to improve their odds for survival.

For many front-line infantrymen and bomber crews, the question wasn't whether or not they would be hit, but where and how. The most prized quality in combat was not patriotism or bravery, but stoicism: to willingly

▲
A Belgian AMC-35 tank engulfed in flames

Nurses preparing for an influx of wounded soldiers
▼

continue in conditions that could not be improved. Many personal accounts of the war discuss the senseless way in which one man would die an unspeakable death while his comrade next to him survived unscathed.

In World War II, protective apparel was rudimentary and inadequate. Soldiers had helmets, but rarely any form of body armour; lightweight bullet-proof materials were not yet invented. Soldiers could keep their heads down and avoid risks, but that was no protection from stepping on a landmine, being strafed by enemy aircraft or being overwhelmed or ambushed by the enemy. Planes were often thin skinned and easily penetrated by flak and shrapnel. Tanks – while armoured against light assault by foot soldiers – could be knocked out by anti-tank guns or specialized hand-held weapons. Additionally, if a tank caught fire, it quickly became a death trap.

Medical treatment

Medical treatment for wounded soldiers varied considerably. Some armies had better medical support than others, while the response of medics was also impacted by the terrain of the battlefield. A soldier evacuated from the field by stretcher was taken first to an emergency first-aid post: an improvised facility in a tent or requisitioned house that had to be

ready to move in the event of an advance or retreat. Patients who couldn't be patched up and returned to the front were sorted – passing through a series of more permanent medical clearing stations until the most serious cases were sent to hospitals back home.

Ironically, the war also stimulated medical research into saving and improving lives. During World War II, a number of important breakthroughs were made that helped reduce casualties. In 1943, penicillin

became available as a way of controlling the infection of wounds. Anaesthetics also improved, as did techniques of blood transfusion: plasma was introduced as a substitute for whole blood since it was easier to transport and store.

Battlefield injuries, however, were just one cause of death on the front line. Not all military casualties were caused by weapons. Avoidable accidents were common, and disease was rife in the unhygienic and crowded conditions of makeshift medical facilities. The hospitals were filled with men suffering from malaria in Italy, dysentery triggered by a poor diet and contaminated water, trench foot brought on by the northern European winter and frostbite induced by freezing temperatures. Venereal diseases caught by soldiers on leave also posed a serious challenge.

Battle fatigue

All armies in World War II and the Liberation did their best to patch up the bodies of wounded soldiers. It was in their interest to keep as many trained men on the battlefield as possible, but they were at a loss when it came to treating the men's injured minds. During World War I, "shell shock" had been observed but often disbelieved. Sufferers were commonly seen as soldiers who were reluctant to return to the front, and the military hierarchy was opposed to giving what they saw as cowardice and malingering a medical name. By World War II, shell shock was beginning to be accepted, though the term was not yet widely used. General Patton almost ended his military career by slapping two soldiers in Sicily because they had no physical injuries but had still been assigned hospital beds.

Most commanders realized that prolonged exposure to life-or-death decisions could unhinge a person's mind. While there was no recognized medical term for war-provoked mental illness, neither was there a definitive set of symptoms. For convenience, the condition became known as "battle fatigue". For the army, the most pressing issue surrounding mental illness was its effect on others. A soldier with battle fatigue was unreliable and a threat to morale. The treatment for anyone in the front line who was unable to do his job due to uncontrollable shaking, relentless moral questioning or acute emotional distress was a period of sedated rest. Once he'd "recovered", the soldier would be returned to the front line – until he was killed or incapacitated with the same condition.

Self-harm

One of the unspoken causes of injury in World War II was self-harm. A soldier injuring himself in order to be removed from the battlefield was in serious breach of army regulations, but it could be hard to prove. In the Battle of the Bulge, the brutality of combat coupled with the intense cold drove some soldiers to the belief that being wounded out of service was preferable to remaining on the front. A soldier would go into the woods – ostensibly to urinate – and stagger back with a bullet to the hand, arm

▲
Exhausted German soldiers resting by the roadside on the Eastern Front, 1941

or leg, claiming there had been a surprise ambush from which he had been lucky to escape alive.

Dealing with the dead

While injuries were complex, death was more straightforward. Wherever an army went on active service, soldiers died in high numbers – whether on the battlefield, in lonely plane crashes or on hospital operating tables. Their corpses had to be dealt with.

Ceasefires were occasionally arranged in the midst of battle – such as at Arnhem (see p.197) – to collect the wounded and the dead, but these were exceptional truces that didn't last long. Mostly, a battle had to reach a final outcome before its dead could be buried. On some occasions it could take months before it was safe to gather the casualties, as at Monte Cassino in Italy. When the time came, the dead were collected, identified (where possible) and buried nearby, sometimes temporarily – until they could be moved to permanent cemeteries.

In some places, as at Anzio, soldiers could see the cemeteries being laid out even as they went into battle. Most of those who died in World War II were buried near where they fell – although there were exceptions. American families were often given the choice of having the bodies of their young men repatriated.

It has become an accepted practice for official agencies to maintain the cemeteries of the men who perished in World War I and World War II. The Commonwealth War Graves Commission (cwgc.org) performs this function for all cemeteries containing British and Commonwealth personnel. US cemeteries are maintained by the American Battle Monuments Commission (abmc.gov), while the German war dead are cared for by the Volksbund Deutsche Kriegsgräberfürsorge (volksbund.de).

Civilian casualties

In parts of Europe, being a civilian during the Liberation was even more hazardous than being a soldier. Civilians were killed in their thousands, both deliberately and as an unfortunate side effect of the military campaigns. Whereas each battle death was recorded and mostly included under the banner of sacrifice and duty, civilians often died inconspicuously with no glory or honour. Entire families were wiped out with no one to mourn them.

Civilians also suffered in a great many ignominious and sordid ways: they were injured, robbed, raped and killed by marauding soldiers on both sides. The hospitals that had survived in war-ravaged nations were overwhelmed by demand. Ordinary, ununiformed victims of war seldom received the same medical or psychiatric treatment as service personnel. Most were forced to cope on their own.

▲
A girl cries over her wounded sister during the Nazi invasion of Poland in 1939

Explore the Atlantic Wall in the Wadden region

During the Second World War, German Army commanders ordered the construction of a defence structure of over 6,000 kilometres. The Atlantic Wall was located on the European coastline, from Norway to Spain, and was made up of over 12,000 heavy bunkers and tens of thousands of lighter bunkers and field enhancements. In ten different locations in the Wadden region, the Atlantic Wall is visible and accessible again. The bunkers tell the history of the Wadden in wartime.

THE WADDEN IN WARTIME

Traces of the Atlantic Wall can be seen in several places in the Wadden region. The bunkers have helped shape the landscape, especially on the islands here.
Visit to discover the heritage and story of the Wadden during the Second World War, a story of military strategy and of daily life under occupation. After the war, many military buildings and personal testimonies were lost or buried. Today, the structures and experiences of local people are once again being uncovered and their importance recognized.

waddenfonds THE ATLANTIC WALL IN THE WADDEN REGION IS A COOPERATION OF CULTURAL AND NATURE ORGANISATIONS, AND THE MUNICIPALITY, WHICH IS SPONSORED BY THE WADDENFONDS AND THE THREE WADDEN PROVINCES.

ATLANTIC WALL

WADDEN REGION

DO IT!

The information centre and museums at the sites are a good starting point for discovering the area's extraordinary military heritage. Several routes begin here, taking in the locations of a number of memorable events during the Second World War. The Atlantic Wall Centre is located in Huisduinen in Den Helder. This is where all the stories come together.

LOCATIONS

HUISDUINEN: **ATLANTIC WALL CENTRE**

TEXEL: **LUCHTVAART- EN OORLOGSMUSEUM**

VLIELAND: **STELLING 12H**

TERSCHELLING: **TIGERSTELLUNG**

AMELAND: **BUNKERMUSEUM**

SCHIERMONNIKOOG: **BUNKERMUSEUM SCHLEI**

TERMUNTEN: **MARINE FLAK BATTERIE**

NOARDERLEECH (NOORDERLEEG)

KORNWERDERZAND: **KAZEMATTENMUSEUM**

DEN OEVER

ADDITIONAL INFORMATION AND STORIES AT WWW.ATLANTIKWALL-WADDEN.NL OR DOWNLOAD THE APP.

The
Netherlands

WAALCROSSING BRIDGEHEAD · KILLED IN ACTION · DIED OF WOUNDS · SEPTEMBER 1944

The Liberation
The Netherlands

GERMANY

NORTH SEA

Schiermonnikoog

Ameland

Terschelling

Vlieland

Texel

Waddenzee

Groningen

Assen

Camp Westerbork
National Memorial Centre

Emmen

Leeuwarden

Fries Verzetsmuseum
(Resistance Museum Friesland)

Sneek

Zwolle

Nijverdal

Almelo

Memory Museum

Holten Canadian
War Cemetery

Holten

Enschede

Deventer

IJsselmeer

Uk

Apeldoorn

Enkhuizen

Putten

Georgian War
Cemetery Loladse

Den Helder

Markermeer

Hilversum

Hoorn

Alkmaar

Zaandam

IJmuiden

Haarlem

Anne Frank House

Verzetsmuseum
(Dutch Resistance Museum)

National Monument on the Dam

Hollandsche Schouwburg

AMSTERDAM

Leiden

N

0   50

kilometres

Anglo-American forces

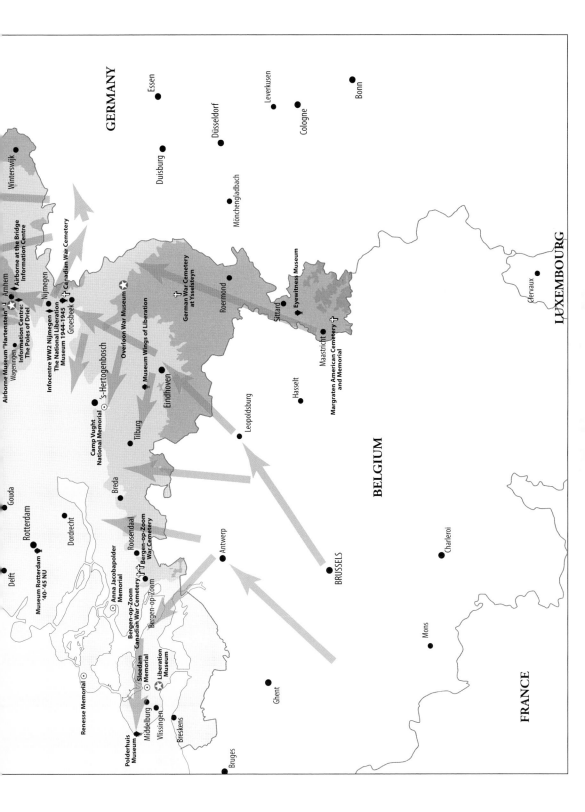

GERMANY

Essen

Leverkusen

Düsseldorf

Cologne

Bonn

Duisburg

Mönchengladbach

Winterswijk

Airborne at the Bridge
Information Centre

Arnhem

Airborne Museum "Hartenstein"

Wageningen

Information Centre:
The Poles of Driel

Canadian War Cemetery

Nijmegen

Infocentre WW2 Nijmegen

The National Liberation
Museum 1944-1945

Groesbeek

German War Cemetery
at Ysselsteyn

Roermond

Eyewitness Museum

Sittard

Overloon War Museum

's-Hertogenbosch

Museum Wings of Liberation

Maastricht

Margraten American Cemetery
and Memorial

Camp Vught
National Memorial

Eindhoven

Tilburg

Hasselt

Gouda

Breda

Leopoldsburg

Rotterdam

Dordrecht

BELGIUM

Delft

Roosendaal

Bergen-op-Zoom
War Cemetery

Antwerp

Museum Rotterdam
'40-45 NU

Anna Jacobapolder
Memorial

Bergen-op-Zoom
Canadian War Cemetery

Bergen-op-Zoom

BRUSSELS

Charleroi

LUXEMBOURG

Clervaux

Renesse Memorial

Sloedam
Memorial

Liberation
Museum

Middelburg

Vlissingen

Breskens

Polderhuis
Museum

Ghent

Mons

Bruges

FRANCE

The Liberation The Netherlands

During the late summer and early autumn of 1944, as the Allies swept through northern France and Belgium, the liberation of the Netherlands seemed close at hand.

In fact, Dutch liberation was only achieved in May 1945 after a tough and frustrated campaign. When the population was finally freed, the Netherlands emerged from almost exactly five years of Nazi occupation.

German invasion and occupation

On 10 May 1940, the German Army crossed its eastern frontier into the Netherlands using the techniques of *blitzkrieg* – fast-mov-

» Liberation Day in the Netherlands

ing war. The Germans viewed the Netherlands as something of an irritation on their path to France, which they sought to reach as soon as possible. Duly taken by surprise, the Dutch Army fought hard for five days, but a flat country with only rivers to act as natural defences was difficult to defend. On 14 May Rotterdam was subjected to heavy aerial bombardment, and when other cities were threatened with the same treatment the Dutch army capitulated. The following day the surrender was signed and the occupation of the Netherlands began. Queen Wilhelmina, a passionate anti-Nazi, had already left the country for London. When her prime minister, Dirk Jan de Geer, tried to negotiate with Hitler, the queen dismissed him and appointed Pieter Gerbrandy to lead the government-in-exile.

The new Nazi overlords, under the leadership of Reichskommisar Arthur Seyss-Inquart, hoped they would find a sympathetic ally in the Netherlands, which they considered a fellow "Aryan" nation. Day-to-day administration continued under the Dutch civil service, but attempts to Nazify the Dutch population met with almost complete failure. German treatment of the civilian population was relatively mild initially, but occupation became increasingly repressive in the face of Dutch non-cooperation and resistance. Nazi economic exploitation of the country included deporting around 400,000 people to Germany as labourers; those who resisted were met with brutal reprisals.

As an extreme anti-Semite, Seyss-Inquart was quick to implement anti-Jewish measures, forcing Jews to register and removing them from all official positions. Of the 140,000 Jews in the Netherlands – many of whom were refugees from Germany – a total of 107,000 were interned in Camp Westerbork, a transit camp in the country's northeast. From here they were transported onwards to concentration and extermination camps across Europe, including nearly 35,000 sent to the extermination camp at Sobibór in Poland between March and July 1943. Seventy-five percent of the Dutch Jewish community died in World War II, a far higher figure than almost all other Western European nations.

As the war progressed and the Nazi grip tightened, the Dutch Resistance grew stronger and more active. Made up of diverse groups across the political spectrum, its activities focused on destroying German supplies and munitions, organizing strikes, hiding Nazi "undesirables" and forging identity papers. Military resistance wasn't easy in a densely populated country with no mountains or large forests to use as hideaways, but there were several successful assassinations, including the death of the collaborationist Dutch officer, General Seyffardt. Unfortunately, the Nazis proved adept at infiltrating resistance movements and by the end of the war around 23,000 resistance fighters had been rounded up and executed,

» LRE audiospots in the Netherlands

There are almost 200 LRE audiospots (see p.6) in the Netherlands, telling stories – both big and small – relating to the war and the Liberation. Throughout this guide, audiospots are marked with the headphone symbol . All the stories can be heard at liberationroute.com; at brabantremembers.com you can view similar experiences online.

Significant sites are marked on the map on pages 186 and 187

✪ **Liberation Museum Zeeland, Nieuwdorp. See p.192**

✪ **Airborne Museum "Hartenstein", Oosterbeek. See p.203**

✪ **Overloon War Museum, Overloon. See p.205**

✪ **Anne Frank House, Amsterdam. See p.206**

✪ **Verzetsmuseum, Amsterdam. See p.206**

Significant sites

«

bringing the total Dutch casualties in World War II to at least 200,000.

Liberation

Allied forces overran northern France and Belgium in the summer and autumn of 1944, and the Dutch expected they would soon be liberated. There was a mood of optimism in the air: 5 September is still known as "Dolle Dinsdag" (Mad Tuesday) after the premature celebrations that rippled through the Netherlands. It was a false dawn, however, and the Dutch would have to wait until May the following year before their country was entirely free.

The liberation of the Netherlands proved to be a slow and protracted grind, beginning with two campaigns: the ambitious – but only partially successful – Operation Market Garden, close to the German border in the east, and the Battle of the Scheldt in the southwest. As the Germans came closer to losing the war, they became increasingly ruthless. Reprisals against the Resistance and civilians grew more frequent, and in the bitter winter of 1944–1945 thousands died from starvation as the result of a German blockade.

Zeeland and South Holland

By the late summer of 1944, the Allies desperately needed a substantial harbour for troop supplies in order to continue their advance. Capturing coastal Zeeland, at the Netherlands' southwestern edge, became vitally important.

The Allies had won the Belgian port of Antwerp, with its docks intact, in early September 1944 (see p.169), but it was of little use while the Nazis still controlled the huge estuary of the River Scheldt in the Netherlands. Taking Zeeland, where the key German defences of the estuary lay, was a strategic necessity.

Despite the importance of the Scheldt estuary, the Allies focused their advance further east, as Operation Market Garden was rolled out – Montgomery's ambitious plan to strike at Germany via an airborne attack deep within the Netherlands (see p.197). As a result, the front line around Antwerp remained almost unchanged for a month. It was finally impressed on Montgomery (by Eisenhower and Admiral Ramsay among others) just how vital control of the Scheldt was, and the difficult task of clearing the German defences fell to the First Canadian Army, commanded – in the absence of General Crerar through illness – by Lieutenant General Guy Simonds.

The Battle of the Scheldt

In order to gain control of the Scheldt, the Allies deployed six divisions tasked with taking four key targets: the area north of Antwerp (to gain access to the South Beveland peninsula); the Breskens pocket, north of the Leopold Canal; South Beveland itself; and Walcheren Island. Much of the terrain was made up of "polders", low-lying fields prone to flooding and protected by dykes, making the movement of men and machines extremely onerous.

The 2nd Canadian Infantry Division set off north from Antwerp on 2 October 1944, heading across the Antwerp-Turnhout canal towards the entrance to South Beveland. Progress was slow and steady, but it came to a halt at the town of Woensdrecht – the key access point at the neck of the peninsula – where the Canadians encountered strong resistance from veteran German defenders, including the elite 6th Fallschirmjäger Regiment. One of the bloodiest engagements was fought on 13 October, when the Canadian Black Watch Regiment attacked well-prepared German positions across an open field, incurring heavy losses. Eventually, on 16 October, the Canadians reached a ridge above the town and succeeded in repelling the fierce German counterattacks.

Following in the wake of the 2nd Canadian Infantry Division was the 4th Canadian Armoured Division which, on 20 October, liberated Bergen op Zoom before proceeding to Sint Philipsland and sinking several German vessels in Zijpe harbour.

Operation Switchback: the Battle of the Breskens Pocket

On the Scheldt's southern shore, meanwhile, to the northwest of Antwerp, the 3rd Canadian Division was encountering similarly dogged opposition from the German 64th Infantry Division. On 6 October 1944, the Canadians had launched their attack – codenamed Switchback – with the aim of establishing two bridgeheads on the opposite bank of the Leopold canal and clearing the so-called Breskens Pocket on the other side. Resistance was stiff, and on 9 October an amphibious assault was made at the small village of Hoofdplaat to help relieve pressure. The town of Breskens finally fell on 21 October, and on 2 November the command-

» Canada's role in World War II

As a British dominion and member of the Commonwealth, Canada declared war on Germany in 1939, shortly after Great Britain. This caused some tension between Canadian anglophones, who were generally pro-war, and francophones, who were reluctant to get involved in another conflict on a distant continent so soon after the horrors of World War I.

Canada's citizens volunteered enthusiastically for army service overseas. Although only one division was initially sent to Europe, the country's contribution to the war effort increased exponentially, despite the huge financial cost to Canada – a country with a low population which had suffered considerably in the Great Depression.

Canadian soldiers first saw action in Europe in the disastrous Dieppe raid of 1942 (see p.81), which resulted in the deaths of 907 Canadian nationals and a further 1882 being taken as prisoners of war. In July 1943 Canadian troops participated in the invasion and liberation of Sicily (see p.42) and then crossed to the Italian mainland with the British Eighth Army in September. They distinguished themselves in the demanding and bloody battles of the Italian campaign, particularly at Ortona (see p.62) in

December 1943, where there were 2339 Canadian casualties. Canadian fighting forces were sustained by a steady stream of volunteers; it wasn't until 1944 that conscription was introduced to counteract the losses in battle.

On D-Day, Canada was allocated Juno Beach, where the 3rd Canadian Infantry Division secured all its objectives. It went on to fight at the Battle of Normandy, notably in the clearing of the Falaise Pocket (see p.132). The First Canadian Army formed the left flank of Montgomery's 21st Army Group as it moved north from France up the Channel coast via Dieppe, Boulogne and Calais into Belgium.

Canadian troops also played a crucial role in the protracted Battle of the Scheldt (see p.190) and contributed three divisions to Operation Veritable (see p.284), the invasion of the Rhineland. In the final months of the war, the First Canadian Army, commanded by Harry Crerar, was tasked with re-entering the Netherlands from Germany.

Over one million men and women – ten percent of the population – served in the Canadian armed forces during World War II. Of those, around 45,000 died, 54,000 were wounded and nine thousand were taken prisoner.

ing German general, Knut Eberding, was captured. The next day the remaining German forces laid down their weapons.

Operation Vitality, the capture of South Beveland

The 2nd Canadian Division – having captured Woensdrecht – moved up the Beveland peninsula on 24 October. Here they engaged the German 70th Infantry Division, many of whom

were weakened by chronic stomach disorders. The first mission of the Canadian division was to cross the Kreekrakdam, which connected South Beveland to the mainland. The difficult terrain resulted in the failure of an initial armoured assault, and it became clear that the infantry would have to capture the dam.

The infantry encountered little resistance before they reached the main German defensive line on the South Beveland canal.

Believing a frontal attack would be costly, the Canadian forces were to outflank the German line with the help of the newly arrived Scottish 52nd Lowland Division. On 26 October, the Scots launched a successful amphibious assault across the Scheldt, forcing the German troops to withdraw to their next line of defence on the Sloedam, the 1.5km causeway linking South Beveland to Walcheren.

The capture of Walcheren

All that remained for the Allies to do was to take heavily fortified Walcheren Island. To limit German defensive options, RAF bombers breached the dykes on 3 October 1944, flooding most of the island.

The Allies had two ways of attacking Walcheren – by sea or land, although the only overland connection to the island was the Sloedam, which had been fortified at both ends. The causeway was attacked on 31 October by the 2nd Canadian Infantry Division, but proved difficult to overcome. To support the stalled offensive, on the night of 2 and 3 November, Scottish soldiers of the 6th Battalion Cameronians crossed the waters 2km south of the causeway in a surprise attack, codenamed Mallard. The successful operation forced a German withdrawal, enabling the 2nd Canadian Infantry Division to gain ground. The causeway finally fell to the Allies on 3 November.

On 1 November, another amphibious landing had taken place at Vlissingen (Flushing), on the southwest of Walcheren. British, French and Dutch commandos were supported by heavy bombardment of the German coastal defences, and within a few hours had captured the centre of Vlissingen – although German resistance continued in the north of the city. A second landing at Westkapelle, northwest of Vlissingen, went less smoothly. Four of the heaviest German batteries were still in operation and engaged a group of 25 British gunboats that had supported the landings. After two hours only five of the Allied boats were operational, but the landing craft survived and the commando forces reached the shore, where they silenced the German guns. Middelburg, the island's main town and the capital of Zeeland, was captured on 6 November. The Scheldt estuary had been cleared of German forces, but it took another three weeks to clear the area of mines and for the first Allied shipping to reach Antwerp.

The Battle of the Schledt had lasted just over a month, and had cost the Allies dearly. The First Canadian Army suffered nearly 13,000 casualties, around half of which were Canadian nationals.

Zeeland and South Holland sites   «

Liberation Museum Zeeland

Coudorp 41, Nieuwdorp,
ⓦ bevrijdingsmuseumzeeland.nl ☺

Located on Walcheren, about 9km east of Middelburg, this ever-expanding museum is dedicated to the story of Zeeland in World War II, with a special focus on the Battle of the Scheldt. The Dutch regard the Scheldt as a "forgotten" battle and compare its significance to the Normandy landings – the only other occasion that the Allies breached the Atlantic Wall. In 2017, a 3-hectare Liberation Park opened on-site, with some fascinating outdoor exhibits including bunkers, a Sherman tank, an original Bailey bridge and a church built from Nissen huts – the replica of an emergency church built at nearby Ellewoutsdijk when the original was hit by a bomb. The museum also draws attention to the Zeeland Battalion, a group of volunteers who, af-

➤➤ The flooding of Walcheren

On 2 October 1944, the Allies dropped leaflets over Walcheren urging its civilians to evacuate the island immediately. No explanation was given – the warning was cryptic and only became understood after the events that followed – and the Germans forbade anyone to leave. The next day, the RAF breached the dyke near Westkapelle in a bombardment that cost the lives of more than 150 civilians and destroyed most of the town. Further attacks followed on the dykes at Veere, Vlissingen and Fort Rammekens. Since about eighty percent of Walcheren lay below sea level, the island was almost completely submerged. Thousands of civilians were forced to abandon their possessions and flee to dry land.

The flooding of Walcheren remains controversial. The operation was designed to disrupt the German lines of communication and prevent the movement of German troops, but in practice, the advantages were negligible. By the autumn of 1944, the Germans had no more reserves to bring in and deploy. It may have been that the flooding of Walcheren was ordered as a preventative measure against Hitler treating Walcheren as a *Festung* – a fortress to be defended at all costs – knowing that if the Germans lost Walcheren then Antwerp would be reopened to Allied shipping.

The damage done to the island was enormous, and it would take until the beginning of 1946 before the dykes were fully closed and the long process of recovery could begin.

ter the liberation of Zeeland, fought alongside the Allied forces to free the rest of the country.

Polderhuis Museum

Zuidstraat 154–156, Westkapelle,
Ⓦ polderhuiswestkapelle.nl

On the west coast of Walcheren at Westkapelle, the Polderhuis Museum covers the history and culture of the area with a special emphasis on the wartime years. Along the dunes around Westkapelle are several monuments relating to the Battle of the Scheldt, including two at the Erika dune where 172 Allied troops lost their lives on 1 November 1944.

Sloedam Memorial

Postweg, Arnemuiden ☻◉

Just off the N665 road, heading east from Arnemuiden, is a turning for the Sloedam Memorial, a group of stone monuments that commemorates two wartime operations. The first was a rearguard action by a French Infantry Division after the Dutch surrender in May 1940; the second was the battle for the causeway, Operation Mallard, fought by Scottish and Canadian troops in November 1944.

Anna Jacobapolder Memorial

Langeweg, Sint Philipsland ☻◉

On the morning of 23 January 1945, German commandos came ashore at Sint Philipsland in an attempted counterattack against the Allied forces. After blowing up a water tower they headed for the town of Anna Jacobapolder but were successfully repelled. In the defence of the town three Poles, two Englishmen and the Dutch section commander, Piet Avontuur, lost their lives. A stone monument

with a carved Phoenix commemorates those killed in the attack.

Renesse Memorial
Oude Moolweg, Renesse ☺﴾

The war memorial in Renesse comprises a stone sculpture of a woman dressed in local costume holding the body of a lifeless man. It commemorates ten captured resistance fighters who, after trying to escape to North Beveland, were hanged by the Germans on 10 December 1944 at the entrance to Moermond Castle. A black stone plaque standing nearby remembers the civilians and soldiers of the area who were killed during World War II and in hostilities that took place in the Dutch East Indies (1945–1962).

Museum Rotterdam '40–'45 NU
Coolhaven 375, Rotterdam,
Ⓦ museumrotterdam.nl/en/bezoek

On 14 May 1940, four days into the German invasion of the Netherlands, the Luftwaffe subjected Rotterdam to a major bombardment. A residential area was hit, and the city's historic centre was largely destroyed. This small museum, located close to the Coolhaven metro stop, relates the devastation and rebirth of Rotterdam, the Netherlands' second-largest city and major port. A film outlines the story of the bombing, while fascinating objects from the period are displayed. Note that individuals can only visit at weekends, as the weekdays are reserved for groups.

At Plein 1940, a twenty-minute walk eastwards from the museum, is the famous Osip Zadkine sculpture-memorial. *The Destroyed City*, depicting a bronze man with a hole in his chest, symbolizes a postwar Rotterdam that had lost its historic heart. The piece was donated to the city in 1953.

Oranjehotel 1940–1945
Pompstationsweg 32, The Hague,
Ⓦ oranjehotel.org

Scheveningen, a seaside resort close to The Hague, is where the Gestapo confined and interrogated political prisoners and resistance fighters in a section of the town's prison. It was given the ironic nickname, the "Oranjehotel" (Orange hotel). Around 25,000 people passed through its gates, of whom 215 were executed. The remainder were sent on to concentration or labour camps. One of the death cells, Cell 601, has been preserved in its original state with messages from prisoners scratched on the walls, a poignant memorial to those who were incarcerated here. The executions are commemorated at the site where they took place, on the dunes at nearby Waalsdorpervlakte.

Limburg

On 12 September 1944, the Allied armies in Belgium crossed the Dutch border near the village of Mesch in South Limburg, initiating the liberation of the Netherlands. They reached Maastricht two days later.

After the Allies had entered the Netherlands and liberated Maastricht, heavy fighting followed throughout the province, with the Maas (Meuse) river becoming a front line. The division that fought the toughest battles in this area was the 52nd British Lowland Division, which counted 752 casualties. Large swathes of Limburg were liberated during the final months of 1944, but early 1945 witnessed further engagement in which numerous soldiers and civilians lost their lives.

It took the Allied forces until 1 March 1945 to liberate Venlo in the north of Limburg, where hostilities centred on the airport – baptized "Yankee 55" after its capture by American troops. Because the Germans had blown up most of the airport before their retreat, the Americans set up a tented camp they called the "Venlo Hilton".

«
Symmetrical lines at Margraten American Cemetery and Memorial

》 War correspondents

A legion of reporters and photographers followed the armies on both sides of the conflict as closely as they could. These unarmed, non-combatants took grave risks – some joined frightened men in landing craft; others jumped out of planes into enemy fire beside seasoned paratroopers. War correspondents often had an ambivalent attitude towards what they saw and experienced. They were attracted by the glamour of war and the number of compelling stories it generated, but were repulsed by the sordid reality of life on the front line.

Truthfulness was always a challenge. Should they tell their readers, listeners and viewers at home what was really happening – including the misjudgments of generals and the substantial deaths by accident and friendly fire – at the risk of undermining commitment to the war effort? Or should they maintain the myths of glory and sacrifice in the interests of patriotism? Even more complicated was the question of whether or not to portray the enemy soldiers as human beings – even the victims of evil leaders – or as two-dimensional villains.

Some correspondents went on to have successfully literary careers; others wrote seminal accounts of the war. A few reporters didn't survive. Working in a dangerous field, the closer journalists got to the story, the greater the personal risk.

》 Limburg sites

Eyewitness Museum

Maastrichterlaan 45, Beek,
Ⓦ eyewitnesswo2.nl/informatie ☺ⁱ⁾

The Eyewitness Museum uses the power of storytelling to bring World War II to life. The "eyewitness" in question is a fictional German paratrooper, August Segel, whose story is told through thirteen dioramas of wartime scenes, peopled by 150 life-sized mannequins and a number of prized objects. Sound effects accompany the battle scenes, and background information is provided throughout.

Margraten American Cemetery and Memorial

Amerikaanse Begraafplaats 1, Margraten,
Ⓦ abmc.gov

Just outside the town of Margraten, the American War Cemetery and Memorial is a moving monument to more than eight thousand US servicemen who died in the Dutch and Belgian campaigns of late 1944 and 1945. The centrepiece is a stone quadrangle recording the names of the fallen soldiers, together with a small visitors' room and a pictorial and narrative description of the ebb and flow of the local campaign. Beyond the quadrangle, white marble crosses stretch into the distance. The cemetery is located near the historic Cologne–Boulogne highway, once trodden by Julius Caesar, Charlemagne, Napoleon and Kaiser Wilhelm II.

German War Cemetery

Timmermannsweg 74, Ysselsteyn ☺ⁱ⁾

This cemetery in Ysselsteyn is the only German military cemetery in the whole of the Netherlands. Eighty-five German soldiers from World War I and 32,000 combatants from World War II are buried here across 28 hectares of land.

Noord Brabant and Gelderland

Most of France and Belgium had been liberated by September 1944, and Eisenhower, Patton and Montgomery were divided about how to progress towards Germany.

Fearing that an orthodox campaign would take many months and cost many lives, Montgomery argued for a pencil thrust north though the Netherlands and then east into the Ruhr, around the back of the heavily fortified Siegfried Line, which he believed offered a good chance of ending the war early.

Operation Market Garden

Despite preferring to advance across a broad front, the cautious Eisenhower eventually agreed to Montgomery's plan: Operation Market Garden. Montgomery's offensive would divert resources from the Scheldt estuary (see p.190), but would bring four immediate benefits: the German army in the western Netherlands would be cut off; V2 rocket launchpads would be overrun and disabled; the Ruhr, Germany's industrial heartland, could be surrounded; and a route to Berlin across north-central Germany would open up. A broad front at the Veluwe, with a deep bridgehead over the Ijssel river, would serve as a springboard for an offensive into the Ruhr. Montgomery (and the Allied planners who supported his idea) had good reason to be confident. The German army had already been pushed back from France and Belgium and was considered a spent force, incapable of mounting a defence against the Allied troops who had the momentum of war with them.

The plan for Market Garden called for the largest airborne operation in the history of warfare (codenamed "Market"). Thousands of British, American and Polish paratroopers would be flown from England and supported by an overland advance (codenamed "Garden") by Brian G. Horrocks' British XXX Corps, setting out from Belgium (see p.169). Three major rivers would need crossing, and nine bridges would have to be either captured or rebuilt. Crucial to the whole plan was the seizure of one of the two bridges across the Neder Rijn, a tributary of the Rhine, by Arnhem. Allied command expected the XXX Corps to reach the Veluwe – and Market Garden to succeed – in no more than three days.

《
American troops in Nijmegen

On 17 September 1944, three airborne divisions were dropped behind enemy lines, responsible for taking and holding selected bridgeheads until the main army could force their way north to join them. The 1st British Airborne Division parachuted into the fields west of Wolfheze and north of Heelsum, a small village near the most northerly target of the operation. Their principal objective was to seize the bridges at Arnhem and establish a bridgehead between the Westerbouwing and the railway bridge at Westervoort. The 101st American Airborne Division was dropped to secure objectives in the area around Veghel, Sint-Oedenrode and Son. The 82nd Division was dropped around Grave and Nijmegen, for the crossings over the Maas and the Waal, and to secure higher ground at Groesbeek.

Stalemate at Arnhem

The landings around Arnhem ran into serious problems. Allied command believed there was no suitable landing zone near the city, so airborne units were dropped 10–15km away.

»
Commemorative event
in Arnhem, 2014

(In fact, assumptions that German anti-aircraft guns were installed in Arnhem and Deelan were incorrect.) A shortage of transport aircraft also meant the units arrived in three waves. The first units to arrive on 17 September were stretched, being forced to capture the road bridge at Arnhem (the rail bridge had in the meantime been destroyed by the Germans) as well as securing the landing site for the second and third waves. Ginkelse Heide (Ginkel Heath) near Ede was the dropping zone on the second day of the operation; again, troops were overextended and had a long way to walk to the bridge at Arnhem. To compound their problems, General Urquhart lost control of almost his entire division after landing because the tactical radios failed. The flat terrain, divided up by an extraordinary number of canals and ditches, was difficult to traverse and offered little cover for the Allied soldiers.

Bad luck dogged the operation. Extensive intelligence work had failed to reveal the strength of the enemy. Allied Command had estimated that opposition was unlikely to exceed three thousand troops, but, as it turned out, the entire 2nd SS Panzer Corps was refitting near Arnhem just when the 1st Division landed. Seasoned SS Panzer (armoured) units put up unexpected and heavy resistance against the lightly armed Allied paratroopers.

Nevertheless, British forces were able to take the enemy by surprise, and the 2nd Parachute Battalion, under Lieutenant Colonel John Frost, did manage to capture the northern end of the road bridge across the Rhine, but it proved impossible to capture the southern end. Frost's paratroopers were forced to wait for reinforcements and heavy weapons that were due to arrive by road. Surrounded, outgunned and outmanned, the 2nd Battalion held their position from September 17th to the morning of the 21st, a feat of extraordinary courage and determination.

The commander and men of the 1st Airborne Division, meanwhile, were besieged in their headquarters at the Hartenstein Hotel at Oosterbeek, just outside Arnhem, with supplies running low and corpses accumulating in the hotel grounds.

The Battle of Nijmegen and crossing the Waal

American troops were having their own troubles trying to capture the two bridges across the Waal at Nijmegen. The first attempt, made by units of the American 82nd Airborne Division on 17 September, managed to get within 400m of the Waal bridge, only to be repelled by German forces. The next day another attack was initiated, but again the paratroopers were unable to secure the bridge.

On 19 September the ground forces of the XXX Corps established contact with airborne units in Grave. A combined attack to secure the bridges was made, this time with tank support from the Guards Armored Division. Again, the Allied advance was halted just before the bridges. German troops had been reinforced by men from the 10th SS Panzer Division and put up stiff resistance. It was becoming clear that the bridges could not be stormed.

A plan was finally made to infiltrate behind enemy lines and attack the bridges from both sides. In a desperate effort to regain the initiative, US paratroopers crossed the Waal in 26 inadequate, canvas-sided boats. Lacking proper oars, some soldiers had to use their rifle butts to row. Half of the 160 US soldiers involved were killed or wounded before, after and during the crossing. Just half of the dinghies could be used for a second crossing.

After four hours of bloody fighting and

›› Nijmegen Sunset March

In 2013, the city of Nijmegen opened a new bridge called the Oversteek (Crossing). Erected close to the place where troops of the US 82nd Airborne Division crossed the River Waal under heavy fire on 20 September 1944, the Oversteek commemorates the soldiers of Operation Market Garden. The bridge is fitted with 48 pairs of specially programmed street lights, which are illuminated at sunset, pair by pair, at the pace of a slow march.

Each evening at dusk, a Dutch military veteran – wearing a beret, insignia and war medals – walks the Sunset March to honour the 48 American soldiers who died trying to cross the river and as a tribute to all Allied personnel who fought for the liberation of the Netherlands. The march takes 12 minutes in total; all are welcome to attend. Any veteran can volunteer to lead the march, although dates get booked up in advance (sunsetmarch.nl).

heavy losses on both sides, the paratroopers, with the help of the XXX Corps, succeeded in capturing the bridges intact. The city of Nijmegen was liberated.

Hell's Highway

Operation Market Garden might still have succeeded had the land forces, with the Irish Guards at the front of the column, been able to relieve the paratroopers. But the ground forces were dependent on a single road between Eindhoven and Nijmegen that was vulnerable to constant fire from both sides; it soon became dubbed "Hell's Highway". Many lives were lost trying to move supplies northwards to the exposed troops, and matters were only made worse when immobilized tanks blocked the road.

»
Sturmgeschütz III
assault gun on
display during an
event in Overloon

Withdrawal and consequences of Operation Market Garden

By the morning of 25 September it was apparent that reinforcements in sufficient numbers would not be able to get through in support. There was no other option but to abandon the operation and evacuate the troops. Under the cover of darkness (during the night of 25–26 September), a dramatic and supremely well-executed withdrawal saved more than two thousand soldiers out of an original force of 10,000 from the perimeter of the Hartenstein villa in Oosterbeek. Historians generally agree that Operation Market Garden was lost within its first hours with the failure to take the bridge at Arnhem, which became known in popular literature as a "bridge too far".

There has been controversy about Operation Market Garden ever since. Some argue that it was poorly conceived, others that it might have worked but for a series of military mishaps and miscalculations. Whatever the case, its failure created mistrust between Montgomery and Eisenhower, and tarnished Montgomery's reputation as an infallible military strategist. Montgomery defended himself by claiming the operation had been "ninety per-

cent successful". Air Marshal Tedder famously retorted, "one jumps off a cliff with an even higher success rate, until the last few inches."

For the Dutch, the consequences were severe. After the Battle of Arnhem, 95,000 civilians living in the area were forced to evacuate as the Germans turned the north bank of the Rhine into a heavily fortified line. Arnhem became a ghost town. The failed military operation also revealed to the Germans just how much of the Dutch population reviled them and were willing to "collaborate" with the enemy. This was a prime motivation for the policy that led to the "Hunger Winter" (see p.210).

Operations Aintree and Veritable

The price had been high, but some benefits were also gleaned from Operation Market Garden. It liberated around one fifth of the Netherlands, including the town of Eindhoven (on 18 September), and gave the Allies a valuable salient from which to launch an offensive into Germany. The salient was vulnerable to German attack, however, by troops operating from a bridgehead over the Maas near Venlo. To deal with this threat, Operation Aintree was devised to clear German troops from Overloon and Venray (which lay en route to Venlo).

The land west of Venlo was marshy and crossed by several canals. At Overloon, Allied forces came up against determined resistance between 30 September and 18 October 1944. In all, 2500 men were killed and a significant number of tanks (mainly American) were lost in what is largely regarded as a forgotten battle in the Netherlands. The Allies were ultimately successful, and managed to drive the Germans back across the Maas.

Not until four months later were the Allies ready to launch an offensive, Operation Veritable, from the Netherlands into northern Germany. British and Canadian troops were assembled in the captured Nijmegen area (Rijk van Nijmegen) and in North Limburg in preparation for Veritable, the opening move in the major Rhineland offensive (see p.284) beginning on 8 February 1945. However, a thaw in the cold weather jeopardized another carefully thought-out plan, as rain and mud made it virtually impossible to push forward. Montgomery was finally able to bypass Arnhem to reach the Rhine.

The liberation of Arnhem

Arnhem was finally liberated, long after the Allies had crossed the Rhine in other places, by Operation Anger in April 1945, sometimes referred to as the Second Battle of Arnhem. The offensive to seize the city was implemented by the First Canadian Army, which incorporated British units. The attack was led by the artillery, armour and infantry of the 49th British (West Yorkshire) Division, nicknamed the Polar Bears, which had been stationed on Nijmegen Island since the previous December. They were supported by the 5th Canadian Armoured Division. Operation Anger began on 12 April 1945 and Arnhem was entered and liberated on 15 April.

Fighting at Otterlo

Arnhem's province, Gelderland, was also the scene of one of the last major battles in the Netherlands. After the breakthrough at the Rhine, the Allied forces where split into three groups. One of these, made up mostly of Canadian forces, swung round and started the liberation of the Netherlands from the east.

On 16 April 1945, the 5th Canadian Armoured Division liberated the village of Otterlo (near Ede) before continuing on to Wekerom and Voorthuizen, leaving the divisional headquarters and an infantry battalion behind in the village. The Germans, meanwhile, were trying to get to safety in the west of the Netherlands, and somewhere between 600 and 900 German soldiers came upon Otterlo on the evening of 16 April. The Canadians fired their guns at short range but were eventually taken out by the German soldiers. The gunners fought on using their hand guns, but groups of German soldiers managed to push through and entrench themselves in the village.

In the early hours of the next morning, the situation had escalated into a serious battle. Canadian tanks had been called in for assistance. Two Wasp flamethrowers fired at the German positions, whereupon the Nazi soldiers panicked and fled. More than three hundred of them were killed, along with twelve Canadians and four civilians.

Noord Brabant and Gelderland sites

Putten

World War II left a deep and indelible mark on the community of Putten. On 2 October 1944, in retaliation for a resistance operation, 659 men were arrested here and more than one hundred homes were subsequently set alight. The men were deported first to Camp Amersfoort; on 11 October, 601 were transported on to Neuengamme concentration camp. More than 550 men died as a result of the round-up, almost Putten's entire male population. Aid was collected from around the Netherlands – and even abroad – to support the women of the village in the following months. On 1 October 1949, Queen Juliana unveiled a memorial to the lost men of Putten – *The Widow of Putten*, handkerchief in hand, is a moving monument to human grief.

Loenen Field of Honour
Groenendaalseweg 64, Loenen

More than 3900 war victims are buried at Loenen Field of Honour. The graves belong to men and women who died in various campaigns around the world, including military personnel, members of the resistance, vic-

tims of reprisal and forced labour, and those who escaped the Netherlands in the first years of the war to join the Allies in England (the "Engelandvaarders"). Casualties from the Indonesian War of Independence and New Guinea, as well as victims of peacekeeping missions in Korea, Lebanon, Yugoslavia, Afghanistan and Mali, are also buried here.

Airborne at the Bridge Information Centre
Rijnkade 150, Arnhem,
Ⓦ airborneatthebridge.nl ☺⑉

With a view of the famous – if unspectacular – John Frost Bridge (the "bridge too far" that was so bloodily contested in September 1944), the Airborne at the Bridge Information Centre explains the story of Operation Market Garden and Arnhem's pivotal role in it. The centre also tells the personal stories of some of the people involved, in-

» German capitulation in the Netherlands

In the first week of May 1945, negotiations were started between the German forces occupying the northern parts of the Netherlands and Germany and the Allies. The end of the war seemed imminent – especially after the forces defending Germany had been divided in two by Eisenhower. On 4 May, Field Marshal Montgomery accepted the official and unconditional surrender of the German army in northwest Europe at his headquarters on Lüneburg Heath in Germany.

In the Netherlands, General Foulkes, commander of the I Canadian Corps, feared that the German Twenty-fifth Army might hold out despite the official surrender. Foulkes drew up a separate surrender document and on 5 May summoned his German counterpart,

General Blaskowitz, to the Hotel de Wereld in Wageningen to sign his capitulation. Prince Bernhard, acting as commander-in-chief of the Dutch Interior Forces, was also present, along with reporters and cameramen.

A detailed document of surrender was passed to Blaskowitz, who asked for 24 hours to assess whether he could meet the Allied demands and to inform his troops of the capitulation. He returned the next day to sign the official surrender of all German forces in the Netherlands.

Today, Wageningen calls itself the "City of Liberation", and is marked by an LRE audiospot. Every year on 4–5 May, it hosts a parade and freedom festival, while the historic Hotel de Wereld (hoteldewereld. nl) remains open for business.

cluding British lieutenant John Grayburn, German Hauptsturmführer Viktor Eberhard Gräbner and the Dutch captain Jacob Groenewoud, who fought and died at Arnhem. The town's tourist information office is also located here.

Airborne Museum "Hartenstein"
Utrechtseweg 232, Oosterbeek,
Ⓦ airbornemuseum.nl ☺⁜

Given the intensity of the battle that raged here in September 1944, it's surprising that the Hotel Hartenstein, just outside Arnhem and the villa-headquarters of the British First Airborne Division during the assault, wasn't razed to the ground. The building, which lies just to the west of the village centre, survived the war; afterwards, it was restored and adapted to house the Airborne Museum.

The museum experience begins with a first-rate battle film, making skilful use of original footage – including a chilling scene in which German machine gunners blaze away at paratroopers dropping from the sky. Ensuing rooms hold a series of small exhibitions on some of the individuals who took part in Operation Market Garden, perhaps most memorably Private Albert Willingham, who died protecting a Dutch woman from a German grenade. There's also a piece of wallpaper salvaged from the hotel, where British snipers marked up the score of their hits and inscribed the words, "Fuck the Gerrys". A further display in the basement (the "Airborne experience") recreates the scene in the hotel as the Germans closed in – the British were besieged at Hartenstein for a week before finally retreating across the river.

The Army Film and Photographic Unit landed with the British forces, and it's their photographs that stick in the memory most of all: grimly cheerful soldiers hauling in their parachutes; tense, tired faces during the fighting; and shattered Dutch villages.

Airborne War Cemetery
Van Limburg Stirumweg, Oosterbeek

This Commonwealth war cemetery contains the graves of 1754 Allied troops, including most of the soldiers who were killed during Operation Market Garden. American remains, meanwhile, were either repatriated or interred in the cemetery of the American Battle Monuments Commission in Margraten. The "Cross of Sacrifice", the cemetery's main monument, supports a bronze sword and is a symbol for all the soldiers who died in the Netherlands during World War II.

Information Centre: The Poles of Driel
Kerkstraat 27, Driel, Ⓦ driel-polen.nl ☺⁜

The Information Centre: The Poles of Driel provides valuable insight into the battle fought by the 1st Polish Independent Parachute Brigade in the village of Driel during Operation Market Garden. Interesting exhibits trace how the brigade was formed, the dishonourable way the Poles were treated after the failure of Operation Market Garden, and the friendship that subsequently developed between the people of Driel and the Polish parachutists.

Infocentre WW2 Nijmegen
Ridderstraat 27, Nijmegen,
Ⓦ infocentreww2.com

Opened in February 2019, this brand-new information centre in Nijmegen is designed to introduce visitors to the wartime history of the region, with an overview of the stories, heritage and museums on offer.

Canadian War Cemetery
Zevenheuvelenweg, Groesbeek

The largest Commonwealth war cemetery in the Netherlands, the Canadian War Cemetery contains the graves of hundreds of men killed in neighbouring regions in the closing months of the war, mostly after Operation Market Garden. Many of the dead were brought here from Germany – General Crerar, commander of Canadian forces in Europe, ordered that no Canadian should be buried on German soil. All the Canadians who lost their lives during Operation Veritable – except for one man – were buried or reburied here.

The cemetery also contains the graves of 267 soldiers from Britain, as well as a few from Belgium, Poland, the Netherlands, Russia, New Zealand and Yugoslavia. Just inside the entrance to the cemetery is a memorial wall bearing the names of 1047 military personnel missing in action.

The National Liberation Museum 1944–1945
Wylerbaan 4, Groesbeek,
ⓦ liberationmuseum.com ☺

During Operation Market Garden, paratroopers from the 82nd US Airborne Division landed in the area where the National Liberation Museum is now located. From here, they started their advance towards the bridges at Grave and Nijmegen; the capture of these would open up the region between the Maas, Waal and Rhine rivers to the Allied advance.

This area, around Groesbeek and Nijmegen, was also the stepping stone from which Operation Veritable, aimed at clearing the Reichswald Forest, was launched in February 1945. By then, the road leading to the museum had become the front line separating the Allied and German forces. Operation Veritable opened with the heaviest artillery bombardment seen on the Western Front during World War II – more than half a million shells were fired at the German front line.

The National Liberation Museum 1944–1945 has recently emerged from a comprehensive rebuild, reopening in mid-2019 to mark the start of the commemorative 75 Years of Freedom programme. A striking new building houses its excellent collection relating to Operation Market Garden, the battle for the Reichswald and World War II more generally. Its new incarnation has been developed with a strong international outlook and a specific focus on Germany.

Camp Vught National Memorial
Lunettenlaan 600, Vught,
ⓦ nmkampvught.nl

Opened in January 1943, Camp Vught was the only official SS concentration camp in the Netherlands. Modelled on camps in Germany, it was divided into two sections, one for political prisoners brought here from Belgium and the Netherlands, the other for Jews.

Most of the Jewish inmates were subsequently moved to Westerbork (see p.211) before being transported to the death camps further east. Predictably, many people died here in the cruellest of circumstances or were executed in the woods nearby. Although it's a reconstruction, and only a fraction of the size it used to be, Camp Vught still makes a vivid impression.

» Men's Island

After the overall failure of Operation Market Garden in September 1944, several front lines were established on the floodplain between the Waal and Rhine rivers. The Betuwe, as this region is known, had suffered little during the initial German invasion of the Netherlands in 1940. During the years of occupation that followed the population had faced hardship, but this was nothing compared to what they had to endure from September 1944 onwards.

Having become the new front line on the Western Front, fighting overwhelmed parts of the Betuwe, with heavy shelling from both sides. The civilian population was caught up in the violence, and the area was soon evacuated. By December 1944, only about 1000 men remained to farm the land and take care of their cattle. The pocket of the region they inhabited, around Lent, Oosterhout and Ressen, became known as "Men's Island".

The affected parts of the Betuwe were liberated in April 1945, just weeks before the German surrender. By then, the inhabitants of this unfortunate region had suffered greatly. Their houses had been damaged or destroyed, their land flooded, and many loved ones lost. For the population of the Betuwe, the Liberation was a bitter-sweet experience.

Overloon War Museum
Museumpark 1, Overloon,
Ⓦ oorlogsmuseum.nl Ⓔ

The affluent little town of Overloon in Noord Brabant was rebuilt after the war, having been devastated in the eponymous battle. The final stages of the Battle of Overloon took place in the woods to the east of town, where hand-to-hand combat eventually secured the area.

The result of a proposal by local resident Harry van Daal, the Overloon War Museum was developed on a section of the former battlefield to commemorate the fighting that took place here. Founded using military hardware left behind in the wake of World War II, this excellent museum is openly didactic, intended as "an admonition and warning, a denouncement of war and violence." The collection is particularly strong on military machinery, with tanks, rocket launchers, armoured cars, a Bailey bridge and a V1 flying bomb on display.

Museum Wings of Liberation
Sonseweg 39, Best,
Ⓦ en.bevrijdendevleugels.com

This museum just outside Eindhoven, located on "Hell's Highway", explores what life was like under German occupation and the final liberation. Expect authentic military equipment, including vehicles, and beautiful dioramas.

Bergen op Zoom cemeteries
Ruytershoveweg 1, Bergen op Zoom,
Ⓦ cwgc.org

Bergen op Zoom is located in Noord Brabant, close to Zeeland and the "neck" of South Beveland. Some 3km east of the town are two adjacent Commonwealth cemeteries: Bergen op Zoom British War Cemetery and Bergen op Zoom Canadian War Cemetery, separated by a thick screen of trees. Many of the dead interred here died in the Battle of the Scheldt and other actions in the southwest Netherlands.

Amsterdam and around

Along with the rest of the country, Amsterdam was occupied in May 1940. It was liberated by the German capitulation that ended the war in the Netherlands on 5 May 1945 (see p.202).

Even after the war was officially over, incidents of violence still occurred. Some German forces simply refused to lay down their arms, and clashed with members of the Dutch Interior Forces or resistance fighters. These incidents led to the death of 19 civilians in Amsterdam.

Unlike Rotterdam, Amsterdam was spared physical damage during the war, but its people still suffered, living in constant fear of attracting the attention of the authorities. As a largely open, tolerant, mercantile community, Amsterdam had attracted many foreign Jews who sought safety here before the war. Nazi Germany's virulent anti-Semitism dealt a devastating blow to the city. After the war, the fate of teenager Anne Frank provided a human face to the impersonal cruelty of the Holocaust, and Amsterdam has several monuments related to its Jewish past.

Several other sites connected to the war and the Liberation, near Utrecht and Amersfoort, are within easy reach of Amsterdam.

» Amsterdam and around sites

Anne Frank House
Westermarkt 20, Amsterdam,
Ⓦ annefrank.org

A poignant memorial to the Holocaust, Anne Frank House is one of Amsterdam's most visited sights. Since the publication of her diaries, Anne Frank has become extraordinarily famous, in the first instance for recording the iniquities of the Holocaust, and latter-

ly as a symbol of the fight against oppression in general and racism in particular.

Anne Frank House is in the premises on Prinsengracht where the Frank and Van Daan families lived in secrecy for two years before being discovered by the Nazis. Well-chosen displays, old offices and filmed interviews with some of the leading characters, including Anne's friend Hanneli Goslar and Anne Frank's father, Otto, fill out the background. There are also displays on the persecution of the Jews – from arrest and deportation through to the concentration camps. Further sections are devoted to Anne as a writer/diarist; information on the Franks' Dutch helpers; and the importance of Anne's diary to other prisoners, most notably Nelson Mandela.

Behind a hinged bookcase are the secret rooms that were occupied in 1942–44 by eight people – only one of whom, Otto Frank, would survive the war. Anne Frank was among 100,000 Dutch Jews who died during World War II, but this, her final home, provides one of the most enduring testaments to its horrors and, despite the number of visitors, most people find a visit very moving.

Verzetsmuseum (Dutch Resistance Museum)
Plantage Kerklaan 61, Amsterdam,
Ⓦ verzetsmuseum.org

The excellent Dutch Resistance Museum, located in a former synagogue, tells the story of the 25,000 Dutch men and women who risked their lives to oppose the Nazi regime. Thoughtfully presented, the main gangway examines the experience of the majority of the population, dealing honestly with the fine balance between cooperation and collaboration. Side rooms are devoted to different aspects of the resistance, from the brave determination of

Biography
Anne Frank

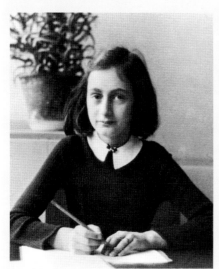

Anne Frank's father, Otto Frank, was a Jewish businessman who fled Germany in December 1933 after Hitler came to power, moving to Amsterdam, where he established a successful spice-trading business on the Prinsengracht. After the German occupation of the Netherlands, Jewish refugees thought they could avoid trouble by keeping their heads down. However, by 1942 Amsterdam's Jews were isolated and conspicuous, being confined to certain parts of the city and forced to wear a yellow star. Round-ups were increasingly common. In desperation, Otto Frank decided to move the family into the unused back rooms of their Prinsengracht premises.

The Franks went into hiding in July 1942, along with a Jewish business partner and his wife and son, the Van Pels (renamed the Van Daans in the *Diary*). Their new "home" was separated from the rest of the building by a bookcase that doubled as a door. As far as everyone else was concerned, they had fled to Switzerland. So began a two-year incarceration in the *achterhuis*, or Secret Annexe, and the two families were joined in November 1942 by a dentist friend, Fritz Pfeffer (the *Diary's* Albert Dussel), bringing the number of occupants to eight. Otto's trusted Dutch office staff continued working in the front part of the building, regularly bringing supplies and news of the outside world. In her diary Anne Frank describes the day-to-day lives of the inhabitants of the annexe: the quarrels, frequent in such a claustrophobic environment, the celebrations of birthdays, or of a piece of good news from the Allied Front; and of her own, slightly unreal, adolescence.

In the summer of 1944, the atmosphere was optimistic; liberation seemed within reach – but it wasn't to happen soon enough. A Dutch collaborator betrayed the Franks, and the Gestapo arrived and forced open the bookcase. The occupants of the annexe were arrested and dispatched to Westerbork – the transit camp in the north of the country where all Dutch Jews were processed before being moved to Belsen, Auschwitz or Sobibór. Of the eight who had lived in the annexe, only Otto Frank survived. Anne and her sister died of typhus within a short time of each other in Belsen, just one week before the German surrender. Remarkably, Anne's diary survived the raid, with one of the family's Dutch helpers handing it to Otto on his return from Auschwitz. In 1947, Otto decided to publish his daughter's diary and, since its appearance, *The Diary of a Young Girl* has been translated into over sixty languages and sold millions of copies worldwide.

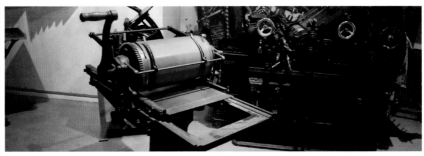

the Communist Party to more ad hoc responses like the so-called Melkstaking (Milk Strike) of 1943, when hundreds of milk producers refused to deliver in protest at the Germans' threatened deportation of 300,000 former (demobilized) Dutch soldiers to labour camps in Germany. A range of ingenious objects – forging tools, a hollow chessboard to hide false documents and a "broadcasting suitcase" containing a radio – depict the challenges of operating undercover. Other poignant exhibits include a farewell letter written by a condemned prisoner and a tiny box of potatoes sent from the country to the city – a godsend to anyone trying to survive the Hunger Winter (see p.210) that the Nazis inflicted from November 1944 until the country was liberated in May 1945.

Hollandsche Schouwburg
Plantage Middenlaan 24, Amsterdam,
ⓦ jck.nl

Originally a Jewish theatre, in 1942 this building was commandeered by the Nazis for use as a holding centre for Amsterdam Jews. An estimated 60,000 Jews passed through here on their way to concentration and extermination camps. After the war, the building was left unused for many years before being turned into a national memorial to the Holocaust. The front of the edifice

has been refurbished to display a list of the dead and an eternal flame along with a small exhibition on the plight of the city's Jews, but the old auditorium out at the back has been left as an empty, roofless shell. A memorial column of basalt on a Star of David base stands where the stage once was, an intensely mournful monument to suffering of unfathomable proportions.

National Monument on the Dam
Dam, Amsterdam

To one side of Amsterdam's main square is the country's National Monument, where two sculpted lions commemorate the Dutch people who were killed during World War II. Every year on 4 May, the day before the war ended in the Netherlands, a ceremony called Dodneherdenking (Remembrance of the Dead) is held here.

National Military Museum
Soesterberg Verlengde Paltzerweg 1,
Soest, ⓦ nmm.nl/en

The National Military Museum, situated in a former airbase between Amersfoort and Utrecht (southeast of Amsterdam), deals with all wars – including World War II. Its main purpose is to demonstrate the importance of the armed forces to modern societies.

Northern Netherlands, western Netherlands and the islands

Most of the Netherlands' south was liberated in September 1944 during Operation Market Garden and the Battle of the Scheldt, but the north remained in German hands for months to come.

After the ultimate failure of Operation Market Garden, Allied commanders decided that the liberation of the Netherlands would require the dispersal of their forces. This would stretch the Allies' limited resources, so priority was first afforded to thrusting eastwards towards the Rhine and into the German heartland. This resulted in a strange situation. When the final drive came to clear the north and west of the Netherlands, it was launched from the east – from Germany.

In March 1945 the Allies breached the German defences and crossed the Rhine. The Allied forces were now divided into three groups: two headed deeper into Germany, while the third swung round to liberate the Netherlands. They found a country in the depths of the so-called Hunger Winter that claimed 20,000 lives (see p.210).

The task of clearing the northern part of the Netherlands was given to the I Canadian Corps. They were assisted by units from the British XXX Corps, the Polish 1st Armoured Division and the Belgian 5th SAS.

Combat at this stage of the war was sporadic and depended on whether individual German commanders chose to keep fighting. In certain areas, the German forces put up stiff opposition (the terrain, with its many streams, canals and waterways, favoured the defenders); elsewhere they chose to surrender. Many ordinary soldiers laid down their arms in the final weeks of the war.

» Texel Uprising

The 822nd Queen Tamar infantry battalion, stationed on the island of Texel, was made up of 800 Georgian and 400 German soldiers. The Georgians had been taken prisoner on the Eastern Front earlier in the war and chose to join the German army rather than go to prisoner of war camps. In early April, the battalion received orders to transfer to the mainland to fight the Allies. The Georgians became worried that if Germany lost the war, as seemed likely, they would fall into Soviet hands and be dealt with as traitors. In the early hours of 6 April, they staged an uprising, led by their commander Shalva Loladze and assisted by the Dutch resistance. On the first morning some 400 German soldiers on Texel were slaughtered, mostly in their sleep. The Georgians were unable to take control of two gun batteries at the north and south of the island, however, and the Germans sent reinforcements from the mainland. It still took five weeks to put the rebellion down. During that time, 565 Georgians, 800 Germans and 120 Texel residents were killed. Fighting continued even as Germany was signing its Instrument of Surrender in Berlin on 8 May; the violence was only stopped by the arrival of Canadian troops on 20 May.

❯❯ The Hunger Winter

In support of Operation Market Garden in September 1944, and in anticipation of imminent liberation, the exiled Dutch prime minister, Pieter Gerbrandy, instructed the resistance to organize a national railway strike that would cripple Dutch infrastructure and hamper German troop movements. When Market Garden failed to achieve its aims, the country was effectively divided into an occupied northern section and a largely liberated southern one. Incensed by what they regarded as Dutch "betrayal", the Germans decided to wreak a slow and cruel revenge by minimizing the already meagre food supplies available to Dutch citizens.

By early October, Gerbrandy was having desperate meetings with Churchill, during which he predicted a humanitarian disaster and suggested that the Swedish government be allowed to intervene with deliveries of food. Churchill was reluctant to comply, believing that relief supplies would simply be consumed by the Germans, but by the end of the month Eisenhower had agreed in principle to such an operation. By this point winter was approaching, and it would turn out to be one of the harshest on record. To make matters worse, transport of coal from the south had stopped and gas and electricity were being cut off. People were resorting to chopping down trees and ransacking abandoned houses – some belonging to deported Jewish families – for fuel.

Throughout the winter the situation worsened, especially in the major towns where people were trying to survive on as little as 400–800 calories per day. There was no meat or milk available, only small quantities of flour and potatoes, forcing people to fall back on sugar beets and tulip bulbs as staples. Many town dwellers headed into the country seeking food, bartering their possessions with farmers for whatever they could get. The agreed relief convoys from Sweden finally began at the end of January 1945, but they only scratched the surface of what was required. People were now starving in large numbers, making them more susceptible to disease, with the elderly and very young particularly vulnerable.

Following negotiations with the Germans not to shoot down relief planes, the Allies began a series of air drops at the end of April: nearly 7000 tons of food were dropped by the RAF and the Canadian Air Force between the 29 April and 8 May, and a further 4000 tons by the USAAF between 1–8 May. But it wasn't until the German surrender on 6 May that a full-scale and systematic relief operation could begin, by which time an estimated 20,000 Dutch citizens had died from starvation.

❯❯ Northern Netherlands, western Netherlands and the islands sites

Holten Canadian War Cemetery

Eekhoornweg 10, Holten

Canadian troops were principally responsible for the liberation of the northern and eastern Netherlands in the spring of 1945. Nearly 1400 soldiers who lost their lives in the campaign are buried here – the headstones belonging to teenagers are especially moving. Adjacent to the cemetery is a visitor information centre, which explains the events of the war through films, personal memoirs and photographs.

Memory Museum

Grotestraat 13, Nijverdal,
🖤 memorymuseum.nl

As its name suggests, the Memory Museum exists to preserve information about World War II, from the rise of National Socialism to the Liberation.

Fries Verzetsmuseum (Resistance Museum Friesland)

Wilhelminaplein 92, Leeuwarden

Objects, photographs, film fragments and documents retell the World War II stories that have been passed down from generation to generation in Friesland. One of the most spectacular acts of the resistance in the area was a raid on the Huis van Bewaring prison in Leeuwarden on 8 December 1944 by members of the armed group known as the Knokploegen ("Strong-arm Boys"). They managed to free 51 captive resistance fighters within half an hour, without a shot being fired.

Camp Westerbork National Memorial Centre

Westerbork Oosthalen 8, Hooghalen,
🖤 kampwesterbork.nl

Shortly before the outbreak of World War II, the Dutch government built a camp near the town of Hooghalen to accommodate (mainly Jewish) German refugees. Camp KZ Westerbork was later used by the German occupiers as a transit camp. Many Dutch Jews, Sinti, Roma, resistance combatants and political adversaries were imprisoned here before being transferred to concentration and extermination camps in Germany and occupied Poland. Anne Frank was deported on the last train leaving Camp Westerbork on 3 September 1944.

» Flying bombs over Overijssel

In the winter of 1944–1945, everyone living in the area between Almelo, Nijverdal, Deventer and Zutphen was used to the sound of sputtering rockets. These were flying bombs, equipped with jet engines, popularly known as the V1 and V2. The Germans called them "weapons of revenge" – launched as retaliation for the invasion of Normandy and the death of German troops.

German engineers developed these weapons under considerable pressure from Hitler. They were built using slave labour, first in Peenemünde on the German north coast (see p.305) and later in abandoned mines in northern France. Working under inhumane conditions, many slave labourers took the opportunity to sabotage production, and many rockets malfunctioned.

On the night of 25–26 March 1945, a week before its liberation, things went terribly wrong above Rijssen in Overijssel, when a V1 fired from Almelo crashed in the town centre. Then, as the flames were being extinguished, a British plane nosedived towards the conflagration and dropped its high-explosive bombs. That night, 23 people were killed, and many more were wounded.

The National Memorial Centre Westerbork explains the history of the camp.

Georgian War Cemetery Loladse

Hoge Berg, Texel, 🖤 texel.net

This cemetery on the island of Texel, which made up part of the Atlantic Wall (see p.115), contains the remains of Georgian soldiers killed in a mutiny within the German army, the Texel Uprising (see p.209).

75 PERSONAL
LIFE CHANGING
WAR STORIES

BRABANT REMEMBERS

40 45

AR
Unique
Augmented
Reality app
for iOS and
Android

EXPERIENCE 75 PERSONAL LIFE-CHANGING WAR STORIES

What's your function?

Spy

Resistance fighter

Person in hiding

Next

ANDROID APP ON
Google Play

Download on the
App Store

Find the *Brabant Remembers – Living History*
AR app in the App Store and Google Play.

The Second World War provided Brabant with countless differing stories. Both anxious and hopeful moments have found their place in history. Brabant Remembers brings this history to life in a poignant Augmented Reality App.

Re-live stories of people in wartime Brabant and visit the places where their lives were changed dramatically. Feel the doubt, the fear, the hope and the courage of people who had to make choices with life-changing consequences for themselves and others.

The *Brabant Remembers – Living History* AR app allows you to step right into these personal stories. Where somebody once had to make a life-changing decision, you are now faced with the same choice. Download the free *Brabant Remembers – Living History* AR app now, and share your experiences on social media.

www.brabantremembers.com

Provincie Noord-Brabant

vfonds
invests in
PEACE

CROSS ✕ ROADS

CELEBRATE
75 YEARS OF
FREEDOM

EUROPE
REMEMBERS

Atrocities

For all its savagery, modern warfare is underpinned by strict rules. Nevertheless, a string of atrocities was committed by both sides during World War II.

The rules laid down by the Hague conventions of 1899 and 1907 and the Geneva Convention of 1929 (see p.286) governed World War II. These international agreements were designed to be heeded as law, but there was no single body capable of enforcing them. Obeying the rubric of the Hague and Geneva conventions was up to the honour and ethics of each country, commander, division and individual.

Throughout the Liberation, and especially at Nuremberg, the Western Allies sought to keep the moral high ground by adhering to the rule of law, but they played a close game. Mustard gas was strictly prohibited by the Geneva protocol on chemical weapons of 1925, but the Allies surreptitiously shipped large quantities of it to Italy. While they claimed the gas was intended only as a "plan B" in case the Germans used it first, the secret was revealed when a ship loaded with mustard gas blew up in an air raid in December 1943 – inadvertently poisoning anyone who came into contact with it.

The behaviour of war was not easily regulated. On the battlefield, conduct was judged by the upper echelons of the military hierarchy – with minimum political involvement. Atrocities, in contravention of international law and moral codes, occurred on both sides of the conflict throughout the Liberation.

On the Eastern Front, in particular, the German and Soviet armies were locked in a savage fight that paid little heed to any international regulations. In many cases, respect for the enemy was condemned outright and all forms of brutality condoned.

Turning humans into soldiers

The common soldier, on the front line, was forced to make many of the hardest moral decisions. Combatants were expected to kill to help secure victory, but no more than was necessary. The job of the army was to mentally equip its cadets to kill. Military training was – and still is today – designed to ease its recruits through the taboo against taking human life, to motivate them to do their duty under a temporary moral code that tips to the other extreme. At the same time, motivation for action must be born of noble reasons, of moral superiority and justified hatred of a corrupt enemy.

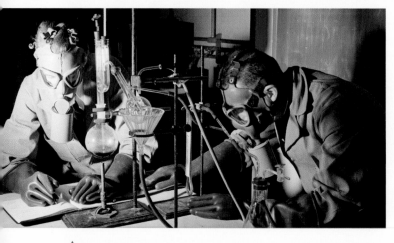

▲
Military chemists don gas masks while purifying mustard gas

In reality, the majority of soldiers were young men with strong emotions who were pushed to the extreme. War demanded difficult choices in complicating and confusing circumstances. None of this condones the atrocities that occurred during World War II and the Liberation; nevertheless, it helps to understand the context in which they took place.

Atrocities against prisoners of war

Taking prisoners in World War II (see p.286) was particularly complex. The conventions related to prisoners of war seemed clear when written down: an enemy soldier with his hands in the air or waving a white flag was not to be harmed. On the battlefield, it was harder for a young recruit – conditioned to loathe the enemy – to switch from murderous hatred to compassion and responsibility in an instant. In addition, some commanders discouraged their men from taking captives because of the inconvenience they caused. In many cases, unarmed men died as the result of split-second decisions in which soldiers were forced to calculate whether taking a prisoner would affect the outcome of a battle. There is no way of knowing exactly how many men were killed in dubious circumstances on either side of the conflict.

On isolated occasions, soldiers took a step beyond the grey area of surrender. In two separate

German POWs watch newsreels of atrocities committed at Buchenwald, Mittelbau-Dora and other Nazi concentration camps
▼

incidents near Biscari in southern Sicily, on 14 July 1943, American infantrymen lined up and killed a total of 73 German and Italian prisoners of war. "Battle fatigue" was cited as one of the principal causes of the massacres. The German armed forces committed numerous atrocities during the war, too. Most took place on the Eastern Front, but the Western Front was not exempt. On 17 December 1944, an SS unit took 84 US prisoners at a crossroads near

Malmédy in Belgium during the Battle of the Bulge (see p.171). Treating the prisoners properly would have handicapped the German offensive, which relied on speed. Instead, as the Americans stood in lines with their hands raised, the Nazi troops opened fire with machine guns and pistols.

Other atrocities

A number of other atrocities were committed in World War II. The German state was responsible for a great number of them as it sought to eliminate its political opponents and anyone who fell foul of its racial policies. The fate of the Jews and other concentration and extermination camp victims, of course, constitutes a category of atrocity apart (see p.252). The liberators of the camps were stunned by what they found: by the depths of depravity human beings in uniforms could sink to when given the upper hand.

Atrocities on the Western Front were more often investigated and documented than those on the Eastern Front, because they were comparatively less frequent. In France, cold-blooded massacres were carried out by German troops at Tulle, Maillé and Oradour-sur-Glane; and in Italy at Sant'Anna di Stazema and Monte Sole. The Wola massacre during the Warsaw Rising, however, dwarfs them all – with 50,000 victims.

Individual atrocities occurred almost everywhere that soldiers went. Civilians were defenceless against under-disciplined troops who sought relief and reward for the miseries they were forced to endure by exploiting the weak and vulnerable. Rape was particularly prevalent: it was difficult to prevent and all too often went unpunished.

▲
**Lines of corpses after
the Wola Massacre**

Defining an atrocity

Some mass killings are harder to classify as atrocities. Should the premeditated firebombing of German cities harbouring tens of thousands of civilians be considered an atrocity or a legitimate military strategy? What are we to make of the generals who ordered their troops to advance towards certain death in battles that could not be won? Can the bombing of the *Cap Arcona* (see p.309), loaded with prisoners, be excused as an understandable mistake? It is worth considering, too, whether extenuating circumstances can ever turn would-be atrocities into tragedies in which no one is to blame. Wartime killings and calamities frequently inhabit a moral grey area.

Within the context of war, an atrocity is defined as excessive cruelty or violence without justification. Atrocities are carried out in situations of unequal power and serve no military or political objective, other than inducing terror and despair. Usually perpetuated for selfish reasons, these acts are executed with complete disregard for the victims. Atrocities violate both the law and common ethical codes.

The committal of atrocities is usually accompanied by a lack of remorse and responsibility, and the perpetrators in World War II often could not understand what they had done wrong. A frequent justification was the "Nuremberg Defence": that they were carrying out orders – implied, verbal, precise or printed. Many perpetrators claimed they were just complying with broad orders from above, and some high-ranking German army commanders escaped prosecution for war crimes in this way.

Other atrocities were justified by necessity. It was claimed, for example, that the bombing of Monte Cassino Abbey in Italy in February 1944 was crucial to the Allied campaign – even if there were civilians sheltered inside. Self-defence was also a common response. "If I hadn't killed him first", a soldier claimed, "he would have killed me."

Atrocities in hindsight

With the benefit of distance and hindsight, it is easy to condemn individual events of the war as atrocities. But it's important to consider whether it's fair to apply the same moral codes that govern modern European society today to a front-line soldier in World War II.

Eisenhower was said to have been mortified when troops under his command went on a killing spree after the liberation of Dachau concentration camp. The soldiers were so appalled and incensed by what they saw that they executed at least 28 SS guards who had already surrendered. Eisenhower understood that the entire rationale of the Liberation was that the Allies – the western democracies at least – would founder if American soldiers sank to the same level as their Nazi foe. He

called for "criminal conduct" to be fully investigated and punished accordingly, but it rarely was. It was difficult for a commander to ask his troops – his brothers in arms – to fight shoulder to shoulder and then discipline them for killing an enemy who had committed barbarous acts but later surrendered.

Long after the war, there were attempts to relativize atrocities and their consequences – to judge the liberators by the same standards with which they judged the defeated Nazis. The results were stark. If the Americans in charge of Biscari were tried in the same way as the Nazi officers who had allowed Malmédy to occur, General Bradley would have received a sentence of ten years' imprisonment; General Patton would have been sentenced to life.

It would be a sad conclusion to concede that every war has its share of atrocities; that the combination of lethal weapons and the stress of battle inevitably leads to appalling acts of carnage. The Liberation certainly witnessed terrible massacres and atrocities by both the Allied and the Nazi armies, which caused immense suffering and loss of life. On the Eastern Front, the Soviets exacted terrible reprisals for the genocidal campaign Nazi Germany had waged there.

At the same time, most soldiers active in World War II – and many with the opportunity to do

▲
Skeletal camp prisoners

so – did not engage in atrocities of any kind. On both sides, the vast majority of individuals adhered to the rules of the Hague and Geneva conventions and their own moral codes, despite finding themselves in extreme circumstances. Maybe there's more to learn from the ordinary men and women who held their heads above water than those who drowned in the mire of war.

Poland

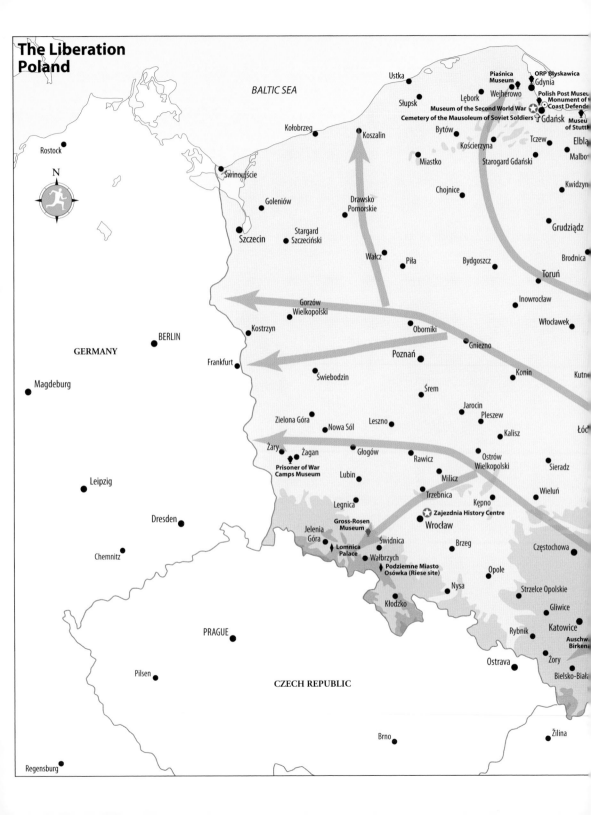

The Liberation
Poland

BALTIC SEA

N

GERMANY

BERLIN

Magdeburg

Leipzig

Dresden

Chemnitz

PRAGUE

Pilsen

CZECH REPUBLIC

Brno

Regensburg

Žilina

Rostock

Świnoujście

Szczecin

Goleniów

Stargard
Szczeciński

Kołobrzeg

Koszalin

Słupsk

Ustka

Piaśnica
Museum

ORP Błyskawica
Gdynia
Wejherowo
Lębork
Polish Post Museum
Monument of
Coast Defence
Museum of the Second World War
Cemetery of the Mausoleum of Soviet Soldiers
Gdańsk
Museum
of Stutt

Bytów

Kościerzyna

Miastko

Chojnice

Starogard Gdański

Tczew

Elbląg

Malbo

Kwidzyn

Drawsko
Pomorskie

Wałcz

Piła

Bydgoszcz

Grudziądz

Brodnica

Toruń

Inowrocław

Włocławek

Gorzów
Wielkopolski

Kostrzyn

Oborniki

Frankfurt

Świebodzin

Poznań

Gniezno

Konin

Kutn

Śrem

Jarocin
Pleszew

Łód

Zielona Góra

Nowa Sól

Leszno

Kalisz

Żary

Żagan

Głogów

Rawicz

Ostrów
Wielkopolski

Sieradz

Prisoner of War
Camps Museum

Lubin

Milicz

Wieluń

Trzebnica

Kępno

Legnica

Jelenia
Góra

Gross-Rosen
Museum

Zajezdnia History Centre

Wrocław

Świdnica

Brzeg

Częstochowa

Lomnica
Palace

Wałbrzych

Podziemne Miasto
Osówka (Riese site)

Opole

Nysa

Strzelce Opolskie

Kłodzko

Gliwice

Katowice

Rybnik

Auschw.
Birkena

Ostrava

Żory

Bielsko-Biała

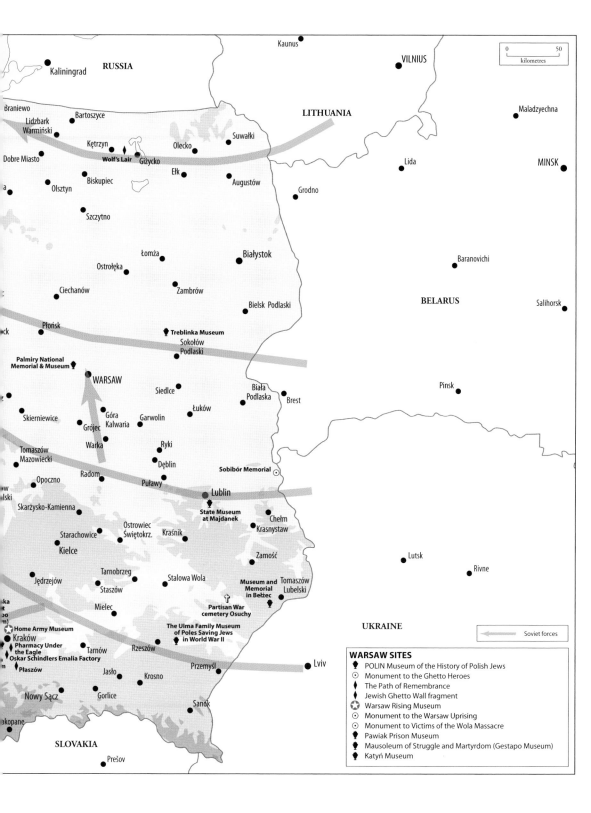

RUSSIA

Kaunus

VILNIUS

Kaliningrad

Maladzyechna

Braniewo
Lidzbark
Warmiński

LITHUANIA

Bartoszyce

Suwałki

Dobre Miasto

Kętrzyn

Olecko

Lida

MINSK

Wolf's Lair

Giżycko

Ełk

Biskupiec

Grodno

Olsztyn

Augustów

Szczytno

Baranovichi

Łomża

Białystok

Ostrołęka

Ciechanów

Zambrów

BELARUS

Salihorsk

Bielsk Podlaski

Płońsk

Treblinka Museum

Sokołów
Podlaski

Pinsk

Palmiry National
Memorial & Museum

WARSAW

Siedlce

Biała
Podlaska

Brest

Skierniewice

Góra
Kalwaria

Garwolin

Łuków

Grójec

Warka

Ryki

Tomaszów
Mazowiecki

Dęblin

Sobibór Memorial

Opoczno

Radom

Puławy

Lublin

Skarżysko-Kamienna

State Museum
at Majdanek

Chełm

Ostrowiec
Świętokrz.

Kraśnik

Krasnystaw

Starachowice

Kielce

Zamość

Lutsk

Tarnobrzeg

Stalowa Wola

Jędrzejów

Staszów

Museum and
Memorial
in Bełżec

Tomaszów
Lubelski

Rivne

Mielec

Partisan War
cemetery Osuchy

Home Army Museum

The Ulma Family Museum
of Poles Saving Jews
in World War II

UKRAINE

Soviet forces

Kraków

Pharmacy Under
the Eagle

Tarnów

Rzeszów

Oskar Schindlers Emalia Factory

Płaszów

Jasło

Krosno

Przemyśl

Lviv

Nowy Sącz

Gorlice

Sanók

akopane

SLOVAKIA

Prešov

WARSAW SITES
- POLIN Museum of the History of Polish Jews
- Monument to the Ghetto Heroes
- The Path of Remembrance
- Jewish Ghetto Wall fragment
- Warsaw Rising Museum
- Monument to the Warsaw Uprising
- Monument to Victims of the Wola Massacre
- Pawiak Prison Museum
- Mausoleum of Struggle and Martyrdom (Gestapo Museum)
- Katyń Museum

0   50
kilometres

The Liberation Poland

Poland was liberated, not by the Americans or the British, but by the Soviet Union. For the Poles this was a bitter irony.

Having had to endure the onslaught of the Nazi invasion on 1 September 1939, Poland underwent a second invasion at the hands of the Red Army just sixteen days later. These two events – and the devastating occupation that followed – were to set the scene for Poland's liberation five years later.

The Polish campaign

Hitler's pretext for invading Poland was Germany's claim to the port of Danzig (modern Gdańsk). In the aftermath of World War I,

» Officials discuss the details of the German–Soviet demarcation line following the invasion of Poland in 1939

when Poland re-emerged as an independent nation, the country's redrawn borders provided access to the Baltic via a "corridor" that separated East Prussia from the rest of Germany. Danzig stood at the top of this corridor, neither Polish nor German, but a free city under the protection of the League of Nations. Many of its citizens, most of whom were German, resented this arrangement.

Hitler used the corridor dispute to try and force the Polish state to hand over Danzig to Germany, but the Poles refused any territorial concessions. For Hitler this was reason enough to invade. The German assault came from several points simultaneously and employed a new tactic, *Blitzkrieg* (lightning war), in which attacks were fast, intense and co-ordinated. The Polish Army was outnumbered and its forces spread out, and despite valiant counteroffensives, was only staving off the inevitable. Poland's military command ordered a retreat to the southwest of the country, at which point the Red Army invaded the country from the East, claiming to be protecting Poland's Ukrainian and Belorusian minorities. After nearly a month of incessant aerial and artillery bombardment, resulting in around 40,000 civilian deaths, Warsaw, Poland's capital, finally surrendered to Nazi invasion on 27 September 1939.

Poland partitioned

Following the two invasions, Poland was divided into three main areas under the terms of the Nazi-Soviet Pact (see p.26): the west of the country was assimilated into the German Reich, with the ultimate aim of full "Germanization": the removal of all Slavs, Jews and other "undesirables" and their replacement with German colonists.

The east of the country, known as Kresy to the Poles, was handed over to the Soviets (though Hitler was to renege on his agreement, invading the Soviet Union in June 1941). This included parts of Lithuania, Belarus and Ukraine, many of whose inhabitants were nationalists who resented rule by Poland, the Soviet Union, or anyone else.

The central territory – the rump of Poland – became a German protectorate, renamed the General Government, with Kraków as its capital. A "dumping ground" for Poles removed from the west of the country, it was to be economically exploited for the benefit of the Reich. It was also where the first death camps were built in the spring of 1942.

Potential opposition was targeted by both invading powers. It is estimated that the Nazis killed a third of all Catholic priests, the same proportion of doctors and around fifty percent of Poland's lawyers. Similarly, the Soviets imprisoned or executed anyone they thought of as ideological enemies, most infamously thousands of Polish army and police officers who were shot and buried in Katyń forest and other sites.

Many of those killed by the Nazis died in concentration camps, labour camps, or in extermination camps, such as Auschwitz-Birkenau. In addition to enslaving the Poles, the Nazis aimed to annihilate Poland's entire Jewish population, murdering them in gas chambers and mass shootings, or working them to death. Those who hid Jews were also executed, as were those who failed to report someone doing so. Little wonder that some turned a blind eye to the fate of former neighbours or, worse, colluded in their persecution.

Significant sites are marked on the map on pages 220 and 221

✪ **Warsaw Rising Museum, Warsaw.** See p.231

✪ **Museum of the Second World War, Gdańsk.** See p.237

✪ **Home Army Museum, Kraków.** See p.242

✪ **Auschwitz-Birkenau, Oświęcim.** See p.245

✪ **Zajezdnia History Centre, Wrocław.** See p.248

Significant sites

«

Resistance and liberation

Several Polish politicians and members of the armed forces managed to escape and establish a government-in-exile in London, which had strong links to the underground government and the Resistance, including the Home Army, or Armia Krajowa (AK), in Poland. For the war's duration, Poles made a major contribution to the Allied cause in Europe; in Britain thousands served in all the armed forces.

Five years after the catastrophic events of 1939, it was the Soviets – having suffered a brutal Nazi invasion of their own – who managed to push the mighty German army all the way back to the border with Poland. Polish armies – formed with soldiers released from Soviet jails and camps – supported the Red Army in its final drive against the Nazis.

While the Armia Krajowa did everything they could to liberate the country themselves, in the end their efforts simply assisted the Red Army in their defeat of the Germans in Poland. The Poles were about to replace one occupier with the another, paving the way for 35 years of Soviet domination.

Lublin and the east

By the end of August 1943, the tide had turned in the Soviets' favour in their fight to repel the Wehrmacht from Russian soil. The Red Army was now on the offensive and it soon became apparent that they, rather than the western Allies, would be the ones to end German occupation in Poland.

enclosed ghettos. The Lublin ghetto was set up in March 1941 in the district of Podzamcze on the site of the former Jewish district; it held in excess of 30,000 people in a handful of streets, mostly Jews but with some Roma people. Though cramped and vulnerable to the spread of disease, it was regarded as less dreadful than other ghettos.

Operation Bagration

On 22 June 1944, two weeks after the Allied landings at Normandy, the Russians launched their own D-Day in Belarus, Operation Bagration. It was made up of several offensives operating concurrently and stretched across a wide front. One of these, the Minsk Offensive, completely destroyed the only major German force left on Soviet soil, Army Group Centre, and was one of the greatest Soviet victories of the war. It was achieved partly by sheer weight of numbers, but also by a deception plan that fooled the Germans into thinking the major attack would happen further south. Minsk was liberated on 3 July, opening the way for the Red Army to enter Poland, and on 18 July an assault was launched on the eastern Polish city of Lublin.

Nazi oppression in Lublin

The Lubelskie province, of which Lublin is the capital, was, and still is, one of the richest agricultural areas of Poland. This made it a prime target for German colonization after the Nazi invasion, the aim being to remove both the Polish and Jewish populations. Jews – targeted almost immediately the war began – were initially sent to the Lublin Reservation – a large segregated Jewish "state" populated by Jews deported from across Europe, and used as a forced labour camp.

When the reservation idea proved unworkable, it was replaced by isolating Jews in

Aktion Reinhard

The Lublin ghetto was liquidated after about a year as part of Aktion Reinhard, the planned extermination of all Jews within the General Government. This entailed the building of a series of death camps. The first, completed in March 1942, was near the village of Bełżec about halfway between Lublin and Lwów (now Lviv in Ukraine). The second at Sobibór was due east of Lublin and close to the border with Ukraine and Belarus, and the third at Treblinka, midway between Warsaw and Bialystok. In addition, the Majdanek concentration camp on the outskirts of Lublin – originally a labour camp for Soviet POWs – was converted into an extermination centre. It is thought that Aktion Reinhard was responsible for the murder of about 1.7 million Jews, and an unknown number of Poles, Roma and Soviet POWs.

Zamość Uprising

In 1942 a mass deportation of Poles from the Zamość region was carried out: inhabitants of around three hundred villages were removed and replaced by German settlers. This prompted a major uprising spearheaded by the Home Army and other groups, who encouraged villagers to destroy their properties before leaving. Some deportees were screened as potential candidates for Germanization on the basis of background or "Aryan" characteristics. Those that failed the test were sent to Majdanek. As many as 250,000 villagers managed to evade capture, seeking shelter wherever they could, some hiding in forests with the partisans. The Resistance continued to harry German troops and colonists over the next two years, but were eventually defeated with heavy casualties at the Battle of Osuchy in June 1944.

The liberation of Poland

On 18 August 1944, Marshal Rokossovsky's 1st Belorusian Front (equivalent to a Western army group) launched the Lublin-Brest Offensive. Part of Operation Bagration, five of its armies – including the Soviet-trained Polish First Army led by General Berling – broke through the German Army Group North Ukraine close to Kovel, 160km east of Lublin.

The River Bug – which marked the border with the General Government – was crossed by the Soviets' Forty-seventh Army and the Eighth Guards Army on 21 July; Chełm was liberated on 22 July. It was here, on the same day, that the Soviet-backed Polish Committee for National Liberation (also known as the Lublin Committee) issued a manifesto, urging support for the Red Army and the Home Army, but at the same time denouncing the London government-in-exile and setting itself up as the new provisional government.

Lublin was entered by the troops of the Second Tank Army the next day. In the fighting, the Army's commander, Soviet General Bogdanov, was wounded. He was replaced by General Radzievsky, who was immediately ordered by the Stavka (the Soviet High Command) to head north with his troops towards the River Vistula and Warsaw.

The Lublin camp of Majdanek was liberated by Red Army troops, but not before the Germans had tried to destroy it, evacuating or killing the remaining inmates. Only a few hundred were left, mostly hospitalized Soviet POWs. Majdanek had been used as a storage depot for objects stolen from victims; the Red Army found thousands of shoes, spectacles and human hair, along with piles of ash. They also found gas ovens. This was the first evidence of mass killings, and was soon reported to a shocked world by journalists flown over from places like Moscow and New York.

Lublin and the east sites   «

Jewish Lublin

Lublin was renowned as a Jewish cultural centre before the war, with a population of

«
The Lublin ghetto

40,000, twelve synagogues and two Yeshivas – schools for religious study. The Jewish district was near the castle where the ancient Grodzka Gate marks the divide between the Jewish and Gentile sections of the city. Part of the gate is now used as a study centre and exhibition space dedicated to Lublin's lost Jewish heritage. It's run by a drama group, Teatr NN, which also organizes performan-

ces, educational events and tours. Both the Old Jewish Cemetery (ul. Kalinowszczyzna) and the New (ul. Walecznych) still survive, despite Nazi desecration. So does the Yeshiva Hahmei Lublin (ul. Lubartowska) and its synagogue. Lublin's Great Synagogue was used by the Nazis during the liquidation of the ghetto as a collection point for Jews prior to transportation; it was then destroyed.

⟫ Poland betrayed

Following the fall of France, Poland became Britain's most important ally. Its government-in-exile, based in London, provided military support and had close links to the resistance Home Army in Poland. But with the Soviet Union's entry into the war everything changed, not least for the Poles: overnight, an enemy – the co-invader of their country – had become an ally, someone they had to negotiate with. General Sikorski, the Polish prime minister, signed a Polish-Soviet Treaty in July 1941 which resulted in the release of over one million Polish citizens from Soviet jails and the formation of a Polish army in Russia, led by General Anders.

What Sikorski completely failed to do was get an agreement with Stalin about the Polish-Soviet frontier, and relations between the two countries soon soured. The situation worsened with the discovery in 1943 of the remains of some four thousand Polish officers murdered by the Russians (see p.233). Stalin used the breakdown in relations to reinforce the activities of the Communist Polish Workers' Party in Poland. When Sikorski was killed in an aircraft accident in July 1943, the new prime minister, Stanisław Mikołajczyk, made a desperate attempt to negotiate with Stalin about the make-up of any postwar Polish government.

By now it was too late. The Red Army had begun to turn back the tide of the invading Germans and was scenting victory. At the Tehran Conference in November 1943 – attended by all the "Big Three" leaders but with the Poles excluded – the Allies decided that the frontier should follow the "Curzon Line" suggested in 1918, in other words the Soviets would retain the territory they seized in 1939 but shift the Polish-German border westwards. By July 1944 Stalin had already established a small group of Polish communists in Poland, known as the Lublin Committee, who issued a Manifesto of the Polish People (despite representing hardly any of them).

Though the Red Army's progress through Poland was aided by the Home Army, Stalin responded by refusing his troops permission to assist in the Warsaw Uprising (see p.228) and then, in the aftermath, arrested thousands of Home Army members. These people were either imprisoned or shot. The Lublin Committee now became a provisional government; other political parties were marginalized; and the government-in-exile ignored. In July 1945 Stalin's ruthless *fait accompli* was reluctantly recognized by Britain and the USA. Poland would remain as a Soviet satellite state until 1989.

State Museum at Majdanek
Droga Męczenników Majdanka 67, Lublin,
Ⓦ majdanek.eu/en

Majdanek is just a few kilometres southeast of the city centre. Tens of thousands of Jews and other "undesirables" were brought here, not just from Lublin but from across occupied Europe. Initially it housed Soviet POWs, most dying of cold or disease. Overall 78,000 people are thought to have been killed here, three-quarters of them Jews. After the Soviets liberated the camp, they used it to imprison members of the Polish Resistance, then opened it as a museum in November 1944. A long path runs through the site, with the Fight and Martydom monument at one end and a domed mausoleum containing the ashes of the dead at the other. Quite a few of the original buildings survive, including the gas chambers and crematoria, and the museum contains a range of displays that record and memorialize the horrors that took place here.

Museum and Memorial in Bełżec
ul. Ofiar Obozu Zagłady 4, Bełżec,
Ⓦ belzec.eu/en

Close to the Ukrainian border, some 40km south of Zamość, the Bełżec extermination camp was only fully commemorated 63 years after the Nazis attempted to erase all traces of it. Mass deportations from the ghettos of Lublin and Lwów began in March 1942 and ended in December, when the camp was closed down. In that ten-month period, around 450,000 people, mostly Jews, were murdered. Because little visible evidence remained, the site has been completely transformed into a powerful memorial, which combines architecture and symbolism to striking effect. As visitors walk the sloping path to the

wall of remembrance, the walls on either side seem to rise up, creating a feeling of claustrophobia. The museum provides a history of the camp and displays objects found during archeological excavations. Guided tours are available but need to be booked in advance.

Partisan War Cemetery Osuchy
Osuchy

About 45km due west of Bełżec is the village of Osuchy, the scene of one of the biggest battles fought by the Polish Resistance. In June 1944, the Germans launched a major anti-partisan offensive, Aktion Sturmwind II, in an attempt to suppress the Zamość Uprising. Much of the fighting took place in the heavily wooded Solska Wilderness. Outnumbered and surrounded, all attempts by the Resistance to break through failed. Around 400 died in the fighting, while the 800 who surrendered were executed or imprisoned. The cemetery contains a memorial and over 300 partisan graves.

Sobibór Memorial
Stacja Kolejowa Sobibór 1, Włodawa,
Ⓦ sobibor-memorial.eu/en

Like Bełżec, the death camp at Sobibór was located at an isolated spot, close to the Ukrainian and Belarusian borders, about 50km north of Chełm. The second of the Aktion Reinhard camps to be operational, Sobibór was completed in May 1942 when the first transports arrived. The number of deaths is estimated at between 170,000 and 250,000. A revolt in October 1943, in which three hundred prisoners managed to escape, led to the camp being closed and largely destroyed. The remaining inmates were transferred to Treblinka. The site is currently closed while a new memorial museum is constructed.

Warsaw and the north

Many Poles realized that the imminent arrival of the Red Army would jeopardize any chance of re-establishing Poland as an independent democratic nation.

Instead of a general insurrection against the Germans, in 1944 the Home Army launched Operation Tempest, a series of assaults in support of the advancing Red Army. It was hoped that this would establish common cause with the Soviets but, at the same time, show the Polish underground to be a significant political and military force in its own right, capable of taking over the country when the war was over.

Despite military success fighting alongside the Soviet forces, the Poles gained no

» Warsaw Ghetto uprising

The Warsaw Ghetto was established in October 1940 in the Muranów district and enclosed within 3-metre-high walls. It was the largest ghetto in Europe, housing over 400,000 people, many living ten to a room. Malnutrition and disease were widespread, and by summer 1942 had reduced the population by twenty percent.

At this point, the Nazis began a mass deportation of Jews from the ghetto to the extermination camp at Treblinka, murdering around 300,000 people. On 19 April 1943, when Waffen-SS troops arrived to remove the remaining inhabitants, armed resistance broke out organized by the Jewish Combat Organization (ŻOB) led by Mordechai Anielewicz. Despite the lack of adequate weapons, the ghetto uprising was sustained for almost a month, its leaders preferring to commit suicide rather than surrender. The 50,000 still alive when the uprising was suppressed were either executed or deported to death camps.

political advantage. On the contrary, when campaigns were finished, Home Army soldiers were disarmed and given a choice by the NKVD (the Soviet Secret Police) of either joining the Polish First Army of General Berling, or facing arrest and almost certain deportation. In some cases, Home Army soldiers were executed.

Having reached Lublin (see p.225), the 1st Belorusian Front continued west and north with the aim of establishing bridgeheads on the Vistula, the river that runs the length of Poland. By the end of July, the Second Guards Tank Army, commanded by Soviet Major General Radzievsky, had reached Garwolin – 60km southeast of Warsaw – where it engaged with and routed the German 73rd Infantry Division. The right flank of the Second Guards Tank Army was meant to be protected by the Forty-seventh Army, but a series of German counteroffensives to the east and northeast of Warsaw, including a major tank battle at Wołomin, forced a Soviet withdrawal.

The Warsaw Uprising

The Red Army was within striking distance of Warsaw, and Moscow Radio urged the city's inhabitants to rise up against their oppressors. This posed a terrible dilemma for the Home Army: should it engage with a ruthless enemy vastly superior in arms and numbers, running the risk of defeat and great loss of life, or do nothing and wait for the Russians to arrive, with the likelihood of being branded as Nazi collaborators? The London government-in-exile approved an uprising, and at 5pm on 1 August the Home Army's commander, General Bór-Komorowski, ordered the go-ahead.

The uprising began with an attack on the German garrison, and for the next 63

«
Sick and starving people emerge from basements and sewers in Warsaw, two months after the start of the Warsaw Uprising

days the Home Army and other insurgents attempted to drive the occupying forces from the city. Though they met with some early success, the odds against them were overwhelming. The Germans had brought in reinforcements and began pushing back the Poles street by street, slaughtering any civilians they encountered. The district of Wola was subjected to the most brutal treatment, with an estimated 50,000 people murdered over ten days in August. Throughout the uprising the insurgents used the city's sewer system as a way of moving from district to district, despite the narrowness of many of the tunnels, and at the end of August the sewers were used to evacuate more than five thousand people from the Old Town to the Zoliborz district.

Although close by, the Red Army failed to assist the uprising. The widely held view is that this was deliberate. Initially Stalin would not even allow American and British supply planes to land in Soviet-held Polish territory. Some Allied air-drops did take place, but they were largely ineffective as much of the material landed in German-occupied areas. Attempts by Berling's Polish First Army to cross the Vistula proved unsuccessful.

By the end of September, the Home Army was running out of weapons and men, and on 2 October Bór-Komorowski signed the capitulation. He and his remaining troops became prisoners of war; most of the civilian population were transported either to concentration camps or as forced labour to Germany. Hitler then ordered the destruction of

≫ Irena Sendler

For any Poles caught assisting Jews, or even suspected of doing so, the sentence was death for them and their family. This was usually immediate, without any legal process. Despite all of this, many Christian Poles risked their lives helping Jews out of a sense of common humanity and moral outrage; Irena Sendler was one of them. Working with Żegota, the codename for the Council for Aid to Jews (Rada Pomocy Zydom), Sendler, a social worker, helped to smuggle babies and small children out of the Warsaw ghetto, and set up a network of private houses, religious institutions and orphanages that could take in and hide them. Many Catholic clergy and nuns assisted her. It was a highly risky enterprise, which involved giving the children Christian names, teaching them prayers, and coaching them how to behave under Gestapo questioning. Often children needed to be moved from one place to another at regular intervals. Sendler was insistent that the children be reunited with their families after the war and wrote all their names down and hid them in bottles which she buried. Nearly all the parents of those children Żegota saved were killed at Treblinka.

Warsaw. One of the most beautiful capitals in Europe was plundered of anything valuable and then systematically dynamited, building by building, by a specialist SS detachment. Three months later, 85 percent of the city had been destroyed, at which point – in January 1945 – the Red Army entered to "liberate" a vast pile of smoking rubble.

≫ Warsaw and the north sites

POLIN Museum of the History of Polish Jews
ul. Anielewicza 6, Warsaw, Ⓦ polin.pl/en

Housed in a striking new building located on the site of Warsaw's Jewish quarter (later the ghetto), the POLIN Museum outlines the history of the Jewish presence in Poland from the early Middle Ages to the present day. Its core exhibition is made up of eight galleries displaying a wealth of artefacts and multimedia displays, including a stunning replica of the ornately painted ceiling of the 17th-century Gwoździec Synagogue, destroyed in 1941. The Holocaust has a whole gallery dedicated to it, but the museum as a whole is as much a celebration of the Jewish contribution to Polish history as it is a memorial to its passing.

Monument to the Ghetto Heroes
ul. Zamenhofa 11, Warsaw

Standing in front of the POLIN Museum, this monument was erected in 1948 on the fifth anniversary of the ghetto uprising. A large monolithic wall, it has sculptural reliefs on either side, one depicting a line of deportees being taken away, the other a group of ghetto insurgents with a defiant Mordechai Anielewicz clasping a grenade. The monument was constructed from stone imported by the Nazis in anticipation of refashioning Warsaw as a German city.

The Path of Remembrance
Warsaw

Beginning at the Monument to the Ghetto Heroes, the Path of Remembrance is a memorial route marked by sixteen granite blocks, each one commemorating a significant person or organization in the ghetto's history. Along the way you pass the bunker of the Jewish Fighters Organization (ŻOB). The route ends at the Umschlagplatz Monument, the assembly point near the train station from where thousands of Warsaw Jews were transported in crowded cattle trucks to the extermination camp at Treblinka.

Jewish Ghetto Wall fragment
Warsaw

A few small sections are all that survive of the 3-metre wall built by the Nazis to enclose the Warsaw Ghetto. Two can be accessed via a courtyard at ul. Sienna 55 and ul. Złota 62. Information plaques provide details of life in the ghetto and a map shows the area it occupied.

Warsaw Rising Museum
ul. Grzybowska 79, Warsaw, ⓦ 1933.pl/en

The aim of this museum is to tell the story of the Home Army and the citizens who supported it in the largest anti-German uprising in occupied Europe. Located in a former power station, the museum contains a wide range of exhibits and experiences, including a recreation of parts of the sewers and a replica B-24 bomber, the plane that took part in the Warsaw airlift. The rooms are arranged chronologically and much of the emphasis is on the activities of ordinary citizens, in the form of audio-visual displays and personal stories. The many photographs by Eugeniusz Lokajski, a commander during the uprising, provide a vivid record of the terrible suffering that Warsaw's population endured in the face of sustained German brutality.

Monument to the Warsaw Uprising
pl. Krasinskich 2, Warsaw

Completed in 1989, this monument was a belated and controversial attempt by the communist regime to acknowledge the heroism displayed in the uprising. It's made up of two separate bronze sculptural groups: one rep-

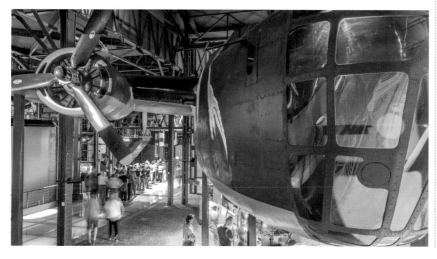

« Warsaw Rising Museum

resenting a group of armed insurgents rushing forward from slabs of a collapsing building, the other showing soldiers assisting a mother and baby descend into the sewers, as a priest prays close by.

Monument to Victims of the Wola Massacre
pl. Solidarności, Warsaw

The Wola massacre ranks as one of the most sadistic and ruthless assaults against civilians of the entire war. Beginning on 5 August, groups of German soldiers moved through the western district systematically killing its inhabitants, irrespective of age, gender or involvement in the uprising. The most notorious unit – led by the sadistic Oskar Dirlewanger –

went on a spree of torture, rape and murder. It is estimated that around 50,000 people were killed. The monument to the massacre, dedicated in 2006, represents a fragment of broken wall, on one side of which are the ghostly indentations of ten human figures.

Pawiak Prison Museum
ul. Dzielna 24/26, Warsaw, Ⓦ muzeum-niepodleglosci.pl/pawiak

A vast, 19th-century Tsarist prison, Pawiak was used by the Gestapo for holding and torturing Polish political prisoners. Over 100,000 people spent time here during the war, of whom around 37,000 were executed within the prison grounds. The Germans dynamited the whole building before retreating

» Memorial tree at Pawiak Prison Museum

in 1944 and now only part of the main gateway and a few cells remain. The museum, housed in a separate building, tells the story of Pawiak and its inmates through photographs of prisoners, their personal effects and some reconstructed cells.

Mausoleum of Struggle and Martyrdom (Gestapo Museum)
ul. Al. Szucha 25, Warsaw

The imposing Ministry of Education building was used as the Gestapo headquarters during the war and now contains a small museum tucked away in a basement (entered through a door in the courtyard). There is only one route through the claustrophobic space, which contains some of the original holding cells and the interrogation room, complete with instruments of torture. The nightmarish atmosphere is heightened by the use of striking visual and sound effects, and some will find the experience distressing. Children under 14 years are not admitted.

Katyń Museum
ul. Jana Jeziorańskiego 4, Warsaw,
Ⓦ muzeumkatynskie.pl

During the spring of 1940, in the Katyń forest near Smolensk and at other locations, more than 20,000 Poles, including 10,000 army and police officers, were executed by the NKVD (the Soviet secret police) – a mass execution known collectively as the Katyń Massacre. The first bodies were discovered by the Germans in 1943, but the Russians only admitted culpability in 1990. The museum commemorating the victims has recently been relocated to the Citadel fortress, where it is housed in a newly designed exhibition space that includes a small park. The displays, which use

« Personal belongings and papers of Polish officers killed in the Katyń Massacre

music and a soundscape, outline the events leading up to the massacre from the Nazi-Soviet pact onwards, but it's the many personal belongings found on the exhumed corpses that have the most powerful impact.

Palmiry National Memorial & Museum
Palmiry, Czosnów, Ⓦ palmiry.
muzeumwarszawy.pl/en

Mass executions of Warsaw's Polish elites were carried out in secret by transporting prisoners to a forest near the village of Palmiry west of the city. The blindfolded prisoners were lined up in front of long ditches which they fell into as they were shot. An estimated two thousand people were murdered

»
Lines of gravestones at
Palmiry National
Memorial & Museum

here, many buried in the nearby cemetery. There is now a striking museum: its austere exterior of rusted steel is punctured by symbolic bullet holes, while the interior creates a more tranquil environment with a glass wall looking out on to the forest. The display contextualizes the murders but also tells how the forest was used by Polish Resistance forces to train and to hide weapons.

Treblinka Museum
Treblinka, Kosów Lacki, Wólka Okrąglik 115, Ⓦ treblinka-muzeum.eu

Located about 100km northeast of Warsaw, Treblinka was, after Auschwitz-Birkenau, the extermination camp that saw the greatest number of killings as part of Aktion Reinhard (see p.224). Around 800,000 Jews were murdered here, along with some 2000 Romani. There were two camps: Treblinka I,

built in November 1941, was a forced labour camp for Poles and Jews; Treblinka II, 2km to the east, was added as an extermination centre in April 1942. Most of the Jews deported here came from the ghettos of Warsaw and Radom. In April 1943 Jewish prisoners organized a revolt and three hundred managed to escape, though most were recaptured. The Germans started dismantling Treblinka II shortly afterwards, forcing surviving inmates to exhume and burn corpses. When the Red Army arrived in July 1944, much of the camp had disappeared.

Today the emptiness and isolation of the site is powerfully affecting. A small museum near the car park has a few exhibits, including archive photos and a scale model of the camps. The large stone memorial is surrounded by a field of smaller stones marked with the names of the cities and villages from where the victims came.

Gdańsk and Pomerania

The capture of Warsaw ended the Lublin–Brest Offensive and signalled the beginning of the Vistula–Oder Offensive, the final massive Soviet thrust against the Germans through Poland to the River Oder and into Germany.

Stalin had over six million soldiers at his disposal; Hitler had just over two million. Nevertheless, Hitler called the Soviet build-up in the central sector of the Eastern Front "the greatest bluff since Genghis Khan", and refused to withdraw troops from any territory where they were active, thus increasing the risk of his armies being isolated, cut off and destroyed.

On 12 January 1945, the Vistula-Oder Offensive was launched in the south by Marshal Konev's 1st Ukrainian Front. Two days later Marshal Zhukov, commanding the 1st Belorusian Front, began advancing due west from the centre. The attack in the north, which began on 13 January, was the responsibility of two fronts: the 2nd and 3rd Belorusian Fronts would advance on East Prussia, after which the Second, commanded by Marshal Rokossovsky, would continue on to East Pomerania.

The Polish part of Pomerania had been annexed by Germany since 1939; for the battle-scarred Soviet troops, Pomerania was, as much as Prussia, the Fatherland of the hated enemy, an enemy that had committed barbaric acts against their country. Most would have witnessed the aftermath of terrible atrocities, and in some cases been personally affected by them. Unsurprisingly, thoughts of revenge were uppermost in many soldiers' minds, and to a large extent were encouraged by Soviet anti-Nazi propaganda. In East Prussia evacuation of civilians was slow in happening, and the inhabitants of many villages and towns were subjected to the full brunt of Soviet carnage, arson and mass rape.

East Pomeranian Offensive

The main strategic aim of the East Pomeranian Offensive was to overcome the German forces in Pomerania so as to eliminate the risk of a counteroffensive against Marshal Zhukov's advance on Berlin. As each town was overcome, the German Army retreated

» Danzig – September 1939

On 1 September 1939, the German battleship SMS *Schleswig-Holstein* opened fire on the Military Transit Depot at Westerplatte peninsula at the mouth of the River Vistula. In the face of heavy bombardment and attacks from the air, the small Polish garrison held out for seven days before the hopelessness of their situation forced their commander to surrender.

At the same time, the Polish Post and Telegraph Office in Danzig was attacked by a local SS unit and the police, a force of around two hundred men. The building had been fortified in anticipation of war and some of its workers had received military training. With a handful of others, they managed to put up fierce resistance which lasted around fifteen hours. It was only overcome when the Germans pumped petrol into the basement and ignited it. Those not killed in the attack were tried and sentenced to death as illegal combatants. Both Westerplatte and the Post Office Siege became potent symbols of Polish resistance.

and many German civilians fled with them. The coastal town of Kolberg (modern Koło-brzeg) experienced a ferocious siege in the first two weeks of March, during which time the Germans evacuated around 70,000 civilians and about 40,000 troops by sea to Germany and Denmark. Many ships carrying thousands of refugees were sunk by Soviet submarines. The other Baltic ports of Gdynia and Danzig (Gdańsk) were no less fiercely defended against the vengeful onslaught of Russian and Polish troops. Apart from a handful of German soldiers on the Hel peninsula who battled on until May, this left Poland free from Nazi occupation. It was a freedom that was shortlived, however, as Nazi subjugation was replaced by Soviet domination.

Gdańsk and Pomerania sites

Monument of the Coast Defenders
Westerplatte peninsula, Gdańsk

Erected in 1966 during the communist era, this monument is a tall, chunky Soviet-style structure dedicated to the coastal defenders of World War II in general, rather than the Westerplatte garrison in particular. Nearby exhibition panels explain the modern history of the peninsula. Some of the ruined guardhouse and barracks are still standing and one building is now a small museum telling the story of the events that took place here in

» Monument of the Coast Defenders

the first week of September 1939 (see p.235). Memorials are spread across the peninsula and it takes a couple of hours to see them all. Westerplatte can be reached by bus or boat from Gdańsk.

Polish Post Museum
pl. Obrońców Poczty Polskiej 1/2, Gdańsk

On the 40th anniversary of the Post Office workers' defence of their building, a small museum was opened to commemorate the events that occurred here, with a monument erected in the adjacent square. The exhibition contains a wealth of documents and evocative photographs, as well as a copy of the plan of the attack, drawn up in July 1939. Other material, including a reconstruction of the postmaster's room, outlines the history of the Polish postal service and the wider Polish community in Danzig/Gdańsk.

Museum of the Second World War
pl. Władysława Bartoszewskiego 1, Gdańsk, Ⓦ muzeum1939.pl

A spectacular tower, tilting at a seemingly impossible angle, is the dominant feature of this new museum, designed by a local architecture firm. Most of the permanent exhibition is actually located underground (the tower is used as offices). The original concept of the displays sought to place the Polish experience of World War II in a broad international context, with an emphasis on the lives of ordinary citizens, while also looking at current conflicts. Immediately after it opened in 2017, the Minister of Culture criticized the museum as insufficiently patriotic and sacked the director and his deputies. Despite the political controversy, the museum is well worth visiting, with

« Museum of the Second World War

thousands of objects imaginatively displayed. It's an immersive experience, with recreations of whole streets, organized in three narrative themes: "The Road to War", "The Terror of War" and "The Long Shadow of War".

Museum of Stutthof
ul. Muzealna 6, Sztutowo, Ⓦ stutthof.org/english

The day after the German invasion, Stutthof, to the east of Danzig, was established – the first Nazi internment camp outside of Germany. It was used to imprison and then kill Polish professionals and the intelligentsia. Less well known than other Nazi camps, Stutthof grew in five years from a camp housing mainly local Poles to an extermination camp, with 39 sub-camps, containing tens of thousands of prisoners from across Europe. The museum researches and displays archival records and historical artefacts relating to the camp and its administration. Exhibitions, films and photographs provide a haunting insight into the lives of the 110,000 people that were imprisoned here during World War II before its liberation by Red Army troops in May 1945.

Piaśnica Museum
ul. Św. Jacka 11/2, Wejherowo,
Ⓦ muzeupiasnickie.pl

In a forest near the village of Piaśnica, close to the port of Gdynia, between 10,000 and 12,000 people are estimated to have been murdered between September 1939 and April 1940. The perpetrators were the SS, assisted by local German paramilitaries. Those killed included Kashubians (a local ethnic group), Polish intellectuals, Catholic priests, Jews, Czechs and patients from mental hospitals. At the end of the war, as the Red Army approached, the Nazis forced Stutthof prisoners to dig up the corpses and burn them. In the forest, 9km to the north of Wejherowo, there is now a commemorative grave site for the victims, with a monument and a nearby chapel. The Piaśnica Museum in Wejherowo is currently housed in a temporary site while its intended location (the former Gestapo headquarters) undergoes restoration.

》 The Wolf's Lair and the July Plot

In the run-up to the 1941 German invasion of the Soviet Union (Operation Barbarossa), a large military complex was built as Hitler's principal command base near Rastenburg in East Prussia (now the Polish town of Kętrzyn). Hidden by thick forest, it was known as the Wolfschanze, or Wolf's Lair. Hitler spent more time here – over 800 days – than at any of his other military bases. In 1944, the living quarters of Hitler and other leading Nazis were replaced with large, heavily reinforced bunkers in anticipation of Allied air attacks.

As it turned out, the attack on Hitler came not from the Allies but from his own side. On 20 July, a staff officer, Lieutenant Colonel Claus von Stauffenberg, attended a meeting at the Wolf's Lair, where he planted a bomb hidden in a briefcase a few feet from where Hitler was sitting. He then left the room and, after the explosion, flew to Berlin in the belief that the Führer was dead. He wasn't, and shortly afterwards Stauffenberg and the other ringleaders of the plot (code-named Valkyrie) were arrested and summarily executed. The Gestapo then pursued anyone connected, even remotely, to this and earlier plots, and around five thousand people were eventually killed, either by suicide or execution.

The conspirators were motivated by a number of factors. As senior officers, they were appalled at the disastrous way in which the war was progressing, especially on the Eastern Front, which they ascribed to Hitler's poor military leadership. To some extent, they were also alarmed at the extremes of brutality meted out by the Waffen SS against Jews and Slavs in the latter years of the war. But they were all conservative nationalists, many of whom had supported the Nazi cause for most of their careers, and their plans for a negotiated peace included retaining Austria and the Sudetenland. Unquestionably the plotters were brave – Stauffenberg in particular – but whether their actions were heroic is something that is still debated by historians and Germans alike.

«
Visitors to the
Wolf's Lair

ORP Błyskawica
al. Jana Pawła II 1, Gdynia,
Ⓦ muzeummw.pl

Built in Britain and launched in 1936, ORP *Błyskawica* was the most modern surface ship of the prewar Polish Navy; today, she's the oldest surviving destroyer in the world. Shortly before the German invasion, she left the Baltic along with two other Polish destroyers and sailed to Britain where she served under the operational control of the Royal Navy. *Błyskawica* took part in several major operations, including the Allied invasion of Normandy where she provided cover for the landing forces. Now a museum, much of the ship can be explored by visitors, including the engine room, and there are displays about *Błyskawica*'s service during the war.

Cemetery of the Mausoleum of Soviet Soldiers
ul. Generała A. Giełguda, Gdańsk

About 600,000 Russian soldiers fell as the Red Army advanced through Poland in 1944–1945. Some 3100 are buried in this cemetery, many of whom died in the bitter fighting to win Gdańsk. Each soldier's grave is marked with a star. Since the fall of communism in 1989, Soviet monuments have become a contentious issue and some of the more political ones have been removed. At the moment Soviet cemeteries continue to be respected, although there have been instances of vandalism.

Wolf's Lair
Gierłoż, Kętrzyn

The ruins of Hitler's secret headquarters (see box, p.238) are located close to the village of Gierłoż, about 225km east of Gdańsk and close to the border with Kaliningrad. Wandering through the compound, which contains around eighty buildings, is an eerie experience. As the Red Army approached, Hitler ordered its complete destruction by an SS team, a difficult task considering that many of the bunkers had walls over five metres thick. Nature has now invaded the remains, covering much of the site in dense foliage. Only a wall survives of Hitler's bunker, but that of Goering is almost complete; a plaque marks the location of the failed assassination attempt and there is a small on-site exhibition.

Kraków and southeastern Poland

On 13 July 1944, at the southern section of the Russian front, a major offensive was launched with the aim of driving the German Army Group North Ukraine from western Ukraine and southeastern Poland.

The Lwów–Sandomierz Offensive, as the plan was codenamed, was also partly conceived as a deception to lure enemy troops down from the north, leaving German Army Group Centre even more vulnerable for attack (see p.224). The operation was assigned to the 1st Ukrainian Front led by Soviet Marshal Ivan Konev. The Germans, commanded by General Josef Harpe, offered strong resistance, but were surrounded and routed near the town of Brody. The Polish Home Army began an uprising in Lwów (Lviv) on 23 July as the Soviets advanced, and the city was liberated three days later. Red Army bridgeheads were estab-

lished on the Vistula on 28 July near Baranów Sandomierz. The Germans launched a major counterattack in August in an attempt to push the Russians back across the river, but the Soviets held their position. Both sides dug in until January, when Konev's troops began their advance across southern Poland.

Kraków liberated

Kraków, rather than Warsaw, had been the capital of the newly formed General Government. It was governed by Hitler's lawyer, Hans Frank, who had installed himself in the magnificent Wawel Castle, the former residence of Poland's royalty. On 17 January 1945, as the Soviets approached, Frank and his administration fled, leaving General Wilhelm Koppe to organize the German military defence and withdrawal. Konev's 1st Ukrainian Front approached from the north

» Soviet soldiers in liberated Kraków

›› Kraków's ghetto and Oskar Schindler

Prior to the 1939 invasion, Kraków had around 70,000 Jewish inhabitants, about a quarter of the population, many of whom lived in the traditional Jewish district of Kazimierz. In March 1941, 16,000 were relocated to a newly created ghetto in the Podgorze district south of the city, housing about five times the number that had lived there previously. Only one non-Jew chose to remain: Tadeusz Pankiewicz, a Catholic Pole who ran a pharmacy, known as the Pharmacy Under the Eagle. As well as providing medical advice and medication to residents – often without charge – Pankiewicz and his three female assistants risked their lives hiding Jews and helping them to escape.

Forced to work in factories both inside and outside the ghetto, after June 1942 many ghetto inmates were sent to the labour camp at nearby Płaszów. Conditions there were harsh and treatment exceptionally brutal, even by SS standards. At the limestone quarry, prisoners were worked to the verge of death, and random beatings and shootings were commonplace – many carried out by Amon Goeth, the camp's sadistic commandant. The Kraków ghetto was liquidated in 1943. The 8000 prisoners still able to work were transferred to Płaszów, the rest were either shot or sent to the death camps of Bełżec or Auschwitz-Birkenau.

One of the factories was Oskar Schindler's Emalia Factory, a previously Jewish-owned enamel business purchased by him in 1939. Schindler, who had once been a spy in Czechoslovakia, was a Nazi Party member and a wheeler-dealer businessman who enjoyed the good things in life. Despite his dubious credentials, he viewed the treatment of the Jews with horror, and did his utmost to protect his workers. When the ghetto was liquidated, he used bribery, contacts and charm to make sure that none of the Emalia Jews were deported. When Płaszów became a concentration camp in August 1943 he had his factory designated a sub-camp where the workers could reside. Arrested three times, he always succeeded in getting the charges dropped. In October 1944, when the arrival of the Red Army seemed imminent, the SS removed all Jews from the Emalia Factory to Płaszów, but Schindler somehow managed to get permission to relocate the factory (now producing armaments) to Brünnlitz in Moravia. "Schindler's List" contained the names of the 1200 workers that he insisted would be needed there – Jews who otherwise would have met their deaths at Auschwitz or Gross-Rosen.

and Major General Ivan Korovnikov's Fifty-ninth Army from the northeast. Soviet accounts of the battle for Kraków claim that the speed of Konev's attack saved it from the destruction suffered by so many Polish cities. In 1987, a statue was raised in Konev's honour. It was pulled down four years later, and most Polish historians now think there were no plans by the Germans to blow up the city, and regard the story of Konev as Kraków's saviour as a myth.

Auschwitz-Birkenau

Early in 1940, a former Polish barracks at Oświęcim, around 70km from Kraków, was converted into a concentration camp and given the German name Auschwitz. For the first year of its existence, most of its inmates were Polish political prisoners. Conditions were extremely harsh and the demands for forced labour at local factories meant that the camp was regularly expanded. In October 1941 work started on another camp nearby, Auschwitz-Birkenau, to accommodate Soviet prisoners of war. Around the same time tests for the gassing of "undesirable" prisoners, using Zyklon B, had already begun. Auschwitz III was a large industrial complex, built for I.G. Farben, which used slave labour.

In the spring of 1942, transports of Jews began to arrive at Auschwitz as part of the Nazis' "Final Solution". As the numbers of Jews from across Europe increased, so the machinery of murder became more efficient. Some prisoners were also selected for cruel and deadly pseudo-medical experiments conducted by camp doctors. An estimated total of 1.3 million people (Poles, Jews, Roma, Soviet POWs and others) were sent to Auschwitz, of whom 1.1 million were killed; of these, 960,000 were Jews.

The Red Army liberated Auschwitz on 27 January 1945. Before they arrived, the Germans scrambled to destroy all evidence of their crimes, killing thousands of prisoners and taking 60,000 others on a forced march westwards. Around 15,000 died, either shot because they couldn't keep up, or simply succumbing to malnutrition, disease and the freezing winter weather.

» Kraków and southeastern Poland sites

Home Army Museum
ul. Wita Stwosza 12, Kraków, Ⓦ muzeum-ak.pl/english

Housed in an austere red-brick former Austrian barracks, and slightly off the beaten track, this is the only museum entirely dedicated to Poland's underground government and resistance army. The many objects on display range from personal memorabilia and photographs to weaponry, including the reconstruction of a V2 rocket (see p.306). You enter through a large, light-filled courtyard, but most of the collection is displayed in the dimly lit basement with only a limited amount of explanation in English. With this in mind, it's well worth taking a guided tour of the museum, which requires advanced booking.

Pomorska Street (Gestapo Museum)
ul. Pomorska 2, Kraków, Ⓦ mhk.pl/branches/pomorska-street

The Dom Śląski (Silesian House) was a hostel for Silesian students before it became Kraków's Gestapo headquarters in 1939. It is now a museum with a permanent exhibition entitled "People of Kraków in Times of Terror 1939-1945-1956", which tells of the suffering endured by Kraków's citizens under both the Nazi regime and during the postwar Stalinist tyranny. The emphasis is on the human cost of institutionalized cruelty: a wall of faces lines the entrance corridor – official mugshots of concentration camp inmates – and in the basement the cell walls are covered with the scratched names of those held and tortured here.

Kazimierz
Kraków

Kazimierz is now one of the most vibrant districts of Kraków, as it was in the prewar years as the city's historic Jewish quarter and one of the great centres of European Jewry. The

«
The haunting entrance
to Auschwitz-Birkenau

Nazis displaced and then murdered its inhabitants, but left most of Kazimierz's buildings standing, although they plundered or destroyed nearly all its treasures. Wandering the streets gives some sense of what was prewar life was like. Of its seven synagogues, two now serve the city's small Jewish community, while the grandest, the Old Synagogue, is a fine Renaissance building, heavily damaged by the Nazis, but restored in the 1950s and now a museum.

Galicia Jewish Museum

ul. Dajwór 18, Kraków,
Ⓦ galiciajewishmuseum.org/en

This museum, housed in a former warehouse, was founded in 2004 by British photographer Chris Schwarz to commemorate the lost Jewish world of Galicia, a Habsburg Empire province and former kingdom that stretched from Oświęcim in the west to Ternopil (now part of western Ukraine) in the east. The main exhibition, "Traces of Memo-

ry", displays Schwartz's poignant photographs, with text by Jonathan Webber, and records the residue of Jewish life – synagogues and cemeteries, some abandoned and decaying – from across this once ethnically diverse region.

Podgórze
Kraków

Just across the river – now conveniently linked by the Father Bernatek Footbridge – is the district of Podgórze, where the Kraków ghetto was crammed into a handful of streets. Fragments of the ghetto wall (built in the shape of tombstones) still exist: a small stretch is visible at ul. Lwowska 25–29 and a longer section at ul. Limanowskiego 60/62. The only surviving synagogue from the ghetto area, the Zucher Synagogue, is now an art gallery. Plac Zgody, the main square of the ghetto, is now named Plac Bohaterów Getta (Ghetto Heroes Square), and is where a recent memorial has been erected in the form of rows of metal chairs – a reference to the Nazi practice of throwing furniture into the square as people were deported from their homes.

Pharmacy Under the Eagle

pl. Bohaterów Getta 18, Kraków, ⓦ mhk.pl/branches/eagle-pharmacy

This museum is located in the original pharmacy building and was inspired by Tadeusz Pankiewicz's memoir, *The Kraków Ghetto Pharmacy*. The interior has been recreated as closely as possible to how it was (based on old photographs) and much of the information is displayed in wooden cabinets and drawers. There are a total of five rooms, each themed slightly differently, covering such topics as Pankiewicz's own story, the history of Kraków's Jews, what life was like in the ghetto, and the role the pharmacy played in helping people survive.

Oskar Schindler's Emalia Factory

ul. Lipowa 4, Kraków, ⓦ mhk.pl/branches/oskar-schindlers-factory

The Schindler Factory – a ten-minute walk from the Pharmacy Under the Eagle – is now a museum with a permanent exhibition on the life of the city during the war. Called "Kraków During Nazi Occupation 1939–1945", as with many of Poland's museums about the occupation, it focuses on the individuals caught up in those nightmarish times, using recorded testimonies as well as documents and artefacts. Schindler and his workers are part of the story, but by no means the main emphasis. The museum is extremely popular and it is essential to book tickets in advance to avoid disappointment. Schindler's now dilapidated villa is close by at Tadeusza Romanowicza 9, but is not open to the public.

» Colourful bottles inside the Pharmacy Under the Eagle

Płaszów
Kraków

Close to Podgórze and the ghetto, Płaszów is the site of the concentration camp where many Jews worked and where many lost their lives. Most of the camp was razed to the ground after the war, and the area is now a wild and overgrown wedge of land between ul. Kamieńskiego and ul. Wielicka. There are plans for a museum, and there are boards explaining Płaszów history, but the area is not yet geared for tourists and feels rather neglected. For the intrepid, however, there is still much to see, including the villa, known as the Grey House, which was once the offices of the Płaszów SS and Amon Goeth.

A vast granite monument commemorating the "martyrs murdered by the Nazi perpetrators of genocide" looms over the site. The camp was built on a former Jewish cemetery and recently a single gravestone has been restored.

Auschwitz-Birkenau
ul. Stanisławy Leszczyńskiej 11, Oświęcim, Ⓦ auschwitz.org/en

The entrance to the original camp is through the infamous main gate bearing the message *Arbeit Macht Frei* ("Work Makes You Free"). The camp itself is made up of a series of barrack buildings divided into blocks, many showing exhibits relating to specific countries, peoples or themes. Several displays show masses of a single object – suitcases, children's shoes, human hair – bringing home in a particularly graphic way the sheer enormity of the Nazis' crimes. Block 11 is where the first tests of Zyklon B took place and where the Polish priest Maximilian Kolbe was starved to death, having taken the place of another prisoner. Outside is the wall where thousands of prisoners were shot by the SS.

Birkenau, about 3km northwest of Auschwitz, is more austere and regimented, with a vast area where the grid of prisoner blocks once stood – by 1944 the camp held as many as 100,000 inmates. Just a few of the huts still stand, allowing visitors to see the cramped and dehumanizing conditions. The railway line ran straight down the middle of Birkenau, ending close to the gas chambers. As the Red Army approached, the Nazis tried to destroy all evidence of what had been happening, but what remains bears powerful testimony to the terrible suffering experienced here. Both camps receive thousands of visitors each year and it is worth booking before you make the journey to Oświęcim.

The Ulma Family Museum of Poles Saving Jews in World War II
37–120 Markowa 1487, Ⓦ muzeumulmow. pl/en

Opened in 2016 and located in the mountainous Podkarpackie region some 190km east of Kraków, this museum is dedicated to those Poles who risked, and often lost, their lives attempting to protect Jews from Nazi persecution. It's named after Jósef and Wiktoria Ulma, who cared for eight Jews at their farm before being betrayed by a neighbour in March 1944. The Ulmas, their six children and those they sheltered were all shot. The museum has been criticized by some for having a nationalist agenda, but there is little evidence of this in the sensitive and balanced displays which make it clear that such principled acts of bravery (see p.230) were the exception rather than the rule.

Wrocław and Lower Silesia

After the liberation of Kraków and Auschwitz, the 1st Ukrainian Front continued its march westward through Lower Silesia, which today is part of Poland, but in 1945 was predominantly German.

The 1st Ukrainian Front's progress was swift, though they were still faced with sporadic opposition from Army Group "A" (formerly Army Group North Ukraine), now under a new commander, the fanatical General Ferdinand Schoerner. Hitler was being encouraged by his generals to withdraw and redeploy his troops, but he continued to advocate a "stand or die" policy, designating certain cities as *Festung* – fortresses to be defended at all costs.

Sandomierz–Silesian Offensive

The Sandomierz–Silesian Offensive was the final push westwards by Marshal Konev's troops towards Breslau (modern Wrocław) and the Oder river, part of the co-ordinated Vistula–Oder Offensive that was operating along the whole of the Eastern Front. As the 1st Ukrainian Front began besieging Breslau on 13 February 1945, General Chuikov's

» Rusting Nazi equipment left behind in a tunnel in Lower Silesia

» Project Riese

Góry Sowie (the Owl Mountains) lie along the Czech-Polish border 80km southwest of Wrocław. Their inaccessibility made this an ideal site for a mysterious, top-secret project ordered by Hitler in 1943 as the war started to turn against him. Using prisoners as slave labour from a Gross-Rosen satellite camp (see p.249), an estimated 213,000 cubic metres of bomb-proof tunnels and halls were dug out from within the mountains. The project was codenamed Riese, meaning "giant".

It remains unclear what this underground complex was used for. The retreating Germans and then the Soviets removed all machinery, few documents seem to have survived, and most of the workers involved perished from the terrible working conditions or were killed by the guards. Armaments were almost certainly produced here, but suggestions that a "wonder weapon" was being developed have never been verified. It may also have been used to store some of the art works and cultural treasures looted by the Nazis, and there is a popular rumour of a hidden train containing Nazi gold. Organization Todt, the Nazi engineering group who worked on the tunnels, had its headquarters at nearby Książ Castle, and it's possible that that castle was intended as the final redoubt of Hitler and his staff.

Eighth Guards Army was engaged in the month-long Battle of Poznań 170km to the north. Poznań was captured on 23 February, opening up a direct route to Berlin. Breslau would take rather longer to overcome.

Siege of Breslau

On the orders of Silesia's Gauleiter, Karl Franke, Breslau was declared a *Festung* ("fortress") to be defended to the utmost by its garrison of 50,000 troops. The street-to-street fighting that ensued was extremely fierce and lasted almost three months, during which most of the city was destroyed. Civilian casualties were huge, possibly as many as 40,000, largely because Franke had been slow to evacuate non-combatants. When he started to do so, after heavy aerial bombardment in January, thousands had to flee on foot in freezing conditions because of a shortage of trains, and many were left behind. Those refugees that headed for Dresden were killed when the city was bombed (see p.294). Bre-

slau finally capitulated on 6 May 1945, the last major German city to do so. As in Pomerania, Red Army troops then went on a brutal rampage of rape and murder against the remaining German inhabitants. This unofficial policy of "retribution" devastated the surrounding lands, making them virtually uninhabitable.

Borders, deportations and repopulation

As early as 1943, Stalin was insisting to his western allies that the Soviet Union be allowed to retain the Polish territory it had invaded in 1939, an area that the Poles called Kresy, and which now makes up of parts of Ukraine, Belarus and Lithuania. After prolonged discussions (which largely excluded the Poles), the partition was agreed and ratified by the Allies at the Potsdam Conference in August 1945. To compensate for this huge loss of territory, Poland was to be given Danzig (now called Gdańsk), part of East Prussia and all the land east of the River Oder and its tributary the River Neisse. It

»
Lomnica Palace

still amounted to an overall loss of nearly 74,000 square kilometres.

What then followed was the removal, often forcibly, of huge numbers of people from their homes – Poles from Kresy, Germans from Silesia and Western Pomerania. The expulsion of German refugees into an already devastated Germany was carried out precipitously and often brutally by the Polish authorities and caused major problems for Allied administrators. In the east it was no less painful and confusing: Ukrainians, Belorusians and Lithuanians living in Poland were transferred east; Poles in Kresy – about 1.5 million – were "repatriated" west. Breslau (now Wrocław) was largely repopulated with families from Lwów (Ukrainian Lviv), nearly 600km away. For many people this displacement, on top of everything else they had suffered, was profoundly traumatic.

» Wrocław and Lower Silesia sites

Zajezdnia History Centre
ul. Grabiszyńska 184, Wrocław,
Ⓦ zajezdnia.org

Occupying an old bus depot (*zajezdnia* is the Polish for "depot"), this enthralling mu-

seum charts the story of the reborn city's inhabitants in a permanent exhibition, "Wrocław 1945–2016". The mass movement of entire populations that took place after the war's end is communicated clearly and sympathetically, albeit from a largely Polish point of view. The multimedia displays focus on the lives of ordinary people, using evocative everyday objects and personal testimonies.

Lomnica Palace
ul. Karpnicka 3, Łomnica,
Ⓦ palac-lomnica.pl/en

Lomnica (formerly Lomnitz) Palace, near the town of Jelenia Góra 95km southwest of Wrocław, is part of a historic estate dating back to the 14th century. From 1835 it was owned by the German von Küster family, but after their enforced departure in 1945 their home was nationalized and used for various different purposes. Abandoned and slowly falling into ruin, it was bought back by the von Küsters in 1991. The Great Palace and its English-style gardens have now been beautifully restored as a museum and cultural centre, a symbol of reconciliation after the horrors of the postwar deportations. The smaller manor house is now run as a luxury hotel.

Podziemne Miasto Osówka (Riese site)
ul. Swierkowa 29d, Sierpnica,
ⓦ osowka.pl

The site, in woodland close to the villages of Sierpnica and Kolce, is the largest of the three Riese tunnel complexes (see p.247) open to the public. Four tours are offered at different prices: the longest is three hours, the shortest one hour. Always book in advance and check when tours in English are available; alternatively, there is an English audioguide. It can get quite cold and slippery, so it's advisable to wear warm clothing and sturdy shoes. It's also worth working out how to get here in advance, as it's rather off the beaten track, with Głuszyca the nearest town.

Gross-Rosen Museum
ul. Szarych Szeregów 9, Rogoźnica,
ⓦ en.gross-rosen.eu

In the summer of 1940, the Germans built a concentration camp about 65km southwest of Wrocław, near the village of Gross-Rosen (now Rogoźnica). Its location was close to an SS-owned granite quarry where the prisoners were made to work twelve hours a day while on minimal rations. The camp eventually became the largest in Lower Silesia, with around one hundred sub-camps. The one at Brünnlitz (Brněnec in the Czech Republic) belonged to Oskar Schindler (see p.241), who had his Kraków factory relocated here in 1944, where he managed to keep the 1200 workers alive. The 70th Motorized Infantry Brigade of the Red Army liberated the Gross-Rosen camps in mid-February 1945, but not before the SS had evacuated about 40,000 remaining prisoners to camps in Germany.

Smaller and not so well resourced as other camp museums, Gross-Rosen is still a fascinating but chilling place to visit, rarely as crowded as the better-known camps. Not many of the buildings remain, but their positions are clearly indicated. One building still standing is the SS Canteen, which now houses the camp's main exhibition, "KL Gross-Rosen 1941–45", outlining the history of the camp. Labelling is in Polish but there is a booklet in English and the helpful staff will answer any questions. Along the road to the right of the main entrance is the quarry where many prisoners were worked to death.

Prisoner of War Camps Museum
ul. Lotników Alianckich 6, Żagań,
ⓦ muzeum.zagan.pl/en

A pine forest 4km to the southwest of Żagań (German Sagan) is the site of two prisoner of war camps. Stalag VIIIC, built in 1939, held over 40,000 prisoners, including many Polish soldiers captured at the start of the war. Conditions were excessively squalid, and the regime was brutal. Stalag Luft III, a separate camp built in 1942 for Allied airmen, was far less primitive. This camp became famous for its many escape attempts. The best known involved digging three tunnels, nicknamed "Tom, Dick and Harry", with the last used for a breakout of 76 men in March 1944. All but three escapees were eventually recaptured, and of these fifty were shot. Paul Brickhill, a former prisoner, later wrote up the story as *The Great Escape*, which was filmed by Hollywood in 1963. The museum site contains a reconstructed hut, a scale model of Stalag Luft III and several memorials to those who died at the camps. Bear in mind that the actual site of the camp is back towards Żagań. For clear directions, ask at the museum.

The Holocaust

Hatred of the Jews was a central strand of Nazi ideology, the Holocaust its genocidal conclusion.

In his 1925 book *Mein Kampf*, Hitler blamed Jews for all the perceived "evils" besetting not just Germany but the world – from the threat of international Bolshevism to the inequalities caused by unbridled capitalism. Above all, he believed that Jews were sullying the "purity" of the German race.

The party propaganda machine, run proficiently by Dr Joseph Goebbels, promoted and reinforced these ideas, which were embraced by many Germans.

After 1933, Hitler began introducing punitive legislation against Germany's 500,000 Jews – less than one percent of the population – restricting access to certain professions. The Nuremberg Laws of September 1935 deprived Jews of their German citizenship and forbade them marrying Germans or having sexual relations with them. Jews were defined not by religion but by race: a person with three Jewish grandparents qualified, those with one or two grandparents were classified as *Mischling* ("mixed-blood") and subject to less severe restrictions.

Nazi persecution extended to many other groups. Roma, Slavs and black people were also regarded as *untermenschen*, or "sub-human", while those with mental and physical disabilities were designated *Lebensunwertes Leben* – unworthy of life. Homosexuals were victimized as sexual deviants and Jehovah's Witnesses for their allegiance to God rather than Hitler. Known communists and trade unionists were also seen as legitimate targets. It's estimated that more than ten million people were killed overall by the Nazis for failing to conform to, or for opposing, their narrow and perverted world view. Six million of these were Jews.

Kristallnacht

Random acts of violence against Jews were carried out by Hitler's thuggish paramilitary bodyguards, the SA (or "brownshirts"), on a regular basis. Such violence reached a climax on 9–10 November 1938 when a wave of anti-Jewish attacks took place across Germany, Austria and the recently annexed Sudetenland. Instigated by Goebbels, this event was known as Kristallnacht, or "Night of Broken Glass", because of the

▲
Pedestrians survey the broken windows of a Jewish-owned shop in Berlin after Kristallnacht, November 1938

thousands of shattered windows of destroyed synagogues, shops and homes.

With the invasion of Poland in September 1939, persecution intensified. Stutthof in Pomerania (see p.237) was one of the first Nazi concentration camps built on foreign soil. Initially such camps were used to imprison political opponents (real or imagined) of the Nazi regime, but these increasingly included Jews. Labour camps were also built to exploit the manpower of Jews and other "undesirables" for the benefit of the Reich. From 1941, all Jews in Reich territories had to wear a badge bearing a yellow star of David so that they were easier to identify.

Various "solutions" to what the Nazis thought of as "the Jewish question" or "problem" were aired. A "territorial solution" was briefly considered, which involved the planned deportation of Jews to the East African island and French colony of Madagascar. The plan was only abandoned because the coastal waters around the island were controlled by the British.

Ghettos

As the war progressed, the segregation of Jews from society increased. It was mainly achieved by creating ghettos, enclosed areas of cities or towns where Jews

Jewish men being transported from the Warsaw Ghetto to work at other sites
▼

were effectively imprisoned and excluded from the outside world. Before being expelled from their homes, they were stripped of almost all their possessions, including any property. Ghettos were nominally self-governing, but in reality they were under strict Nazi control, with their inhabitants exploited as slave labour. Conditions were appalling: overcrowding and malnourishment increased the likelihood of disease, and mortality rates were extremely high.

In the minds of some senior Nazis, the inevitable next step was the total eradication of all the Jews of Europe. The German invasion of the Soviet Union in June 1941 provided a pretext for putting this genocidal policy into practice. In the wake of the German advance, mobile killing units, called *Einsatzgruppen*, targeted anyone seen as enemies. This included the entire Jewish and Roma populations – men, women and children were executed, either by gassing in special customized trucks, or by shooting. One of the single biggest massacres took place in Ukraine, at Babi Yar in September 1941 when more than 33,000 Jews from Kiev were shot over the course of a couple of days.

At the same time, a project was conceived to build new camps in Poland (and adapt existing ones) for the purpose of murdering large numbers of Jews as quickly and efficiently as possible. The order came from Heinrich Himmler, Reichsführer of the SS and chief architect of the Holocaust. The ghettos would be emptied and their inhabitants transported to labour camps or the new death camps. Gas was the favoured killing method – either carbon monoxide or the cyanide-based pesticide, Zyklon B. Gas chambers, usually disguised as shower units, were installed at the new camps of Bełżec, Sobibór and Treblinka, and at Majdanek and Auschwitz-Birkenau. The official stamp of approval for the mass killing programme, euphemistically called "the Final Solution", was given at the Wannsee Conference in Berlin in January 1942.

Industrialized murder

All camps were built close to railway lines to facilitate transportation from across the Reich. Cattle wagons were used, with people packed in so tightly that many died during the journey. On arrival at a camp, a selection process would occur: those deemed fit to work would be identified, the remainder – small children, the old and the sick – would be made to strip off and taken to the gas chambers. At Auschwitz, some children were selected for gruesome medical experiments carried out by camp doctors. Anything that victims had with them – clothes, luggage, jewellery – was utilized. After a killing session, bodies were disposed of by mass burial or cremation, but only after hair and gold from teeth had been removed.

Prisoners selected for work at the extermination camps rarely lived more than a few months. Conditions were appalling, food was minimal and of poor quality, and diseases such as typhus, pneumonia, dysentery and tuberculosis were widespread. Prisoners were subjected to petty rules with brutally disproportionate punishments, often applied at the whim of a guard. Work was exhausting and, in combination with all the other privations, could have fatal consequences.

Some prisoners were eligible for "privileges" because of the type of work they did. *Kapos* were prisoners promoted to the role of a functionary, who supervised the work of fellow inmates. They were often former criminals and could be even crueller than the guards. *Sonderkommandos* were Jewish prisoners forced to assist in the killing process by clearing bodies from the gas chambers and then burning them. Some women were allocated to the camp brothel. But none of these activities meant that a person was more likely to live; those who did survive relied on a mixture of guile, opportunism, luck and sometimes the help of others. Possessing a valued skill was an advantage – at Auschwitz most of the members of the all-female Jewish orchestra managed to stay alive.

▲
The arrival of Hungarian Jews in Auschwitz-Birkenau

Reactions from outside

Although what was happening inside the camps was communicated to the outside world, many people found the news too extreme to believe. Polish resistance fighters had infiltrated ghettos and concentration camps, and one of their agents, Jan Karski, travelled to Britain and the USA with detailed accounts of mass extermination. Debate still continues about the Allied reaction. Could bomber aircraft have destroyed parts of the camps or, at least, bombed the railway lines that led to them – as requested by Jewish organizations?

There was resistance from Jews themselves, not just by partisans or in the ghettos (see p.228), but also in the camps, most notably at Treblinka, Sobibór and Auschwitz-Birkenau. The revolt at Sobibór in October 1943 involved the murder of eleven SS officers before a mass breakout of about three hundred prisoners. Though most were either killed while escaping or on recapture, around 58 prisoners got away, including Alexander Pechersky, the Jewish-Soviet POW who led the uprising. Shortly afterwards, Himmler ordered the camp to be closed down and destroyed.

With the approach of the Red Army, the Germans made a desperate attempt to remove evidence of their crimes. Some surviving prisoners were executed in the last months of the war, while many at the larger camps were evacuated, forced into long arduous "death marches" further be-hind German lines. In January 1945, in the depth of winter, about 60,000 prisoners made the 53km journey from Auschwitz to Wodzisław on foot, just ten days before Soviet troops liberated the camp. Many died en route, shot by guards for failing to keep up. From Wodzisław the remainder were taken to camps across a disintegrating Germany.

Liberation

Liberation, when it arrived, could be a traumatic experience for both soldiers and prisoners. When British troops got to Bergen-Belsen in Lower Saxony they found a camp that was vastly overcrowded, having been used as a collection point for thousands of evacuated prisoners from elsewhere. Many of the 60,000 prisoners still alive seemed barely recognizable as human beings, and thousands of skeletal corpses lay piled up around the camp. Over 13,000 more would die in the next few weeks. Feelings of compassion were mixed with shock and, in some cases, fear and disgust.

For the prisoners that lived, the nightmare may have been over, but they still had much to endure. On top of the institutionalized degradation that they had been through – with the prospect of death a constant fear – they had no homes to go to and most had lost loved ones, or even witnessed their deaths. Not surpris-

▲
Young prisoners interned at Dachau cheer the liberating American troops

ingly, a huge psychological barrier existed between the prisoners and their liberators. This was exacerbated by the fact that nearly all surviving Jews remained behind barbed wire for months, sometimes years, in Displaced Persons camps run by the Allies (see p.323). The task of rebuilding their lives seemed almost insurmountable.

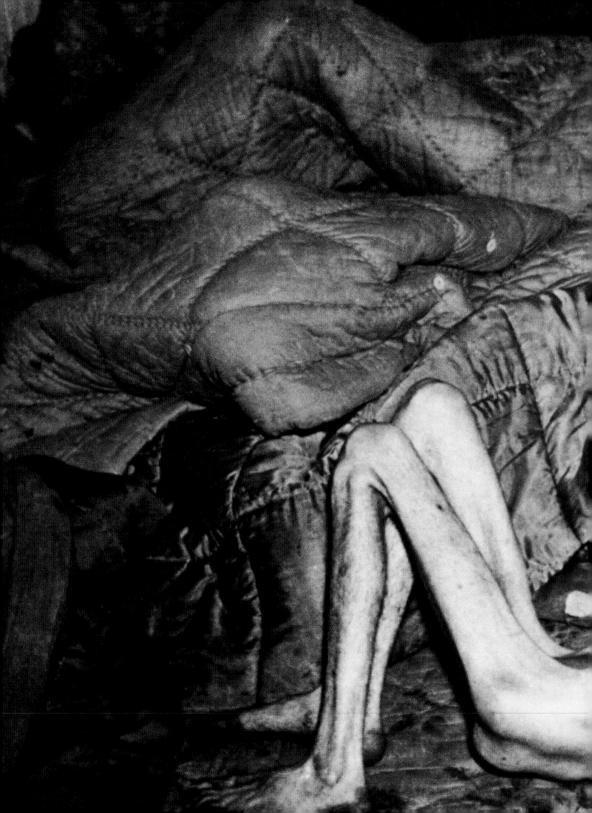

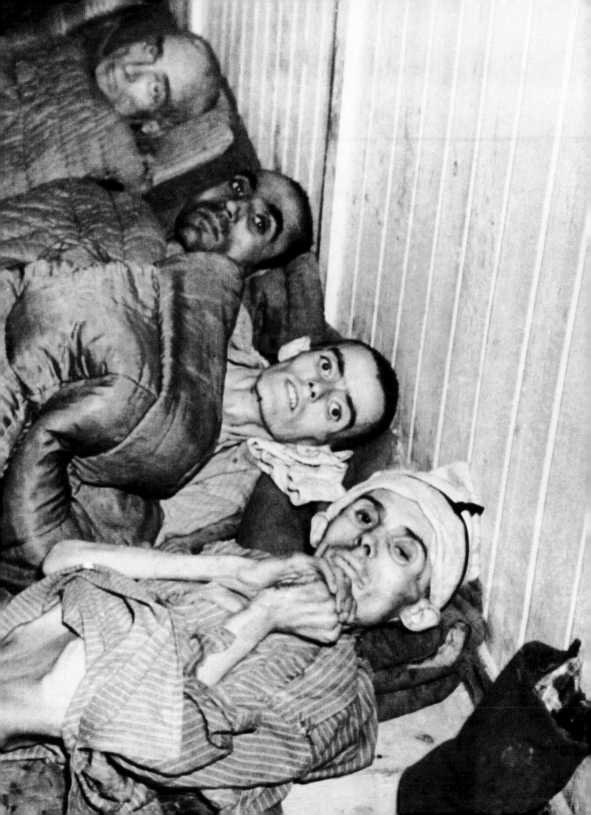

Czech Republic

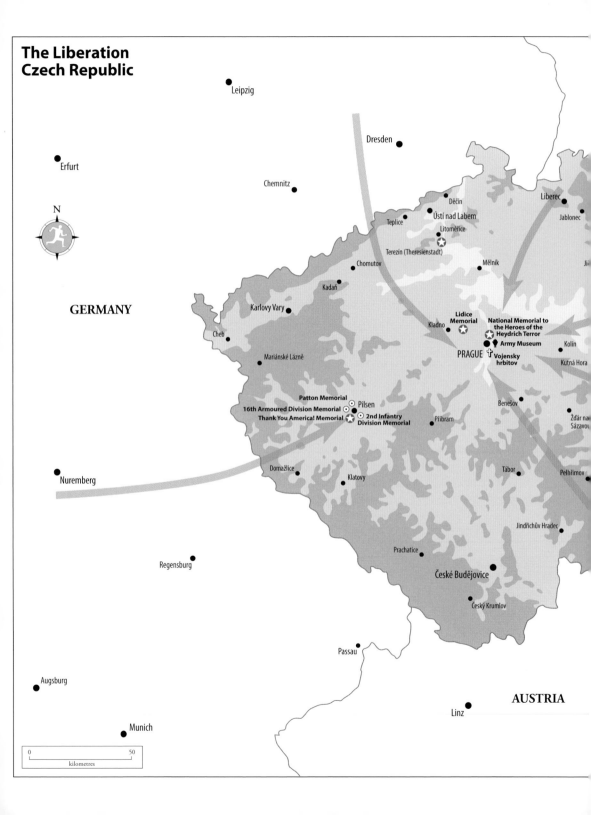

The Liberation
Czech Republic

N

GERMANY

AUSTRIA

Leipzig

Dresden

Erfurt

Chemnitz

Děčín

Liberec

Jablonec

Ústí nad Labem

Teplice

Litoměřice

Terezín (Theresienstadt)

Mělník

Ji

Chomutov

Kadaň

Karlovy Vary

Cheb

Kladno

Lidice
Memorial

National Memorial to
the Heroes of the
Heydrich Terror

Army Museum

Kolín

Mariánské Lázně

PRAGUE

Vojensky
hrbitov

Kutná Hora

Patton Memorial

16th Armoured Division Memorial

Thank You America! Memorial

Pilsen

2nd Infantry
Division Memorial

Příbram

Benešov

Žďár na
Sázavou

Nuremberg

Domažlice

Klatovy

Tábor

Pelhřimov

Jindřichův Hradec

Prachatice

Regensburg

České Budějovice

Český Krumlov

Passau

Augsburg

Linz

Munich

0   50
kilometres

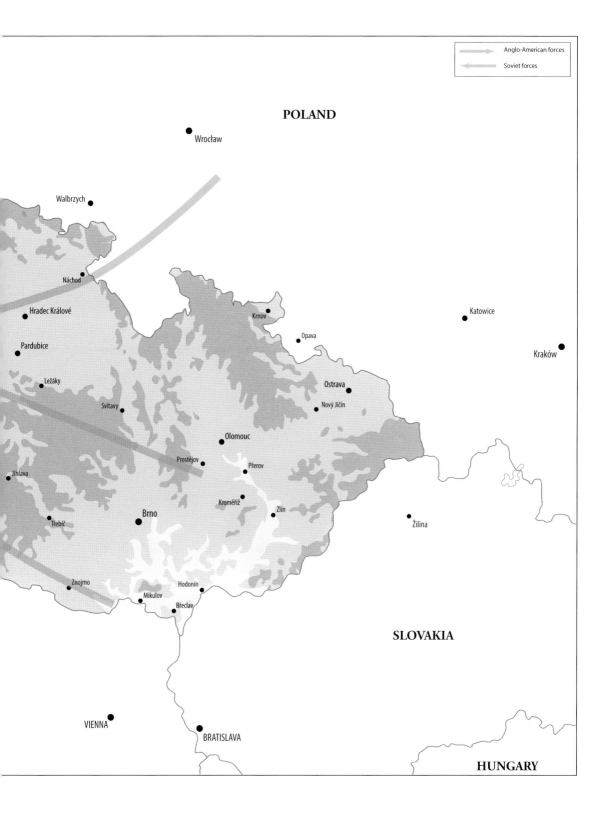

POLAND

Wrocław

Walbrzych

Náchod

Hradec Králové

Krnov

Opava

Katowice

Pardubice

Kraków

Ležáky

Ostrava

Nový Jičín

Svitavy

Olomouc

Prostějov

Přerov

Jihlava

Kroměříž

Zlín

Brno

Žilina

Třebíč

Znojmo

Hodonín

Mikulov

Břeclav

SLOVAKIA

VIENNA

BRATISLAVA

HUNGARY

The Liberation
Czech Republic

The liberation of Czechoslovakia (modern Czech Republic and Slovakia) came from two different directions: Soviet troops advanced on the capital, Prague, in early May 1945, while US troops headed towards the industrial city of Pilsen.

Popular uprisings helped oust the German occupiers, who had been present in Czechoslovakia since the invasion of the Sudetenland in 1938.

The Munich Agreement

Today the Czech Republic and Slovakia are two separate nations; in 1938 they were part of a single nation, Czechoslovakia, that included Czechs, Slovaks and Germans. Many of the country's German speaking citizens lived in areas – collectively called the Sudetenland – that bordered Germany.

Hitler saw this as a pretext for occupation. Presenting himself as the champion of the "oppressed" Sudetenland Germans, he demanded these areas be incorporated into Germany. Desperate to avoid war, the British and French caved in to his demands and persuaded the reluctant Czechoslovak president, Edvard Beneš, to do the same.

Hitler claimed the Sudetenland was the last of his territorial demands. Less than six months later, on 15 March 1939, German troops occupied the rest of the country. Offered the choice of cooperating or facing a full-scale invasion, the Czechoslovaks put up little resistance. The country was then divided: Slovakia became the Slovak Republic, a puppet state of Germany under the leadership of the fascist priest Jozef Tiso;

» Markers of the Czech–German border are pulled down after the Munich agreement

the main Czech-speaking areas were turned into the Nazi-controlled Protectorate of Bohemia and Moravia.

To some extent, life for many Czechs continued as normal. The collaborationist government functioned under German control, but at the same time its prime minister was communicating with Beneš and the government-in-exile, supplying them with important intelligence.

Things changed in the Autumn of 1941 when the Head of Reich Security, Reinhard Heydrich, became the *de facto* ruler of Bohemia and Moravia. As an ardent advocate of Nazi racial beliefs, he regarded around half the Czech population as potential for Germanization; the rest were expendable. The small fortress town of Theresienstadt (Terezín) was converted into a transit camp/ghetto for the Protectorate's Jews, and labour camps were established at Lety (southwest Prague) and Hodonín to intern the Romani population.

Many exiled Czechs and Slovaks served in the Allied armed forces, and in May 1942 two British-trained Czech agents assassinated Heydrich in one of the most daring resistance operations of the war (codenamed Anthropoid). Nazi reprisals, on Hitler's instructions, were extremely brutal and included the total destruction of two Czech villages, Lidiče and Ležáky. Despite the loss of life, both the assassination of Heydrich and the later Prague Uprising of 1945 were seen as worthwhile, because they reinforced the validity of the Czech exiles in London and Moscow, and made them active partners in Allied discussions about their country's future.

Liberation

In early May 1945, as the Soviets advanced on Prague and US troops on Pilsen, popular

Significant sites are marked on the map on pages 258 and 259

 Thank You America! Memorial, Pilsen. See p.264

National Memorial to the Heroes of the Heydrich Terror, Prague. See p.266

Terezín (Theresienstadt). See p.266

Lidice Memorial, Lidice. See p.267

Significant sites «

uprisings broke out across the country in expectation of imminent freedom, including at Pilsen and Prague on 5 May. Almost all the fighting in Prague ended on 8 May with the German capitulation and withdrawal. The first troops from the Soviets' 1st Ukrainian Front did not arrive in the city until the following morning.

« Commemorative celebrations of the Liberation, Pilsen

Biography
» **Edvard Beneš**

Edvard Beneš was one of the founding fathers of the new state of Czechoslovakia, a country born – like Poland – out of the wreckage of the Austro-Hungarian Empire in 1918. A socialist, but not a Marxist, his vision for Czechoslovakia was as a multi-ethnic state, which would act as a bridge between the communist east and the capitalist west. Beneš acted as foreign minister from the country's founding in 1918 until 1935 when he became president.

By then, there was already discontent among Czechoslovakia's minorities, especially the Germans and the Slovaks, who made up 22 percent and 16 percent of the population respectively. Beneš resisted Nazi Germany's demand that the predominantly German areas, the so-called Sudetenland, be ceded to Germany. Italy, France and the United Kingdom disagreed, approving Germany's annexation of the Sudetenland in the Munich Agreement of September 1938; Beneš was not invited to attend. Pressurized by France and the UK into agreeing the decision, and by Germany into resigning as president, he went into exile in October.

When war broke out, Beneš set up the Czechoslovak National Council as a provisional government-in-exile in Paris, transferring it to London after the Fall of Paris. He encouraged acts of sabotage and subversion by the remnants of the army at home, but the Czechoslovak Resistance was never as active as its Polish equivalent; its importance largely derived from its intelligence work, organized from London by František Morávec.

Beneš's major foreign-policy aim was the re-establishment of Czechoslovakia after the war. Convinced that the Soviet Union would emerge as a dominant force in the postwar political landscape (and embittered by his country's 1938 betrayal by Britain and France), he did his best to maintain good relations with Stalin, signing a Czech-Soviet Treaty of Alliance in July 1941. Beneš hoped that this would guarantee his own return after the war and the preservation of democracy.

Beneš did return to Czechoslovakia in April 1945, and later presided over the expulsion of 2.5 million Sudeten Germans. Democracy, however, only survived until 1948, when a communist coup established a one-party state – controlled by Moscow – that would last until 1989. Beneš, now a sick man, witnessed the loss of his country's independence for the second time. He resigned in June 1948 and died a few months later. For Czechs, he remains a highly controversial figure.

Pilsen

On 4 May 1945, the 9th Infantry Regiment of the US 2nd Infantry Division – part of General Patton's Third Army – broke through the eastern frontier of the Third Reich and entered occupied Czechoslovakia. Shortly before noon the regiment set up its command base in Neukirchen (Czech Nový Kostel).

The following day, the population of Pilsen (Czech Plzeň) rose up against the Nazi occupation. Citizens entered the streets and began to tear down Nazi symbols. As the Germans attempted to suppress the uprising, the civilian population called on the Allies for immediate assistance.

Early in the morning of 6 May, tanks from the US 16th Armored Division set out for Pilsen, reaching the city and its grateful citizens around 8.00am. The first unit into town was Combat Command B, led by Colonel Charles Noble. The Americans encountered sporadic resistance from German soldiers, and were fired on from the tower of the cathedral, but it soon became apparent that further fighting was futile. Around 2.15pm, Lieutenant Colonel Perkins, Noble's second-in-command, received the capitulation signed by the German commander, General von Majewski, who then shot himself. The 16th Armored Division was relieved by the 2nd Infantry Division (nicknamed the "Indianheads") and the 17th Belgian Fusilier Battalion, which included 700 volunteers who had joined the US Army after the liberation of Liège.

Many Sudeten Germans and German soldiers were desperate to avoid falling into the hands of the Soviet troops, and significant numbers fled into the US zone of occupation; once there, they had to be protected by the Americans from vengeful attacks by the Czechs.

General Patton was eager for his men to continue on to Prague to prevent Czechoslovakia falling into the hands of the Soviets. Churchill and many senior Americans were of the same opinion, but such a move (though easily achievable) was vetoed by Eisenhower as the western Allies' supreme commander. Czechoslovakia had been designated within

«
US General George S. Patton makes a farewell speech to men of the 8th Armored Division prior to their demobilization in Rokycany

>> **Porajmos: the forgotten Romani Holocaust**

Romani people use the term *Porajmos*, meaning "the Devouring", to refer to the Nazi attempts to exterminate them. Two labour camps, at Lety and Hodonín, were built by the Czechs in March 1939. From 1942 these were used to intern the Romani of Bohemia and Moravia, most of whom were later transported to the so-called "Gypsy family camp" at Auschwitz-Birkenau. Exact numbers are un-known, but an estimated four thousand were killed at Auschwitz and about 95 percent of Czech Romani perished over-all. Recognition of the degree of persecution suffered by the Romani people has been slow to happen, and prejudice is still widespread. In 1971 a pig farm was built on the site of the camp at Lety; its removal was only agreed by the Czech government in 2017 after years of campaigning.

the so-called Soviet sphere of interest at the Yalta Conference (see p.271) and he felt that to renege on this would create all sorts of political complications in the future.

>> Pilsen sites

Patton Memorial Pilsen
Probřežní 10, Ⓦ patton-memorial.cz/en

The Patton Memorial Pilsen museum was opened on 5 May 2005 to coincide with the 60th anniversary of the liberation of the city and southwestern Bohemia by the US Army. It contains over a thousand exhibits drawn from private collections, including archive photographs showing the war's final days, with the arrival of US troops and their enthusiastic reception by the local population. Much of the exhibition focuses on General Patton and General Ernest N. Harmon, who assisted the postwar recovery of the country. The museum underwent a major refit in 2018–19, so check it's open before visiting.

Thank You America! Memorial
Americká třída

On a street named America, close to the junction with Klatovská třída, is the Thank You America! Memorial, erected to honour the US liberation of Pilsen. Two tall granite stelae with gold-leaf inscriptions in both Czech and English stand side by side up a small flight of steps opposite a fountain. In front of them is a separate smaller block dedicated to the 16th Armoured Division bearing the words, "We'll Never Forget".

2nd Infantry Division Memorial
Chodské náměstí (Chodské Square)

A wedge of land at the junction of Klatovská and E. Beneše is the site of the memorial to the 2nd Infantry Division. Conceived and designed by Dr Pershing Wakefield, a veteran of the division, it was erected in 1990 and takes the form of a small black obelisk with the division's insignia – the head of an American Indian superimposed on a star (the division was known as the "Indianheads").

16th Armoured Division Memorial
Husova

This memorial, located opposite the Czech National Bank, is in the shape of a metal-framed glass pyramid. Etched on the glass is the division's emblem.

Prague and around

Having been major participants in the fall of Berlin (see p.314), Marshal Konev and the Soviet 1st Ukrainian Front were ordered to head southwest towards Czechoslovakia and on to Prague.

In support of Konev's forces were Marshal Malinowsky's 2nd Ukrainian and General Eremenko's 4th Ukrainian fronts, advancing towards the southern and eastern borders of Czechoslovakia. This combined Soviet force of over two million men was opposed by around half that number of soldiers from the German Army Group Centre, commanded by the staunch Hitler loyalist, Field Marshal Schörner.

Prague Uprising

Before the Soviet advance had reached Czechoslovakia, Prague's citizens spontaneously rose up against the Germans on 5 May – ahead of a planned operation by the Czech Resistance. German signs were ripped down and Czech flags raised. Radio Prague broadcast requests for Allied assistance, but although General Patton's forces were closer to the capital than the Red Army, they were prevented from advancing by General Eisenhower.

Once German reinforcements arrived from Army Centre North, the reaction to the uprising was wholehearted and vicious. Help for the Czechs came from an unlikely source when, on 6 May, a division of the Russian Liberation Army (ROA) arrived. This anti-communist army – known as "Vlasov's Army" after its commander, General Andrey Vlasov – had been fighting for the Nazis, but changed sides in a desperate attempt to save its own skin.

Although the German unconditional surrender was signed on 7 May (see p.320), a short period had been granted for ongoing offensives to be terminated. The SS in Prague used this time to wreak as much murderous havoc as possible. In one instance, they mas-

---

❯❯ Theresienstadt: the "model" camp

In November 1941, the 18th-century garrison town of Theresienstadt (Terezín), 64km north of Prague, was converted into a camp for Jews. The Nazis described it as a ghetto, but it was used as a transit camp for those ultimately destined for the gas chambers. The inmates included a large number of intellectuals and artists. Run by the SS, the camp was administered by a Jewish Elders Council who organized and encouraged a wide range of cultural activities. These were permitted by the SS, who used it to their advantage when an investigative commission of the International Red Cross visited the camp in June 1944. Theresienstadt was presented as a "model Jewish settlement", complete with schools and gardens, an image reinforced by a Nazi propaganda film that was intended to counter the rumours of mass killings.

The day-to-day reality was very different: the camp was overcrowded, food was minimal, medical care inadequate and there were regular deportations to Auschwitz-Birkenau and other death camps. The SS fled on 5 and 6 May and Soviet troops arrived on 8 May. More than 155,000 Jews passed through Theresienstadt; around 35,440 perished there and 88,000 were deported to extermination camps.

sacred around fifty resistance fighters who had surrendered. Although the ROA proved effective at thwarting some German progress, by the 8 May its troops had abandoned the city to surrender to the Americans. German troops were similarly reluctant to fall into the hands of the Soviets and fought on before an agreement was brokered with the Resistance. This allowed most of the Germans to evacuate westwards on the morning of 9 May before the arrival of the Red Army's 3rd and 4th Guards Tank Armies – the first Soviet troops to enter the city. The precise casualty figures of the uprising remain unknown: an estimated 1700 Czechs were killed and around the same number wounded; the Germans lost around 900 men; troops from the ROA about 300; while Red Army casualties in Prague were no more than thirty.

Over the next two days, Soviet forces to the east of Prague battled against the remaining Wehrmacht troops in the Protectorate, taking about 600,000 as prisoners-of-war. On 11 May the Soviets met up with elements of the US Third Army near Pilsen. While the war in Europe was officially over, hostilities continued against Sudeten Germans and Czech collaborators, violent attacks that were encouraged by Beneš and the Soviets. Thousands were killed and even more – perhaps as many as 2.5 million – were forcibly expelled from the country.

» Prague and around sites

National Memorial to the Heroes of the Heydrich Terror
St Cyril and St Methodius Cathedral, Resslova 307/9a, Prague

Built for Catholic worship in the 18th century, this building became the cathedral of Czech Orthodox Christians in the 1930s. It was the only church to give refuge to the escaping Operation Anthropoid agents after their assassination of Heydrich in 1942. A section of the crypt contains an exhibition outlining the events, with memorial busts and brief biographies of the seven paratroopers who took part. Outside, on the bullet-marked south wall, is a plaque that commemorates those who died. A separate memorial in the Libeň district, on the actual site of the attack, is near a very busy road intersection and difficult to access.

Vojensky hrbitov (Military cemetery)
Jana Želivského, Prague

Part of the vast Olšany cemetery, created in 1680 for plague victims, the military cemetery is within the northeastern section, 200m along Jana Želivského. Its centrepiece is the monument to the 436 Soviet soldiers killed during the liberation of Prague and its aftermath. There is also a mass grave containing two generals and 187 soldiers of the Russian Liberation Army who aided the Czechs during the Prague Uprising, and the graves of 256 British and Commonwealth soldiers gathered from across the Czech Republic.

Terezín (Theresienstadt)
Ⓦ pamatnik-terezin.cz

In 1941, the population of Terezín was ejected and the garrison town turned into a Jewish ghetto and transit camp. Today, some of it functions as a museum, memorializing those who lived and died here. Made up of two fortresses, the larger is laid out in a grid plan. Near the main square are the remains of the railway siding where prisoners arrived and departed. The ghetto museum, housed in a large

›› Operation Anthropoid: the plot to kill Heydrich

In October 1941, František Moravec, the Czech head of military intelligence in London, devised a plan (codenamed Anthropoid) to assassinate Reinhard Heydrich, whose ruthless control of the Protectorate had earned him the nickname "the Butcher of Prague". Trained by the British Special Operations Executive (SOE), two agents, Jan Kubiš and Jozef Gabčík, landed near Prague. After various failed attempts, the pair ambushed Heydrich's open-topped Mercedes in the Prague suburb of Libeň on 27 May 1942. When Gabčík's sten gun jammed, Kubiš threw a grenade, injuring both Heydrich and himself. An exchange of fire followed before the injured Kubiš escaped by bicycle. Heydrich died eight days later from sepsis after his wounds became infected.

Furious that so senior a Nazi had been attacked, Hitler ordered massive reprisals. The villages of Lidice and Ležáky – thought to have links to the assassins – were singled out for particularly brutal treatment. Both villages were completely destroyed and most of their inhabitants murdered. The Gestapo tortured and executed many others suspected of involvement; as many as 1300 were killed.

Kubiš and Gabčík, along with five other Anthropoid agents, managed to evade capture until 18 June. They ended up sheltering in the cathedral of Sts Cyril and Methodius in Prague, but were betrayed by fellow agent Karel Čurda. The group held out against Waffen-SS troops for a few hours, but their situation was hopeless. The Germans were keen to capture them alive, but on entering the building they found Kubiš dying from his wounds, and Gabčík and the other five dead by their own hands.

neo-classical building, outlines the history of the ghetto and its place in the "Final Solution". The Magdeburg Barracks site, south of the museum, was where the self-governing Jewish council was located. The displays here focus on the camp's remarkable cultural life (see p.265), but there is also a reconstructed women's dormitory – the three-tier bunks, luggage and belongings conveying some idea of the cramped conditions. The smaller fortress, just across the River Ohře, was built as a prison and used by the Gestapo to intern around 32,000 prisoners – mostly non-Jews active in the Resistance.

Lidice Memorial
Tokajická 152, Lidice, ⓦ lidice-memorial.cz/en

The massacre at Lidice – ordered as a reprisal for Operation Anthropoid – so horrified world opinion that several places were renamed after the village so that its name wouldn't disappear. During the attack, 173 men were shot; the same number of women were sent to Ravensbrück; and 82 children were gassed at Chełmno extermination camp. The village itself was rebuilt nearby in 1945 and the site of the old village turned into a memorial and a museum. There's a paved "reverent" area and mausoleum close to the museum, but much of the site is a green open space dotted with sculptures, including a poignant bronze group of the 82 murdered children. The museum uses archive material and film to evoke the everyday existence of those who lived here. Recently, one of the houses in the new village opened as a museum, continuing the Lidice story after the war, when 143 of its original female inhabitants returned.

EUROPE
REMEMBERS
CELEBRATE
75 YEARS OF
FREEDOM

Official Member of the
Liberation
ROUTE
EUROPE
www.liberationroute.com

LIBERATION FESTIVAL PILSEN

CELEBRATING THE 75TH ANNIVERSARY OF THE LIBERATION BY THE US ARMY

MAY 1–6, 2020

- **The City of Pilsen** – the last major European city liberated by the US Army and its allies on May 6, 1945
- **Since 1990 – Liberation Festival Pilsen** – a rich and varied cultural and social programme, with a spectacular vintage military vehicles parade, re-enactment camps, competitions for kids and public discussions with WWII veterans, in milestone anniversaries attended by 200,000 spectators
- **2005 – Patton Memorial Pilsen museum** opened by the grandson of General Patton
- **2009 – From D-Day to V-Day** international project launched
- **Since 2009** – Liberation Festival Pilsen provides **educational trails and educational materials** for schools
- **2018** – Pilsen becomes member of the international foundation Liberation Route Europe

EARL INGRAM, US Army WWII veteran, liberator of the city of Pilsen:

"We should never forget that one of the worst men who ever walked planet earth in the 20th century came to power through ballots. By taking more interest in who is leading us today, we can guard against repeating the mistakes of history and ensure there is never again the need to reflect on monuments like that of Pilsen."

More information: www.liberationfestival.com, www.facebook.com/slavnostisvobody

The Soviet Union

Western consciousness of the war's end, in particular the Liberation of Europe, is strongly focused on the Anglo-American achievement. But the actions of the Soviet Union were highly significant too.

The Soviet contribution, if acknowledged in western discourse at all, is coloured by the fact that in "liberating" the countries of Central and Eastern Europe, the Red Army overthrew one kind of brutal tyranny, Nazism, only to re-place it with another – Stalinism. And yet the extent to which the Soviet Union suffered in helping to defeat the Nazis is truly staggering. During the four years of its war with Germany, in which it came perilously close to defeat, the country lost an estimated 26 million of its citizens – around fourteen percent – of which some 10.5 million were soldiers. The land war was fought, for the most part, on Soviet territory; something that the country's two main allies never had to experience.

Operation Barbarossa

The German invasion of the Soviet Union in June 1941, codenamed Operation Barbarossa, came as a surprise to Stalin, despite many reliable warnings from his and other intelligence agencies. His armies were mostly unprepared. The invasion began less than two years after the signing of a non-aggression pact between the Nazis and the Soviets, who – though ideological enemies – were willing to make an agreement in order to divide up Central Europe between them. Hitler reneged on the pact in the confident belief that his seemingly invincible armies would reach Moscow before winter set in. Initially at least, his confidence was rewarded. During the summer, three German Army Groups of 153 divisions and 3.5 million soldiers (around eighty percent of Hitler's total forces) swept eastwards in a series of fronts that stretched from Finland to the Black Sea.

Nazi terror

Because they regarded Slavic people as barely human, the Nazis treated those they conquered with extreme barbarism, ransacking and burning villages, raping and murdering at will. Commissars, and any officials connected to the Communist Party, were automatically executed, and millions of POWs and workers were transported back to Germany as forced labour. Organized executions were carried out by Himmler's mobile death squads, the *Einsatzgruppen*, with the most systematic violence directed against Jews and Romani. Some of these murders were on an unbelievably

▲
Troops in action during Operation Barbarossa

massive scale, such as the Rumbula massacre near Riga in which 25,000 people (nearly all of them Jews) were shot over two days. In many cases the Nazis recruited locals both to assist in the killings and to fight against the Soviets.

Stalin's response

Why was the Red Army, despite its size, at first so inadequate to the task of defending the country? One answer is the sheer efficiency of the Wehrmacht which, once again, employed the tactic of *blitzkrieg* (see p.27) to devastating effect. Another is that Stalin's purging of the officer corps in 1937 had seriously undermined the Red Army's effectiveness and weakened morale. Among the many executed were three Soviet marshals, including Marshal Tukhachevsky, a key strategist and expert on armoured warfare. Other senior officers were imprisoned, such as Mikhail Rokossovsky, who after his release became one of the key commanders in the eventual defeat of Germany.

Shortly after the invasion, the Supreme Command Headquarters (the Stavka) was established to improve and coordinate the running of the armed forces, with Stalin as its Supreme Commander. Stalin then had something of a personal crisis, retiring to his dacha for a few days and only returning when asked to by the Politbu-

Joseph Stalin (centre), flanked by his Foreign Minister Molotov (left) and General Zhukov (right)

ro. Like Hitler, Stalin felt he knew how to conduct a war better than his generals, and (also like Hitler) would not countenance the idea of a tactical retreat. But at least at this point he was surrounding himself with some talented advisers: notably Georgy Zhukov, who would emerge as the Soviets' most successful commander. Stalin's interference was initially incessant, with NKVD men appointed to check and monitor the behaviour and performance of senior officers. General Pavlov's failure to defend the Western Front in the first week of the invasion led

to his arrest and execution within a month. As the war progressed, Stalin started to listen to his generals more intently.

Fighting for the motherland

With many Soviet troops surrendering in the face of the Germans' implacable advance, Stalin issued Orders 227 and 270, authorizing extreme measures against any soldiers (and their families) who were captured or retreated. At the same time, Stalin was calling on the population to defend "Mother Russia" in terms of an apocalyptic fight for survival. For the Soviets – and for many Russians today – the conflict was thought of not as World War II but as the Great Patriotic War. Stalin recognized that appealing to the national pride of his citizens would have better results than any ideological arguments, even softening his attitude to the Orthodox Church. His citizens responded, and millions fought with dogged resilience. Even so, the forward thrust of the German Army Group Centre towards Moscow looked unstoppable, and was only ended when Hitler (to the frustration of his generals) ordered some of its divisions south to the Ukraine and north to attack Leningrad. The subsequent Siege of Leningrad would last nearly two and a half years and result in over half a million deaths, mostly from disease and starvation.

What halted the advance and scuppered Hitler's plan for early victory was the weather. By early October the rains had begun, reducing the roads to quagmires of thick, sticky mud; the conflict became literally bogged down. In addition, the German supply lines were badly stretched, the Soviets were now launching counteroffensives and had upped their industrial production levels, relocating their armaments factories further east and out of bombing range. They were also receiving much-needed materials and equipment from the British, and later the Americans, as part of the Lend-Lease scheme (see p.28). Above all, with a population of around 190 million, Soviet frontline troops – which included women in important combat roles – could always be replaced, as soldiers were killed or captured. They needed them, as by December the ratio of soldiers killed was twenty Russians to every one German.

Turning points

As the ground froze in November 1941, it seemed inevitable to almost everyone involved that Moscow would finally be taken by the Germans. That it didn't happen was due to a resolutely determined defence, organized by Zhukov, that at times bordered on the suicidal. In December, the Russians launched a counteroffensive, followed by a large general offensive – ordered by Stalin – which met with failure. As Russian troops ventured into territory that had until recently been behind German lines, they witnessed the devastation and carnage that the invading forces had brought to villages and towns. What they saw inspired a deeply held thirst for revenge that would manifest itself

▲
Children hide in an air-raid shelter during Nazi air strikes

in extreme reprisals (including systematic rape) as soon as Soviet troops reached those Reich-occupied territories beyond the Soviet Union, intensifying as they encountered actual Germans – whether soldiers or civilians.

Significant though the defence of Moscow was, the true turning points on the Eastern Front occurred in 1943: first came the terrible, attritional 23-week grind of the Battle of Stalingrad (modern-day Volgograd) which ended in February 1943; followed five months later by the Battle of Kursk, a vast armoured encounter involving 6000 tanks, 4000 aircraft and around two million troops. These two battles ended in Soviet victories, with massive losses suffered on both sides. They marked the end of the vast German campaign in the east and shattered the myth of the Wehrmacht's invincibility. From now on it would be the Soviets who would be on the offensive.

Outwitting his allies

As the Red Army pushed the Wehrmacht back and the defeat of the Axis seemed highly likely, Stalin began negotiating with his two allies about how the war would end and what a postwar Europe would look like. The first of the so-called "Big Three" conferences, at which Stalin, Roosevelt and Churchill convened together for the first time, took place in Tehran at the end of No-

vember 1943. Although military matters were the main discussion point, in particular the timing of Operation Overlord, Stalin was insistent that the frontiers gained by the Soviet Union's invasion of Poland should be retained and signalled his contempt for the Polish government-in-exile.

In February 1945, at Yalta in the Crimea, the three leaders met again. Roosevelt, now clearly a very sick man, wanted to secure Soviet assistance against the Japanese and was largely uninterested in European affairs. Once again, Stalin quietly manipulated the other two leaders, managing to secure a dominating role for the Soviet Union in Eastern and Central Europe, with the matter of the precise makeup of the Polish government to be decided later in Moscow – something most Poles saw as a betrayal (see p.226). Churchill also agreed to the enforced repatriation of all former Soviet POWs, including those who fought for the Nazis (which would guarantee their certain death). The Potsdam Conference held later in the year confirmed many of the decisions reached at Yalta and established precise zones of occupation in Germany (see p.312).

A vast Soviet victory parade took place in Moscow in June 1945. Marshal Zhukov, who had played such a major role in the defeat of Germany and who had accepted the country's surrender, was con-

▲ An armoured fighting vehicle at the Battle of Stalingrad

spicuous on a white horse, but his triumph proved relatively brief. Although he attended Potsdam and was put in charge of the Soviet zone of occupation, the NKVD was already pursuing him. An incriminating trainload of war booty led to his downfall. The ever-paranoid Stalin, who saw Zhukov as a rival, was almost certainly behind the general's fall from grace.

БЬЁМСЯ МЫ ЗДОРОВО,
КОЛЕМ ОТЧАЯННО –
ВНУКИ СУВОРОВА,
ДЕТИ ЧАПАЕВА

Germany

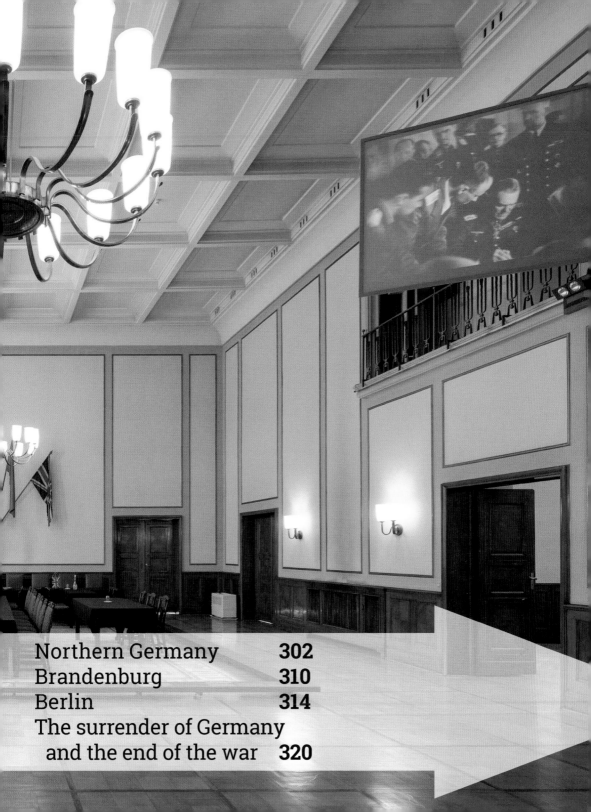

The Liberation Germany

BERLIN SITES

- Allied Museum
- Anti-War Museum
- Bebelplatz
- Berliner Unterwelten Museum
- Memorial to the Murdered Jews of Europe
- Flak Tower
- "Mother and Child" Bunker
- German Historical Museum
- Forced Labour Documentation Centre
- German Resistance Memorial Centre
- German-Russian Museum
- Kaiser Wilhelm Memorial Church
- Jewish Museum
- Reichstag
- Soviet Memorial Tiergarten
- Topography of Terror
- House of the Wannsee Conference

Anglo-American forces
Soviet forces

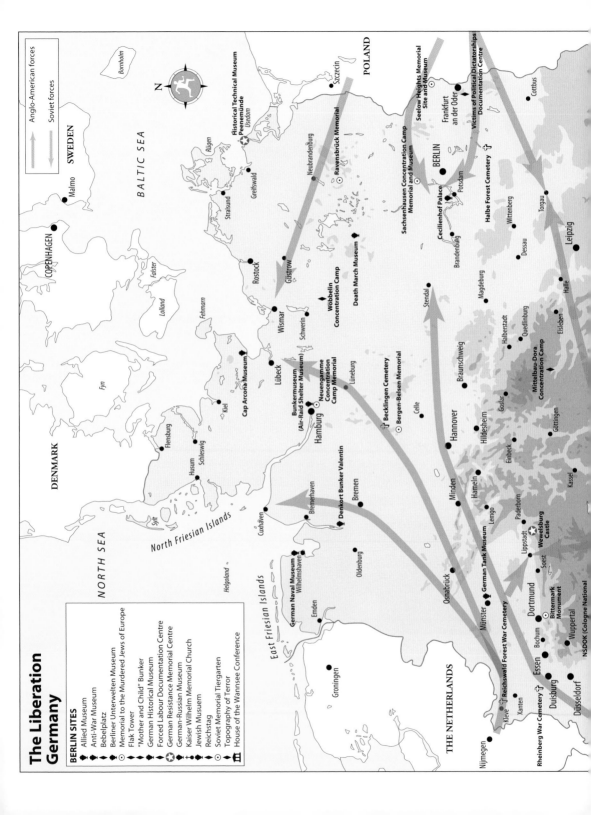

DENMARK

SWEDEN

POLAND

THE NETHERLANDS

BALTIC SEA

NORTH SEA

COPENHAGEN

Malmo

Bornholm

Fyn

Lolland

Falster

Rügen

Usedom

Sylt

Helgoland

East Friesian Islands

North Friesian Islands

Fehmarn

Flensburg
Husum
Schleswig
Kiel
Emden
Groningen
Nijmegen
Xanten
Kleve
Wilhelmshaven
Oldenburg
Bremerhaven
Cuxhaven
Bremen
Osnabrück
Münster
Bochum
Duisburg
Düsseldorf
Essen
Dortmund
Soest
Lippstadt
Paderborn
Lemgo
Minden
Hameln
Hannover
Hildesheim
Einbeck
Göttingen
Goslar
Kassel
Celle
Lüneburg
Hamburg
Lübeck
Wismar
Schwerin
Güstrow
Rostock
Stralsund
Greifswald
Neubrandenburg
Szczecin
Braunschweig
Magdeburg
Halberstadt
Quedlinburg
Dessau
Wittenberg
Brandenburg
Potsdam
BERLIN
Frankfurt an der Oder
Cottbus
Torgau
Leipzig
Halle
Eisleben
Stendal

Historical Technical Museum Peenemünde
Ravensbrück Memorial
Seelow Heights Memorial Site and Museum
Victims of Political Dictatorships Documentation Centre
Sachsenhausen Concentration Camp Memorial and Museum
Cecilienhof Palace
Halbe Forest Cemetery
Death March Museum
Wöbbelin Concentration Camp
Cap Arcona Museum
Bunkermuseum (Air-Raid Shelter Museum)
Neuengamme Concentration Camp Memorial
Becklingen Cemetery
Bergen-Belsen Memorial
Denkort Bunker Valentin
German Naval Museum
German Tank Museum
Reichswald Forest War Cemetery
Rheinberg War Cemetery
Bittermark Monument
NSDOK (Cologne National
Wewelsburg Castle
Mittelbau-Dora Concentration Camp

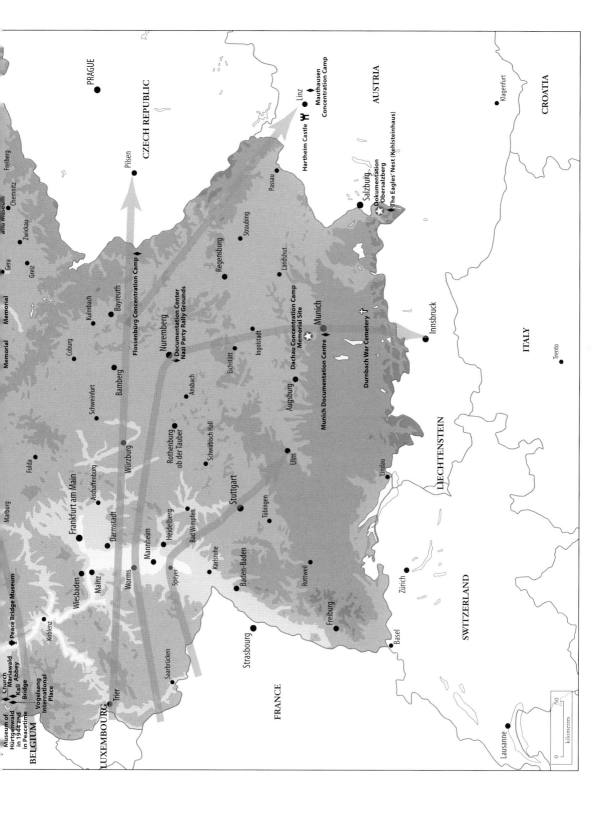

PRAGUE

CZECH REPUBLIC

Freiberg

Chemnitz

Zwickau

Gera

Greiz

Pilsen

Mauthausen
Concentration Camp

Linz

AUSTRIA

Hartheim Castle

Klagenfurt

CROATIA

Passau

Salzburg
Dokumentation
Obersalzberg
The Eagles' Nest (Kehlsteinhaus)

Straubing

Regensburg

Landshut

Bayreuth

Kulmbach

Flossenburg Concentration Camp

Coburg

Nuremberg
Documentation Center
Nazi Party Rally Grounds

Eichstätt

Ingolstadt

Dachau Concentration Camp
Memorial Site

Munich

Durnbach War Cemetery

Innsbruck

ITALY

Trento

Schweinfurt

Bamberg

Ansbach

Augsburg

Munich Documentation Centre

Würzburg

Rothenburg
ob der Tauber

Schwäbisch Hall

Marburg

Fulda

Frankfurt am Main

Aschaffenburg

Darmstadt

Heidelberg

Bad Wimpfen

Stuttgart

Tübingen

Ulm

Lindau

LIECHTENSTEIN

Mannheim

Wiesbaden

Mainz

Worms

Speyer

Karlsruhe

Baden-Baden

Rottweil

Freiburg

Zürich

Basel

SWITZERLAND

Koblenz

Saarbrücken

Strasbourg

FRANCE

Trier

LUXEMBOURG

Lausanne

BELGIUM

Museum of
Hürtgenwald
in 1944 and
in Peacetime

Church
Mariawald
Abbey

Peace Bridge Museum

Vogelsang
International
Place

Kall Abbey
Bridge

Memorial

Memorial

and Museum

0   50
kilometres

The Liberation Germany

In the autumn of 1944, six British, American, Canadian and French armies advanced on Germany from the west, while three Red Army fronts approached from the east.

Numerically, the Allies had overwhelming superiority. Their uniformed combatants numbered well over five million – the US and the Soviets fielded more than two million soldiers each – and they were backed by almost 20,000 aircraft. British and American planes controlled Germany's skies, from which they bombed towns and cities remorselessly in the hope of weakening the country's industrial base and demoralizing the population. Germany's forces, meanwhile, were dwindling in number, as its soldiers were killed or captured and its planes shot down. Persistent Allied bombing had devastated the German oil fields and synthetic oil plants were only producing a fraction of what was needed to keep the country's tanks and other military vehicles on the move.

To an outside observer it was an unequal fight with a certain outcome. Some German generals believed the war was lost as early as July 1944. Each month that passed, each kilometre of retreat, seemed to bring further proof of the country's inevitable defeat.

The invasion of Germany

The odds may have been heaving in the Allies' favour, but Eisenhower in the west and the commanders of the Russian fronts (army groups) in the east knew that Germany was not a military power to be underestimated. Only a well-coordinated and tenacious attack would succeed. The campaign began inauspiciously, however, with a battle that would prove unexpectedly bloody, brutal and futile.

❯❯ Civilian responsibility

Before and during the invasion of Germany there was much discussion about the culpability of the German population, and how they should be treated in defeat. It was easy to see the entire German people as responsible – and it might have been necessary for soldiers to accept this as a simple truth – but the reality was far more complex. There was some opposition to Hitler in Germany, and plenty of people wanted the war to end or the Führer replaced with a peacemaker. Unfortunately, few of them had any real power. The Nazis were ruthless in jailing and executing their political opponents, and expressing scepticism of Hitler's leadership was to risk death. Only the military had any chance of controlling Hitler, but the failed coup d'etat of 20 July 1944 proved just how difficult a takeover would be.

As the Allies gathered on Germany's borders for the final assault, Wehrmacht officers and civilians found guilty of plotting against Hitler were still being executed. The 20 July assassination attempt had resulted in an escalation of terror operations: more than 7000 were arrested and nearly 5000 were executed in its aftermath. The failed plot also led to obligatory fanaticism, as every high-ranking German officer was made to swear personal allegiance to Hitler. In the defence of the Fatherland, any unauthorized surrender – and Hitler did not authorize surrender – was punishable by death.

» Hitler's failure to negotiate

With the advantage of hindsight, it's hard not to ask why Nazi Germany carried on fighting rather than negotiating a peace with the Allies.

Before the war, Hitler had proudly proclaimed the start of a thousand-year Reich. In his mind, Germany's territorial expansion into Central and Eastern Europe – and the war that followed – was just the beginning. Even as he was forced to fight on multiple fronts, unable to mount a new offensive, Hitler still talked and behaved like a man who thought he could win the war.

Hitler trusted in himself and his mission, and believed it was Germany's destiny to be victorious under his leadership. Faced with mounting German losses, Hitler responded by branding his generals incompetent and his people irresolute. He was dismissive of anyone who expressed pessimism towards the Nazi cause, and made it clear that his confidence on winning the war rested on three expectations. Firstly, Hitler believed that the Allies would argue among themselves and that these divisions could be exploited. This was possible: at times, the American and British generals carped at each other, and the only motivation they shared with the Soviets was a desire to see the end of Nazism. Secondly, Hitler hoped that the introduction of new weapons would swing the balance of power in Germany's favour or terrorize Britain's population into demanding peace. Had Germany perfected the atomic bomb before the USA, the outcome of the war may indeed have been different.

If none of these hopes was realized, Hitler was certain that providence would step in to save Germany, killing one of his enemies or dealing a similarly devastating blow to the Allies.

Significant sites are marked on the map on pages 276 and 277

 Wewelsburg Castle, Wewelsburg. See p.293

✪ **Dachau Concentration Camp Memorial Site, Dachau. See p.297**

✪ **Dokumentation Obersalzberg, Berchtesgaden. See p.300**

✪ **Historical Technical Museum, Peenemünde. See p.305**

✪ **German Resistance Memorial Centre, Berlin. See p.317**

Significant sites

«

«
Adolf Hitler on his 55th birthday, 1944

Hürtgen Forest

On the evening of 11 September 1944, a US patrol crept across the German border from Luxembourg. The following day, US General Courtney Hodges' First Army pushed forward towards Aachen with the intention of breaking through the Siegfried Line to reach the Rhine.

Eisenhower's overall plan was to co-ordinate and advance his three army groups together, liberating German territory without committing troops too far ahead of a broad north-south front. The setback around Colmar (see p.149) and Axis resis-tance in the Netherlands (see p.197) meant that the corps in the centre of the Allied front were moving slightly faster than the rest. Reluctant to halt the advance of Hodges' American troops – who could make a spectacular breakthrough and shorten the war – the Allies decided to press on, but Hodges realized he must first protect his right flank. This meant taking control of the Hürtgen Forest (Hürtgenwald), and its high point, crowned by the village of Schmidt. This ostensibly simple operation would prove anything but. The Germans lay in wait in the forest, and the ensuing six-month battle was the longest the western Allies would fight on German soil.

>> Logistics

One reason for the delay in launch-ing the final assault on Germany was the perennial, unseen problem of all armies: getting supplies to the front line in sufficient quantities and at the right time. It is no exaggeration to say that logistics was as vital a part of the Lib-eration as events on the battlefield. For every combat soldier, up to eight oth-ers were needed to staff supply chains stretching back to ports and across the seas to Britain and the USA.

Every need had to be foreseen and ca-tered for by clerks and logistics manag-ers. Thousands of men in the field need-ed nutritious food provided on time and in quantity; tanks and other vehicles required refuelling if they were to keep asserting pressure on the enemy; and survival and success in battle depend-ed on the ready availability of ammuni-tion. The further the army drew from its ports of supply, the more difficult it be-came to keep them functioning at peak efficiency. Each hungry town conquered and each battalion of new prisoners simply increased the demand for Allied provisions.

The Battle of Hürtgen Forest

The forest constituted unfamiliar and for-bidding terrain, and its defenders were eas-ily concealed. These gloomy evergreen woods, bare hilltops and deep gorges bounded by Aachen, Duren and Monschau were of no obvious strategic importance, but the natural landscape provided a per-fect snare. The Germans had scattered the thickets with pillboxes, machine-gun nests, barbed wire and minefields, while the woods were difficult to penetrate, either on foot or by vehicle. Heavy rainfall and then snow compounded the formidable task of the American soldiers.

Underestimating the German defences and the difficulties of the terrain, the Ameri-cans suffered heavy losses, particularly during a bitter confrontation from 2 Novem-ber 1944 for the village of Schmidt, north-west of the Rur Reservoir. The US 28th In-fantry Division committed three regiments to the advance on Schmidt. On the second day, one managed to reach the village church. The other two regiments struggled in the thick woods, sustaining substantial casualties. The American units in Schmidt then came under artillery fire from the German 89th Infantry Division and the 272nd "People's Grenadier" Division, while American tanks sent in as support were disabled by the terrain.

All Allied attempts to resupply Schmidt failed. The American troops on the bare ridge between Vossenack and Schmidt were pounded by German artillery until 8 November, when their withdrawal was finally ordered. The reason for the unexpectedly tenacious defence of the woods became clear only later: the Germans needed to hold the Hürtgen Forest as a marshalling area for their planned offensive in the Ardennes – the Battle of the Bulge (see p.171). It was only after the Battle of the Bulge was concluded in early 1945 that the Allies were finally able to take possession of the forest that had cost so many lives.

» Hürtgen Forest sites

Museum of Hürtgenwald in 1944 and in Peacetime
Pfarrer-Dickmann-Str. 21–23, Vossenack,
Ⓦ museum-huertgenwald.de

The Battle of Hürtgen Forest in the autumn and winter of 1944 claimed the lives of thousands of German and American soldiers, as well as leaving villages, farmland and forest utterly devastated. Evacuated inhabitants returning to their homes at the end of the war saw the labour of generations annihilated. During the summer of 1945, forest fires burned for months and spontaneous explosions of unspent ammunition killed many men, women and children. Displaying immense courage and ded-

ication, the local population set about the daunting task of rebuilding their lives and their land from scratch.

The Museum of Hürtgenwald explores the military confrontation as well as the plight of the civilian population during and after the battle. It is run entirely by volunteers, and most of its objects were collected in the Hürtgen Forest area after the war.

Vossenack Church
Baptist-Palm-Platz, Vossenack

Vossenack was almost completely destroyed between November 1944 and February 1945. The village changed hands nearly thirty times between German and American forces, while the front ran straight through its parish church, which witnessed close-quarters combat and was reduced to rubble.

The church was rebuilt and newly consecrated after World War II. An inscription on the door commemorates 68,000 soldiers who died in Hürtgen Forest, but this figure is inaccurate. Current estimates suggest around half that number perished here; 68,000 is most likely a mix-up of the dead and injured.

Vogelsang International Place and The Torchbearer
Vogelsang 70, Schleiden,
Ⓦ vogelsang-ip.de

The Vogelsang complex was built between 1934 and 1936, on a wooded mountain spur above the Urfttal dam, as a National Socialist training institution for young party fanatics. The imposing buildings were intended to show the dominance of state and party over nature, and great trouble was taken to create a relief effect on the hillside. Those who came here adhered to a cult of prowess and virility: physical health, beauty and strength were equated with the ideal of the "Aryan race".

Around the park are several sculptures depicting favourite Nazi images of the master race, the *Herrenmensch*. The most conspicuous of these is Willy Meller's *The Torchbearer*, which borrows heavily from Christian and Greek mythology. The raised torch references the ancient Greek myth of Prometheus, bringing fire to mankind; the flame symbolizes the rebirth of the nation through the victory of Nazi Germany; while the chilling inscription echoes Jesus's words in the Sermon on the Mount, directly addressing the cadets: "You are the torchbearers of the Nation, you carry forth the light of spirit in the fight for Adolf Hitler". When American soldiers captured Vogelsang in 1945, they fired on *The Torchbearer* and the site's other sculptures. Look out for the bullet marks, which are still clearly visible today.

Field Hospital Bunker Simonskall

Simonskall, Ⓦ museum-huertgenwald.de

This medical aid bunker is the only bunker of its type in all Nordrhein-Westphalia, and its inventory is almost completely original. Conditions were very cramped, with four medics caring for twenty or thirty infirm soldiers. Visits can be arranged via the Museum of Hürtgenwald in Vossenack, which is run by the same volunteer organization that renovated the bunker.

Kall Bridge

In November 1944, several units of the 28th US Infantry Division advanced towards the village of Schmidt via the so-called "Kall Trail", a rough road cutting through the dense forest. After eight days of fighting, the Battle of Schmidt ended in German victory and the exhausted US soldiers were forced to fall back on their front line in Vossenack. On their return, the troops had to cross the Kall Bridge, leaving them vulnerable to German forces who had retaken the surrounding valley. Between 7 and 9 November, Dr Stüttgen, a German captain in the medical corps, managed to negotiate a series of short ceasefires at this bridge, allowing wounded soldiers from both sides to be treated. While the effect of these ceasefires was limited, the lives of numerous US soldiers were saved by German doctors and paramedics. After the war, Dr Stüttgen was honoured by the Governor of the State of Pennsylvania for his act of humanity. The events at Kall Bridge are immortalized in the painting *A Time for Healing*, which is displayed at the National Guard Museum in Washington DC; a replica can be seen at the Museum of Hürtgenwald in Vossenack (see p.281).

A simple sculpture by Michael Pohlmann marks today's bridge.

Vossenack German Cemetery

Thousands of American and German soldiers died during the six months of bloody fighting for Hürtgen Forest. Most American servicemen were repatriated to the US for burial, but some of the German soldiers who lost their lives during the campaign were laid to rest in German war cemeteries at Hürtgen or Vossenack, or at communal cemeteries in the area. Many more were transferred to German war cemeteries in Belgium and the Netherlands.

The Vossenack German Cemetery was constructed on a hill by the German War Graves Commission (Volksbund Deutsche Kriegsgräberfürsorge) between 1949 and 1952. Today, the cemetery contains the graves of 2347 war dead, among them 35 men who lost their lives during postwar operations as members of an "Ammunition Search and Removal Team". A monument at the entrance commemorates Julius Erasmus, a German engineer captain who – at great risk – recovered the remains of around 1500 of his former comrades from the Hürtgen Forest battlefields and personally buried them on this hill.

Mariawald Abbey
Heimbach, Ⓦ kloster-mariawald.de

During the battle for Hürtgen Forest, this 15th-century Trappist abbey served as a hospital for casualties on both sides. The Nazis closed the abbey before the war because of its opposition to their regime, arresting some brothers and conscripting others. A few were allowed to stay on as farmhands, working the fields of the monastery.

Not all the wounded treated here could be saved – 414 men are buried in the military cemetery nearby.

Ochsenkopf pillboxes

When Hodges' American soldiers arrived at Hürtgen Forest, they had to adapt quickly to fighting in the wooded terrain. Their German counterparts, meanwhile, were reinforced by troops returning from the Eastern Front who were familiar with the tactics demanded by forest warfare. In areas such as Ochsenkopf and Peterberg, the Germans had another advantage: they could withstand American fire in the pillboxes that

» The Siegfried Line
In 1936, Nazi Germany began to build a line of defences along its western border to match the French Maginot Line. The Germans know it as the Westwall, but in English it is the Siegfried Line, a reference to the Wagnerian hero who didn't know what fear was.

The Siegfried Line consisted of a series of fortifications with interlocking fields of fire, minefields and anti-tank obstacles. In 1939, construction of the structures used up one third of all cement production in the Reich.

The conquest of France in 1940 rendered the Siegfried Line redundant: henceforth occupied Europe would be defended against its enemies by the Atlantic Wall (see p.115). As a consequence, its fortifications were neglected and its guns removed. In autumn 1944, however, the Siegfried Line rediscovered its purpose when it was required to delay the invading army until reinforcements could be brought up from the front. Determined German soldiers held the American and British troops at bay for several months, until the line was breached and overrun in February 1945. Several components of the Westwall survive, particularly near Aachen.

dotted the hills. These formed part of the Westwall, or Siegfried Line – the last line of defence of Hitler's Third Reich. In the northern Eifel, the pillboxes were generally situated in dense spruce forests, where trees doubled up as tank obstacles. In the bewildering forest, every German company and regiment could hide behind the pillboxes' massive concrete walls.

The scant remains of a number of pillboxes can still be made out in the forest.

The Rhineland

The Allied operation to reach the Rhine – codenamed Veritable – was a campaign fought with grit and zeal on both sides.

As the Allies battled on at Hürtgen Forest, another unsuccessful attempt to invade Germany was being launched in the northern Netherlands. Operation Market Garden (see p.197) failed to capture the bridge across the Lower Rhine at Arnhem, but it did give the Allies a salient extending to Nijmegen. This was chosen by General Montgomery as the starting point for another assault, Operation Veritable, but the surprise German offensive in the Ardennes – the Battle of the Bulge – intervened. Allied resources became tied up in the Ardennes and the start of Veritable was delayed until the German troops had been driven back to the Siegfried Line, where they'd launched their initial attack, in January 1945.

The aim of Veritable was for Montgomery's British and 21st Canadian Army Group to advance swiftly to reach the Rhine at the far north of the Allied front. The troops would then cross the river and attack the Ruhr conurbation from the north, making a concentrated thrust at Germany's industrial centre.

Veritable was entrusted to the First Canadian Army (under General Crerar), supported by the British XXX Corps commanded by General Horrocks. Its instructions were to clear the area between the rivers Maas (Meuse) and Rhine of German forces, so that a crossing of the latter could be organized. To assist in the task, the US Ninth Army was to simultaneously implement Operation Grenade, approaching from the south to meet the British and Canadians.

As a prelude to Operation Veritable, the historic town of Kleve (Cleves) was heavily bombed. Veritable proper began on 8 February 1945 with a massive artillery barrage.

The Reichswald

When the Allies crossed the border into Germany they entered the Reichswald, a densely

» Kleve was pulverized by Allied bombardment in October 1944 and again in February 1945

wooded area 10km wide and 15km deep. German units had turned the forest into a death trap. Their commanders knew that the Rhineland was the last chance to organize an effective, spirited defence before the Allies penetrated the heart of the Reich. The natural obstacles of the forest were heavily reinforced by German troops and rigged with trenches, mortar pits, barbed wire, mines and anti-tank ditches. Two major roads provided the only means of an Allied approach, while inside the forest there were virtually no other surfaced roads. The paths leading through the woods snaked and zig-zagged – ideal for laying ambushes. The British and Canadian troops were forced to advance on a narrow front, while movement was further restricted by bad weather and the control of large areas by the German army.

As at Hürtgen Forest, the wooded terrain naturally favoured the German defenders, who could only be dislodged after close-quarters combat. Deep in the forest, infantry units fought hand-to-hand, where risk, bravery and tenacity were as important as technical skill. At times, the struggles in the Reichswald resembled the battles of attrition fought between opposing trenches in World War I.

Operation Grenade

To the south, Simpson's US Ninth Army made good progress under Operation Grenade, until the German troops flooded the lands in its path. Simpson was forced to wait two weeks for the water levels to subside. He resumed his march on 23 February 1945, and by 2 March his troops had reached the Rhine opposite Düsseldorf.

The conclusion of Veritable

With relentless determination, the advancing troops of Operation Veritable fought their way eastward past Kleve (Cleves) to reach the Rhine opposite Emmerich. To the south, they met the US troops of Grenade at Geldern on 3 March. As the Allies approached the river, the Germans were ordered to evacuate their forces to the other bank and destroy the bridges behind them. By mid-March the Rhineland had been cleared, although at great cost, with heavy casualties to both military and civilian populations.

Montgomery would later conclude that the Germans had made three major mistakes while defending occupied Europe: fighting the battle of France south of the Seine rather than using it as a defensive line; launching a counter-offensive in the Ardennes without air support or fuel to sustain it; and lastly, deciding to stand and fight in the Rhineland – west of the river – in order to mask the Ruhr.

The Allies were finally ready to cross the Rhine, threaten the Ruhr and take the battle into the heart of Germany.

The Rhineland sites

Kleve

The town of Kleve (Cleves) was repeatedly bombed as part of the invasion of Germany. On 7 October 1944, a major bombardment by the RAF using Lancaster and Halifax bombers left Kleve devastated and an estimated five hundred civilians dead. The historic centre was mostly destroyed, including Schwanenburg castle and its imposing tower, the Schwanenturm. Just four months later, on 7 February 1945 (the eve of Operation Veritable), Kleve was bombed again and the upper town was ravaged. The civilian population had largely been evacuated, leaving only military personnel, members of the Hitler Youth and firefighters behind. One hundred Ukrainian slave labourers, locked in the prison on Krohnestrasse, were killed in the raid.

Reichswald Forest War Cemetery
Grunewaldstr, Kleve

The Reichswald Forest War Cemetery,

designed by Philip Hepworth, is the largest Commonwealth cemetery in Germany. It holds the remains of 7654 soldiers, mostly airmen from the Royal Air Force and paratroopers; 176 burials remain unidentified. Wheelchair access is possible. The cemetery is situated in the Reichswald itself, an ancient forest on the Dutch-German border and the scene of heavy fighting in February 1945.

» Prisoners of war

The rules on taking prisoners of war, as laid out in the Third Geneva Convention of 1929, were easily stated but just as easily broken. All countries in World War II were obliged to adhere to the Geneva Convention, both during fighting and occupation.

One of the most fundamental directives made it unlawful to kill a soldier who had surrendered on the battlefield. There were instances of misuse, however, when capitulators would fly a white flag only to fight on against their unwitting opponents. Abuses of the Geneva Convention made some combatants cynical about honouring its legal and ethical procedures. In certain cases, commanders on both sides indicated that prisoners were an inconvenience, and that it was better to annihilate the enemy completely. Even when the framework was upheld, excuses were often made for soldiers who vented their bitterness by killing unarmed prisoners in cold blood.

Once in custody, prisoners of war were property of the state to which they had surrendered, not of any individual soldier. They were to be securely and safely incarcerated for the duration of the conflict, treated humanely and their wounds tended to. No physical or mental torture was permitted to extract information from them. The transporting, housing and

feeding of prisoners of war made great demands on the resources of every army.

An exception was made by the convention to "unlawful" combatants: those who participated in battle without a uniform or visible insignia, and who were not part of a clear hierarchy of command. This meant that saboteurs, spies, ununiformed snipers, plain-clothed commandos and resistance fighters were not protected under international law. Many were summarily shot.

Thousands of Polish officers and men captured in 1939 spent nearly six years in prisoner of war camps, a few months longer than the unlucky French and British soldiers captured in the brief battles of 1940. Generally, officers were kept separate from enlisted men in the camps and treated with more respect. The International Red Cross did what it could to ensure that the rules of holding prisoners of war were complied with – for instance, that letters and parcels from home could reach men in custody – but experiences of captivity were varied, ranging from the tolerable to the unspeakable. Much depended on the nationality of the prisoner, and where they were captured: around 3.5 million Soviet POWs taken by the Nazis are estimated to have died from cruelty, neglect or overwork.

Crossing the Rhine

The course of war is sometimes dictated not by strategy, the technical skill of soldiers or even the quality of equipment, but by luck – and knowing how to exploit a small stroke of good fortune.

As a German retreat from the Rhineland became increasingly likely, the Nazi high command issued orders to lay explosive charges on the bridges across the Rhine. If it proved impossible to hold the west bank, the German troops and vehicles should be evacuated and the charges detonated.

When General Hodges' US First Army approached the Rhine on 7 March 1945, they expected to find all the bridges blown. But the defenders of the Ludendorff rail bridge at Remagen were surprised by the approach of the first American patrols; their bridge, situated between Koblenz and Bonn, was not on any strategic route of conquest. German soldiers scrambled to detonate the charges, which caused only partial damage to the bridge, which was subsequently seized. An Allied bridgehead was quickly established on the east bank. One bridge was not enough to win the war, but it was a prize to boost morale and discourage the Germans, who discussed flying kamikaze missions into the bridge and even targeted it with V2 rockets. The bridge eventually fell of its own accord ten days later, but not before the Allies had erected temporary bridges beside it. Their forces were now building on the east side of the river, although Eisenhower chose to wait for further bridgeheads to be established before pushing forwards into central Germany.

«
American Navy LCM landing craft being loaded with a tank to cross the Rhine as part of Operation Plunder

» Inside the Cologne
National Socialism
Documentation Centre

The Allies across

On the night of 22–23 March, US General Patton's Third Army reached the Rhine at Oppenheim, south of Mainz, and crossed it using boats and later a floating bridge. The next day, British Field Marshal Montgomery breached the Rhine in an elaborate "invasion within an invasion", Operation Plunder. One million ground troops stormed across the river, supported by 14,000 paratroopers who landed on the opposite shore.

The US Seventh Army crossed the river on the night of 24–25 March near Worms. The Free French Army, delayed by the Colmar Pocket, made the crossing at sites between Mannheim and Karlsruhe between 31 March and 2 April.

Crossing the Rhine sites　　«

NSDOK (Cologne National Socialism Documentation Centre)

Appellhofplatz 23–25, Cologne,
Ⓦ nsdok.de

From 1935 to 1945, the EL-DE House functioned as the headquarters of the Cologne Gestapo. Many victims of the German secret police were held in its basements – with up to 25 people sharing one cell – and executions were carried out in the courtyard. The last Gestapo officers fled when American troops entered the city. Cologne, which straddles the Rhine, was officially taken on 6 March 1945 by the US First Army, the day before they crossed the Rhine at Remagen.

The documentation centre was founded in 1979 and serves both as a memorial to the victims of the Nazi regime and as a research centre documenting Cologne's history during the Nazi era.

Peace Bridge Museum
An der Alten Rheinbrücke 11/ Rheinpromenade, Remagen, Ⓦ brueckeremagen.de

Although the Ludendorff railway bridge spanning the Rhine at Remagen collapsed in 1945, two of its towers remain intact.

》 Bridges
Every river on the liberation route was both a line of defence for the retreating German army and an obstacle for the Allied advance. Strategy demanded careful planning as to whether a bridge should be preserved or demolished, and when. A key bridge blown up at the right time could prolong a battle by days or even weeks – as the Germans expertly demonstrated in Italy and in the battle for the Rhineland. A priority for the liberators was taking bridges intact before they could be destroyed, but this was seldom possible. If Allied ground forces couldn't reach a bridge quickly enough to save it, they were forced to cross the river by boat under heavy fire. Only when they had established control of the opposite bank could engineers begin to build a makeshift military bridge capable of carrying tanks and other vehicles across. Failing to destroy a bridge was a costly mistake, for which the Germans paid the price at Remagen.

Today, they contain a museum recalling the bridge's history and its role in the Liberation through photos, newspaper clippings, a video documentary and a selection of other artefacts.

Bittermark Monument
Theodor-Freywald-Weg, Dortmund

Between December 1944 and March 1945, the Dortmund State Police, a branch of the Gestapo, arrested thirty known members of the Resistance in the region. They were imprisoned, along with around two hundred others (including non-German forced labourers and prisoners of war) before being taken to sites south of Dortmund, including Bittermark Forest, where they were ordered to stand in bomb craters and shot. The last mass execution was carried out on 12 April 1945, the day before a division of the US Ninth Army – who had crossed the Rhine with Montgomery in Operation Plunder – arrived in Dortmund.

The Bittermark Memorial is a stark bunker-like slab, with haunting relief images depicting the condemned.

Rheinberg War Cemetery
Am Englischen Friedhof, Rheinberg

The majority of the 3330 people buried in this cemetery are airmen whose graves were brought in from Düsseldorf, Krefeld, Mönchengladbach, Essen, Aachen and Dortmund. Four hundred and fifty are from Cologne alone. Men from other branches of the armed forces interred here mostly lost their lives during the battle of the Rhineland, or in the advance from the Rhine to the Elbe. There are also nine war graves of other nationalities, most of them Polish.

Central Germany

After the Allies had breached the Rhine, they had a chance to regroup and take stock before marching on central Germany.

By the end of March 1945, General Eisenhower was drained; the Rhine had finally been crossed, but only after months of difficulties and reversals. Since D-Day there had been several moments in which the Allies had assumed the collapse of Germany was imminent and the war was close to an end, and Eisenhower had learned not to celebrate too soon. Once the Allies had successfully crossed the great river, Eisenhower had time to rethink his strategy. The weight of responsibility had depleted his mental and physical resources, however, and he took five days off in Cannes, which he used mainly to sleep.

For most of the war, Eisenhower had favoured an advance in Germany on a broad front, and for several months had encouraged Montgomery's belief that his 21st Army Group would be the main invasion force, with a mandate to thrust across northern Germa-ny towards Berlin. When Eisenhower returned to his headquarters at Reims, he revised his strategy, partly because of the capture of the bridge at Remagen and partly because of the rapid progress of the Red Army from the east. He realized that there was no point in competing with the Soviets to take Berlin, who were much closer to the German capital than the Anglo-American forces. In addition, committing US troops to an attack on Berlin would risk heavy casualties for a city that was steadily being reduced to rubble.

Instead of looking to Berlin, Eisenhower nominated Montgomery's rival, US General Omar Bradley, as the vanguard. His US 12th Army Group would traverse Hessen and Thuringia, making for Leipzig and Dresden in Saxony, before meeting up with the Soviets on the Elbe. Once Germany was defeated, it would be divided into zones assigned to the western Allies and the Soviets (see p.312). Montgomery's role would be to protect Bradley's northern flank, while the south was assigned to Devers' 6th Army Group.

» A German civilian carries her belongings from a burning building in newly liberated Siegburg

» Occupation zones

In September 1944 – when Allied victory was still uncertain – American, British and Soviet politicians began to plan the fate of a defeated Germany. Designed to prevent the dominance of a single power and international disputes after the war, Germany was to be divided into three zones of occupation, assigned to each of the "Big Three" victors.

The zones were reaffirmed at the Yalta Conference in February 1945, but with a difference. The Americans and British insisted that the French be given their own zone in the west of Germany. Stalin reluctantly agreed, so long as the French zone was carved out of the American (southern German) and British (northern German) zones. Berlin, located within the Soviet sector, would also be split into four zones of occupation.

No firm "stopping" lines were drawn up at the conference, which would have prevented the western Allied troops from liberating parts of Germany in the Soviet zone. At the time of Yalta, the British and Americans were still west of the Rhine, recovering from the Ardennes offensive and anxious about the existence of a southern redoubt (see p.296). They didn't expect to reach beyond the Elbe before the Red Army took Berlin.

In April 1945, however, the pace of the British and American advance took them further than expected. Eisenhower restrained his armies from continu-ing further east, leaving some Allied planners disappointed, who wanted to see General Patton liberate Prague. Instead, Eisenhower established stopping lines, beyond which only reconnaissance patrols were permitted to venture. Churchill remarked that Eisenhower's decision must have been political, thinking ahead to the new world order. Yalta, he claimed, left a loophole: occupation zones were not to affect strategic military decisions, so Berlin, Vienna and Prague could be liberated by whichever army got to them first.

By the end of the war, both the British and Americans had advanced into territory far beyond their zones of occupation. The "line of contact" – where the western Allies met the Soviets – ran from Wismar on the Baltic, through Schwerin and Magdeburg, to the east of Leipzig and through Pilsen (in modern-day Czech Republic) to Linz (in Austria).

In July 1945 the British and Americans withdrew from the territory they had taken in the Soviet zone. The Soviet Union, in turn, honoured the division of the city of Berlin into four sectors. Austria was treated in a similar fashion to Germany, except that the centre of Vienna was declared a fifth, international zone to be governed by each of the occupying powers in turn. The postwar Potsdam Conference in August (see p.312) ratified the occupation zones.

The Ruhr Pocket

Having successfully crossed the Rhine, the Allies were presented with an opportunity they had anticipated for some time. The cities of the Ruhr made up the industrial heartland of the German Reich, and although they had been damaged by Allied bombing, the factories were still of great symbolic importance. Hitler would defend them with force, but that incurred a risk: the Allies may be able to surround the Ruhr and capture the German troops within their cordon.

The German Army Group B, led by Walter Model, defended the Ruhr. Model was aware of the risk of encirclement, but was told by Hitler to make the Ruhr into a fortress that would not yield. Model was outmatched. His men were poorly trained: they included numerous Volkssturm militia volunteers, some of whom were unarmed, and members of the Hitler youth who – though enthusiastic and ready to die for the Fatherland – were unlikely to offer any serious resistance.

On Easter Sunday, which fell on 1 April 1945, US troops travelling north met their counterparts travelling south at Lippstadt, and the Ruhr was enveloped. Model's predicament worsened, and on 14 April the US divisions split the Ruhr Pocket into two further sections, east and west. The next day Model formally dissolved his army group, a move to make his coming surrender seem less calamitous. He made provisions for the safety of his family before committing suicide on 21 April to avoid the shame of capitulation. More than 300,000 prisoners were captured in the Ruhr Pocket, a much higher number than the Allied planners had predicted. In total, one and a half million German prisoners were taken on the Western Front. Incarcerating all of them in safe conditions was a major problem for the Allies, a common issue throughout the Liberation.

Meeting on the Elbe

While the events of the Ruhr Pocket were being concluded, Hodges' US First Army advanced rapidly across land to the south of the Harz mountains, until it neared the Elbe river. On 25 April, forward American patrols met Soviet scouts at Torgau, a meeting of great significance. German forces in the north of the country were cut off from those in the south, and Berlin was surrounded. The war could only have days left.

» Establishing the bridgehead across the Rhine at Remagen

«
Wewelsburg Castle

» Central Germany sites

Military History Museum
Olbrichtplatz 2, Dresden, Ⓦ mhmbw.de

Dresden, in the far east of Germany's central belt, was one of the last cities to be taken by the Allies on 8 May 1945. It had already suffered enormously as the result of a ruthless bombing campaign in February of the same year (see p.294).

The Military History Museum in Dresden is one of the few museums in the country that has German military equipment from both world wars. The largest items on display include a V2 ballistic missile and Germany's first submarine. The museum aims to explain how armies and war influenced politics and society in the twentieth century, and vice versa.

Colditz Castle and Museum
Schlossgasse 1, Colditz, Ⓦ schloss-colditz.com

Fifteenth-century Colditz Castle was used to incarcerate political prisoners in the early years of the Nazi regime. At the outbreak of war, it was designated "Oflag IV C" and claimed to be "escape-proof", serving as a prisoner of war camp for Allied officers until it was liberated on 16 April 1945. Life inside was relatively comfortable, but thirty prisoners still defied the camp's guards, barbed wire, searchlights and reputation to break free. A British escapee later wrote *The Colditz Story*, which was subsequently adapted into the film that turned the castle into a household name in Britain. The museum displays artefacts and uniforms of Allied POWs as well as detailed information on their legendary breakouts.

Wewelsburg Castle
Burgwall 19, Büren-Wewelsburg,
Ⓦ wewelsburg.de

Heinrich Himmler had big plans for this triangular castle. It was used in the 1930s and the early years of the war as an SS ideological training site, a meeting place of high-ranking officers and a base for Himmler's military and racial elite. The north tower was planned as the focal point of a vast complex consisting of a series of concentric installations.

Slave labourers, housed in a specially commissioned concentration camp nearby, began construction work, but it was never finished. The intended purpose of the circular crypt and Hall of the Supreme SS Leaders above it is unknown.

In the guardhouse, a permanent exhibition entitled "Ideology and Terror of the SS" tells the story of the SS and its relationship with Wewelsburg between 1933 and 1945.

Buchenwald Memorial
Gedenkstätte Buchenwald, Weimar,
Ⓦ buchenwald.de

"Nothing has shocked me as much as that sight," wrote Eisenhower of his visit to Buchenwald, the largest concentration camp in Germany, shortly after its liberation on 11 April 1945. At its height, Buchenwald and its 139 subcamps held a staggering 280,000 prisoners. An estimated 56,000 people died here – some as the result of torture or medical experiments – including eight thousand Soviet prisoners who were shot in a specially built killing facility. There was an underground resistance organization operating in the camp, but it was unable to prevent the worst excesses.

Mittelbau-Dora Concentration Camp
Kohnsteinweg 20, Nordhausen,
Ⓦ buchenwald.de

Mittelbau-Dora Concentration Camp was established in 1943 near Nordhausen in Thuringia and served as a subcamp of Buchenwald. Like Buchenwald, it was liberated on 11 April 1945. The memorial includes one permanent collection and several changing exhibits with information on the camp's history.

Topf & Söhne Memorial
Sorbenweg 7, Erfurt, Ⓦ topfundsoehne.de

"Always happy to be at your service" was the slogan of Topf & Söhne, the leading company for the supply, installation and maintenance of crematorium incinerators under the Weimar Republic. The creation of the Nazis' extermination camps boosted business for Topf & Söhne, whose engineers installed corpse incinerators and ventilation systems for gas chambers at Auschwitz-Birkenau and serviced their upkeep. The management knew what its products were being used for;

≫ The bombing of Dresden

Dresden, capital of Saxony state, had little industry of value to the Reich. It was known for its production of china, and yet it was repeatedly bombed in February 1945 by the British and Americans, igniting a firestorm. While emergency workers tried to control the fires caused by one raid, another wave of bombers arrived overhead. Whether the bombing of Dresden was a legitimate act of strategic warfare or a terrible atrocity – even a war crime – is hotly debated. The number of casualties is also controversial, but 25,000 civilian deaths is probably a fairly low estimate.

One of the men ordered to dig bodies out of the rubble was Kurt Vonnegut, an American intelligence scout who had been taken prisoner in the Battle of the Bulge (see p.171). During the bombing he took refuge in an underground meat store; he would later use his experiences in his cult novel, *Slaughterhouse-Five*.

» The SS

The Nazi regime relied on violence and terror perpetrated by a fanatical paramilitary organization called the SS (or Schutzstaffel). The SS was founded in 1925 as a personal protection force to escort the Führer, and each member swore unconditional loyalty to him.

In 1926, Heinrich Himmler, a former chicken farmer, was appointed as Reichsführer – head of the SS. After he had employed his storm-troopers to eliminate a competing paramilitary wing of the Nazi party, the SA (in 1934), he transformed the SS into a vast structure that infiltrated the lives of ordinary German people and spread terror across Europe. "I know there are many people who fall ill when they see this black uniform," Himmler remarked; "we don't expect that we will be loved."

The SS was divided into units. One squad enforced Nazi racial laws; another ran the concentration and extermination camps; while the Gestapo – the official secret police – carried out investigations, acts of torture and executions in Germany and its occupied territories. The SS had its own system of ranks, which deliberately differed from those of the army, and a variety of distinctive insignia, most notably a double "S" in German runes and an ominous skull and crossbones.

In keeping with Nazi ideology, the SS recruited according to a policy of racial selection. It excluded non-Aryans from its ranks, relaxing this rule only when it urgently needed new recruits – later accepting foreigners with proven fascist sympathies.

The SS branch known as the Waffen-SS occupied a blurred space between paramilitary and military organization. Known as the "Black Order", its series of 38 fully equipped divisions worked alongside and sometimes rivalled units of the regular army, the Wehrmacht. Because fearlessness and fanaticism were prized traits in the Waffen-SS, where surrender was deemed a fate worse than death, its units suffered particularly high casualty rates. The Waffen-SS was also notorious for its brutal reprisals against acts of resistance, and for initiating its own bloodthirsty atrocities.

The SS was largely responsible for the horrors of the extermination camps. A number of other sites and monuments, including the ruins of Oradour in France (see p.146), are further testament to their ruthlessness. Because of their reputation for cruelty, SS men were regarded with special contempt by the Allied troops as they fought to liberate Europe. After the war, many former SS members claimed they were guilty only of efficiency and patriotism, and that their "crimes" were exaggerations and lies circulated by their enemies.

demand for better efficiency led one of the company's engineers to design and patent a horrifying "continuous operation corpse incineration oven for mass use". Even as late as February 1945 Topf & Söhne was planning a new extermination centre for Mauthausen camp in Austria, reusing machines that had to be dismantled at Auschwitz-Birkenau because of the approach of the Red Army. The company was closed down after the war, and its former premises are now a memorial to those who died as a consequence of the Holocaust and – more directly – as a result of Topf & Söhne apparatus.

Southern Germany

While Allied commanders encountered the bulk of German forces where they expected to find them – concentrated in the centre of the country blocking the route to Berlin – they still harboured a fear that everything might not be as it seemed.

For some time, murmurings of a Nazi contingency plan had been rippling across Europe. They hinted that Germany's retreating armies could be set to regroup at an *Alpenfestung* (also known as the "National Redoubt"), an impregnable Alpine fortress that would function as a final holdout. Many Allied politicians and military planners believed the rumours. The strategy seemed consistent with the Nazi psyche. Moreover, Berlin was not a city with natural defences, and once the Oder had been crossed in the east and the Rhine in the west, there was little to stop a large army taking the capital by force. Southern Germany and Austria, meanwhile, were more easily defended as a result of their mountainous terrain. It was plausible that Hitler – an Austrian by birth – had made plans for a last stand in a landscape more friendly and familiar.

A trickle of intelligence reports were read as indicating German plans for the Na-

tional Redoubt: the stockpiling of arms, equipment and food; the excavation of tunnels; the building of fortifications; and even the construction of subterranean factories to continue building Messerschmitt planes and V2 rockets. Meanwhile, Goebbels' propaganda hinted that all was not lost for National Socialism. The National Redoubt grew in the Allied imagination into a potential reality that could not be ignored.

Even the Allied commanders who treated the idea of a last great stand by Hitler with scepticism could not afford to dismiss it completely. If the rumours were true, their clean victory would be frustrated by a determined garrison of well-armed, fanatical troops. Hitler could hole up and rebuild his regime or, at the very least, subject Europe to years of guerrilla warfare.

The three armies of the south

The task of overwhelming resistance in southern Germany and neutralizing the prophesied National Redoubt was assigned to three Allied armies.

The First French Army under de Lattre was given the extreme southwestern corner of the country, adjacent to France. Having

» The Eagle's Nest, Hitler's retreat near Obersalzberg

been delayed by the Colmar Pocket (see p.149), de Lattre's troops crossed the Rhine later than the other armies, between 31 March and 2 April 1945, at Germersheim and Speyer, before liberating Stuttgart on 21 April and Ulm on 24 April. To its northwest, Patch's US Seventh Army was directed to work its way along an arc from its Rhine crossing site at Worms through western Bavaria and into Austria. It liberated Nuremberg on 20 April, Dachau concentration camp on 29 April and Munich on 30 April, before its advance eventually came to a halt at the Brenner Pass, where it met American troops of the US Fifth Army heading towards Germany from northern Italy.

Further northwest still, protecting the flank of the US First Army as it made its way across central Germany, was the US Third Army under Patton. Patton travelled quickly, leaving Mainz on 22 March; Frankfurt was reached on 29 March and Linz (Hitler's hometown) in Austria on 5 May. He was only stopped by Eisenhower when he reached Pilsen, on the border of Czechoslovakia, deep inside the designated Soviet zone of occupation.

German General Hermann Foertsch and American General Jacob Devers signed an instrument of surrender covering the southeastern areas of the Reich at 2.30pm on 4 May 1945.

The National Redoubt resolved

After a thorough search, the existence of the National Redoubt turned out to be unfounded. It suited the moribund Nazi regime for its enemies to believe it had a final, elusive plan, but the Allies had misread Hitler this time. He had always dismissed his commanders' pleas for a last stand. Sometimes history leans towards anti-climax, and Hitler remained in Berlin where he let the inevitable run its course.

» The Eagle's Nest

The Eagle's Nest or Kehlsteinhaus is a chalet poised atop an 1834m-high rock outcrop near Obersalzberg in Bavaria, designed by Nazi acolyte Martin Bormann and gifted to Adolf Hitler on his 50th birthday in 1939. It was a prized trophy when it was captured by the US 3rd Infantry in early May 1945, and is one of the few monuments to Nazi arrogance that has survived intact. A truly outstanding spot, with breathtaking panoramas over the surrounding mountains, the Eagle's Nest – now a restaurant run by a charitable trust – would be truly idyllic if not for its origins and associations. A guided tour includes an ascent in the original brass elevator.

Southern Germany sites   «

Dachau Concentration Camp Memorial Site

Alte Römerstr. 75, Dachau,
Ⓦ kz-gedenkstaette-dachau.de

On 22 March 1933, soon after Hitler came to power as Chancellor, Dachau concentration camp opened to receive political opponents of the new regime, who were incarcerated in indefinite "preventive custody". They were joined over the following years by Jehovah's Witnesses, homosexuals, Roma, Sinti, Poles and Soviet prisoners of war. Dachau spawned 150 subcamps, an empire of misery, exploitation and death. On 29 April 1945, US troops arrived at Dachau and were aghast at the sight of 33,000 starving and mistreated survivors. Some American soldiers were so horrified that they gunned down the SS guards who had already surrendered.

Biography
» **Dietrich Bonhoeffer**

Protestant pastor Dietrich Bonhoeffer (1906–1945) was a prominent critic of the Nazi party. Its racist policies and their violent enforcement directly opposed the pastor's Christian ethics. As the war progressed, Bonhoeffer came to consider passive resistance an insufficient response to the evils of Nazism. He was an active member of the Resistance and plotted against Hitler before being arrested and imprisoned in April 1943. After the 20 July plot in 1944, Bonhoeffer was found guilty of conspiracy and hanged at Flossenbürg on 9 April 1945, two weeks before its liberation by the Allies and less than a month before the collapse of the Nazi regime. Bonhoeffer's life and fate illustrate the great sacrifice of many Germans who resisted the Nazis at great personal cost.

Munich Documentation Centre
Brienner Str. 34, Munich,
Ⓦ ns-dokuzentrum-muenchen.de

The capital of Bavaria, Munich played a key role in the development of National Socialism; this documentation centre charts the details. It was here that the German Workers' Party was founded shortly after World War I. In 1920 it changed its name to the National Socialist Workers' Party (NSDAP), although it had nothing to do with socialism. Initially the party was a marginal group that struggled for publicity and popularity – it achieved the former on 9 November 1923, when the Nazis attempted a coup d'état known as the Beerhall Putsch. Hitler received a mild jail sentence, during which he wrote *Mein Kampf*. Even after Hitler's rise to power in 1933 the party headquarters re-

mained in Munich, and the first concentration camp was built at nearby Dachau.

Flossenbürg Concentration Camp
Gedächtnisallee 5, Flossenbürg,
Ⓦ gedenkstaette-flossenbuerg.de

As the Soviets continued their advance into Germany and concentration camps in the occupied territories were evacuated, the number of prisoners in Flossenbürg, northeast of Nuremberg, rapidly increased. By March 1945, there were 15,000 people in the main camp and a further 37,000 in satellite camps. At the beginning of April, the SS executed resistance fighters here, including some high-ranking participants in the attempt to assassinate Hitler on 20 July 1944. An estimated 30,000 other people died at Flossenbürg because of the appalling living conditions and hard labour. The camp was liquidated between 16 and 20 April 1945, and the remaining prisoners organized into "death marches" heading southwards. When the US 90th Infantry and 97th Infantry arrived on 23 April, the camp was mostly empty, except for 1500 critically ill prisoners who had been left behind.

Durnbach War Cemetery
Gmund am Tegernsee

The site for this cemetery to the south of Munich was chosen shortly after hostilities had ceased. The great majority of the 2934 people buried here (93 unidentified) are airmen who were shot down over Bavaria, Württemberg, Austria, Hessen and

›› Concentration camps

Nazi Germany wasn't just a police state, it was a prison state too. The regime's grip on power depended on incarcerating millions of innocent people who fell foul of the party's ideology. As the Allies moved across Germany dismantling the Nazi regime, they liberated its many concentration camps. Finally open to the scrutiny of the outside world, the inhumane conditions suffered by camp inmates appalled people around the globe.

Mass arrests of Hitler's political opponents began soon after he came to power, and Dachau concentration camp housed the first undesirables as early as 1933. As the regime became bolder, ever greater numbers were installed in a burgeoning system of camps and subcamps in which ill treatment, malnutrition, disease, forced labour, summary justice and death were commonplace.

The SS ran the concentration camps (*Konzentrationslager*) with ruthless administrative efficiency. Labour camps differed from extermination camps, although the two often existed within the same complex, such as at Auschwitz-Birkenau (see p.241). There were no death camps in Germany designed expressly as places of mass murder. The inmates of labour camps were incarcerated indefinitely without trial but were rarely subject to systematic killings.

Prisoner of war camps (Stalags or Oflags) were something else again, conforming, at least nominally, to international law.

Nazi concentration camp prisoners wore uniforms with a badge indicating their offence. Jews, for example, were made to wear a yellow Star of David. Inside the camps, inmates existed outside the law, and camp guards frequently committed horrific acts of violence against them. Many were used as slave labour, others as disposable fodder for medical experiments.

The outside world knew little about the concentration camps until the invasion of Germany beyond the Rhine in April 1945. With the discovery of the camps and the depravity they witnessed, any illusion that Nazism was simply a different – pragmatic and authoritarian – approach to organizing modern society was quickly dispelled. Evidence from the camps, their abysmal conditions, ruthless cruelty and mass killings, changed perceptions of human nature forever.

While the liberation of the camps brought some survivors hope, others found it hard to adjust to civilian life. Many had no home or family to return to; some suffered from survivor's guilt; others were in such poor health that they never recovered, but died in freedom rather than captivity.

Thuringia, brought from their scattered graves by the Army Graves Service. The remainder are men who were killed while escaping from prisoner of war camps in the same areas, or who died towards the end of the war on forced marches from the camps to more remote areas.

Documentation Center Nazi Party Rally Grounds
Bayernstr. 110, Nuremberg, ⓦ museen. nuernberg.de/dokuzentrum

The city of Nuremberg had great significance for the Nazis. In the 1930s, the famous Nuremberg Rallies were held here, during which Hitler perfected his oratory skills to massed ranks of the faithful. It was here too, during a rally in 1935, that Hitler proclaimed the discrimination and persecution of German Jews in the infamous Nuremberg Laws.

The city's final service to the Nazis was as a place of postwar trials and executions. The Documentation Center has a permanent exhibition that seeks to explain the hold the Nazis had on German society up until the end of the war.

Dokumentation Obersalzberg
Salzbergstr. 41, Berchtesgaden, ⓦ obersalzberg.de

After his rise to power, Hitler bought a holiday home in Obersalzberg, near the town of Berchtesgaden, with the proceeds of *Mein Kampf*. He called his house the Berghof. Obersalzberg's residents were gradually driven out as other Nazi leaders moved in, buying up its properties. Their presence turned this inconspicuous corner of Bavaria into a second seat of Nazi government, close to their powerbase in Munich. From here, Hitler presented himself to the world – often through film – as a dictator at ease, as a good neighbour and as

» Eva Braun and Adolf Hitler on the terrace of the Berghof

» Austria

One of Hitler's key ambitions when the Nazi party rose to prominence was to reunite his native Austria with Germany, a move that would break the treaties that had ended World War I. In 1938, he defied the world and joined the two countries in a union known as Anschluss. Austria became a province of Greater Germany, subject to its repressive racial laws.

A number of concentration camps were built in Austria. The most visited today is Mauthausen (southeast of Linz, mauthausen-memorial.org), which, together with its various subcamps, processed almost 200,000 displaced and detained persons, including political prisoners. A group of exiled Spanish Republicans was even sent to Mauthausen as a courtesy to General Franco – despite technically being citizens of a neutral country. As the war drew towards its conclusion, overcrowding increased as inmates from other camps were evacuated and transported here, either on forced "death marches" or in cramped railway wagons.

During its seven years of existence, Mauthausen earned a reputation as one of the harshest Nazi camps, where throngs of inmates were worked to death and 3500 people, including a high proportion of Soviet prisoners of war, were exterminated in a single gas chamber.

As the Reich crumbled, SS guards tried to destroy the evidence before they fled. An estimated 90,000 people died at Mauthausen, including some after US troops liberated the camp on 5 May 1945.

Hartheim Castle (Schloss Hartheim, schloss-hartheim.at) is another infamous Austrian site, which acted as a euthanasia centre from 1940 to 1944. Some 30,000 people with mental and physical disabilities were murdered here under the auspices of psychiatrist Dr Rudolf Lonauer from Linz, who committed suicide in May 1945. An elaborate cover-up was organized, including false death certificates which claimed the victims died of tuberculosis.

Four different armies liberated Austria in 1945. The Soviets' Second Ukrainian Front (under Marshal Malinovsky) and the Third Ukrainian Front (commanded by Marshal Tolbukhin) combined to take Vienna on 13 April 1945. Patton's US Third Army invaded eastern Austria, while Patch's US Seventh Army entered western Austria from Bavaria, advancing as far as the Brenner Pass (see p.297).

When the war ended, Vienna was divided into five zones of occupation, a tense arrangement that is brilliantly evoked in Carol Reed's 1949 film, *The Third Man*. In the postwar settlement, Austria became an independent republic again.

a lover of nature, children and the ordinary people of rural Germany.

On 25 April 1945, while Hitler was ensconced in Berlin, Obersalzberg was bombed by British and American forces and mostly destroyed. When the US 3rd Infantry arrived on 4 May, plunderers had already picked over the ruins, leaving a smattering of memorabilia behind.

A museum was built on this site long after the war, which explains the development of Nazism and its association with Obersalzberg and Bavaria in meticulous detail. Beneath the museum, a bunker complex built in 1943–5 survives. Its dank stairs and passageways give an idea of the realities of war, a stark contrast to the bucolic mountain world above.

Northern Germany

Despite being relegated to a subordinate role in the conquest of Germany by Eisenhower, General Montgomery acquitted his responsibilities in the north of the country with diligence.

After crossing the Rhine, Montgomery's 21st Army Group separated into three parts. The First Canadian Army turned north to liberate the northern Netherlands and the northwest corner of Germany (including the principal German naval base of Wilhelmshaven); command of the US Ninth Army was passed to Bradley and sent south to meet up with the First Army and encircle the Ruhr (see p.291); while the British Second Army headed for the Baltic coast.

The Second Army at the Elbe river

The bulk of Montgomery's forces, the British Second Army, moved in an oblique line across the plains of northern Germany towards the Baltic coast. The Bremen–Hamburg autobahn was crossed on 19 April 1945.

A number of watercourses – the Ems and Weser rivers and two canals – presented obstacles for Montgomery's army, and five hundred bridges were built to carry its men and vehicles forwards. Its greatest challenge was crossing the Elbe on 29 April. Montgomery met with limited resistance from German Army Group H, under the command of General Johannes Blaskowitz; by now, Nazi military strength was thinly spread and fuel in short supply. As Montgomery proceeded, he was able to take the Luftwaffe's last operational airfields. Aided by the arrival of the first RAF jets, the Allies established control of the airspace over northern Germany.

Reaching the Baltic

Eisenhower urged Montgomery to quicken his progress. Now that the defeat of Nazism appeared inevitable, British and

» Liberated Allied POWs

American politicians turned their thoughts to the occupation of Germany and the order of the postwar world. Stationing their troops in the liberated territories would give the Allied nations clout after the war, and although the Soviets were their allies, the Anglo-American commanders would readily take lands in the designated Soviet zone and return them later on to serve their own interests.

Advancing from the Elbe, Montgomery took both Lübeck and Wismar on 2 May 1945, just hours before the Russian troops of Marshal Konstantin Rokossovsky arrived from Mecklenburg-Vorpommern in north-eastern Germany. British troops were now deep inside the Soviet zone of occupation agreed at the Yalta Conference in February (see p.271), but were unable to prevent the Soviets reaching Schleswig-Holstein, the Jutland peninsula and Denmark. Montgomery halted on a line through Hamburg (liberated on 3 May) and Lübeck. The new German head of state, president Karl Dönitz, was left stranded in Flensburg on the Danish border.

The end of the war in northern Germany

On 4 May, a delegation of high-ranking German officers arrived at Montgomery's tactical headquarters on Lüneburg Heath. It was led by Admiral Hans-Georg von Friedeburg on behalf of Karl Dönitz and Wilhelm Keitel, Commander-in-Chief of the German armed forces. Dönitz was still hoping for a negotiated armistice with the Anglo-American allies, but Montgomery convinced von Friedeburg that Germany's situation was hopeless. Berlin had capitulated (see p.315), Germany had been organized into zones of occupation, and – in any case – Montgomery could not accept the surrender of any armies engaged with Soviet forces. After some discussion, Dönitz and Keitel authorized von Friedeburg to sign an instrument of surrender of all German forces in the Netherlands, northern Germany and Denmark; the document was officially signed at 6pm on 4 May. War in northern Germany was over. Islands and ships were included in the capitulation and all U-boats were ordered to return to base.

» Peenemünde's former power station

Withdrawal from the Baltic coast

On 7 May, Montgomery formally met his Russian counterpart, Marshal Konstantin Rokossovsky, in Wismar. Two months after the end of the war, the British withdrew from the Baltic ports.

» Northern Germany sites

Historical Technical Museum

Im Kraftwerk, Peenemünde, Ⓦ museum-peenemuende.de

In the late 1930s, the thickly wooded island of Peenemünde, at the mouth of the Oder river on the north coast of Germany, was chosen as the secret location for a weapons research centre and test site. It became the largest installation of its kind in Europe, employing 12,000 people, including forced labourers.

The Polish Resistance (AK) managed to infiltrate Peenemünde and, in April 1943, information about the research centre and the progress of its work on the V1 and V2 was smuggled out of Poland via Switzerland and delivered to Britain. On the night of 17–18 August 1943, the RAF attacked Peenemünde with almost six hundred heavy bombers, dropping more than 1600 tons of bombs over the site. Many German personnel were killed, but one of the leading scientists on the programme, Wernher von Braun, survived. The raid was considered a success: development of the V1 and V2 was halted at Peenemünde and moved to other sites in a response estimated to have delayed the first offensive launch of the V1 by six months.

The Historical Technical Museum in Peenemünde was built in 1991 on the grounds of the former research centre where the rockets were constructed. As well as information on the programme and the weap-

onry, displays also focus on the people who lived and worked at Peenemünde.

Neuengamme Concentration Camp Memorial

Jean-Dolidier-Weg 75, Hamburg, Ⓦ kz-gedenkstaette-neuengamme.de

Opened in 1938 as a subcamp of Sachsenhausen (see p.311), Neuengamme became an independent camp in 1940. More than half of its 100,400 prisoners, mostly foreign nationals, died under Nazi persecution. The memorial,

» The Hamburg Firestorm

In the early hours of 28 July 1943, the RAF unleashed Operation Gomorrah upon the city of Hamburg. The campaign lived up to its name, a reference to the biblical city consumed by fire and brimstone. Dropping a mass of highly explosive and incendiary bombs over Hamburg, so many fires were started that they soon fused together to form a single, monstrous blaze. The fire sucked in so much oxygen that hurricane-force winds were generated, and temperatures rose to a staggering 800°C. The Hamburg Fire Department was forced to coin a new term: *Feuersturm* (firestorm).

Bombing had reached its nadir: survival was almost impossible for those on the ground and 40,000 people – mainly civilians – were killed. After Hamburg, other deliberately provoked firestorms would follow.

German bombers were responsible for the deaths of 60,500 British civilians in World War II. During the Liberation, British and American bombers would kill many times that number of German nationals.

which was inaugurated on the 60th anniversary of the camp's liberation in May 2005, encompasses the entire grounds and seventeen of Neuengamme's original buildings.

Becklingen Cemetery
Lüneburg Heath, Wietzendorf

Becklingen Cemetery is located on a hillside overlooking Lüneburg Heath, at the site where Field Marshal Montgomery accepted the German surrender from representatives of Admiral Dönitz on 4 May 1945. Burials were transferred to Becklingen from isolated German and POW cemeteries located within an 80km radius; most of those interred here died during the last two months of the war.

Wöbbelin Concentration Camp
Ludwigsluster Str. 2b, Wöbbelin

Wöbbelin Concentration Camp existed for just ten weeks from 12 February to 2 May

» German military technology

Hitler recognized that the development and availability of technology could have a profound impact on the war's outcome, and would transform the face of modern warfare. He hoped that a series of new weapons would swing the war in the Nazis' favour, but was unable to perfect his V1 and V2 missiles before the Allied victory. The USA remained the frontrunners in nuclear development throughout the war. Their atomic bombs would devastate the Japanese cities of Hiroshima and Nagasaki in August 1945.

The Nazis invested heavily in technology. The Peenemünde facility (see p.305) was the largest armaments centre in Europe; in the 1930s, its team of experts worked on new inventions and machines they hoped would deliver the Nazis a decisive victory. Towards the end of the war, as the German army yielded ground to the advancing Allies, Hitler was convinced that several newly perfected weapons would reverse his fortunes. An "electro" submarine was preparing to come into service, and the first military jet aircraft were already flying over Germany.

The future of modern warfare, Hitler realized, was the pilotless aircraft – what we now call the cruise missile. Priority was afforded to the development of so-called *Vergeltungswaffe* (Retaliation weapons), which were given a variety of nicknames by the Allies, generally with the prefix "V". After Peenemünde was destroyed by Allied bombing, the manufacture and evolution of the V weapons was moved to secret locations around Germany.

The V1 was a cruise missile launched by catapult or dropped from an aircraft, with a range of 200km. The first V1 fell on London a week after D-Day, renewing the terror of the Blitz. The V1 was later fired at Antwerp, with similarly devastating results. The Allies' main tactic against the V1 was to find its launch bases and destroy them.

The first V2 was deployed on 18 September 1944. It could go higher and faster than the V1, which meant it was impossible to shoot down. The V2 could be launched from almost anywhere within its 320km range using minimal equipment, making the Allies' task even harder.

Both the V1 and V2 weapons were of variable accuracy and reliability, however, and eventually the advance of the liberating armies overran all of Germany's launch sites.

«
Junkers aircraft
factory at Tarthun

1945. Constructed under extremely harsh conditions by inmates from Neuengamme and Bergen-Belsen camps, it was originally intended to house American and British prisoners of war. As the Allies advanced, the still incomplete camp was used between 15 and 26 April 1945 as a reception camp for various evacuation transports, mainly from the satellite camps of Neuengamme. Nearly 5000 inmates from at least 25 nations were interned at Wöbbelin, more than one thousand of whom died as a result of exhaustion, maltreatment and starvation.

On 2 May, units of the 82nd US Airborne Division and 8th Infantry reached the region. The guards left the camp around noon; in the early afternoon American soldiers stumbled upon Wöbbelin, which was not marked on any maps.

A circular path lined by information panels takes the visitor through the grounds of the former camp.

Bunkermuseum (Air-Raid Shelter Museum)
Wichernsweg 16, Hamburg,
Ⓦ hh-hamm.de

This four-chamber air-raid shelter, built in 1940–41 in the Hamm district of Hamburg and complete with restored furniture, gives a lasting impression of what it would have

»
Bergen-Belsen
Memorial

been like during the bombing raids that racked the city in the summer of 1943 (see p.305). A further exhibit displays the personal effects of people who lived through the war.

German Naval Museum
Südstrand 125, Wilhelmshaven, Ⓦ marinemuseum.de

Germany's military maritime museum recalls the history of the naval town of Wilhelmshaven, beginning in 1869 and covering both world wars. The World War II artefacts collection includes a Seehund (a two-man submarine), a barrel of the German cruiser *Köln* and a ship's bell. Boat tours leaving from the museum are also available.

Bergen-Belsen Memorial
Anne-Frank-Platz, Lohheide, Ⓦ bergen-belsen.stiftung-ng.de

In early 1945, no Allied soldier, commander or politician suspected the number of concentration camps that existed in Germany. Nor were they prepared for their inhumanity, which would shock even the most battle-hardened troops. On 15 April, the 11th British Armoured Division opened the gates of a camp whose name was to become notorious throughout the world. Overcrowded and underfed, Bergen-Belsen's 40,000 emaciated prisoners could hardly comprehend liberation after the horrors they had lived through. Some had resorted to cannibalism to survive, while more than 12,000 corpses were left unburied and had to be bulldozed into immense mass graves. When the British had evacuated the survivors and buried the dead, they razed this "horror camp".

The site and museum give a good understanding of the events that occurred here. Note that, as with most of the concentration camps, exhibits may not be appropriate for children; much of the material is chilling.

Denkort Bunker Valentin

Rekumer Siel, Bremen-Farge, Bremen,
Ⓦ denkort-bunker-valentin.de

Europe's second-largest above-ground bunker was begun in 1943 using forced labour; around two thousand people died during its construction. Planned as a production site for type XXI submarines, it was bombed by the RAF in March 1945 and never served its intended purpose.

Cap Arcona Museum

Haakengraben 2/Kremper Tor, Neustadt in Holstein, Ⓦ museum-cap-arcona.de

On 26 April 1945, SS guards loaded prisoners from Neuengamme and several other concentration camps onto three unmarked ships. One of them was the SS *Cap Arcona*, an ocean liner and former flagship of the Hamburg–South America Line. No one is certain where the ships were headed, but on the afternoon of 3 May, RAF fighter-bombers attacked the convoy and the ships were sunk almost immediately. Afterwards, both the pilots and SS lifeboat crews shot drowning prisoners in the water. Over six thousand prisoners from 24 different European nations were killed in what came to be known as the *Cap Arcona* disaster.

This museum explains the whole story – or at least what's known of it.

German Tank Museum

Hans-Krüger-Str. 33, Münster,
Ⓦ daspanzermuseum.de

The German Tank Museum in Münster was constructed in 1983. Its military hardware – tanks, uniforms, small arms, medals and so on – covers World War I to the present day.

Ravensbrück Memorial

Str. der Nationen, Fürstenberg/Havel,
Ⓦ ravensbrueck.de

Ravensbrück was the largest concentration camp for women on German soil. Between 1939 and 1945 around 133,000 women and children as well as 20,000 men were imprisoned here. Ravensbrück Memorial presents the camp's history in various exhibitions and commemorates the fate of its former prisoners.

« Denkort Bunker Valentin

Brandenburg

Stalin was eager to reach Berlin before the Americans and the British. To take the city, he would first have to penetrate Brandenburg, the German province surrounding Berlin.

Stalin hoped that the conquest of Berlin would demonstrate Soviet military might and help lever a favourable negotiating position after the war. In the event, by the spring of 1945 there was little competition for the city. US President Franklin Roosevelt, whose troops were deep in the heart of Germany, was happy to ignore Berlin so long as Nazi Germany was defeated. His main interest was keeping the Soviet Union as an ally in the war against Japan, and as a willing partner in the creation of a stable postwar world order. Roosevelt's death on 12 April and the accession of Harry S. Truman to the presidency

had little impact, and the Red Army was left to capture the city via Brandenburg.

The Seelow Heights

In mid-April 1945, Marshal Georgy Zhukov, commander of the 1st Belorusian Front, and Ivan Konev, leading the 1st Ukrainian Front, began their offensive campaign against Berlin. Zhukov hoped to advance directly on the city, but had underestimated the obstacle formed by the Seelow Heights, 70km east of Berlin in Brandenburg.

On the morning of 16 April, the 1st Belorusian Front attacked several German positions in the Seelow Heights, but met with little success. The intensity of German defensive fire took the Soviet troops by surprise. To make matters worse, nearly 150 anti-aircraft defence searchlights placed in the Soviet

» Soviet artillery at the Battle of the Seelow Heights, April 1945

front lines to blind the Germans caused disorientation among Zhukov's own troops instead. His tanks attempted to scale the Heights but found the incline so steep that the Soviet commanders had to search for alternative routes through, frequently meeting German defensive positions in the process.

After several fruitless days of fighting, Zhukov realized he needed to change course, to go around the Heights and approach Berlin from the north. Konev, meanwhile, swung his forces round after crossing the Neisse to attack Berlin from the south.

The two Russian fronts advanced and surrounded the German Ninth Army under General Theodor Busse, which was positioned in the Spree Forest southeast of Berlin. Busse attempted to break out of the Halbe Pocket – as the encirclement became known – to the west, and join up with Wenck's Twelfth Army with the intention of surrendering to the Americans rather than the Soviets. While a few thousand Ninth Army soldiers were successful, the rest were killed or captured.

The last days of April
On 20 April, Adolf Hitler's 56th birthday, the Führer awarded medals to members of the Hitler Youth and addressed key members of the Nazi elite for the last time in Berlin. The Soviets would soon take the city, and Hitler finally gave his followers permission to try to steal through their offensive lines.

By 25 April, Soviet troops belonging to the 1st Belorusian Front and the 1st Ukrainian Front met to completely surround Berlin. With the defeat of the Ninth Army, German resistance outside Berlin was over. All that was left was for Zhukov, who had been granted the honour of delivering the coup de grâce, to enter Berlin.

Brandenburg sites

Seelow Heights Memorial Site and Museum
Küstriner Str. 28a, Seelow,
Ⓦ gedenkstaette-seelower-hoehen.de

The Seelow Heights Museum, built in 1972 and expanded in 1985 with a semicircular entry area, was inspired by Soviet Marshal Georgy Zhukov's command bunker, which he established on Reitwein Heights and used as a forward command post on 15 and 16 April 1945. The permanent exhibition, presented in both English and German, provides information on the Battle of Seelow Heights, with text, pictures and sound documentation, as well as expert accounts of the events of 1945. It also shows how the battle was incorporated into East German historiography.

Parked in front of the museum are several large military vehicles and artillery pieces. Situated on the plateau above is the Kerbel Memorial, designed in 1945, together with the military cemetery. A Russian Orthodox cross, dedicated in 2003 and restored in 2013, has consciously been placed on an axis leading to the graves of the fallen Soviet soldiers. From this "Place of Rest", visitors can take in a sweeping view of the Oder Marsh area all the way to Küstrin (Kostrzyn) and the Reitwein Heights. The panorama includes part of the historical battlefield.

Sachsenhausen Concentration Camp Memorial and Museum
Str. der Nationen 22, Oranienburg,
Ⓦ sachsenhausen-sbg.de

The closest concentration camp to Berlin and the first to be constructed after Himmler became chief of police, Sachsenhausen was opened in the summer of 1936 in Oranienburg. Himmler intended it to serve as a model camp.

Between 1936 and 1945, more than 200,000 people, including 20,000 women, were imprisoned here. The museum was inaugurated in 1961, after Sachsenhausen had been used by the Soviet secret police for its own nefarious purposes. The remnants of buildings and other relics of the camp are augmented by several interesting permanent exhibitions.

Cecilienhof Palace
Am Neuen Garten, Potsdam, Ⓦ spsg. de/schloesser-gaerten/objekt/schloss-cecilienhof

This vast mansion was built from 1913–17 in the style of a country manor. It was the last palace to be commissioned by the Hohenzollerns before their fall from grace at the end of World War I; Emperor William II had it built to accommodate his eldest son, Crown Prince William. From 17 July to 2 August

≫ Potsdam Conference

Between 17 July and 2 August 1945, the Potsdam Conference was held at Cecilienhof Palace (see above) in Potsdam, southwest of Berlin. It was here that the three leaders of the dominant Allied victors (Britain, the USA and the Soviet Union) met to discuss the new order in Europe and Germany. The results of the conference were contained in the Potsdam Agreement.

In the summer of 1945, world history was written. To the "Big Three" – Harry S. Truman (who had become president of the USA in April), Winston Churchill and Joseph Stalin – was added Clement Attlee, who had just won the British general election and would be replacing Churchill as prime minister. These men came to an agreement about the political principles that would govern Germany during its occupation: decentralization, demilitarization, denazification and democratization. The German-Polish border would be provisionally shifted westwards to the Oder-Neisse Line, but the final boundary would be decided at a later peace conference. The expulsion of German populations from Poland, Czechoslovakia and Hungary was to be suspended to ensure an orderly transfer.

It was also decided that each occupying power was to take reparations from its designated zone. Additional reparations would be provided to the Soviet Union from the Western sectors.

Although France was informed of the outcomes of the Potsdam Conference, it took no part in the decision-making process. On 7 August 1945, the French government acceded to the Potsdam Agreement, albeit with reservations about a number of points.

At the Potsdam Conference it became clear that the end of the war also meant the end of a common policy shared by the Allies, and the beginning of new and unpredictable disputes between them. There was repeated discussion about how the details of the Potsdam Agreement were to be interpreted.

Less than one week after the conference broke up, the first atomic bomb was dropped on Hiroshima, a demonstration of US power that was intended not only to bring the Japanese government to the negotiating table, but also to impress upon the Soviets that although World War II had ended, they would still face opposition to their envisioned world order. Rumblings of the Cold War had begun.

1945, it was used as the venue for the Pots-dam Conference (see p.312).

Halbe Forest Cemetery
Ernst-Teichmann-Str, Halbe

More than 40,000 people were killed in the Battle of the Halbe Pocket at the end of April 1945. The bodies of the fallen had to be buried quickly – the first warm days of May were accelerating their decay, and the risk of disease and epidemic was high. The local Soviet occupying authority stipulated that the dead were to be interred immediately and where they lay, be it in mass graves, front gardens or shell craters. As a result, numerous provisional gravesites were cleared in the forests and along pathways, while many single graves were dug in the gardens of local villagers.

   In 1951, six years after the battle, a local Protestant minister, Ernst Teichmann, initiated the gathering of bodies buried in and around Halbe into a central cemetery. The result, Halbe Forest Cemetery, is the resting place of 24,000 victims of the Battle of the Halbe Pocket, including soldiers, civilians and Soviet forced labourers. There are also a number of graves holding people killed at the German execution site in Berlin-Tegel and at the Ketschendorf internment camp.

Victims of Political Dictatorships Documentation Centre
Carl-Philipp-Emanuel-Bach-Str. 11, Frankfurt (Oder), Ⓦ museum-viadrina.de

Located in a former prison, this documentation centre records the fate of those who were persecuted for political reasons, not only in Nazi Germany but also during the

«
Tableau at the Death March Museum

subsequent Soviet occupation and in the East German GDR.

Death March Museum
Belower Damm 1, Wittstock, Ⓦ stiftung-bg.de

This little museum in the Below Forest commemorates the prisoners of Sachsenhausen camp who were forced to march through this area in April 1945 after Himmler ordered the evacuation of the camps. The Reichs-führer-SS didn't want any "human evidence" of the horrifying conditions to fall into the hands of the Allies as they advanced and the camps were liberated.

   An estimated 33,000 prisoners were marched in columns towards the Baltic. According to the camp commander, they were destined to be loaded onto ships and sunk at sea. The marchers got as far as Schwerin before their guards deserted them and the Allies found their columns.

Berlin

By the end of April 1945, Berlin was no longer much of a prize. The Prussian and imperial capital that Hitler dreamed of making the fulcrum of an ordered, authoritarian world had been reduced to a state of ruin and rubble by sixteen months of Allied bombing.

As the Soviet troops approached Berlin, most of its inhabitants cowered underground, safe from the effects of Soviet shelling. Those who were able manned the concentric lines of defence that ringed the city, but they did little to slow the advance.

The front line crept inexorably inwards from the suburbs, despite the efforts of an ad hoc army of regular soldiers, SS fighters and Volkssturm (home guard) units. There was no longer an age limit for military service: young

» The Soviet flag is raised over the Reichstag in a popular propaganda photo

boys who had grown up in a warring country fought and died in Berlin supporting Hitler's desperate last stand. Most of the combatants defending Berlin had little or no training. They fired anti-aircraft guns or whatever weapons they had at the advancing Russian soldiers.

The Führer and his government took refuge in a subterranean bunker, where they received sporadic intelligence from the outside world. They knew that the Soviets had reached the outer suburbs and were making progress street by street, house by house, towards Berlin's centre and the remaining trappings of the Nazi state.

Hitler still hoped that salvation would come from outside the city – that General Walther Wenck would rally the remaining German soldiers for a do-or-die attempt to break the Soviet throttlehold. Hitler's commanders, confined to the bunker, knew there wasn't enough military manpower or order left in Nazi Germany to organize an effective opposition.

Without outside assistance, Berlin could not hold out. However much courage its citizens' army displayed, the city's arsenal was running out of ammunition; food was also becoming increasingly scarce.

In the early hours of 29 April, the Soviet troops managed to cross the Moltke Bridge and attack the Interior Ministry. After capturing the Secret State Police headquarters later that day, the Soviets pressed on towards the Reichstag. Only now did Hitler begin to envisage a Germany without himself in command. He dictated his will and a political testament, which made provisions for continuing the governance of a Reich that no longer existed. Reichsmarschall Göring and Himmler, the minister of the interior, were both dismissed from the Nazi party. Each had tried to take control of the Reich and still hoped to come to an agreement with the British and the Americans. Hitler appointed Admiral Karl Dönitz as his successor – with the title of president of Germany – and Joseph Goebbels as Chancellor.

The next day, Hitler killed himself. Goebbels poisoned his own family and followed suit on 1 May, leaving Dönitz, who was absent from Berlin, in charge of the closing stages of Germany's war.

The Battle for the Reichstag was one of the last fights in the conquest of Berlin. Two soldiers raised the Soviet flag on its roof, while heavy fighting still raged below. The city's remaining 10,000 German soldiers, now commanded by General Helmuth Weidling, were forced into a shrinking area in the city centre.

On 1 May, the German garrison tried and failed to negotiate a conditional surrender; the Reichstag was occupied and German defeat was imminent. Weidling agreed to the Soviet demand for an unconditional ceasefire, saving the lives of the remaining inhabitants of Berlin, and an armistice was signed on 2 May that handed control of the city to Vasily Chuikov, commander of the Soviet armies. The commanders of the two German armies closest to Berlin – the Twenty-first Army and Third Panzer Army – simultaneously surrendered to the western Allies.

The Battle for Berlin is estimated to have cost the lives of 80,000 Soviet troops and 50,000 German soldiers and civilians.

» Berlin sites

Allied Museum
Clayallee 135, Ⓦ alliiertenmuseum.de

The Liberation was the end of one story and the beginning of another. This museum explains what happened next, from the defeat of Germany in World War II to the division of West and East Berlin between the three Western powers and the Soviet Union.

Anti-War Museum
21 Bruessler Str.

This delightfully idiosyncratic museum was originally founded in 1925 by anarchist-pacifist Ernst Friedrich. It was destroyed in 1933 by stormtroopers, for whom war was to be admired rather than vilified. The building was used as an SS torture chamber in the following years, when Friedrich emigrated to Belgium and then France. The museum has since been revived and is run by Friedrich's grandson, with the help of volunteers. There are exhibits on both wars, as well as displays dedicated to current global conflicts.

Bebelplatz

A modern work of art marks the spot at Bebelplatz where a Nazi book burning took place in May 1933, when 20,000 books were engulfed by flames. Today's memorial takes the form of a sunken library of empty shelves.

Berliner Unterwelten Museum
Brunnenstr. 105, Ⓦ berliner-unterwelten.de

The Berliner Unterwelten Museum is located in a former air-raid shelter at Gesundbrunnen underground station. Visitors can explore the site by guided tour to see bunkers from the former government quarter, war rubble and archeological finds. The museum also explores the difficult topic of military construction and historic preservation.

The permanent exhibition, "Myth of Germania – Vision and Crime", explores Hitler's grand plans for Berlin, which he envisioned as an architectural showcase of Nazi

strength and power. Several displays focus on the expulsions, deportations and use of forced labour that were implemented to make his vision a reality.

Memorial to the Murdered Jews of Europe
Cora-Berliner-Str. 1, Ⓦ holocaustmahmal. de

The block of land immediately south of Brandenburger Tor and Pariser Platz is officially called the Memorial to the Murdered Jews of Europe, and general known as the Holocaust Memorial. It involves 2711 dark grey oblong blocks (stelae), evenly and tightly spaced but of varying heights, spread across an area the size of two football pitches. As there is no single entrance, visitors make their own way through the maze to the centre where the blocks are well above head height, tending to convey a sense of gloom, isolation and solitude. An underground information centre relates the life stories and plight of Jewish victims of the Holocaust.

Undeniably powerful, the memorial has faced various criticisms: for being unnecessarily large in scale; for its use of prime real estate with little historical significance; and for its incredible costs. Also contentious was the hiring of German company Degussa (now Evonik) to supply the anti-graffiti paint for the blocks, since they are a daughter company of I.G. Farben – the company that produced Zyklon B, the gas used in the Nazi gas chambers.

Flak Tower
Humboldthain Park, Brunnenstr.

This ruined 42m-high tower is normally inaccessible, but can be visited on a tour arranged by Berlin Unterwelten (see p.315). Equipped with heavy anti-aircraft guns, Berlin's flak towers were supposed to protect its city centre from bomb attacks.

"Mother and Child" Bunker
Fichtestr.

To see this bunker, located in a former gasometer, you will need to ask for details at Berlin Unterwelten (see p.315). The six-storey bunker – with a 3m-thick ceiling – was installed in 1940 to shelter 6500 mothers and children. Later in the war, as many as 30,000 people crowded into its interior.

German Historical Museum
Unter den Linden 2

The German Historical Museum tells the comprehensive story of 2000 years of German history. The permanent exhibition comprises around seven thousand historical exponents providing information on the individuals, ideas, events and developments that have shaped the nation. The main floor is devoted to the Weimar Republic, the Nazi regime, the postwar period and the two German states that existed from 1949 to the reunification in 1990.

Forced Labour Documentation Centre
Britzer Str. 5, ⓦ dz-ns-zwangsarbeit.de

This centre in Schöneweide is the last well-preserved Nazi forced labour camp. "Barack 13", one of the first camp buildings, is open to the public on guided tours. Two permanent exhibitions document the fate of the resident forced labourers during World War II.

German Resistance Memorial Centre
Stauffenbergstr. 13–14, ⓦ gdw-berlin.de

This slick exhibition centres on German resistance to the Nazi regime. It is an important reminder that not all Germans were Nazis, and that many stood up to Hitler and paid with their lives. Note the name of its street, which honours the man who tried to assassinate Hitler in the summer of 1944.

German-Russian Museum
Zwieseler Str. 4, Berlin-Karlshorst, ⓦ museum-karlshorst.de

A unique bilateral institution sponsored by the Federal Republic of Germany and the Russian Federation, this museum marks the spot where the unconditional surrender was signed on 8 May 1945 signalling the end of World War II in Europe. The war caused an unprecedented amount of death and destruction across the continent, but fighting was especially brutal during Operation Barbarossa, the German invasion of the Soviet Union that began on 22 June 1941.

This is the only museum in Germany with a permanent exhibition recalling the war of annihilation in Eastern Europe. It documents wartime events from the perspective of both parties, German and Soviet, as well as exploring the consequences of World War II as they continue into the present day.

Kaiser Wilhelm Memorial Church
Breitscheidplatz, ⓦ gedaechtniskirche-berlin.de

This church, named after the Emperor Wilhelm, was badly damaged in a raid on 23 November 1943. After the war, its surviving sections were left standing as a reminder of the catastrophic events of 1939–1945.

Jewish Museum
Lindenstr. 9–14, Ⓦ jmberlin.de

Berlin's Jewish Museum is the place to go to reflect on Jewish history and culture. Changing temporary exhibitions, from cultural history displays to contemporary art installations, cover a broad range of interesting themes.

Reichstag
Platz der Republik 1, Ⓦ bundestag.de

Seizing the Reichstag – already heavily damaged by bombing and shelling – was one of the final victories in the Battle of Berlin. Storming the iconic building on 30 April 1945, two soldiers raised the Soviet flag on its roof, although fighting continued below for another two days. The scene was re-enacted for a well-known propaganda photo on 2 May.

≫ The last days of Hitler

The exact truth of what happened in the Führerbunker at the end of April 1945 can never truly be known. But by piecing the most reliable sources together, it is at least possible to get a good approximation.

With the Soviets advancing through the streets of Berlin, Hitler knew that the war was lost. He had become a sick man, dependent on medication and suffering from serious delusions. Refusing to accept any personal culpability, Hitler blamed the Nazi defeat on military setbacks and on the incompetence and betrayal of his generals.

On 29 April, Hitler had poison administered to his beloved dog, Blondi: a prussic acid capsule was forced into the dog's mouth and crushed with a pair of pliers. That evening he received the news that Mussolini and his mistress had been shot by partisans and their bodies hung upside down at a petrol station in Milan; Hitler resolved not to suffer the same fate.

On the afternoon of 30 April he sat with Eva Braun, who he had recently married. Braun took a capsule of prussic acid while Hitler shot himself in the right temple with a pistol. Following the Führer's orders, his subordinates took both bodies outside the bunker, doused them with petrol and set them alight.

Rumours immediately began to circulate, suggesting that a body double had died in Hitler's place and that the Führer had managed to escape. This ruse is highly improbable: several witnesses saw Hitler's body, and the Soviets carried out a post-mortem as soon as they took the Führerbunker.

Today, there is nothing left of Hitler except for photographs, film footage, assorted Nazi memorabilia and copies of his anger-filled book, *Mein Kampf*. The man who wanted to rule the earth left no descendants, and there is no grave or memorial to mark his death. None of Hitler's schemes endured for more than a handful of years. His followers were disbanded and many of them tried and executed as war criminals, while the apparatus of the Reich was dismantled and destroyed by his enemies.

Hitler wanted history to remember him as a visionary. Instead, his life is a cautionary tale to the consequences of megalomania, a mass murderer in pursuit of futile ends.

After the war, the Reichstag fell into disrepair as an enduring symbol of the Weimar Republic that was abused and manipulated by Adolf Hitler. The Neoclassical building had been ravaged by a fire in 1933 which had completely destroyed the plenary chamber; this was one of the defining moments in Hitler's rise to power, who used the fire as an excuse to persecute his political opponents.

The reunified German parliament moved back into the building in 1999 after extensive renovations and the addition of a flashy cupola by British architect Sir Norman Foster.

Soviet Memorial Tiergarten
Str. des 17 Juni

This war memorial near the Brandenburg Gate is one of several monuments erected by the Soviets after the war. It commemorates the 80,000 Soviet soldiers who fell during the Battle of Berlin. Erected in 1945 as a semicircular stoa (covered walkway), it resembles other Soviet World War II monuments in the former Eastern bloc. On top of the stoa is a large bronze statue of a Soviet soldier, rifle slung over his shoulder, flanked by two T34 tanks and two howitzers used in the Battle of Berlin. Though the memorial was located in the former British sector of Berlin, Soviet honour guards were sent every day to perform guard duty, a tradition that was stringently maintained even during the harshest Cold War periods.

Topography of Terror
Niederkirchnerstr. 8, Ⓦ topographie.de

Standing on the site of Berlin's Gestapo headquarters, the Topography of Terror has a main permanent exhibition on the Nazi

» The fate of Hitler's henchmen
Following Hitler's death, the remaining Nazi leaders either committed suicide or survived to face punishment for their crimes. Joseph Goebbels, loyal to the last, had his six children murdered and then killed himself with his wife on 1 May. Heinrich Himmler, head of the SS, was captured by the Allies and killed himself in prison at Lüneberg on 23 May by cyanide. Göring was sentenced to death at Nuremberg; he asked to be shot as a soldier but was refused, instead swallowing cyanide on the night before he was due to hang. Von Ribbentrop did hang at Nuremberg, on 16 October 1946, as did Jodl and Keitel. Martin Bormann went missing in May 1945, but it was later proven that he had been shot by the Soviets as they took Berlin. Some Nazis – Dönitz, Hess, Speer – survived the war and their imprisonment.

state's institutions of repression. A second exhibition examines the city's role as the capital of the Third Reich.

House of the Wannsee Conference
Am Grossen Wannsee 56–58

The House of the Wannsee Conference was used as an SS guesthouse during World War II. It is most remembered, however, as the setting for the Wannsee Conference of January 1942, where high-ranking Nazi officials planned the Final Solution. Its permanent exhibition, "The Wannsee Conference and the Genocide of European Jews", fleshes out the details of this grim meeting and the story of the persecution of Jews using original documents and audiovisual displays.

The surrender of Germany and the end of the war

With Adolf Hitler dead, the other Nazi leaders discredited, Berlin in Soviet hands and Italy reconquered by a combination of British, Americans and partisan troops, the only remaining question on 2 May 1945 was how Germany as a whole would surrender to the Allies.

The few remaining armies of the Wehrmacht were dispersed and unable to fight on a co-ordinated front. Their strategic positions were weak and the German troops were diminished by the breakdown of their supply chains. Faced with the inevitable, commanders of individual units in the field surrendered to their victorious opposite numbers, as at Lüneburg Heath (see p.304).

Peace in Reims

Admiral Karl Dönitz, Hitler's nominated successor as head of state and commander of the armed forces, was ensconced at Flensburg near the Danish border. He still hoped to negotiate an honorable, conditional surrender with the British and Americans as opposed to the Soviets.

On 5 May, Dönitz dispatched a delegation to Eisenhower's headquarters, the Supreme Headquarters Allied Expeditionary Force (SHAEF) at Reims in France (see p.150) to see what terms could be arranged. Eisenhower refused to discuss anything less than unconditional surrender and threatened to close American lines to Germans fleeing west. The next day Dönitz sent his deputy, Wehrmacht Chief of Staff General Alfred Jodl to Reims in an increasingly desperate attempt to play for time, allowing more of his solders to escape from the encroaching Soviets. Again, the

Americans insisted there was no negotiation to be had.

Göring, Hitler's erstwhile deputy, now a fugitive from both the Allies and the Nazi party, was forced to give himself up to the Americans on 6 May on the German–Austrian border.

On Dönitz's instructions, Jodl ceded to Eisenhower's demands and signed the German surrender at 2.41am on 7 May, stipulating a ceasefire at 11.01pm on 8 May – which would become Victory in Europe (VE Day) in the west.

Peace in Karlshorst

The Soviets were not satisfied with Jodl's surrender, chiefly because they were absent at the signing and because a surrender on French soil did not carry the same weight as one performed in Berlin.

The definitive surrender of all German military forces therefore took place in Berlin's Karlshorst district, where the Soviet forces had set up their main headquarters after taking the city. Shortly after midnight on 8 May, the surrender was signed on behalf of the German High Command by Field Marshal Wilhelm Keitel, Colonel General Hans-Jürgen Stumpff and General Admiral Hans-Georg von Friedeburg. Soviet Marshal Georgy Zhukov signed the document on behalf of the Supreme High Command of the Red Army and British Air Marshal Arthur W. Tedder as deputy of the Supreme Commander Allied Expeditionary Force. Because of this second signing of the armistice, Russia celebrates the end of the war in Europe on 9 May.

Even before the Reims ceremony, news of peace had swept across Europe, the

British Empire and the USA, and celebrations were widespread and spirited. For the hordes who had been displaced by the war, there was both relief and anxiety about the future. Many would remain burdened by unspeakable memories.

The end of Nazism

Peace was not quick and clean everywhere. Although most German commanders obeyed the orders issued by the Oberkommando der Wehrmacht (OKW), some fought on, extending hostilities by several days. The Second Army in the Vistula delta held out until 9 May, while the last battle in Czechoslovakia was fought on 12 May. The Atlantic pockets of France (see p.152) capitulated after the armistice, while the German garrison on Alderney in the Channel Islands surrendered on 16 May.

The Allies occupied Germany but allowed Dönitz's government in Flensburg to conclude its business before it was declared illegal and disbanded on 23 May. Several of Dönitz's cabinet – including the admiral himself – were immediately arrested as war criminals, to be tried at Nuremberg.

A great many SS members and other Nazis who believed they would be indicted for war crimes – perhaps as many as 10,000 – took advantage of the chaos that followed the first days of peace to adopt new identities and flee south on "ratlines", a system of escape routes that connected Nazi safe houses. If they were lucky, they quietly crossed the Alps into Italy, where the fascists were still willing to help them. From here, they travelled to safety in Franco's Spain or South America. Many Nazis who could not escape, or chose not to, committed suicide rather than facing the justice of their accusers. With the death or execution of its hallowed leadership, Nazism disintegrated, leaving people all over Europe to pick up their lives in the new conditions of the postwar world.

«
Nazi criminals Irma Grese (the "Hyena of Auschwitz") and Josef Kramer (the "Beast of Belsen") in British custody at the end of the war

PEENEMÜNDE
Historical Technical Museum
MUSEUM

The Peenemünde Historical Technical Museum

From 1936 to 1945, the Peenemünde Military Test Site formed the largest armaments centre in Europe. Up to 12,000 people worked on guided weapons, most famously the world's first cruise missiles and large-scale rockets. Both were designed as weapons of terror for use against civilian populations, made mostly by forced labourers. From 1944, they began to be used as "Vergeltungswaffen" (V-weapons).

The Peenemünde Historical Technical Museum reconstructs the history of the creation and use of these weapons. The exhibitions document those who worked in Peenemünde, how these people lived and why the enormously elaborate weaponry projects were carried out.

The permanent exhibition in the Peenemünde power plant presents the history of German rocket technology, from its inception in the 1920s through the work at Peenemünde, the mass production of A4 rockets in Mittelbau-Dora and their use against large towns and cities in Western Europe. The two most important weapons of the Peenemünde Test Site, the Fi103/"V1" cruise missile and the A4/"V2" rocket, can be seen, as well as other large exhibits and replicas in the outdoor areas.

Historisch-Technisches
Museum Peenemünde
Im Kraftwerk
17449 Peenemünde
GERMANY

Tel.: +49(0)38371/505 0
E-Mail: htm@peenemuende.de

Member of

European
Route
of Industrial
Heritage

ERIH

www.erih.net

EUROPEAN
UNION PRIZE FOR
CULTURAL HERITAGE
EUROPA NOSTRA AWARD
2013

Nagelkreuzgemeinschaft
in Deutschland

www.museum-peenemuende.de

Displaced persons and refugees

Deciding what to do with Europe's displaced persons and refugees was a pressing issue after the Liberation.

As the last German soldiers surrendered in May 1945 and the fighting in Europe drew to a close, a whole new set of problems presented themselves to the Allies. Foremost among these was how to deal with the millions of sick, malnourished and homeless people now either wandering around Europe or stuck in displaced persons' camps.

The scale of the problem was colossal. Across those countries occupied by the Nazis, and in Germany itself, there were huge numbers of deportees who had been forcibly removed from their homelands to work as slave labour for the Reich (with their houses taken over by immigrant Germans). In addition, there were all those prisoners of war and concentration camp survivors who had been left behind in Germany and its occupied territories as the Wehrmacht fled the Soviet advance.

Deportation continues

Strange as it seems, at the conferences of Yalta in February 1945 and Potsdam in July, the "Big Three" powers decided to adopt a policy of mass deportation themselves in order to solve the ongoing problem of ethnic strife in Central Europe. The consensus was that the redrawn national boundaries of 1918 had exacerbated ethnic tensions, and that the new postwar settlement was a unique opportunity to avoid the same mistakes. This would be achieved, it was hoped, by making those countries in which conflicts were most extreme as ethnically homogeneous as possible. This meant removing between 12 and 14 million people from their homes – "ethnic cleansing" on a massive scale.

Redefining Poland

In Poland, where the borders had been almost completely redrawn, this involved the mass deportation of both Poles and non-Poles. About a million Poles living in what had been the eastern side of the country – now absorbed into the Soviet Republics of Lith-

▲
German refugees sleeping in the hay

uania, Belarus and the Ukraine – were transferred, voluntarily or otherwise, to its western side. Similarly, as many as half a million ethnic Lithuanians, Belarusians and Ukrainians were forced out of Poland. In both cases, these were mostly people who had strong traditional ties to areas in which they had been living for many generations. Unsurprisingly, many did not want to leave and had to be forced to do so.

Other people who had once lived in eastern Poland now found themselves in newly annexed Soviet territory and were forced to stay. Many still thought of themselves as Polish but had been given Soviet citizenship against their will and were prevented from making their way back to Poland.

Expelling the Germans

To compensate for the loss of the eastern borderlands, the western side of Poland had been extended up to the Oder and Neisse rivers, into lands which had previously been German. Many of the inhabitants of these areas had already fled to Germany as the Red Army advanced, with thousands dying in the attempt to do so. On 30 January 1945, a Soviet submarine sank a German military transport ship, the MV *Wilhelm Gustloff*, with the loss of around 9500 lives, half of whom were children. Despite the exodus, parts of Silesia and Prussia were still home to

A young Holocaust survivor at roll call
▼

many Germans. These people were now expelled (or "transferred" in the official jargon). A similar situation played out in Czechoslovakia after the return of the so-called Sudetenland.

According to what was agreed at Potsdam, all transfers of Germans were to be "effected in an orderly and humane manner." The opposite was more often the case, as Poles, Czechoslovaks, Hungarians and the Soviets used the expulsions as an opportunity to inflict revenge for the years of murderous oppression they had suffered during Nazi

occupation. Random acts of violence, even murder, were not unusual and the rape of German women was commonplace. Official reparations by Germany, as agreed at Yalta, included using both soldiers and civilians – women as well as men – as forced labour. By far the greatest number, around 200,000, were transferred to the Soviet Union by the Allies to add to the three million German prisoners of war already held there. Some of these spent more than fifteen years in the gulag and many have never been accounted for.

Emptying the camps

It might be assumed that the victims of Nazism, once liberated from the various labour, POW, concentration or extermination camps fared rather better. In fact, for many the nightmare continued almost as before, despite the Allies' best intentions. These were the people designated as Displaced Persons (DPs) by the Allies and, as more countries were liberated, their numbers substantially increased. Some of them simply decided to make their own way home, but did so through a chaotic, war-ravaged landscape in which much of the infrastructure of Europe had been destroyed. The functioning roads that still existed were clogged with military vehicles and long lines of desperate refugees.

A military problem

Those DPs with no homes to go to, or who were too sick and malnourished to move, remained in camps, often for several years. Initially, it was the task of the Allied armies to shelter them and distribute food and medical aid. But because the Anglo-American forces had plenty of other things to do – not least continuing with the Liberation – DPs tended to be seen as a logistical, rather than a human, problem. Systems were set up to repatriate as many as possible in the shortest possible timeframe. Military resources were so stretched that often just one officer and a handful of soldiers would be in charge of thousands of DPs, who would be treated as recalcitrant children, with little understanding of the degradations they had experienced. DPs were often blamed for looting and criminality, when these actions were actually widespread across all sections of society. Despite all the problems, the repatriation process worked with surprising efficiency and within a few months of VE Day, several million people had been returned home.

UNRRA

The Allied authorities had thought long and hard about the human damage, both physical and psychological, that they would encounter as the Liberation unfolded across Europe. In November 1943, the United Nations Relief and Rehabilitation Administration (UNRRA) was founded, an organization supported by 44 different nations (primarily the USA, the UK and Canada). UNRRA's mission was to coordinate relief operations and provide much-needed food, clothing and medical supplies at a time when such things were in short supply. It was a massive operation: thousands of staff were recruited from all walks of life and sent into the field after the briefest of training. UNRRA provided not just goods, but the professional compassion which the Allied armies, with their different priorities, could not be expected to supply. There were inevitable problems, and frequent clashes between UNRRA's needs and those of the military, but the organization made a huge and vital contribution to the mending of broken lives, running hundreds of camps that accommodated almost seven million people. The organization closed in 1947 when most of its responsibilities were

▲
United Nations Relief and Rehabilitation Administration truck loaded with displaced persons

absorbed into the European Recovery Program, or Marshall Plan (see p.334).

Jewish demands

With the liberation of Auschwitz in January and Bergen-Belsen in April 1945, it became absolutely clear the extent to which the Jews had been singled out by the Nazis, but initially this did not affect how they were treated. At Belsen, the obvious priority for the British liberators was to improve the horrific conditions and attempt to stem the daily death rate. But once this emergency situation had been stabilized, Jewish DPs began to organize themselves politically. The DP camps and repatriation had been established along national lines, but soon Jews were demanding to be treated as a distinct group. This was something the Allies resisted because it seemed to echo Nazi thinking. But the reality was that very few Jews wanted to return to lands where they had been – and were still being – persecuted. What they wished for was to emigrate, primarily to Palestine, which since 1923 had been mandated by the League of Nations as "a national home for the Jewish people".

British resistance

The Jewish desire to leave for Palestine was one that the British – who were responsible for rule in Palestine – strongly resisted, restricting the number of immi-grants on the grounds that mass migration would enflame Arab opinion in the region. The Jewish Agency – the organization responsible for establishing a Jewish homeland – and US politicians castigated the British government for its position, especially after it began deporting illegal Jewish immigrants from Palestine to camps in Cyprus. Two-thirds of the remaining Jewish DPs emigrated to the State of Israel when it was founded in 1948, with the rest heading mostly to the USA after it relaxed its own immigration quotas.

Soviet POWs

As many as three million Soviet POWs are thought to have died or been killed in captivity by the Germans, but a further 2.5 million were liberated by the Allies in the last years of the war. At the Yalta Conference, Churchill had agreed to Stalin's request that all former Soviet POWs should be repatriated, believing that not doing so would jeopardize the return of British POWs freed by the Red Army. For those Soviet citizens and Russian exiles who had fought for or collaborated with the Nazis – either because they were forced to or for ideological reasons – return meant an inevitable, and often brutal, death. For those who had fought loyally for the USSR, the outcome was better but still grim for many. Stalin regarded surrender as tantamount to

▲
Jewish illegal immigrants protesting their political situation

treason, and all returning former POWs were interrogated at NKVD screening camps. Of these, about a quarter of a million – the exact figures are disputed – were sent to the Gulag (the Soviet system of forced labour camps). Their release only came in 1953, following the death of Stalin, when the extremes of repression in the country began to be eased.

Conclusion

Conclusion to the Liberation of Europe

When the bombs stopped falling and the peace treaties were signed, the world began to question what the war – and the Liberation – meant.

The same questions that were being asked in 1945 are still being asked today. Have national narratives been fairly shaped by the war and the Liberation? Do people remember the war and the liberators as they really were – or how they want to see them? Can we learn any universal lessons from World War II, or was it an episode of history that is inseparable from time and place?

How to remember

The Liberation, as explored in this book, is at once a series of battles culminating in the defeat of Nazi Germany and a vastly complicated web of decisions and deeds. If World War II is reduced to a simple narrative, governments and citizens across Europe risk ignoring the lessons learned by those who lived through the war and the Liberation. Countless soldiers, politicians, civilians, victims and survivors have done their best to communicate their experience through written, recorded and filed accounts – it's up to the new generation to listen.

As people today sift through evidence and consider its meaning, it is important to be wary of two distractions: patriotism and moralizing. Each country involved in World War II remembers its catastrophic events and the Liberation in a different way; national memories are not always universally true and are rarely compatible with each other.

The countries that were occupied in 1939–40 remember the Liberation very differently to how the same events are perceived in the UK, which stood apart. In the USA, the view of the Liberation is different again, sometimes reduced to a story of America selflessly intervening to save the Europeans from misfortunes that they had brought upon themselves. Within each country, too, experiences were extremely varied. Listening to as many stories as possible can help understand what the war meant and means in the past, present and future.

Just as historical memory is shaped to fit a national narrative, the historian – and reader – is influenced by their own conscious and unconscious biases, as well as by who they choose to read or listen to.

It is tempting to see World War II and the Liberation as nothing more than a morality tale of good versus evil, in which young men from across the seas – often without a clear idea of why they were in Europe at all – sacrificed their lives to deliver freedom. In the 21st century, people have the advantage that distance brings, the benefit of hindsight and the ability to consider the war and the Liberation from multiple angles. It is hard to imagine the complex forces that acted on an individual soldier, occupier, collaborator, citizen or victim at the time. Acts of barbarism and atrocity were committed on both sides; so were acts of humanity and heroism.

Lessons for the future

Despite the problems associated with remembrance, some basic principles can be garnered from World War II and its conclusion. There are always exceptions, and the actions of the USSR during and after the war

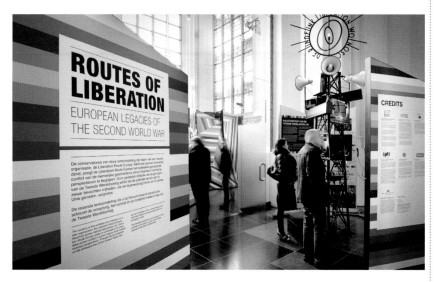

<< Routes of Liberation, a travelling exhibition created by the Liberation Route Europe Foundation

are extremely problematic, but three statements are tentatively true.

Firstly, the Allies' aim – or at least the western democracies' – was broadly noble: for stronger states to restore autonomy to weaker ones and to foster international diversity. The Allies fought to prevent military might from dictating international relations.

Secondly, the Liberation succeeded because a variety of nations were able to temporarily set aside their individual interests and cooperate to achieve a shared goal. This collaboration paved the way for the creation of the United Nations and the European Union.

Thirdly, in the case of the western Allies, the Liberation was – for the most part – ethical and law-respecting in its methodology. Terrible atrocities were committed, but they were recognized and condemned. The concept of human rights emerged as a result.

Still, it is hard to see the Liberation as essentially hopeful. Europe had failed to prevent the outbreak of World War II in 1939, and by 1945 the war had cost more than fifty million lives. The damage and destruction wreaked by World War II remains a powerful cautionary tale.

It must also be emphasized that while the Allies proved themselves adept at the military challenges of liberation, the process of freeing the occupied states of Europe was far from perfect. Many of the liberators vilified the entire German population and the Allies also did little to nurture homegrown resistance movements within Germany that might have succeeded in shortening the war.

To continue learning from World War II, it is important to remember its events in as many ways as possible. The monuments, museums, battlefields and cemeteries that mark the Liberation Route across Europe all tell a different story from a different perspective, contributing to a shared European history. Each one is a potent reminder of the lessons learned by previous generations, and a prompt to apply them to the tensions of international affairs that characterize our complex modern world.

Reconstruction

After the destruction of World War II and the Liberation came the formidable task of rebuilding Europe.

Throughout the war, a great deal of permanent damage was caused by the armies of the Allied and Axis powers, as well as by their air forces. Total war had left structures of every kind – houses, roads, railways, factories, schools, hospitals and churches – scarred, demolished or obliterated. The unprecedented number of explosives and incendiaries had razed entire towns and villages to the ground, and many cities lay in rubble. Roads and fields were cratered. Every bridge across the Rhine had been blown up, as well as countless bridges across smaller rivers.

Some of this damage was inflicted deliberately, as military and economic targets were pummelled relentlessly in order to drive the enemy back. Scorched earth policies were used to great effect by the Red Army in 1941 – devastating crops, bridges and factories as they retreated from the Germans – and Hitler frequently ordered the destruction of a city before the Allies moved in. Much of the damage, however, was unintentional, the collateral effect of armies passing through and the aftermath of bombing missions of varying accuracy. Munitions were occasionally fired or dumped in strategically insignificant locations – or on residential areas to sap civilian morale – producing nothing but more loss and misery.

The toll of war was staggering. The success of a bombing campaign on a German city was measured in a percentage of obliteration. Bremerhaven, for instance, was judged to have only 21 percent of its prewar buildings standing at the end of World War II. In the UK, London sustained serious damage under the rain of German bombs and missiles. Other towns and villages – Ortona in Italy, Caen in France and Bastogne in Belgium – were pulverized by close-quarters combat between two armies determined not to yield.

Surviving cities

Incredibly, for all the destruction wrought along the routes of the Liberation, there were places that survived more or less unscathed. Paris was treated as a shrine of civilization; it was spared in 1940 and – despite Hitler ordering its destruction – again in 1944. In Poland, Warsaw was almost totally obliterated, while Kraków was barely touched.

Enormity of the task

In 1945, a decision had to be made over whether ruined landscapes should be left as they were, swept away or reconstructed. Nature – the ploughed-up fields and the woods shattered by tanks – would repair itself over time. The manmade infrastructure that sustained civilization, however, could only be revived through a colossal reconstruction effort. This task was undertaken by ravaged local populations and liberators alike.

In addition to the physical landscape, Europe also needed reconstructing in other, less material, ways. Societies had been polarized by the promises and threats of Nazism; political institutions had been suspended, exiled or replaced; people's belief in human morality had been shaken; and bonds of cooperation and trust had been worn. In all these ways, Europe needed reconstructing too. If the war-torn nations of Europe couldn't rebuild their democracies and networks of self-help, the Liberation would have failed in its final aim.

World War II left a legacy of unseen traumas which would take a long time to heal, but beginning Europe's physical reconstruction would improve living standards while politics and society returned to some kind of normalcy. Immediately after the war, the Allies repaired and rebuilt what was needed in the short term. Roads, railways and bridges were essential for the Allies to move about, for refugees to be relocated and for food (in scarce supply) to be distributed.

There was also a pressing need to demilitarize Europe, which was awash with munitions. After the armistice, people were still being killed by landmines, and farmers frequently turned up unexploded bombs in their fields. Even today, lost bombs dropped decades ago are occasionally found in unexpected places.

Paradoxically, reconstruction also involved more destruction, as the vainglorious monuments and statues of the Third Reich were torn down.

The role of the USA

Once the immediate needs of Europe were met, long-term planning could begin. The USA had ended the war with its homeland entirely unscathed, and – unlike much of Europe – its economy hadn't been completely decimated by military demands. The debate in Washington towards the end of the war, and immediately after the armistice, centred on how to deal with a shattered postwar Europe. It was generally agreed that since the USA had nobly helped liberate Europe, it should have a hand in the continent's recovery, too. There were also pragmatic reasons for the USA's continued involvement. The Americans were fearful that if Europe wasn't helped back to its feet, chaos or – worse still – Soviet communism might take hold. A recovered Europe would also be able to trade with the USA – and buy its goods.

«
Russian and British staff in Berlin, led by Montgomery (centre, in beret) and Zhukov to his right, 1945

The treatment of Germany

Aiding the reconstruction effort in France or Belgium was one thing, but it was harder to know what to do with Germany – the instigator of the war, disgraced and defeated. Should its surviving population, purged of Nazis, be held responsible for the events of World War II and punished accordingly?

For most of the war, the general feeling among the Allies was that Germany should pay for its transgression against the international order, just as it had in 1918. In the summer of 1944, US Secretary of the Treasury Henry Morgenthau Jr. forwarded a proposal to deal harshly with a post-surrender Germany. He argued that the country had to be prevented from instigating a third world war. To this end, it had to be broken up – parts of its territory should be awarded to Poland and France, and the remainder divided into two autonomous, largely agrarian states. The industry of the Ruhr – the manufacturing heart of the German war machine – should be dismantled and given to the victors (mainly the USSR) as reparations, and all its mines destroyed. This plan was discussed at the Quebec Conference of September 1944, where it found some sympathy with Roosevelt, who insisted that the German people should not be allowed to think of themselves as innocents of their government's crimes. The Morgenthau Plan, however, was quickly utilized by Nazi propaganda: if this was Germany's fate, what choice was there but to fight on?

As peace became a reality, a more considered policy emerged. World War II had been caused, at least in part, by German resentment at the punitive way it had been treated at the end of World War I. They would not make the same mistake twice.

The Marshall Plan

The USA's attitude towards reconstruction was settled by the emergence of the Cold War. The Soviets made it clear they intended to "Bolshevize" the territories in eastern Europe that they had acquired by liberation-conquest. Russia reconstructed these new zones of influence in its own image.

In response, the Americans began to see the advantages of a proactive plan to help Europe recover and rebuild as part of the capitalist world. An ambitious programme of financial assistance, known as the Marshall Plan (named after the US secretary of state but officially called the European Recovery Program), provided the means for western Europe to rebuild (physically and economically) after the ravages of war. Britain, France and Germany were all leading beneficiaries of Marshall money. Much of this was "tied aid" – money lent on the condi-

» Marshall Plan truck carrying tractors

« Women form a human chain to carry bricks during the reconstruction of Dresden, March 1946

tion that a proportion would be used to buy from American businesses. The Marshall Plan benefited the USA by increasing its influence in Europe and creating willing trading partners equipped with the money to buy American consumer goods. Only Spain, still under fascist rule despite the defeat of Nazism, was denied Marshall funds.

Construction work

The people of postwar Europe took the help they were offered and set about rebuilding. Construction work took different forms in different places. Historic buildings and medieval quarters were sometimes painfully reproduced, but where the destruction had been almost absolute the opportunity was taken to give full expression to stark modernist visions of concrete architecture. The heavily bombed port of Le Havre in France is considered a masterwork of postwar re-planning. German towns, too, often chose resolute futurist solutions to plugging the gaps in streets created by bombs: better to build looking forwards than to reconstruct the edifices of a past of which no one wanted to be reminded.

Building to remember

Immediately after the war, the prevalent attitude in Europe was to forget what had happened in the terrible years of 1939–1945. Gradually, however, it became clear that covering up the tragedy would not erase the memories of World War II, nor prevent a similar event in the future. There was a need to remember the past, but in the right way. In a few places – Oradour-sur-Glane in France and San Pietro Infine in Italy – the ruins were deliberately preserved as a warning to future generations against succumbing to an ideology of militarism and hate. Similarly, although most concentration camps were razed by the liberators as abominations that should never have existed, a few were preserved and opened to visitors as proof that the unspeakable and unimaginable really had happened.

As memories of the war receded, Europeans were increasingly able to come to terms with what they or their parents had lived through, and it seemed vital to build monuments and museums along the Liberation routes. All around, postwar buildings celebrated contemporary life, but space was found to honour the memory of World War II, too.

Justice and retribution

Towards the end of World War II and the Liberation, people around the globe turned their attention to how the Nazi perpetrators and collaborators should be dealt with.

As the extermination camps began to be liberated at the end of 1944 and the world became aware of the full extent of the horrors committed by the Nazi regime, so the call for justice and retribution became louder. Many Germans who lived near the death camps were forced to enter them and witness what had taken place there. And as the war ended, thousands of extrajudicial summary executions took place across Europe, both spontaneous revenge attacks on, for example, concentration camp guards, as well as more organized round-ups of those known to have collaborated within occupied countries. In France, an estimated 10,000 people were executed without trial before the Provisional Government took control and established a legal process for trying alleged collaborators.

Officially, it was widely felt that war crimes should be punished only after due process, and that a fair trial was one of the things that distinguished the western democracies from Nazi Germany, a country whose notorious People's Court presumed guilt rather than innocence, rarely admitted evidence and executed thousands. As early as November 1943, the "Big Three" Allied powers issued the joint Moscow Declaration stating that those who had taken part in "... atrocities, massacres and executions will be sent back to the countries in which their abominable deeds were done in order that

they may be judged and punished according to the laws of these liberated countries."

Senior Nazis on trial

The question of what to do with the senior Nazi hierarchy and those who had committed war crimes in Germany had been raised at the Yalta Conference of February 1945. Churchill's view that at least some of the top Nazis should be executed or imprisoned without trial was opposed by Roosevelt, who felt that this would be unacceptable to the US public. Stalin was in favour of a trial because of the humiliation it would impose on the vanquished. But this was another concern for the British who worried that Soviet involvement might bring to mind the notorious 1930s Moscow show trials of Stalin's Russia, in which thousands were imprisoned or killed on little or no evidence.

On 8 August 1945, the three main Allied powers plus France drew up the London Charter, a protocol for the trial of 24 Nazis to take place before an International Military Tribunal at Nuremberg – a former heartland of Hitler supporters where massive Nazi rallies had taken place. The charter defined three types of crime: crimes against peace (waging wars which violated international agreements); war crimes (acts in violation of the rules of war); and crimes against humanity (these included murder, extermination, enslavement and deportation).

Nuremberg trials

The first and most famous of the trials began on 20 November 1945. The judges and prosecutors were selected from each of the signatory countries of the London Charter, while the defence lawyers came from Germany. Films of the concentration camps were shown as evidence and witnesses testified to what they had had to endure. It was the first time that the newly coined term "genocide" was used in a court case. The trial lasted almost a year and ended with three of the defendants being acquitted, three getting life imprisonment, four receiving sentences of 10–20 years, and the remaining twelve sentenced to death by hanging.

Some of the defendants, in particular generals Keitel and Jodl, attempted to use what became known as the Nuremberg Defence, that they were "only obeying orders". They too were executed. The most effective defence was conducted by Albert Speer, Hitler's architect and armaments minister, who accepted responsibility for his crimes and came across as candid, although he claimed to know nothing of the slave labour in the arms factories he ran. Speer received a sentence of twenty years in prison.

Though few doubted the moral justice of the first Nuremberg trial, it met with plenty of legal criticism, not least for being "retrospective justice" – the punishment of actions not deemed crimes when they were committed. The US Chief Justice Harlan Stone called it a "sanctimonious fraud". In addition, the presence of a Soviet legal team – including a judge active in the show trials – was thought to compromise the integrity of the proceedings. While three defendants were charged over the German invasion of Poland, there was no mention of the Soviets doing the same. Soviet prosecutors also attempted to indict defendants for perpetrating the Katyń Massacre (see p.233), even though the killing of 20,000 Poles had been carried out by the NKVD.

There were a further twelve trials held at Nuremberg, which targeted high-ranking officials and professionals who had committed crimes in their work for the Reich. These included doctors, industrialists, civil servants, members of the legal profession and Einsatzgruppen members. The trials were administered entirely by the US, as Nuremberg was within the US occupied zone.

Other trials

According to where they took place, there was a great deal of variation in the way trials were conducted. In Czechoslovakia a huge outbreak of violent summary justice against Sudetenland Germans and collaborators oc-

« Rudolf Hess (front) and Karl Dönitz (with headphones) at the Nuremberg trials, September 1946

curred in the spring of 1945, which was largely sanctioned by the government-in-exile. The situation was later put on a more legal basis, but many courts used unqualified judges who had been selected from the resistance. On the order of prime minister Edvard Beneš, those sentenced to death had to be executed within two hours, resulting in a total of seven hundred deaths – the same number as in the much larger France.

The British insisted on conducting court proceedings as rigorously and fairly as possible, but they were under-resourced and with insufficient time to process the thousands of potential cases. The trial of 44 camp personnel from Bergen-Belsen took place in June 1945 under enormous press scrutiny. It lasted seven weeks and resulted in eleven death sentences, but also fifteen acquittals. Many people, including survivors, felt that the prison sentences were too mild and that defence teams had been obstructively legalistic.

Denazification

At the Potsdam Conference, the Allies had made a commitment that all Nazis should be "removed from public or semi-public office." But, like the war crimes trials, how this process of "denazification" was carried out differed in each zone of occupation. And, once again, the number of cases was enormous. There were around eight million registered Nazi party members at the end of the war, over ten percent of the German population. At the same time, there was a pressing imperative to get essential services up and running. Questionnaires were used to establish a person's activities during the period of the Third Reich, and to ascertain current attitudes. At the end of the process a person would be categorized in one of five ways, ranging from "Major Offenders" to "Exonerated Persons".

Inevitably, many perpetrators of war crimes slipped through the net, either by lying or because paper work had been destroyed. There were massive inconsistencies in who got rehabilitated, too. If you were useful to the Allies in any way, you might find your crimes overlooked. Wernher von Braun, the brains behind the V2 rocket programme, which subjected its enslaved workers to the most degrading of conditions, surrendered to the Americans and was spirited away with other scientists to the US where he went to work on what eventually became NASA's moon mission.

Denazification ended in West Germany in 1951, with the government deciding to concentrate on reparations and compensation to the victims of Nazism instead. At the Potsdam Conference it had been decided that Germany must pay compensation to the countries they had occupied and exploited, as well as to the Allies. The exact amounts varied from country to country and were agreed at subsequent meetings and in treaties.

All but the worst Nazi offenders were now permitted to re-enter public life – if they weren't already there. In 2011 the German Interior Ministry published a list of all former members of the postwar German government who had a Nazi past. This revealed that 25 cabinet ministers, one president and one chancellor of the Federal Republic of Germany had been members of Nazi organizations, along with ninety leading lawyers and judges.

Hunting those that got away

The fact that perpetrators of war crimes were still at large, many having escaped abroad with help from networks of fascist sympathizers, prompted individuals – working in co-operation with state organizations – to start tracking down Nazis and gathering information about them. One of the best known and successful of these Nazi hunters was Simon Wiesenthal, a Polish Jew who had survived several concentration camps. Through his persistence, and in the face of many death threats, his investigations helped with the arrests and prosecution of many significant figures. These included Adolf Eichmann, a key figure in the Nazis' "Final Solution", who was tracked down to Argentina and kidnapped by Israeli agents in 1960. His trial in Jerusalem and later execution generated massive press coverage and reawakened public interest in the Holocaust. Other important war criminals captured with Wiesenthal's help were Franz Stangl, the commandant of Treblinka, and Hermine Braunsteiner, a notoriously sadistic female guard who had worked at Majdanek and Ravensbrück.

Issues of wartime culpability and the demand for justice have continued into the 21st century and show no signs of waning. As recently as April 2018, the US ordered the deportation to Germany of 95-year-old Jakiw Palij, a former guard at Trawniki, one of many such cases. State demands for reparations remain an issue, with Israel, Poland and Greece pressing for further compensation, even though successive German governments believe that all claims "have been legally and politically resolved." And while most of the general funds compensating Holocaust survivors have now expired, individuals remain eligible for restitution payments and pensions from the German and Austrian governments, and from a fund established by Swiss banks. Soviet war crimes, meanwhile, have never been punished.

The world at war

Although the Liberation took place in Europe, it was part of a global conflict that drew combatants from a great number of countries across the world.

Battle accounts often reduce the Allied armies to a small number of national and ethnic identities, but the truth is more complex. World War II was in fact fought by people of around fifty different nationalities. Argentina was the 53rd – and last – country to join the conflict on 27 March 1945. Military intervention, outside the main Allied and Axis forces, was frequently preceded by a national debate over whether Europe's troubles were relevant to the nation in question. Some countries stalled but eventually committed themselves, if only to a token degree.

Every nation remembers its involvement in World War II in a different way. The war didn't only affect distant governments, it also touched ordinary people who volunteered for the cause, many of whom simulta-

neously questioned the injustices of their own societies. The inhabitants of the colonies of France and Great Britain, for instance, fought bravely for their rulers while also challenging the inequalities of empire.

Women all over the world contributed to the war in a number of uncelebrated ways (see p.87). They enthusiastically entered the workforce, made vital contributions to industry and advocated how important it was that the events of World War II were never repeated.

The USA

The USA began the war as an (officially) neutral, isolationist state. American policy was directed to help the Europeans – and particularly the British – in cash and kind, without sending any troops into active service. This changed spectacularly after Pearl Harbor, when the USA entered the war following a Japanese attack on the American naval base in Hawaii.

The USA made an invaluable contribution to the Liberation. They supplied its supreme commander – General Eisenhower – and had a decisive impact on its outcome. The country fielded six armies in Europe, each consisting of at least two corps. Like the USA itself, these armies were far from homogenous. Italian Americans participated in the invasion of Sicily, for example, and second-generation Japanese Americans also fought in the Italian campaign.

African Americans participated in the war in significant numbers, including the so-called "buffalo soldiers" of the 92nd Infantry Division. Many of them, however, later spoke of fighting two enemies at once – fascism abroad and racism within their own army. In parades, campaigns, church services and fighting units, black and white

» Soldier of the Moroccan French Expeditionary Corps in Italy

soldiers were segregated. The irony of a segregated division fighting for equality and unity in Europe was obvious, and an executive order officially ended segregation in the US armed forces in 1948 – although other forms of racism continued.

The British Commonwealth

During World War II, Britain relied heavily on the manpower and supplies provided by its remaining colonies and the British Commonwealth.

Across the Commonwealth it was generally agreed that whatever grievances were harboured against Britain as the motherland, it was important to help win the war. Canada in particular (see p.191) made vital contributions to the Italian campaign, D-Day and the liberation of the northern Netherlands. Today, Canada's main war museum is located in Ottawa (warmuseum.ca). Australia's land units sent to the European theatre of war were all withdrawn by 1942 in order to counter the Japanese threat. New Zealand and South Africa fielded land troops in the African and Italian campaigns, while their trained aircrews formed RAF squadrons.

During the war, it became clear to Churchill that it would be impossible for the British Empire to survive in the new world that was being created. He knew Britain was gravely dependent on the military help of the colonies, but that their involvement would be paid for – directly or indirectly – by grants of independence.

British India, "the Raj", formed the largest volunteer army in the world. Almost 2.5 million men were drawn from various regions and ethnic groups, and a number of Indian units took part in the liberation of Italy. India's National War Museum is currently located in New Delhi.

French colonies

When France fell in 1940, its armies were split and reduced in size. The Armée d'Afrique (Army of Africa), made up of colonial troops, was initially loyal to the Vichy government, but after the Allied invasion of North Africa (Operation Torch) in 1942 it became available to de Gaulle's Free French forces. They formed eight army divisions to fight for the liberation of France. Algerian, Moroccan and west African soldiers were indispensable to France's ability to resume the fight. They witnessed action in the Italian campaign of 1945–1944, and made up part of French Army B that landed on the Riviera in the summer of 1944 and liberated southern and eastern France (see p.140). In 1945, they campaigned in southern Germany.

War-torn France emerged from World War II and the Liberation as a ravaged country unable to maintain its empire. Its colonial troops had mixed feelings about the war; they had fought bravely, but many felt their contribution was insufficiently recognized by "European" France.

Armies in exile

Numerous soldiers and citizens of countries occupied by Nazi Germany wanted to fight on. Some chose the ranks of the resistance, others escaped the Wehrmacht and joined their governments-in-exile to form their own armed forces fighting under Allied command. Towards the end of the war, Free French, Belgian, Dutch, Greek and Norwegian forces took part in the liberation of their native countries. The fate of the Polish Armed Forces in the west, the largest of the armies in exile, was tragic. Despite having fought bravely for the freedom of others, they never took part in the liberation of their homeland. Many could never return to their new communist country for fear of political reprisals.

Reflections on the Liberation

A series of personal reflections on the Liberation, considering the importance of the Liberation in the past, present and future.

Maeve Fennelly
History student at the University of Bristol

As a History student, I have studied World War II more times than any other period. This is unsurprising, given its historical significance in shaping Europe and the wider world. Its impact remains tangible; the scars of the Blitz are everywhere in London, the city where I grew up. There are still prefabs – "temporary" bungalows to replace houses destroyed by bombs – at the end of my road and the remnants of an air-raid shelter in our garden. For me, they are daily reminders of the struggle that took place. It is an important memory to keep alive, it stops us from taking for granted the hard-won joy of growing up in a diverse

» Prefab housing built for London's Blitz victims, 1946

city. The "never again" message of the Holocaust should not only be remembered but be at the forefront of our minds. The sacrifices of those in the past inspire my generation to not be complacent, and remain resilient in the face of intolerance.

Judge Robert S. Croll
Chairman of the Dutch National Fund for Peace, Freedom and Veteran Care (vfonds)

Vfonds has proudly supported the Liberation Route Europe since its conception and we believe that the LRE has an important role to play in remembrance. To remember is to make people aware that living in a peaceful society, democratically run and governed by the rule of law, is not the experience of everyone and should never be taken for granted.

For the majority of western European nations, who have lived in peace for 75 years, it's easy to think that our comfortable society is guaranteed. That would be a fatal mistake. Humankind tends towards realizing what it has – youth or health, for instance – only at the moment when it is lost. The same goes for fundamental human rights. The desire for freedom was never felt so gravely as in 1945, when Europe was liberated by Allied armed forces and resistance fighters. As Alsatian theologian Albert Schweitzer said, "the best plea for peace is a war grave".

Vincent J. Speranza
World War II veteran

One who refuses to learn the lessons of history is doomed to repeat them. The 20th century witnessed two of the most devastating wars in history, including the most cataclysmic event of the modern age: World War II. People today tend to distance themselves from the grim realities of war, when I believe they need to be reminded. The further away we get from the misery of global conflict, the more important it is to make sure that people – especially the younger generations – understand the causes of World War II and how to avoid the repeat of such a catastrophe.

No one hates war more than the men and women who have fought in them. With this in mind, I decided to dedicate myself to travelling the world – and along the Liberation Route Europe – in an attempt to educate people from inciting war and generate support for our veterans.

Daniel Libeskind
**Founder and Principal Architect
at Studio Libeskind**

The idea behind the Liberation Route Europe speaks not only of the past, but also of the future – it communicates the dark history of war, while telling the story of unity against the currents of hatred. The project has strength and modesty because it is based on a simple thing: the human foot. To experience the story of the Liberation does not require complex tools – it requires nothing more than to walk in the footsteps of those who went before.

I hope the trail will be a reminder to all visitors, residents and leaders that we must never forget the vastness of catastrophe and the ultimate triumph of the Liberation.

Mathieu Billa
Bastogne War Museum Director

To me, the Liberation of 1943–1945 represents the end of one of the darkest periods in European history. Besides the well-known images of happiness and joy that surround the Allied liberators, the Liberation also evokes feelings of pain and suffering. In the Ardennes, Hitler's troops left in the autumn of 1944 only to return three months later; the "second" liberation in January 1945 brought death and destruction. Similar experiences abound, of a hard-won liberation born of violence and loss. Considering the world's long history, these events are not that old. No one knows what tomorrow will bring, but by understanding the past we can certainly work towards a brighter future.

Hervé Morin
President of Normandy

In my family, as in all Norman families, the D-Day landings and the Battle of Normandy are the subject of discussions, testimonies and stories that we all share. The Liberation of Europe, because it started in Normandy, is particularly important to us. With our history, Normandy and the Normans carry a collective and permanent commitment to peace. For that reason, I believe in passing the torch of memory to our new generations. Through numerous initiatives and annual events, including the World Peace Forum, Normandy consistently communicates the values of peace and freedom to the general public and especially to young people.

Martin Schulz
Former President of the European Parliament and member of the Bundestag

I grew up in a region where Germany, the Netherlands and Belgium meet: a European crossroads. But for a long time, borders shaped our outlook.

I was fortunate enough to witness European unification and later to help shape it. People in the European Union are now enjoying living in both unity and peace, but to maintain these achievements we must be aware of the past. We must never forget.

Remembrance gives rise to memory. And with memory comes one warning, that those who close their eyes to the past will be blind to the present. If you do not want to remember the inhumanity, you will be vulnerable to new contagion. So it is important to remember together.

Prof. Dr Sönke Neitzel
Historian and Chair of War Studies at the University of Potsdam

The Liberation Route Europe fosters a common European commemoration of the final period of World War II. This doesn't mean that everyone has to share the same approach and the same view of the Liberation. But the project does bring together people from all over Europe, who can learn about the different experiences endured in other European countries. In France, Netherlands, Poland or Germany, the war had many faces.

I think that more than seventy years after the end of World War II, it is time to overcome easy black and white perceptions. We should strive for a more differentiated picture that doesn't exclude painful topics which are sometimes omitted from official narratives. Remembering the Liberation in this way can help us to come to a better understanding of our common history.

Sebastiaan Vonk

**Chairman of the Foundation United Adopters
American War Graves**

As a young boy, I looked at the books on the library shelves. I always wanted one with a war story; those fascinated me. When I grew older, however, I came to learn that war is anything but fascinating. Pretending to be a soldier, playing with my friends, was fun as a child. Being an actual soldier, fighting a real war, is not.

Studying the stories of real people, involved in real conflict, gave these men and women a "face". American soldier Lawrence Shea, for instance, died when he was just 21. I was thirteen when I read about him and "adopted" his grave through the Foundation United Adopters American War Graves. When I looked at Lawrence, it felt like looking at myself in the mirror. How would I feel if I was sent to war? What would I do?

The story of every individual soldier is powerful. The stories help us to remember, to nurture compassion and understanding and inspire us to do good in the world.

« US soldier taking a nap in a foxhole near Stolberg, Germany, 1944

Resources

Understanding armies

To understand the troop movements of the Liberation, it is necessary to know how World War II armies were organized.

Each national army was organized differently and used its own terminology, but some general observations hold true. To complicate things, Nazi Germany effectively had two armies. The Wehrmacht and the Waffen-SS deliberately distinguished themselves by giving different names to their ranks and units.

Divisions

The most important concept in military terminology is that of a division. This was the key fighting element of every army in World War II. A division was capable of acting autonomously; it represented the prime "chess piece" that a commander in chief could shift from place to place, front to front and even from one theatre of war to another, according to the changing needs of strategy. The numerical strength of divisions typically varied between 10,000 and 20,000 men.

Each division was recognized by an ordinal number and a type name, such as the 33rd German Infantry Division. Most divisions were made up of a mixture of subunits carrying out specific functions, such as infantry, armoured (tank) and motorized transport brigades. Fire support for the division was provided by artillery and anti-aircraft regiments, while engineer regiments built bridges, cleared obstacles and carried out other necessary tasks. Signals regiments provided communications.

Divisions were not fixed, making it hard to quantify exactly how many each army had during the war. New divisions were created according to need; existing ones were amalgamated; and sometimes entire divisions were not only defeated in battle but annihilated. The USA alone fielded 91 divisions, while Germany had hundreds of divisions at its disposal, enabling it to put up sustained resistance to the liberating armies. One reason for the Red Army's ultimate success in the east was that it had more available divisions than its opponent.

Non-combat personnel

Accounts of World War II are dominated by the experience of front-line troops, followed by those involved in the most strategically significant actions. Behind them, however, was a huge and highly organized system working to provide essential combat supplies – ammunition, rations, water and fuel – and every other detail necessary to keep an army in the field.

No army could function for long without an efficient logistical machine and its accompanying bureaucracy. Estimates suggest that for every soldier in active combat, a further eight people were needed behind the lines to provide medical services and to maintain and repair equipment.

Special forces

Not all fighting units fit into an easy scheme of army organization. World War II involved many exceptional and irregular units. Some of these – the British Commandos and the Special Air Service (SAS) – were elite troops that operated in their own way within the overall military hierarchy. Other units were irregular in the extreme. French, Polish, Soviet and Italian partisans organized themselves into paramilitary bands with no official supervision, at least to begin with. Another example of an irregular unit active behind enemy lines was the one formed by

Chart of military units in World War II

Name of unit	Numerical strength	Commanding officer	Additional information
Army group	Two or more armies	Field marshal or general	In the Red Army, an army group was known as a front.
Army	100–300,000 soldiers	General	Made up of two or more corps.
Corps	20,000–50,000 soldiers	Lieutenant general	The main subdivision of an army, consisting of two or more divisions or a branch of the army assigned to a particular function. A corps could contain divisions of different nationalities.
Division	6000–20,000 soldiers	Lieutenant general or major general	A group of brigades or regiments.
Brigade	3000–5000 soldiers	Brigadier or brigadier general	Typically a small number of infantry battalions or other units, forming part of a division.
Regiment	300–3000 soldiers	Colonel or lieutenant colonel	A term whose use varied greatly from army to army.
Battalion	300–1000 soldiers	Lieutenant colonel	Three or more companies.
Company, squadron or battery (artillery)	80–250 soldiers	Captain or major	Usually known by a letter ("C Company") or by a number or name.
Platoon or troop	25–50 soldiers	First lieutenant or second lieutenant	Subunit of a company.
Section, patrol or squad	7–24 soldiers	Corporal or sergeant	Commanded by a non-commissioned officer.

Otto Skorzeny that wreaked havoc during the Battle of the Bulge by impersonating American soldiers (see p.171).

Political control

It is sometimes hard to determine exactly who was in charge of each army. There was always a tension between meeting the objectives dictated by politicians and allowing commanders in the field to give quick orders in the changing and confusing conditions of war.

The chain of command itself could also be complicated. Eisenhower was responsible for the overall command of the land armies converging on Germany, but he was answerable to the combined chiefs of staff in Washington, who were in turn accountable to the president of the USA and the prime minister of Great Britain. Hitler, meanwhile, was both a political and military dictator, but he relied on the generals of the Wehrmacht to translate his desires into reality. When they were unable to do so, many German generals were used as scapegoats and disgraced.

Tailor-made trips

The following trips stretch right across Europe, taking in a range of evocative Liberation-themed sites – from big-name attractions to poignant memorials and little-visited monuments. There are as many potential itineraries as there are visitors fascinated by the Liberation, and you'll no doubt want to create your own tailor-made tour to reflect your interests. The trips described in this section should begin to give you a flavour of what each European region has to offer and what we can plan and book for you at www.roughguides.com/trips.

» D-Day tour

This route takes in key D-Day sites in England and France.

❶ Imperial War Museum London
Page 86. London's main military museum houses a huge collection and gives a sober account of the horrors of World War II and the Holocaust.

❷ Churchill War Rooms, London
Page 86. Where Winston Churchill directed operations and held Cabinet meetings for the duration of World War II.

❸ The D-Day Story Portsmouth
Page 92. This newly renovated museum contains plenty of interactive material to bring Operation Overlord to life. Its *pièce de résistance* is the splendid 90m Overlord Tapestry.

❹ Grand Bunker Atlantic Wall Museum, Normandy
Page 129. Recreated wartime tableaux – complete with newspapers, cutlery and cigarette packets – give an idea of what life was like in this six-floor bunker, just one of the formidable defences that made up the Atlantic Wall.

❺ Memorial Pegasus, Normandy
Page 127. On the night before D-Day, twin bridges across the Caen canal and the River Orne were the target of a daring Allied glider assault. The fine Memorial Pegasus museum,

dedicated to men of the British 6th Airborne Division, marks the spot.

❻ Juno Beach Centre, Normandy

Page 125. This high-tech, high-calibre museum is dedicated to the role Canada's troops played in D-Day and World War II more generally.

❼ D-Day Museum, Normandy

Page 124. Normandy's first museum built specifically to commemorate the D-Day landings.

❽ Normandy American Cemetery

Page 123. World War II cemeteries dot the Normandy countryside. This one contains the graves of 9380 US soldiers; a memorial remembers 1557 more recorded as missing in action.

❾ Pointe du Hoc and Omaha Beach, Normandy

Page 121. At the promontory of Pointe du Hoc on Omaha Beach, the cliff heights are still deeply pitted with German bunkers and shell holes.

❿ Bayeux British Military Cemetery, Normandy

Page 133. The largest British World War II cemetery in France. In fact, it holds the graves of men from more than ten different countries.

⓫ La Cambe German Cemetery, Normandy

Page 122. Headstones hewn of dark stone mark the graves of 21,200 fallen German soldiers.

⓬ Airborne Museum, Normandy

Page 117. The collection of uniforms,

weaponry and other military hardware at this excellent museum is crowned by a trio of planes – a Douglas C-47, Waco glider and Piper Cub.

⓭ Utah Beach D-Day Museum, Normandy

Page 119. Sited on a former German strongpoint, the highlight of this museum is a rare American twin-engined Martin B26 G "Marauder".

Experiences

There are plenty of unique experiences themed on D-Day. In the UK, **Visit Kent** (visitkent.co.uk) organizes an exciting ten-day itinerary exploring the county's role in World War II and the Liberation. You can also take a ride on the miniature **Romney, Hythe & Dymchurch Railway** (rhdr.org.uk; see p.91) or discover Churchill's former home at **Chartwell**, where there's a family trail titled "Who was Winston Churchill?" – both will appeal to visitors with children in tow. In London, guided World War II-themed walks are run by **Blitz Walkers** (blitz-walkers.co.uk).

In Normandy, the annual **D-Day Festival** commemorates the landings with an excellent programme of events, including military parades, firework displays, concerts, discussions with veterans and elaborate re-enactments. At Carentan, a 40km **trail** (carentan-circuit-44.com) takes in thirteen sites related to D-Day and the Liberation, while nearby in Angoville-au-Plain, **Domaine Airborne** (domaine-airborne.com) offers tasteful rooms in a historic house in the landing area of the 101st Airborne Division. Cosy B&B accommodation is provided at the **Batterie du Holdy**, where staff can also arrange **jeep tours** around select D-Day sites. **Café Gondrée** in Bénouville, near Pegasus Bridge, was the first café to be liberated, and is still open for business today.

» The liberation of France

A tour tracing the Allied campaign through France, covering Normandy, Paris, Provence, Alsace and Lorraine.

❶ Caen Memorial Museum, Normandy

Page 135. Displays start with the rise of fascism in Germany, follow with resistance and collaboration in France, then chart all the major battles of World War II, with a special emphasis on D-Day and its aftermath.

❷ Civilians in Wartime Museum, Normandy

Page 133. Falaise was almost entirely destroyed during the climax of the Battle of Normandy in August 1944. The Civilians in Wartime Museum here charts the life of ordinary French civilians during World War II.

❸ Army Museum and Historial Charles de Gaulle, Paris

Page 136. This fascinating museum in the Hôtel des Invalides gives comprehensive coverage of World War II, explaining all the battles, the Resistance and the slow, final liberation.

Experiences

There are a number of remembrance trails in Alsace that provide the perfect way to explore the region. Three different themed trails are available. The "**Pathway of the Phoney War**" is a 2km walking trail with an audio-guide companion; the "**Route of the 5th Army**" takes in eight sites in four hamlets – a day-tour on foot, half-day by bike or a two-and-a-half-hour journey by car; while the "**Smugglers' Trail**" is a 20km hiking trail focused on the liberation of Alsace. The latter takes seven hours and requires a good level of fitness.

❹ Museum of the Order of the Liberation, Paris

Page 139. Housing the collections of the Companions of the Order of the Liberation, a little-known decoration created by Charles de Gaulle and bestowed on fewer than 1500 wartime heroes.

❺ Champs-Elysées, Paris

Page 139. The celebrated Champs-Elysées, a popular rallying point at times of national crisis and the site of de Gaulle's victory parade on 26 August 1944.

❻ Camp des Milles Memorial, Provence

Page 141. Once an internment and transit camp, this memorial and museum warns against racism, anti-Semitism and other forms of extremism.

❼ Memorial of the Landing in Provence, Provence

Page 141. This memorial pays homage to the French and American armies who landed and fought in Provence during the Liberation.

❽ Rhône American Cemetery and Memorial, Provence

Page 141. Lines of white crosses mark the graves of more than 850 American soldiers who died during the invasion of Provence, Operation Dragoon.

❾ Memorial-Museum of the Colmar Pocket, Alsace

Page 151. An 18th-century arched vault and former air-raid shelter has been transformed into a museum exploring the events of the Colmar Pocket.

❿ Natzweiler-Struthof Concentration Camp, Alsace

Page 152. The first concentration camp to be liberated by Allied troops, with various evocative items from the camp on display.

⑪ Alsace-Moselle Memorial, Alsace
Page 153. Informative memorial-museum

dedicated to French-German reconciliation.

⑫ Lorraine American Cemetery and Memorial, Lorraine
Page 152. Contains the graves of nearly 10,500 American soldiers who were killed fighting in Lorraine and Alsace.

The Low Countries and Germany

This trip covers a pocket of Europe that witnessed heavy fighting during World War II – crossing Belgium, Luxembourg, Germany and the Netherlands.

❶ Bastogne War Museum, Belgium

Page 175. Immersive experiences take visitors though wartime Belgium at this high-tech museum. The imposing Mardasson Memorial is just across the road.

❷ Bastogne Barracks, Belgium

Page 175. A key command centre during the Ardennes Offensive, with an impressive collection of military vehicles.

Experiences

A range of exciting experiences are offered in the Low Countries and Germany. Experiences in the Netherlands are covered on p.356 and p.357.

During the **NUTS weekend** in December, the city of Bastogne in Belgium heralds a range of events to commemorate the Battle of the Bulge. Parades, veteran talks and re-enactments are joined by a festive market with 1940s music. There's a good Liberation trail in **Leopolsburg**, while in Luxembourg the **Schumann's Eck Memorial Trail** takes in a poignant monument in the woods. Two World War II-related accommodations are worth checking out in Belgium: **Hotel Prachthof** in Borlo (pachthof.com) and **Hotel du Moulin** in Ligneuville (hoteldumoulin.be).

In Germany, several excellent short hiking paths run through Hürtgen Forest, including the "**Westwall-Weg**" (No. 86) and the "**Kall Trail**" (No. 66). Nearby, a 41.5km **cycling trail** links three sites along the Siegfried Line.

❸ National Museum of Military History, Luxembourg

Page 177. Focuses on the Battle of the Bulge and the Liberation. Atmospheric photographs bring the facts and figures to life.

❹ Luxembourg American Cemetery

Page 177. General Patton is buried at the Luxembourg American Cemetery along with 5000 other American servicemen.

❺ Vogelsang International Place and The Torchbearer, Germany

Page 281. Built as a National Socialist training centre, the imposing Vogelsang complex still contains a scattering of bullet-holed sculptures exulting the Nazi ideology.

❻ Kall Bridge, Germany

Page 282. Where German Captain Dr Stüttgen organized a series of temporary ceasefires to save the lives of countless US and German soldiers.

❼ Vossenack German Cemetery, Germany

Page 282. German engineer captain Julius Erasmus risked his life to recover more than 1500 war dead from the Hürtgen Forest battlefields and bury them at Vossenack.

❽ Margraten American Cemetery and Memorial, the Netherlands

Page 196. White marble crosses mark the burial places of more than 8000 American servicemen who died in the Netherlands and Belgium, and cover a depressingly huge area.

❾ Eyewitness Museum, the Netherlands

Page 196. This museum uses the power of

storytelling – following the experiences of a fictional German paratrooper called August Segel – to great effect.

⑩ Overloon War Museum, the Netherlands
Page 205. One of the biggest war museums in the Netherlands, with a fascinating array of military machinery.

⑪ Ysselsteyn German War Cemetery, the Netherlands
Page 196. The only German military cemetery in the Netherlands.

» # The Netherlands: in Canadian footsteps

This itinerary follows the route of the Canadian liberators in the Netherlands, who made an invaluable contribution to the Dutch campaign.

Experiences

The **Liberation Concert** in Margraten (liberationconcert.nl) is a musical tribute held every year at Margraten American Cemetery and Memorial, remembering the fallen soldiers of World War II. An annual commemorative event is also held at Sloedam. Every Christmas Eve at the **Canadian War Cemetery** in Holten, meanwhile, schoolchildren place burning candles at the headstones. The flickering lights add to the reflective atmosphere and the event is followed across the Netherlands. **Camp Westerbork**'s annual commemoration takes place on 4 May.

A great **LRE audiospot** (see p.6) in Woensdrecht provides information on "Black Friday". An online equivalent to the audiospots, **Brabant Remembers** (brabantremembers.com), tells the personal stories of 75 people whose lives were changed forever by World War II.

There are several fine accommodation options in Noord Brabant. **Hotel Restaurant la Sonnerie** (sonnerie.nl), housed in an old nunnery and a 15-minute drive from Eindhoven, makes a wonderfully atmospheric base. **Landgoed Huize Bergen** (huizebergen.com), near 's-Hertogenbosch, is where German General Kurt Student located his headquarters; today it offers a two-day "History Package" including meals in the monumental villa. At Bergen op Zoom, meanwhile, the **Grand Hotel de Draak** (hoteldedraak.nl) occupies an old German command centre. Mr Oirbans, the hotel's former owner, was a member of the Dutch resistance who hid Jewish refugees in a secret compartment in the double ceiling while the Nazis plotted in the rooms below.

❶ # Liberation Museum Zeeland

Page 192. Highlights include a range of outdoor exhibits, including bunkers, a Sherman tank and an original Bailey bridge.

❷ # Sloedam Memorial, Zeeland

Page 193. A group of stone monuments commemorates two wartime operations fought here.

❸ # Bergen op Zoom Canadian War Cemetery, Noord Brabant

Page 205. A moving memorial to the Canadian nationals who died in the Battle of the Scheldt and other Dutch operations.

❹ # National Liberation Museum 1944–1945, Groesbeek

Page 204. Interactive displays evoke the sights, sounds and even smells of the military campaign in the Netherlands.

❺ # Canadian War Cemetery, Groesbeek

Page 204. The biggest Commonwealth war cemetery in the Netherlands.

❻ # Holten Canadian War Cemetery, Overijssel

Page 210. Its information centre has a good selection of films, personal stories, anecdotes and photographs of the fallen soldiers.

❼ # Memory Museum, Overijssel

Page 211. Impressive dioramas cover the Nazi occupation, D-Day and the most significant Dutch campaigns.

❽ # Camp Westerbork National Memorial Centre, Drenthe

Page 211. This centre commemorates the Netherlands' largest concentration camp, with deeply affecting displays.

The Netherlands: Operation Market Garden ≪

Operation Market Garden was General Montgomery's ambitious plan for the Netherlands (see p.197). This route takes in several sites connected to the unsuccessful Allied offensive.

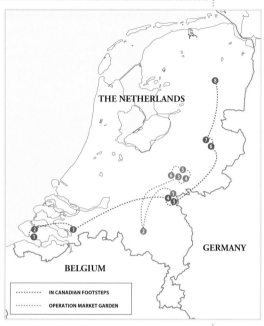

❶ The National Liberation Museum 1944–1945, Groesbeek

Page 204. This state-of-the-art museum provides a comprehensive overview of Operation Market Garden.

❷ Museum Wings of Liberation, Best

Page 205. Military equipment, vehicles and beautiful dioramas explain the Nazi occupation and the Liberation.

❸ Airborne Museum "Hartenstein", Arnhem

Page 203. The Allied command post at Oosterbeek was located in the Hotel Hartenstein, now housing this top museum.

❹ Airborne at the Bridge Information Centre, Arnhem

Page 202. Good information centre focused on Operation Market Garden.

❺ Airborne War Cemetery, Arnhem

Page 203. Containing the graves of 1754 Allied troops, many of them killed during Operation Market Garden.

❻ Infocentre: The Poles of Driel, Gelderland

Page 203. Fascinating little information centre chronicling the actions of the 1st Polish Independent Parachute Brigade during Operation Market Garden.

Experiences

One of the best Liberation-themed experiences in the Netherlands is the **Sunset March** at Nijmegen (sunsetmarch.nl), which is explained in full on p.199. The **Bridge to Liberation Experience** (bridgeto-liberation.nl) in Arnhem is a multimedia show telling the story of the Battle of Arnhem through music, dance, film and light, while there's a fantastic annual **Liberation Parade** in Wagening. Several LRE **audiospots** near Hell's Highway bring the history of Market Garden to life.

Accommodation is offered near Nijmegen at **Hotel Erica** (hotelerica.nl); near Arnhem at **Hotel Avegoor** (landgoe-davegoor.nl); and in Wageningen at **Hotel de Wereld** (hoteldewereld.nl). The latter (see p.202) is famous as the place where General Blaskowitz signed the German surrender in the Netherlands on 6 May.

≫ Wartime Poland

Poland suffered a particularly brutal invasion and occupation during World War II. This tour explores the Polish experience.

❶ Monument of the Coast Defenders, Westerplatte peninsula
Page 236. Grim 1960s slab built by the Soviets to commemorate the coastal defenders of World War II.

Experiences
Every year throughout Poland, a number of significant events commemorate various episodes of World War II. Some of these are thematic, others are military re-enactments. These events come and go with fluctuations in interest, funding and volunteers to organize them. In Warsaw, the annual **"W-Hour" commemoration** remembers the Warsaw Uprising with ceremonies, services and a march of remembrance. You can also book onto the **Warsaw Rising 1944 private tour** (toursby-locals.com), a five-hour unpicking of the events of 1 August 1944. In Kraków, Viator organizes comprehensive World War II tours in the vicinity.
Two historic hotels are located near the Wolf's Lair (see p.239). **Hotel Wilczy Szaniec/Wolfsschanze** offers accommodation in one of the lair's surviving buildings; nearby, **Ksiezycowy Dworek** (ksiezycowydworek.pl) is the hotel where Eva Braun supposedly stayed during her visits here. In Lower Silesia, near the Riese Complex, **Hotel Ksiaz** is located inside Ksiaz Castle (Fürstenstein). During the war, the castle was requisitioned by the Luftwaffe and served as a command post.

❷ Museum of the Second World War, Gdańsk
Page 237. This new museum is one of the most striking buildings in Europe. Using films, graphics, personal memories and dramatic use of exhibits (for instance a whole tank in a recreated city street), it's a tour-de-force of history-telling.

❸ Polish Post Museum, Gdańsk
Page 237. Gdańsk's Post Office put up a spirited resistance to the Nazi invasion on 1 September 1939. The whole event is commemorated by the small Polish Post Museum.

❹ Museum of Stutthof, Sztutowo
Page 237. At its height, Stutthof had 39 sub-camps and held tens of thousands of prisoners from all over Europe. Moving exhibitions, films and photographs explore what life was like here.

❺ Monument to the Ghetto Heroes, Warsaw
Page 230. Unveiled in 1948 on the fifth anniversary of the Ghetto uprising, this monument recalls both the immense courage of the Jewish resistance and the helplessness of deportees to moving effect.

❻ POLIN Museum of the History of Polish Jews, Warsaw
Page 230. The kind of museum that gets you excited as soon as you see it looming in front of you. A panorama of Jewish-Polish history.

❼ Monument to the Warsaw Uprising, Warsaw
Page 231. This important memorial was unveiled by Poland's communist authorities in 1989 – a belated response to years of campaigning by veterans and their families.

❽ Warsaw Rising Museum
Page 231. Housed in a former power station, the Warsaw Rising Museum honours the heroism of August 1944 with a compelling and highly moving multimedia display.

❾ Oskar Schindler's Emalia Factory, Kraków
Page 244. Made famous by Spielberg's blockbuster, this superbly arranged permanent collection is housed in the building where German industrialist Oskar Schindler employed hundreds of Kraków Jews in order to keep them off the Nazi deportation lists.

❿ Pharmacy Under the Eagle, Kraków
Page 244. Former ghetto pharmacy run by Dr Tadeusz Pankiewicz and his three assistants – the only Gentiles permitted to live in the ghetto. Inside lies an intimate and affecting portrayal of wartime pharmacy life.

⓫ Auschwitz-Birkenau, Oświęcim
Page 245. The infamous Nazi death camp, on the outskirts of Oświęcim, is a compelling memorial to man's inhumanity.

« Child survivors of Auschwitz

» The Italian campaign

This route uncovers the wealth of World War II and Liberation sites offered around Italy, including on its beautiful southern island, Sicily.

❶ Historical War Museum of the Landings in Sicily 1943, Sicily

Page 48. The Sicily campaign is colourfully illustrated with exhibits including video footage, waxwork statues and an air-raid simulator.

❷ Motta Sant'Anastasia German War Cemetery, Sicily

Page 48. More than 4500 German soldiers who died in Sicily are buried in this cemetery, designed with multiple "rooms" to represent different parts of the island.

❸ Siracusa Commonwealth Cemetery, Sicily

Page 46. Where around 1000 men – most of them Britons and Canadians who lost their lives during the landings on Sicily – are buried.

❹ San Pietro Infine Historical Memory Park, Campania

Page 55. The village of San Pietro Infine was reduced to rubble in 1943; the ruins have been left exactly as they were as a testament to what happened here.

❺ Monte Cassino Abbey

Page 53. This abbey came to be the lynchpin of German presence in this part of Italy. After a battle that lasted nearly six months, the Allies bombed it to ruins in May 1944, sacrificing hundreds of lives in the process.

❻ Monte Cassino Polish Military Cemetery

Page 54. Polish Cemetery with a gatepost that reads, "For our freedom and yours, we soldiers of Poland gave our soul to god, our life to the soil of Italy and our hearts to Poland."

❼ Sicily-Rome American Cemetery, Anzio

Page 56. The cemetery complex includes a cenotaph, memorial, chapel, pool and map room, as well as a visitor centre telling the individual stories of soldiers.

❽ Anzio Beachhead Museum

Page 57. A small museum bears witness to the difficult Allied landing at Anzio in January 1944.

❾ Beach Head Cemetery, Anzio

Page 57. Planted with roses, pansies, impatiens, wisteria and jasmine, this Commonwealth cemetery is awash with colour.

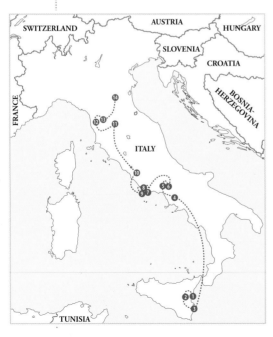

⑩ Historical Museum of the Liberation, Rome

Page 58. Occupying two floors of the building in which Nazi prisoners were held and interrogated during the wartime occupation. It's a moving place and deliberately low key, with the original cells left just as they were.

⑪ Florence American Cemetery and Memorial

Page 65. Built across a series of wooded hills.

⑫ Sant'Anna di Stazzema, Tuscany

Page 65. The place of a brutal massacre in 1944, when the Waffen-SS killed the village's 560 inhabitants for allegedly supporting the Resistance.

Experiences

Several walking and biking trails exist along the **Gothic Line** (camminolineagotica.it). Along the Gustav Line, meanwhile, a guided leisure walk operated by **History & Geo Tours** (historyandgeotours.com) follows a route from Ortona in the east to Cassino in the west.

⑬ Borgo a Mozzano, Tuscany

Page 65. Visible bunkers, tank walls and trenches can be seen just south of this Tuscan village.

⑭ Monte Sole, Tuscany

Page 68. More than 750 people, including 150 children and infants, were killed at this spot in Marzabotto, south of Bologna, in the largest single massacre carried out by the Waffen-SS.

The Czech Republic: Pilsen and Prague

A tour of the major war-themed sites in and around the Czech capital and the city of Pilsen, which was liberated by US troops amid much celebration.

❶ Patton Memorial Pilsen

Page 264. This fine military museum takes a detailed look at the liberation of Pilsen, homing in on General Patton and Major General Ernest N. Harmon, who served with distinction in both World War I and World War II.

❷ Thank You America! Memorial, Pilsen

Page 264. Renovated in May 2018 and dedicated to the American troops who liberated Pilsen, bearing the message "We'll Never Forget".

Experiences

The annual **Liberation Festival Pilsen** (held in May) celebrates the city's liberation by US troops in 1945. Residents and veterans unite to participate in parades, memorial meetings and discussions.

❸ 2nd Infantry Division Memorial, Pilsen

Page 264. Monument to the 2nd Infantry Division designed by one of its veterans, Dr Pershing Wakefield.

❹ National Memorial to the Heroes of the Heydrich Terror, Prague

Page 266. Detailed exhibit in the church where the Operation Anthropoid agents sheltered after their assassination of Reinhard Heydrich in 1942.

❺ Terezín (Theresienstadt)

Page 266. Museum marking the Nazi's "model camp", where a rich cultural scene flourished despite the dire conditions.

» Berlin and Brandenburg

Berlin was where Nazi Germany made its last stand. This trip includes selected sites in the German capital and the surrounding state of Brandenburg.

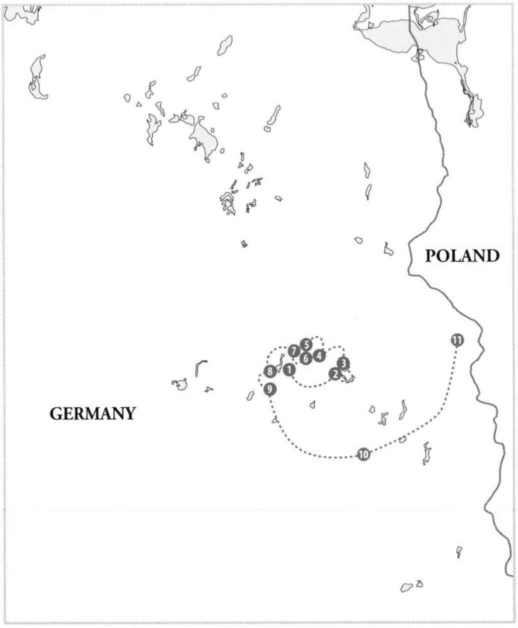

POLAND

GERMANY

❶ Allied Museum, Berlin

Page 315. Well-presented museum on what came after World War II – the Cold War. Highlights include the original Checkpoint Charlie guard cabin, an aeroplane used during the Berlin Blockade and a reconstruction of the famous spy tunnel used in Operation Gold, the largest CIA/MI6 operation of the era.

❷ Forced Labour Documentation Centre, Berlin

Page 317. Exhibits tell the moving stories of the inmates of this forced labour camp at Schöneweide.

❸ German-Russian Museum, Berlin

Page 317. A self-consciously balanced view of tumultuous German-Russian relations in the twentieth century, with poignant photos, books and propaganda posters from both sides of the Iron Curtain.

❹ Jewish Museum, Berlin

Page 318. Housed in an extraordinary building by Daniel Libeskind. Uneven angles and severe lines create a disturbed and uneasy space that mirrors the difficult story portrayed inside: the history and culture of German Jewry.

❺ Memorial to the Murdered Jews of Europe, Berlin
Page 316. Powerful and controversial monument taking inspiration from the densely clustered gravestones of Prague's Jewish graveyard.

❻ Topography of Terror, Berlin
Page 319. Germany's most significant museum on the perpetrators of Nazi terror.

❼ Soviet Memorial Tiergarten, Berlin
Page 319. Crafted from the marble of Hitler's destroyed Berlin headquarters, the Reich Chancellery, this memorial commemorates the Red Army troops who died in the Battle of Berlin.

❽ House of the Wannsee Conference, Berlin
Page 319. Where the Nazi elite planned the "Final Solution".

❾ Cecilienhof Palace, Potsdam
Page 312. Resembling a Tudor mansion and where the Potsdam Conference – confirming decisions made at Yalta about the postwar European order – was held from 17 July to 2 August 1945.

❿ Halbe Forest Cemetery, Halbe
Page 313. The final resting place of some 40,000 people who died in the Battle of the Halbe Pocket in April 1945.

⓫ Seelow Heights Memorial Site and Museum, Seelow
Page 311. Explains the last major Soviet offensive on German soil.

《
Cecilienhof Palace in Potsdam

Experiences
In the German capital, **Berliner Unterwelten** (Berliner-unterwelten.de) organizes guided tours of underground Berlin. Their "Dark Worlds" route focuses on the experience of World War II bombing raids, while "From Flaktowers to Mountains of Debris" explores the ruins of a World War II fortress. **Secret Tours** (secret-tours.berlin), meanwhile, gives exclusive access to several of Berlin's historical sites and buildings. Other good operators include **Humboldt Tours**, running excellent and comprehensive Battle of Berlin and World War II routes, and **Berlins Taiga** (berlins-taiga.com), whose informed staff lead a range of interesting tours with an emphasis on the capital's Soviet history. Guided routes cover Potsdam and the Battle for Berlin; individual tailor-made itineraries are also available.

Films and books

Au revoir les enfants
1987; dir, Louis Malle

At a Catholic boys' boarding school in the country, Julien forms a friendship with quiet new boy, Jean, about whom the headmaster seems especially protective, and whose painful secret Julien slowly uncovers. Malle's partly autobiographical film, set in France in 1944, delicately explores the moral confusions and compromises of life under occupation.

The Bridge at Remagen
1969; dir, John Guillermin

Based on real events (see p.289), this is a Hollywood war film 60s style – strong on action, with plenty of macho cynicism and some completely gratuitous "romantic" moments. Nevertheless, it contains some of the most convincing battle scenes prior to *Saving Private Ryan*. Filmed in Czechoslovakia, it had to be completed elsewhere when Soviet tanks invaded the country.

Carve Her Name With Pride
1958; dir, Lewis Gilbert

The radiant Virginia McKenna plays Violette Szabo, a bilingual Englishwoman married to a French soldier. When he is killed, she joins the Special Operations Executive (SOE) as an agent and is posted to France. Much of the film's effectiveness lies in the contrast between Violette's quiet life with her parents and the violent and perilous work she carries out with the Resistance.

Downfall
2004; dir, Oliver Hirschbiegel

Mostly set in the *Führerbuker* in Berlin and based on eyewitness accounts, this is a powerful and disturbing film. Bruno Ganz's mesmerizing performance as Hitler was criticized by some as too sympathetic, but it brilliantly conveys the paranoia, delusion and self-pity of the ailing dictator in his final days as the Soviets advance and Berlin collapses around him.

Films

The Great Escape
1963; dir, John Sturges

Based on the real 1944 mass escape that took place at Stalag Luft III (see p.249), but with Hollywood embellishments to crank up the excitement. Dramatic tension is brilliantly sustained by director Sturges, both in the tunnel-building and escape itself, and – most exhilaratingly – in the cross-country chase in which Hilts (Steve McQueen) attempts a getaway by motorbike.

Ivan's Childhood
1962; dir, Andrei Tarkovsky

A visionary and poetic evocation of the blighted Eastern Front towards the end of the war, in which a young boy – seeking revenge for the death of his family – acts as a scout for the Russian partisans, slipping back and forth through enemy lines. Dreams about his mother and his previous idyllic life are intercut with the harshness of his current reality.

Kanal
1956; dir, Andrzej Wajda

This Polish-language film, set during the Warsaw Uprising, focuses on a unit of Home Army resistance fighters as they attempt to evade the Germans by escaping though the city's sewers. The air of resigned desperation adds to the poignancy, as does the fact that some of the actors participated in the actual events depicted.

The Longest Day
1962; dirs, Ken Annakin, Andrew Marton, Bernhard Wicki

This black-and-white account of Operation Overlord was the grandest of the Hollywood war epics and is still one of the best, with particularly convincing footage of the D-Day beach landings. As much weight is given to the German view of the battles as the Allied, while the cast of A-list stars provide the more intimate and personal stories.

Films

Patton
1970; dir, Franklin J. Schaffner

For many, Patton was the Allies' most talented general, but he also bordered on the craziest, with his belief in reincarnation, talks with God, and an overwhelming sense of his own greatness. The film covers the campaigns and the controversies. That it rarely tips into caricature is due to George C. Scott's utterly convincing and charismatic portrayal of the great man.

The Pianist
2002; dir, Roman Polanski

Władysław Szpilman, played by Adrien Brody, was a concert pianist who survived the Warsaw ghetto and spent two years in hiding, protected for some of the time by a German officer. Polanski, himself a Holocaust survivor, recreates a convincingly bleak vision of war-torn Warsaw, where who survives and who doesn't seems completely arbitrary.

Rome, Open City
1945; dir, Roberto Rossellini

This is raw and edgy film-making, made shortly after the Germans left Rome, with Rossellini using any film stock he could get hold of. Filmed on the streets of Rome, it tells of a group of ordinary people caught up with the resistance, while at the same time trying to get on with their lives under the privations of occupation.

Saving Private Ryan
1998; dir, Steven Spielberg

Having survived Omaha beach, a group of rangers is sent to save a paratrooper stranded behind enemy lines, whose three brothers have been killed in action. A fascinating contrast with *The Longest Day*, the first half-hour of the film must rank as one of the most visceral and violent recreations of modern warfare, in which the sheer effort involved in killing comes across with a stark power.

Films

Schindler's List
1993; dir, Steven Spielberg

The Holocaust is an almost impossible subject for a feature film, and Spielberg's epic account of Oskar Schindler's rescue of his Jewish workers (see p.241) only half succeeds. Much of the emotionalism feels manipulative, and focusing the story on two Germans – one good, one bad – seems simplistic and reduces the Jewish characters to ciphers.

The Third Man
1949; dir, Carol Reed

Reed's masterpiece is set in a ravaged, postwar Vienna, whose citizens are at the mercy of black-market racketeers like Harry Lime, played with an insouciant charm by Orson Welles. The sense of desperation and a world out-of-joint is enhanced by Grahame Greene's fatalistic script and the skewed camera angles of Robert Krasker's cinematography.

The True Glory
1945; dirs, Garson Kanin, Carol Reed

An Anglo-American co-production introduced by General Eisenhower, this fascinating 80-minute documentary presents the western Allies' own account of the liberation of Europe. Using multiple narrators who give personal accounts of their experiences – from the Normandy landings to Berlin – it is propaganda that largely avoids triumphalism. Available on Youtube.

The World at War
1973–74; prod, Jeremy Isaacs

Made for British TV, this 26-part documentary series was made 45 years ago but is still the best and most detailed overview of the war on film. Authoritatively narrated by Laurence Olivier, its great strength – apart from some remarkable archive footage – is the number of interviews with important eyewitnesses and participants.

Books

The Liberation Trilogy
Rick Atkinson (Henry Holt & Co, 2002–2013)

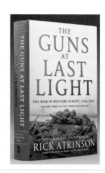

Atkinson's outstanding three-volume history of the liberation of Europe actually begins in North Africa, moves to Italy for volume two, before culminating in the invasion of Normandy in volume 3. Although the focus is primarily on the Americans, the author is even-handed in his account of the sometimes fractious Anglo-American relationship.

Liberation: The Bitter Road to Freedom, Europe 1944–1945
William I. Hitchcock (Faber & Faber, 2009)

A sensitive and moving account of the Liberation told from the point of view of civilians. It brings home just how tough it was for people living under German occupation and how the huge Allied offensive to drive out the Wehrmacht brought problems of its own, often caused by the unremitting bombing of strategic sites by the Allied air forces.

The End: Germany 1944–45
Ian Kershaw (Penguin Books, 2011)

Why did Nazi Germany carry on fighting even when it became clear that the war was lost? Ian Kershaw's attempt to answer the question covers the period from the assassination attempt on Hitler to the final surrender of the Nazi leadership. The impeccable scholarship and analysis is occasionally compromised by unnecessary repetition, but it is still a rewarding read.

Belonging: A German Reckons with History and Home
Nora Krug (Penguin Books, 2018)

In this highly personal book, which is part memoir and part scrapbook, author and illustrator Nora Krug explores Germany's Nazi past and her family's involvement. Though born decades after World War II, Krug describes how the guilt generated by those years has impacted on her life and sense of identity as a German.

Books

Russia's War
Richard Overy (Penguin Books, 1998)

A view of the war as experienced by the Soviet Union, the third of the "Big Three" Allies. Many archives in Russia remain unopened, but Overy does an excellent job at marshalling the facts and showing how the Red Army and the Soviet people were the crucial factor in winning the war – but at a terrible cost and while terrorized by a dictator every bit as ruthless as Hitler.

If This is a Man and The Truce
Primo Levi (Abacus, 1991)

Two memoirs, published in 1947 and 1963 respectively, written by an Italian chemist and former partisan. The first deals with his time as a prisoner at Auschwitz, the second recounts the long, circuitous journey back to Italy across a war-ravaged Europe. The dispassionate objectivity with which Levi describes his struggles for survival intensifies the extremity of his experience.

The Storm of War: A New History of the Second World War
Andrew Roberts (Penguin Books, 2010)

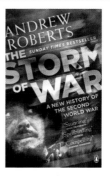

For a lively and well-organized account of the entire war, Roberts' book is hard to beat. He has a knack of highlighting a fact that will suddenly illuminate how or why something happened the way it did. His conclusion that Hitler lost the war as much as the Allies won it – through bad decisions, inflexibility and thinking he knew better than his generals – is convincing.

The Holocaust: A New History
Laurence Rees (Penguin Books, 2017)

One of the best single-volume histories of the subject, drawing on recent scholarship. Rees's study seamlessly combines the stark and hideous facts of the Nazis' genocidal plan – from its origins in 19th-century anti-Semitism to the industrial-level killings of the death camps – with moving first-hand testimonies by survivors.

Index

Acknowledgements and credits

Photo credits

(Key: T-top; C-centre; B-bottom; L-left; R-right)

Adel Csala 194
Alamy 48, 62, 95, 135, 143, 147, 169, 214, 239, 246, 296, 313, 364T, 364CT, 364CB, 364B, 365T, 365CT, 365CB, 365B, 366T, 366CT, 366CB, 366B, 367T, 367CT, 367CB, 367B
Clara Villanueva 381T
Edwin van Wanrooij/PicsPoint Fotografie & Zo 117, 119, 121, 122, 126, 127, 128, 134, 174, 184/185, 316
Ellie Chesshire 342TL
Faber and Faber 368CT
George Staines 381B
Gerben Pul 342R
Getty Images 10/11, 13, 14, 15, 23, 27, 29, 32/33, 34/35, 40, 47, 49, 57, 60, 61, 63, 66, 70, 71, 72, 73, 74/75, 76/77, 80, 83, 88, 91, 93, 99, 102, 103, 104, 105, 106/107, 108/109, 112, 131, 132, 138, 148, 150, 154, 155, 156, 157, 158/159, 164, 166, 178, 179, 180, 181, 182/183, 188, 197, 207, 212, 213, 215, 216/217, 218/219, 222, 225, 229, 233, 240, 244, 250, 251, 252, 253, 254/255 , 256/257, 260, 262, 263, 267A, 268, 269, 270, 271, 272/273, 279, 284, 287, 289, 290, 292, 298, 300, 302, 303, 305, 310, 314, 321, 322, 323, 324, 325, 326/327, 328/329, 333, 334, 335, 337, 338, 340, 342BL, 345B, 346/347, 359, 368TR, 384/385
iStock 25, 53, 54, 56, 59, 89, 90, 95, 101A, 152, 200, 236, 237, 308, 309, 363
IWM 86
Jean-Pierre Geusens 345T
Liberation Route Europe 8, 9B, 17, 64, 113, 118, 120, 140, 160/161, 195, 198, 243, 261, 343TL, 343BL, 344BL
Little, Brown 369TC
Mathieu Billa 343CR
Mike Bink 331
Normandy Regional Council 344TL
Particular Books 368B
Penguin 368CB, 369T, 369CB, 369B
Photo HTM Peenemünde GmbH 321A
PicsPointNL 24
Portsmouth City Council 92
Public Domain 344CR
Richard Overy 5T
Shutterstock 36/37, 96, 98, 116, 137, 151, 208, 231, 232, 234, 248, 293, 304
Studio Libeskind 6, 9
Thomas Bruns 274/275
Trevor Leighton 4T
Cover: The Mardasson Memorial **Alamy** TL, **Jimmy Israel** TC, Dragon's teeth **Shutterstock** BC, Abbey of Monte Cassino **iStock** TR, The Normandy American Cemetery and Memorial **Shutterstock** C & back cover, **D-Day Museum-Portsmouth Museums** BL, Woman Kisses American Soldier **Getty Images** BC, Warsaw Uprising Monument **Shutterstock** BR

Rough Guides credits

Senior Editor: Helen Fanthorpe
Managing Editor: Carine Tracanelli
Proofreader and Indexer: Stewart Wild
Head of Production: Dan May
DTP: Pradeep Thapliyal
Design: Slawek Krajewski
Cover Design: Nicola Erdpresser
Picture Editor: Aude Vauconsant
Cover Photo Research: Tom Smyth
Cartography: Katie Bennett

Liberation Route Europe credits

Chairwoman: Victoria van Krieken
Managing Director: Rémi Praud
Program Manager: Peter Kruk
Project and Communications Manager: Scott Durno
Project Assistant: Roxane Biedermann
Historical Advisors: Jory Brentjens, Jan Szkudliński, Joël Stoppels, Carlo Puddu
Strategic Partner: vfonds

Publishing information

First edition 2019

Distribution

UK, Ireland and Europe
Apa Publications (UK) Ltd; sales@roughguides.com

United States and Canada
Ingram Publisher Services; ips@ingramcontent.com

Australia and New Zealand
Woodslane; info@woodslane.com.au

Southeast Asia
Apa Publications (SN) Pte; sales@roughguides.com

Worldwide
Apa Publications (UK) Ltd; sales@roughguides.com

Special Sales, Content Licensing and CoPublishing
Rough Guides can be purchased in bulk quantities at discounted prices. We can create special editions, personalized jackets and corporate imprints tailored to your needs. sales@roughguides.com.

roughguides.com

Printed in Poland by Pozkal

A catalogue record for this book is available from the British Library
ISBN 978-178-919-430-2

The publishers and authors have done their best to ensure the accuracy and currency of all the information in **Rough Guides Travel the Liberation Route Europe**, however, they can accept no responsibility for any loss, injury, or inconvenience sustained by any traveller as a result of information or advice contained in the guide.

Help us update

We've gone to a lot of effort to ensure that **Rough Guides Travel the Liberation Route Europe** is accurate and up-to-date. However, if you feel we've got it wrong or left something out, we'd like to know. Please send your comments with the subject line "**Rough Guides Travel the Liberation Route Europe Update**" to mail@uk.roughguides.com.

About the authors

Nick Inman

Nick Inman is a travel writer who specializes in France (where he lives) and Europe in general. Writing this book gave him an opportunity to do research into the wartime service of his late father, David Inman, who enlisted in the summer of 1943, two months before his eighteenth birthday. In January 1945, he was posted to the Netherlands for service in the Royal Artillery. He was initially stationed at Nijmegen and in April his division took part in the liberation of Arnhem and Ede. Following the defeat of Germany, his unit guarded a refugee camp. He spent the aftermath of the war in Trieste and then in Gaza, where he was promoted to sergeant, before being demobbed in September 1947. Nick would like to dedicate this book to him.

Joe Staines

Joe Staines is a freelance editor and author specializing in art, culture and history. Joe worked at Rough Guides from 1999 to 2012. He has a keen interest in World War II. His mother, the actress Pauline Letts, took part in an ENSA tour of newly liberated France, Belgium and the Netherlands in the winter of 1944, as part of the cast of the West End play *A Soldier for Christmas*.

Author acknowledgements

Nick Inman: This book is the result of teamwork. It took shape through discussions with Rémi Praud at LRE, my co-writer Joe Staines (always to be relied on for his eclectic knowledge and perceptive ideas) and the team at Rough Guides – Agnieszka Mizak, Carine Tracanelli and Helen Fanthorpe. Our collective challenge was to explain the Liberation (past) and Liberation Route (present) in the clearest possible way. The hard task of managing and editing the book was undertaken by Helen Fanthorpe, exemplary in her dedication to the project. Katie Bennett helped us translate complicated instructions into clear maps. I'd also like to thank James Overton for sharing his knowledge of Sicily with me; John Dixon for helping me understand military organization; the staff of the Commonwealth War Graves Commission for their help in documenting an important aspect of the Liberation; and Scott Durno, Jory Brentjens and Carlo Puddu who contributed their expertise when and where needed.

Joe Staines: Thanks to my co-author Nick Inman for many stimulating exchanges about World War II, and to Jory Brentjens and Jan Szkudliński for advice about the Netherlands and Poland respectively. Thanks to all those at Rough Guides involved in creating the book, especially to Helen Fanthorpe for her diligent and supportive editing.